Study Guide

Principles of Finance

THIRD EDITION

Dr. Scott Besley

University of South Florida

Eugene F. Brigham

University of Florida

THOMSON
SOUTH-WESTERN

Australia · Brazil · Canada · Mexico · Singapore · Spain · United Kingdom · United States

THOMSON

SOUTH-WESTERN

Study Guide to accompany Priciples of Finance, Third Edition
Scott Besley and Eugene F. Brigham

VP/Editorial Director:
Jack W. Calhoun

VP/Editor-in-Chief:
Alex von Rosenberg

Executive Editor:
Mike Reynolds

Developmental Editor:
Jennifer E. Baker

Marketing Manager:
Heather MacMaster

Production Project Manager:
Cliff Kallemeyn

Technology Project Editor:
Matthew McKinney

Manufacturing Coordinator:
Sandee Milewski

Printer:
Globus Printing
Minster, OH

Cover Designer:
Craig Ramsdell/Ramsdell Design

Internal Designer:
Craig Ramsdell

Cover Image:
Getty Images, Inc.

COPYRIGHT © 2006
Thomson South-Western, a part of The
Thomson Corporation. Thomson, the
Star logo, and South-Western are
trademarks used herein under license.

Printed in the United States of America
1 2 3 4 5 08 07 06

ISBN 0-324-23263-2

ALL RIGHTS RESERVED.
No part of this work covered by the
copyright hereon may be reproduced or
used in any form or by any means—
graphic, electronic, or mechanical,
including photocopying, recording,
taping, Web distribution or information
storage and retrieval systems, or in any
other manner—without the written
permission of the publisher.

For permission to use material from this
text or product, submit a request online
at http://www.thomsonrights.com.

For more information about our
products, contact us at:

Thomson Learning Academic Resource
Center

1-800-423-0563

Thomson Higher Education
5191 Natorp Boulevard
Mason, OH 45040
USA

STUDY GUIDE

TABLE OF CONTENTS

PREFACE

This *Study Guide* is designed primarily to help you develop a working knowledge of the concepts and principles of financial management. Additionally, it will familiarize you with the types of true/false and multiple-choice test questions that are being used with increasing frequency in introductory finance courses.

The *Study Guide* follows the outline of *Principles of Finance, Third Edition.* You should carefully read the next section, "Suggestions for Students Using The Study Guide," to familiarize yourself with its specific contents and to gain some insights into how it can be used most effectively.

We would like to thank Dana Aberwald Clark and Susan Whitman for their considerable assistance in the preparation of the *Study Guide*.

We have tried to make the *Study Guide* as clear and error-free as possible. However, some mistakes may have crept in, and there are almost certainly some sections that could be clarified. Any suggestions for improving the *Study Guide* would be greatly appreciated and should be addressed to Scott Besley at the address given below. Because instructors almost never read study guides, we address this call for help to students!

Scott Besley

College of Business Administration
BSN 3403
University of South Florida
4202 E. Fowler Ave.
Tampa, FL 33620-5500
E-mail: sbesley@coba.usf.edu

Eugene F. Brigham

College of Business Administration
University of Florida
PO Box 117167
Gainesville, FL 32611-7167

November 2005

SUGGESTIONS FOR STUDENTS USING THE STUDY GUIDE

Different people will tend to use the *Study Guide* in somewhat different ways. This is natural because both introductory finance courses and individual students' needs vary widely. However, the tips contained in this section should help all students use the *Study Guide* more effectively, regardless of these differences.

Each chapter contains (1) an overview, (2) an outline, (3) definitional self-test questions, (4) conceptual self-test questions, (5) self-test problems, and (6) answers and solutions to the self-test questions and problems. You should begin your study by reading the overview; it will give you an idea of what is contained in the chapter and how this material fits into the overall scheme of things in financial management.

Next, read over the outline to get a better feel for the specific topics covered in the chapter. It is important to realize that the outline does not list every facet of every topic covered in the textbook. The *Study Guide* is intended to highlight and summarize the textbook, not to supplant it. Also, note that appendix material is clearly marked as such within the outline. Thus, if your instructor does not assign a particular chapter appendix, you may not want to study that portion of the outline.

The definitional self-test questions are intended to test your knowledge of, and also to reinforce your ability to work with, the terms and concepts introduced in the chapter. If you do not understand the definitions thoroughly, review the outline prior to going on to the conceptual questions and problems.

The conceptual self-test questions focus on the same kinds of ideas that the textbook end-of-chapter questions address, but in the *Study Guide*, the questions are set out in a true/false or multiple-choice format. Thus, for many students these questions can be used to practice for the types of tests that are being used with increasing frequency. However, regardless of the types of tests you must take, working through the conceptual questions will help drive home the key concepts of financial management.

The numeric problems are also written in a multiple-choice format. Generally, the problems are arranged in order of increasing difficulty. Also, note that some of the *Study Guide* problems are convoluted in the sense that information normally available to financial managers is withheld and information normally unknown is given. Such problems are designed to test your knowledge of a subject, and you must work "backwards" to solve them. Furthermore, such problems are included in the *Study Guide* in part because they provide a good test of how well you understand the material and in part because you might see similar problems on your exams.

Finally, each *Study Guide* chapter provides the answers and solutions to the self-test questions and problems. The rationale behind a question's correct answer is explained where necessary, but the problem solutions are always complete. Note that the problems in the early chapters generally provide both "numerical" and "financial calculator" solutions. In later chapters, only calculator solutions are shown. You should not be concerned if your answer differs from ours by a small amount due to rounding.

Of course, each student must decide how to incorporate the *Study Guide* in his or her overall study program. Many students begin an assignment by reading the *Study Guide* overview and outline to get the "big picture," then read the chapter in the textbook. Naturally, the *Study Guide* overview and outline is also used extensively to review for exams. Most students work the textbook questions and problems, using the latter as a self-test and review tool. However, if you are stumped by a text problem, try the *Study Guide* problems first because their detailed solutions probably will help you get you over stumbling blocks.

CHAPTER 1
AN OVERVIEW OF FINANCE

OVERVIEW

This chapter provides an overview of finance and should give you a better understanding of the following: (1) career opportunities in finance, (2) the importance of finance in non-finance careers, (3) what forces will affect finance in the future, (4) the role of managerial finance in business decisions, and (5) how financial decisions affect value.

OUTLINE

The study of finance consists of three interrelated areas: financial markets, investments, and managerial finance. Career opportunities within each field are varied and numerous, but financial managers must have a knowledge of all three areas.

☐ Many finance majors go to work for financial institutions, including banks, insurance companies, savings and loans, and credit unions, which are an integral part of the financial marketplace.
  ~ For success in the financial services industry, one needs knowledge of the factors that cause interest rates to rise and fall, the regulations to which financial institutions are subject, and the various types of financial instruments. One also needs a general knowledge of all aspects of business administration.

☐ Finance graduates who go into investments generally work for stock brokerage firms, financial institutions, investment companies, or insurance companies.
  ~ The three main functions in this area are sales, the analysis of individual securities, and determining the optimal mix of securities for a given investor.
  ~ A basic knowledge of finance will help you understand how to (1) review companies and industries to determine prospects for future growth and the ability to maintain the safety of your investment, (2) determine how much risk you are willing to take with your investment position, and (3) evaluate how well your investments are performing so you can better ensure your funds are invested appropriately.

☐ Managerial finance, the broadest of the three areas, and the one with the greatest number of job opportunities, involves decisions firms make concerning cash flows.
  ~ Managerial finance is important in all types of businesses.
  ~ The types of jobs one encounters in this area range from decisions regarding plant

1

expansions to choosing what types of securities to issue to finance expansion.

There are financial implications in virtually all business decisions, and nonfinancial executives simply must know enough finance to work these implications into their own specialized analyses. As a result, every student of business, regardless of major, should be concerned with finance.

- ☐ Financial management concepts are very important to making informed decisions in the management area.
  - ~ Personnel decisions such as salary, hiring new staff, and bonuses must be coordinated with financial decisions to ensure any needed funds are available.
  - ~ Strategic planning cannot be accomplished without considering how such plans impact the overall financial well-being of the firm.

- ☐ Coordination of the finance and marketing functions is critical to the success of companies, especially small, newly-formed firms, because it is necessary to ensure the firm generates sufficient cash to survive.
  - ~ People in marketing must understand how marketing decisions affect and are affected by funds availability, inventory levels, excess plant capacity, and so on.

- ☐ In many firms it is difficult to differentiate between the finance and accounting functions. Often, accountants make financial decisions, and vice versa, because the two are closely related.
  - ~ It is important that accountants understand how financial managers use accounting information in planning and decision making so that it can be provided in an accurate and timely fashion.
  - ~ Accountants must understand how accounting data are viewed by investors, creditors, and other outsiders interested in the firm's operations.

- ☐ Without appropriate information, decisions relating to finance, management, marketing, and accounting could be disastrous.
  - ~ Information system specialists work with financial managers to determine what information is needed, how information should be stored, how information should be delivered, and the impact of information management on the firm's profitability.

We provide a brief overview of each of the three areas in finance in terms of its evolution in the twentieth century and its role in the current business world.

- ☐ Because the financial markets in the United States are well developed, we have been able to achieve a higher standard of living than otherwise would be possible. During the twentieth century, financial markets and financial institutions have experienced substantial changes.
  - ~ In the early 1900s, the banking community consisted of thousands of independent banking organizations. By 1920, many of the large commercial banks included investment departments and affiliated organizations that helped companies issue stocks and bonds.

~ A series of financial catastrophes resulted in legislation that severely restricted where and how banks could operate and formed the foundation of our current banking structure. During this period, branch banking as we know it today did not exist because it was either prohibited by law or condemned by the banking industry.

~ The restrictions imposed on banking operations placed banks at a competitive disadvantage in the financial markets, both domestically and abroad. A great deal of deregulation has occurred in the banking industry since the 1970s.

~ Recent legislation and legislative proposals have helped tear down barriers to national branch banking and have permitted banking organizations to venture into such financial areas as investments and insurance, which have been prohibited since the 1930s.

~ Deregulation has been supported as a means to improve competition; proponents argue that severely restrictive regulation threatens the existence of financial institutions.

☐ We have experienced a variety of types of stock markets since the beginning of the twentieth century. In addition, participation in investments and the types of instruments offered have changed considerably.

~ In the early 1900s, the investments area was dominated by a small group of very wealthy investors and opulent corporations. Few small, individual investors ventured into corporate stocks and bonds because managers rarely disclosed financial information to the public. Thus, most individuals invested in instruments considered relatively safe, such as savings accounts at banks or government securities.

~ Industrialization and government financing of World War I resulted in increased financial prosperity and provided substantial wealth for those who had invested in the financial markets. The performance of the markets attracted greater interest from individual investors. By the 1920s, the number of investment firms had grown substantially, and corporate stocks and bonds were no longer viewed as investments for the elite only.

~ From 1929-1932, the stock market declined by more than 80 percent. Many felt that the market crash was precipitated by unethical trading practices and abuses of investment organizations and individuals. Consequently, during the 1930s, there was significant pressure to regulate the behavior of the participants in the financial markets, and much of the legislation that forms the foundation of the regulatory tenor that exists today was enacted at the time. The principal impetus of the regulation was to ban fraudulent behavior and abusive practices of investors and investment organizations and to require greater disclosure of financial information by issuers of securities.

~ Prosperity after World War II and a growing interest in investments by the average individual helped popularize mutual funds in the 1950s and 1960s. But, the 1970s was a period of rising interest rates and high inflation, which created a great deal of uncertainty in the economy and very volatile securities markets.

~ Since World War II, both institutional investors—which include pension funds, mutual funds, insurance companies, and the like—and individual investors have increased their presence in the securities markets.

~ As the attitudes of both investors and regulators have changed, so have the types of investments and the methods used to evaluate investment opportunities. As information disclosure became standardized and the common investor obtained greater investment knowledge, greater varieties of investment instruments and investing techniques were introduced.

~ Investment analysis has evolved into a more sophisticated process. The analytical tools we use today find their roots in theory developed in the 1930s. Although the valuation techniques used today are much more sophisticated, we still use the same general approach developed during that period to analyze investments.

☐ When managerial finance emerged as a separate field of study in the early 1900s, the emphasis was on the legal aspects of mergers, the formation of new firms, and the various types of securities that firms could issue to raise funds.

~ During the Depression era of the 1930s, an unprecedented number of business failures caused the emphasis in managerial finance to shift to bankruptcy and reorganization, to corporate liquidity, and to regulation of security markets. New rules were enacted that required firms to maintain and publicly disclose certain financial information.

~ Finance was mostly a descriptive discipline that emphasized organizational relationships of firms and legal matters. During the 1940s and early 1950s, finance continued to be taught as a descriptive, institutional subject, viewed more from the standpoint of an outsider rather than from that of management.

~ In the late 1950s and the 1960s, increased competition in established industries reduced the profit opportunities available to corporations. Financial managers shifted their focus toward techniques used to evaluate investment opportunities. Emphasis was given to finding investments that would improve the firm's ability to generate profits in the future.

~ A movement toward theoretical analysis began during the 1960s, and the emphasis of managerial finance shifted to managerial decisions regarding the choice of assets and liabilities necessary to maximize the firm's value. This era is considered the birth of modern finance, from which many of the decision-making techniques we use today evolved.

~ During the late 1970s, firms discovered innovative ways to manage financial risk and finance the firm. Stockholders became more concerned with how firms were managed and how managers' actions affected the firm's value.

~ The focus on valuation continued through the 1980s, but the analysis was expanded to include (1) inflation and its effects on business decisions; (2) deregulation of financial institutions and the resulting trend toward large, broadly diversified financial services companies; (3) the dramatic increase in both the use of computers for analysis and the electronic transfer of information; (4) the increased importance of global markets and business operations; and (5) innovations in the financial products offered to investors.

~ In today's fast-paced, technologically driven world, the area of managerial finance continues to evolve. Mergers and acquisitions are still an important part of the financial world. The most important trends in the 1990s, which have continued into the new millennium, include (1) the continued globalization of business, (2) a further increase in the use of electronic technology, and (3) the regulatory attitude of the government.

~ Four factors have made the trend toward globalization mandatory for many businesses:

- Transportation and communications improvements have lowered shipping costs and made international trade more feasible.
- Increased political clout of consumers has also helped lower trade barriers.
- Due to increased technology, higher product development costs have resulted, necessitating increased unit sales for a firm to remain competitive.
- Competitive pressures have forced companies to shift manufacturing operations to lower-cost countries.

~ As we begin the next millenium, we will see continued advances in the use of electronic technology in managerial finance and this technology will revolutionize the way financial decisions are made, just as it has in the past.

- One result of this "electronic revolution" during the last couple of decades is the increased use of quantitative analysis via computer models for financial decision making.
- The next generation of financial managers will need stronger computer and quantitative skills than were required in the past.

~ In the past 20 years, the government has taken fairly friendly positions with respect to legislative enactments and regulatory enforcements affecting businesses. Much of the legislation has focused on deregulation of highly regulated industries. In addition, for the most part, the government has not discouraged mergers and acquisitions.

- In the future, if economic conditions sour, causing decreases in the securities markets, you can bet legislators will favor re-regulation if they believe deregulation contributed to the economic woes of the country. Historically, after the country has experienced economic tragedy, cries for new, tougher regulations have been abundant, and for the most part, Congress has obliged.

The historical trends discussed above have greatly increased the importance of finance, especially managerial finance. Today the financial manager must make decisions in a much more coordinated manner, and he or she generally has direct responsibility for the control process.

☐ Today, companies are greatly concerned with financial planning, and this has increased the importance of corporate financial staffs.

~ The value of managerial finance is reflected in the fact that more chief executive officers in the top 1,000 U.S. companies started their careers in finance than in any other functional area.

Financial decisions affect the value of the firm. Thus, we need to understand how value is determined. Valuation and the factors that affect value are discussed throughout the book. In general, the value of an investment (asset) is based on the following:

☐ The cash flows an asset is expected to generate during its life—if an investment generates zero cash flows to investors, then it has a value equal to zero.

☐ The timing of the cash flows the asset is expected to generate—everything else equal, the sooner cash flows are received, the more valuable the asset.

☐ The riskiness of the expected cash flows—everything else equal, the riskier an investment is, the lower its value. Investors require (demand) higher returns to invest in riskier assets.

SELF-TEST QUESTIONS

Definitional

1. The study of finance consists of three interrelated areas: (1) _____ _____, (2) _____, and (3) _____ _____.

2. The most important trends affecting managerial finance in the 1990s, which have continued into the new millennium, include the continued _____ of business, a further increase in the use of _____ _____, and the _____ attitude of the government.

3. The three main functions in the investments area are _____, the _____ of individual securities, and determining the _____ _____ of securities for a given investor.

4. Recent legislation and legislative proposals have helped tear down barriers to _____ _____ _____ and have permitted banking organizations to venture into such financial areas as _____ and _____, which have been prohibited since the 1930s.

5. Prosperity after World War II and a growing interest in investments by the average individual helped popularize _____ _____ in the 1950s and 1960s.

6. Since World War II, both _____ investors—which include pension funds, mutual funds, insurance companies, and the like—and individual investors have increased their presence in the _____ _____.

7. When managerial finance emerged as a separate field of study in the early 1900s, the emphasis was on the legal aspects of _____, the _____ of new firms, and the various types of _____ that firms could issue to raise funds.

8. During the Depression era of the 1930s, an unprecedented number of business failures caused the emphasis in managerial finance to shift to _____ and _____, to corporate _____, and to regulation of security markets.

9.   In the late 1950s and the 1960s, increased _____ in established industries reduced the profit opportunities available to corporations.

10.   The focus on valuation continued through the 1980s, but the analysis was expanded to include (1) _____ and its effects on business decisions; (2) _____ of financial institutions and the resulting trend toward large, broadly diversified financial services companies; (3) the dramatic increase in both the use of _____ for analysis and the electronic transfer of information; (4) the increased importance of _____ markets and business operations; and (5) _____ in the financial products offered to investors.

11.   The _____ _____ task is to make decisions concerning the acquisition and use of funds for the greatest benefit of the firm.

12.   _____ _____, the broadest of the three areas in finance, and the one with the greatest number of job opportunities, involves decisions firms make concerning cash flows.

13.   During the 1940s and early 1950s, finance continued to be taught as a(n) _____, institutional subject, viewed more from the standpoint of a(n) _____ rather than from that of management.

14.   The era of the 1960s is considered the birth of _____ _____, from which many of the _____-_____ _____ we use today evolved.

15.   The value of an asset is based on the _____ it is expected to generate during its life.

Conceptual

16.   Because the financial markets in the United States are well developed, we have been able to achieve a higher standard of living than otherwise would be possible.

        a. True   **b.** False

17.   In the early 1900s, the investments area was dominated by a large group of individual investors because managers regularly disclosed financial information to the public.

        a. True   **b.** False

18.   As information disclosure has become standardized and the common investor has obtained greater investment knowledge, greater varieties of investment instruments and investing techniques have been introduced.

        a. True   **b.** False

19. There are financial implications in virtually all business decisions, and nonfinancial executives simply must know enough finance to work these implications into their specialized analyses.

   a. True   **b.** False

20. Investors are generally risk averse, which means that they are willing to pay more for investments with more certain (less risky) cash flows than for investments with less certain (riskier) cash flows.

   a. True   **b.** False

21. Which of the following has *not* made the trend toward globalization mandatory for many businesses:

   a. Reduced political clout of consumers.
   b. Transportation and communications improvements.
   c. Increased technology.
   d. Competitive pressures.
   e. None of the above; i.e., all have contributed to the trend toward globalization.

22. Which of the following statements is true?

   a. Personnel decisions such as salary, hiring new staff, and bonuses need not be coordinated with financial decisions.
   b. Strategic planning has no impact on the overall financial well-being of the firm.
   c. Marketing decisions affect and are affected by funds availability, by inventory levels, and by excess plant capacity.
   d. A firm's finance and accounting functions are not closely related.
   e. All of the statements above are false.

ANSWERS TO SELF-TEST QUESTIONS

1.	financial markets; investments; managerial finance	8.	bankruptcy; reorganization; liquidity
2.	globalization; electronic technology; regulatory	9.	competition
		10.	inflation; deregulation; computers; global; innovations
3.	sales; analysis; optimal mix	11.	financial manager's
4.	national branch banking; investments; insurance	12.	Managerial finance
		13.	descriptive; outsider
5.	mutual funds	14.	modern finance; decision-making techniques
6.	institutional; securities markets		
7.	mergers; formation; securities	15.	cash flows

16.   a.   This statement is correct.

17.   b.   This is exactly the reverse of the actual situation. The investments area was dominated by a small group of wealthy investors because managers rarely disclosed financial information to the public.

18.   a.   This statement is correct.

19.   a.   This statement is correct.

20.   a.   This statement is correct.

21.   a.   Increased political clout of consumers has lowered trade barriers. Statements b, c, and d are all factors that have contributed toward the trend of globalization.

22.   c.   Statement c is the only true statement. Personnel decisions must be coordinated with financial decisions to ensure any needed funds are available. Strategic planning cannot be accomplished without considering how such plans impact the overall financial well-being of the firm. In many firms it is difficult to differentiate between the finance and accounting functions because they are so closely related.

CHAPTER 2
FINANCIAL ASSETS (INSTRUMENTS)

OVERVIEW

In this chapter, we describe various financial assets that exist in the financial markets, some of which are created by financial intermediaries and others by businesses and governments.

Different groups of investors prefer different types of financial instruments, and investors' tastes change over time. Thus, corporations and governments offer a variety of securities, and they package their new security offerings at each point in time to appeal to the greatest possible number of potential investors. For the most part, a financial asset can be classified as debt, equity, or a derivative.

To give some perspective of the role of financial instruments in business, we discuss some accounting issues relating to securities used (issued) by firms. Then, we describe the various securities and derivatives in which individuals can invest either through direct investment or through intermediaries, such as pension or mutual funds. Finally, we discuss financial instruments in international markets.

OUTLINE

Two general categories of asset classification in the business world are real assets and financial assets. Although any asset generally is regarded as something that provides value to its owner, there is a significant difference between how value is provided by a real asset and by a financial asset.

☐　A *real asset,* sometimes called a physical asset, is typically a tangible, or physically observable item.

☐　A *financial asset* is intangible: It represents an expectation, or promise, that future cash flows will be paid to the owner.

　　~ A financial asset can be classified as debt, equity, or a derivative.

A firm issues financial instruments so that the assets necessary to produce and sell inventories can be purchased. In addition, firms use derivatives to hedge, or insure, against a variety of risks.

☐　An understanding of the legal and accounting terminology and explanations of financial instruments issued by firms is vital to both investors and financial managers if they are to avoid misinterpretations and the possibility of costly mistakes.

~ A simplified balance sheet shows a firm's assets and how the firm's assets were financed by either (1) *debt* in the form of *current liabilities* (which are short-term) and *bonds* (which are long-term) and (2) *equity*.

- *Total liabilities* represent funds borrowed from such creditors as banks, materials suppliers, and bond investors.

☐ Common equity is the sum of the firm's common stock, paid-in capital, and retained earnings, which equals the common stockholders' total investment in the firm stated at book value.

~ Shares of common stock are authorized by the owners of a business and issued by management.

~ *Par value* is the minimum amount for which new shares of common stock can be issued.

~ *Retained earnings* is the balance sheet account that indicates the total amount of earnings the firm has not paid out as dividends throughout its history; these earnings have been retained and reinvested in the firm.

~ Any difference between the common stock's par value and what stockholders paid for new common stock is shown on the balance sheet as *additional paid-in capital*.

☐ The debt and equity instruments issued by a firm to raise funds to support its operations are purchased by individuals, other corporations, or financial institutions.

~ These instruments represent some of the financial assets that are traded in the financial markets.

Debt is a loan to a firm, government, or individual. There are many types of debt instruments, such as: home mortgages, commercial paper, term loans, bonds, secured and unsecured notes, and marketable and nonmarketable debt.

☐ When we refer to debt we often identify it using three major features: principal repayment value, interest payments, and the time to maturity.

☐ The *principal value* of debt represents the amount owed to the lender, which must be repaid some time during the life of the debt.

~ For much of the debt issued by corporations, the principal amount is repaid at maturity, so the principal value is often referred to as the *maturity value*.

~ The principal value generally is written on the "face" of the debt instrument, so it is also called the *face value*.

~ When the market value of debt is the same as its face value, it is said to be selling at par, thus the principal amount also is referred to as the *par value*.

~ These terms generally are used interchangeably to indicate the amount repaid by the borrower.

☐ Owners of debt instruments may receive periodic payments of interest, which are computed as a percent of the principal amount.

~ Some debt does not pay interest; to generate a positive return for investors, these financial assets must sell for less than their par, or maturity, values.

~ Securities that sell for less than their par values are said to be selling at a discount, and are called *discounted securities*.

☐ The maturity date represents the date the principal amount of a debt is due.
~ As long as interest has been paid when due, once the principal amount is repaid, the debt obligation has been satisfied.
~ Some debt instruments, called *installment loans,* require the principal amount to be repaid in several payments during the life of the loan. The maturity date of an installment loan is the date the last installment payment of principal is made.
~ Time to maturity varies among the different debt instruments. We often refer to debt instruments as either short-term or long-term debt.

☐ Debtholders have priority over stockholders with regard to distribution of earnings and liquidation of assets.
~ Debtholders must be paid before stockholders can be paid.

☐ Debtholders do not have voting rights, so they cannot attain corporate control of the firm.
~ Debtholders can affect the management and the firm's operations by including restrictions on the use of the funds as part of the loan agreement.

Short-term debt generally refers to debt with a maturity of one year or less. A list of the more common short-term debt instruments are included below.

☐ *Treasury bills (T-bills)* are discounted securities issued by the U.S. government.
~ Prices are determined by an auction process—interested investors and investing organizations submit competitive bids for the T-bills offered.
~ T-bills are issued with face values ranging from $10,000 to $1 million, and with maturities of 13, 26, or 52 weeks at the time of issue.

☐ A *repurchase agreement (Repo)* is an arrangement in which one firm sells some of its financial assets to another firm with a promise to repurchase the securities at a higher price at a later date.
~ A firm agrees to sell securities because it needs funds, while another firm agrees to purchase the securities because it has excess funds.
• The repo seller effectively borrows funds from the repo buyer.
~ The maturity of most repurchase agreements is overnight.

☐ *Federal funds* represent overnight loans from one bank to another.
~ Banks generally use the fed funds market to adjust their reserves—banks that need additional funds to meet the reserve requirements of the Federal Reserve borrow from banks with excess reserves.
~ The interest rate associated with this debt is known as the *federal funds rate.*

☐ A *banker's acceptance* is a time draft, which is an instrument that has a future payment date, issued by a bank that obligates the bank to pay the owner of the bankers' acceptance a specified amount at some future date.

~ Generally used in international trade, the arrangement is established between a bank and a firm to ensure that payment for goods and services is guaranteed at some future date.

~ Banker's acceptances are sold at discounts because they do not pay interest.

☐ *Commercial paper* is a type of promissory note, or legal IOU, issued by large, financially sound firms.

~ Commercial paper does not pay interest, so it must be sold at a discount.

~ The maturity on commercial paper varies from one to nine months, with an average of about five months.

~ It is issued in denominations of $100,000 or more, so few individuals can afford to directly invest in the commercial paper market; instead, it is sold primarily to other businesses, insurance companies, pension funds, money market mutual funds, and banks.

☐ A *certificate of deposit* represents a time deposit at a bank or other financial intermediary.

~ Traditional CDs generally earn periodic interest and must be kept at the institution for a specified time period.

~ *Negotiable CDs* can be traded to other investors prior to maturity because they can be redeemed by whomever owns them at maturity.

• They are often called jumbo CDs with denominations of $1 million to $5 million, and maturities that range from a few months to a few years.

☐ A *Eurodollar deposit* is a deposit in a bank outside the U.S. that is not converted into the currency of the foreign country; instead it is denominated in U.S. dollars.

~ These deposits are not exposed to exchange rate risk, the risk associated with converting dollars into foreign currencies.

~ Eurodollar deposits earn rates offered by foreign banks and are not subject to the same regulations imposed on deposits in U.S. banks.

☐ *Money market mutual funds* are investment funds pooled and managed by investment companies for the purpose of investing in short-term financial assets.

~ They offer individual investors the ability to indirectly invest in short-term securities such as T-bills, commercial paper, and Eurodollars, which they otherwise would not be able to purchase because these investments are sold in denominations that are too high or are not sold to individuals.

Long-term debt refers to debt instruments with maturities greater than one year. There are many types of long-term debt; some of the more common types are listed below.

☐ A *term loan* is a contract under which a borrower agrees to make a series of interest and principal payments on specific dates to the lender.

~ Term loans usually are negotiated directly between the borrowing firm and a financial institution, such as a bank, an insurance company, or a pension fund.

~ Term loans are often termed private debt.

~ The maturity is generally from 3 to 15 years, but it may be as short as 2 or as long as 30 years.

~ Term loans have three major advantages over public offerings: speed, flexibility, and low issuance costs.

~ The interest rate can either be fixed for the life of the loan or variable.

☐ A *bond* is a long-term contract under which a borrower agrees to make payments of interest and principal on specific dates to the holder of the bond.

~ Interest payments are determined by the coupon rate and the principal value of the bond.

- The *coupon rate* represents the total interest paid each year stated as a percentage of the bond's face value.

- Interest generally is paid semiannually, although bonds that pay interest annually, quarterly, and monthly also exist.

☐ Some of the more common types of bonds issued by both governments and corporations are listed below.

~ *Government bonds* are issued by federal, state, and local (municipal) governments.

- U.S. government bonds are issued by the Treasury, and are called either *Treasury notes* or *Treasury bonds*.

- The primary difference between Treasury notes and Treasury bonds is the length of the maturity when the debt is issued: The original maturity on notes is from greater than one year to ten years, while the original maturity on bonds is greater than ten years.

~ *Municipal bonds,* or *munis,* are similar to Treasury bonds, except they are issued by state and local governments. Generally, the income an investor earns from munis is exempt from federal taxes. The two principal types of munis are revenue bonds and general obligation bonds.

- *Revenue bonds* are used to raise funds for projects that generate revenues that are used to make interest and principal payments.

- *General obligation bonds* are backed by the government's ability to impose taxes.

~ *Corporate bonds* are issued by businesses called corporations. These bonds are similar to term loans, but a bond issue is generally advertised, offered to the public, and actually sold to many different investors.

- The interest rate generally is fixed, although there has been an increase in the use of various types of floating rate bonds.

~ With a *mortgage bond*, the corporation pledges certain assets as security (collateral) for the bond.

- *Second mortgage bonds* have claim against property, but only after the first mortgage bondholders have been paid off in full. These bonds are often called *junior mortgages*, because they are junior in priority to the claims of senior mortgages, or first mortgage bonds.

~ A *debenture* is an unsecured bond, and as such, it provides no lien against specific property as security for the obligation.

- Debenture holders are general creditors whose claims are protected by property not otherwise pledged as collateral.
- In practice, the use of debentures depends both on the nature of the firm's assets and on its general credit strength.

~ *Subordinated debentures* are unsecured bonds that have claims on assets, in the event of bankruptcy, only after senior debt has been paid off. Subordinated debentures may be subordinated to designated notes payable or to all other debt.

~ There are several other important types of corporate bonds:

- *Income bonds* pay interest only when the firm has sufficient income to cover interest payments.
- *Putable bonds* may be turned in and exchanged for cash at the bondholder's option; generally, the option to turn in the bond can be exercised only if the firm takes some specified action, such as being acquired by a weaker company or increasing its outstanding debt by a large amount.
- *Indexed, or purchasing power, bonds* have their interest rate payment tied to an inflation index; thus, protecting the bondholders against inflation.
- *Floating rate bonds* are similar to indexed bonds except the coupon rates on these bonds "float" with market interest rates.
- *Original issue discount bonds (OIDs)*, commonly referred to as *zero coupon bonds,* are offered at substantial discounts below their par values because they pay little or no interest.
- The *junk bond* is a high-risk, high-yield bond issued to finance mergers, leveraged buyouts, or troubled companies.

A firm's managers are concerned with both the effective cost of debt and any restrictions in debt contracts that limit the firm's future actions. There are a number of features that could affect either the cost of the firm's debt or the firm's future financial flexibility.

☐ Bondholders attempt to reduce the potential for financial problems by use of legal restrictions designed to insure, insofar as possible, that the company does nothing to cause the quality of its bonds to deteriorate after they have been issued.

~ The *indenture* is the legal document that spells out any legal restrictions associated with the bond, as well as the rights of bondholders and the issuing corporation.

~ A *trustee* is assigned to represent bondholders and to make sure that the terms of the indenture are carried out.

~ *Restrictive covenants* are provisions in a debt contract that constrain the actions of the borrower.

☐ A *call provision* gives the issuing corporation the right to call the bonds for redemption prior to maturity. Call provisions allow firms to refinance existing high-cost debt and replace it with lower-cost debt.

~ When a bond is called, the company must normally pay an amount greater than the par value.

- This extra payment is referred to as a *call premium.* It is typically set equal to

> one year's interest if the bonds are called during the first year a call is permitted, and the premium declines at a constant rate each year thereafter.
>   ~ Bonds usually are not callable until several years (generally five to ten) after they are issued; bonds with these *deferred calls* are said to have *call protection.*

☐   A *sinking fund* facilitates the orderly retirement of a bond issue. It is a required annual payment designed to amortize a bond.
   ~ Failure to meet the sinking fund requirement causes the bond issue to be thrown into default, which might force the company into bankruptcy.
   ~ Generally, sinking funds permit the firm to call a specific number of bonds for redemption at par value or to buy the required number of bonds in the open market.
     • The firm will select whichever method is the least expensive.
   ~ A sinking fund call requires no call premium, but only a small percentage of the issue normally is callable in any one year.

☐   A *conversion feature* permits the bondholder (investor) to exchange (convert) the bond for shares of common stock at a fixed price.
   ~ Investors have flexibility with convertible bonds because they can choose whether to hold the company's bond or convert it to common stock.

Since the early 1900s, bonds have been assigned quality ratings that reflect their probability of going into default.

☐   The two major rating agencies are Moody's Investors Service and Standard & Poor's Corporation.
   ~ Aaa (Moody's) and AAA (S&P) are the highest ratings. Triple-A and double-A bonds are extremely safe.
   ~ Single-A and triple-B bonds are strong enough to be called *investment grade bonds,* the lowest-rated bonds that many banks and other institutional investors are permitted by law to hold.
   ~ Double-B and lower bonds are speculative, or junk bonds; they have a significant probability of going into default, and many financial institutions are prohibited from buying them.

☐   Rating assignments are based on both qualitative and quantitative factors including financial strength of the company, collateral provisions, seniority of the debt, restrictive covenants, sinking fund provisions, and regulation.

☐   Bond ratings are important both to firms and to investors.
   ~ Because a bond's rating is an indicator of its default risk, the rating has a direct, measurable influence on the bond's interest rate and the firm's cost of debt.
   ~ Most bonds are purchased by institutional investors, and many institutions are restricted to investment-grade securities.
   ~ As a result of their higher risk and more restricted market, lower-grade bonds offer higher returns than high-grade bonds.

- Risk premiums fluctuate from year to year, and are higher the steeper the slope of the Security Market Line.
- When there is fear of an increase in inflation, there is a "flight to quality;" Treasuries are in great demand, and the premium on low-quality over high-quality bonds increases.

☐ Changes in a firm's bond rating affect both its ability to borrow long-term capital and the cost of those funds. Rating agencies review outstanding bonds on a periodic basis, occasionally upgrading or downgrading a bond as the issuer's circumstances change.

Preferred stock is a hybrid security, because it represents an equity investment in a business, yet it has many of the characteristics associated with debt. Preferred stock is equity that has preference over common stock in the distribution of dividends and assets, and has fixed dividend payments. Although preferred stock has a fixed payment like bonds, a failure to make this payment will not lead to bankruptcy.

☐ Accountants classify preferred stock as equity and report it in the equity portion of the balance sheet.
  - ~ If an analysis is being made by a common stockholder, preferred stock is treated like debt because it entails fixed charges that must be paid ahead of common stock dividends.
  - ~ However, if the analysis is being made by a creditor studying a firm's vulnerability to failure in the event of a decline in sales and income, preferred stock is viewed as part of the equity base.
  - ~ From management's perspective, preferred stock lies between debt and common equity.
    - Because failure to pay dividends on preferred stock will not force the firm into bankruptcy, preferred stock is safer to use than debt.
    - If the firm is highly successful, common stockholders will not have to share the success with preferred stockholders because preferred dividends are fixed.
    - Preferred stockholders do have a higher priority claim than common stockholders.
    - Preferred stock is used in situations where neither debt nor common stock is entirely appropriate.

☐ Preferred stock has the following important features:
  - ~ Preferred stockholders have priority over common stockholders with regard to earnings and assets.
    - To reinforce this feature, most preferred stocks have coverage requirements similar to those on bonds.
  - ~ Unlike common stock, preferred stock always has a par value (or its equivalent under some other name).
    - The par value establishes the amount due to preferred stockholders in the event of liquidation.
    - The preferred dividend generally is stated as a percentage of par value.
  - ~ Most preferred stock provides for *cumulative dividends*. This is a protective feature on preferred stock that requires preferred dividends previously unpaid to be paid

before any common dividends can be paid.

~ Some preferred stock is *convertible* into common stock.

~ Other provisions such as voting rights, participating stock, sinking funds, call provisions, and an effective maturity date, are occasionally found in preferred stock.

The corporation's common stockholders are the owners of the corporation, and as such, they have certain rights and privileges. Common stock is equity that represents ownership in a corporation.

☐ Common stockholders have the last claim on the distribution of earnings and assets.

☐ The firm has no obligation to pay common stock dividends.

~ The return investors receive when they own a company's common stock is based on both the change in the stock's market value (capital gain) and the dividend paid by the company.

• *Income stocks* are stocks that traditionally pay large, relatively constant dividends each year.

• *Growth stocks* are stocks that generally pay little or no dividends in order to retain earnings to help fund growth opportunities.

☐ Common stock has no specified maturity; it is perpetual.

~ Repurchases of common stock do occur in the financial markets. Repurchases might be undertaken when:

• A firm has excess cash and no good investment opportunities.

• The price of the firm's stock is undervalued.

• Management wants to gain more ownership control of the firm.

☐ Common stockholders have control of the firm through their election of the firm's directors, who elect officers to manage the business.

~ Stockholders who are unable to attend annual meetings may still vote shares of common stock by means of a *proxy*.

• A proxy is a document giving one person the authority to act for another, typically the power to vote shares of common stock.

• A *proxy fight* is an attempt by a person or group of people to gain control of a firm by getting its stockholders to grant that person or group the authority to vote their shares in order to elect a new management team.

• A *takeover* is an action whereby a person or group succeeds in ousting a firm's management and taking control of the company.

• *Poison pill provisions* allow stockholders of a firm that is taken over by another firm to buy shares in the second firm at a reduced price. This provision makes an acquisition unattractive, and wards off hostile takeover attempts.

☐ The *preemptive right* gives current shareholders the right to purchase any new shares issued in proportion to their current holdings.

- ~ The inclusion of the preemptive right in a corporate charter may or may not be required by state law.
- ~ The preemptive right enables current owners to maintain their proportionate share of ownership and control of the business.
- ~ It protects stockholders against a dilution of value that occurs if new shares are sold at relatively low prices.

☐ *Classified stock* is common stock that is given a special designation, such as Class A, Class B, and so forth, to meet special needs of the company. The use of classified stock enables the public to take a position in a conservatively financed growth company without sacrificing income, while founders retain absolute control during the crucial early stages of the firm's development.
- ~ Note that Class A and Class B have no standard meanings. One class will typically receive dividends, while the other class will retain voting control.
- ~ *Founders' shares,* owned by the firm's founders, have sole voting rights but generally have restricted dividends for a specified number of years.
- ~ A privately owned, or *closely held corporation* is a corporation that is owned by a few individuals who are typically associated with the firm's management. Their stock is called *closely held stock.*
- ~ A *publicly owned corporation* is owned by a relatively large number of individuals who are not actively involved in its management. Their stock is called *publicly held stock.*

The term derivatives refers to financial assets that have values dependent on, or derived from, the value of some other asset(s), such as stocks or bonds. Because their values depend on the values of other assets, derivative securities are rather complex investments.

☐ An *option* is a contract that gives its holder the right to buy (or sell) an asset at some predetermined price within a specified period of time.
- ~ "Pure options" are instruments that are created by outsiders. They are bought and sold primarily by investors (or speculators).
- ~ There are many types of options and option markets.
  - • *Call options* convey the right to buy a share of stock at a set price called the *exercise*, or *striking*, *price*.
  - • *Put options* give the holder the right to sell the stock at the striking price.
- ~ Corporations are not directly involved with the options market—they do not raise money in this market.

☐ *Convertible securities* are bonds or preferred stocks that can be converted into common stock at the option of the holder.
- ~ Conversion does not produce additional capital for the issuing firm. However, this reduction of debt or preferred stock will strengthen the firm's balance sheet and make it easier to raise additional capital.
- ~ The *conversion ratio (CR)* specifies the number of common shares that will be received for each bond or share of preferred stock that is converted.

~ The *conversion price, P_c,* is the effective price paid for the common stock when conversion occurs.

- For example, if a bond is issued at its par value of $1,000 and can be converted into 40 shares of common stock, the conversion price is $25 = $1,000/40.
- If the stock's market value rises above $25 per share, it would be beneficial for the bondholder to convert (ignoring any costs associated with conversion).

☐ A *futures contract* represents an arrangement for delivery of an item at some date in the future, where the details of the delivery, including the amount to be delivered and the price that will be paid at delivery, are specified when the futures contract is created.

~ Multinational corporations often enter into futures contracts for foreign currencies used in their transactions.

- The futures contract provides the company with insurance against unfavorable changes in exchange rates—the company has hedged its risk.

☐ A *swap* is an agreement to exchange cash flows or assets at some time in the future.

Different investors have different risk/return tradeoff preferences, so to appeal to the broadest possible market, a firm must offer securities that attract as many different types of investors as possible.

☐ Different securities are more popular at different points in time, and firms tend to issue whatever is popular at the time they need money.

☐ Used wisely, a policy of selling differentiated securities to take advantage of market conditions can lower a firm's overall cost of funds below what it would be if the firm used only one class of debt or equity.

It is important to consider when firms might prefer to use debt and equity to raise funds, as well as when investors might have a preference for one of these investments compared to another.

☐ A principal advantage to debt issues is that a firm can limit its financial costs, which is beneficial when the firm prospers because earnings above the interest payments can be distributed to stockholders or reinvested in the firm to fund growth opportunities.

~ Another advantage of using debt financing is that it does not represent ownership, so debtholders do not have voting rights, and thus there is no dilution of ownership when additional debt is issued.

☐ Debt can be a drawback during times of economic and financial adversity because the interest obligation must be paid even if the firm's operating earnings are very low.

~ In addition, bond indentures and other debt contracts generally contain clauses that restrict certain actions the firm can make. Violations of these contractual provisions may force liquidation of the firm.

☐ A firm might consider issuing preferred stock if prosperous times are expected so that existing common stockholders do not have to share the prosperity.

~ Preferred stock does not "legally" obligate the firm to make payments to stockholders, and it has no maturity date.

☐ Preferred stock does have a major disadvantage from the issuer's standpoint: It has a higher after-tax cost than debt.

~ The major reason for this is preferred dividends are not deductible as a tax expense, whereas interest expense is deductible.

☐ Common stock financing has both advantages and disadvantages from the viewpoint of the corporation as well as from a social perspective.

~ Financing with common stock has the following advantages to the corporation:

• Common stock does not legally obligate the firm to make fixed payments to stockholders.

• Common stock has no fixed maturity date.

• Common stock increases the creditworthiness of the firm, because common stock cushions creditors against losses.

• Common stock can often be sold on better terms than debt if the firm's prospects look bright.

~ Stock appeals to certain groups of investors.

• Stock typically carries a higher expected total return (dividends plus capital gains) than does preferred stock or debt.

• It provides investors with a means to hedge against unanticipated inflation because common dividends tend to rise during inflationary periods.

~ Financing with common stock has the following disadvantages to the corporation:

• Issuing common stock extends voting rights, and perhaps even control, to new stockholders.

• Common stock gives new stockholders the right to a percentage of profits rather than to a fixed payment in the case of creditors.

• The costs of underwriting and distributing common stock usually are higher than those for debt or preferred stock.

• Dividends paid to stockholders are not tax deductible as is interest paid to creditors.

☐ Convertibles can be used to take advantage of some of the benefits associated with both debt and equity.

~ Debt with a conversion feature offers investors greater flexibility by providing them the opportunity to be either a debtholder or a stockholder. This feature generally allows the firm to sell debt with lower coupon interest rates and with fewer restrictive covenants.

~ Convertibles help the firm achieve "delayed equity financing" when conversion takes place.

~ Convertibles are generally subordinated to senior debt, so financing with convertibles leaves the company's access to "regular" debt unimpaired.

~ Convertibles provide a way of selling common stock at prices higher than those prevailing when the issue was made.

☐ Convertibles are useful, but they do have important disadvantages.
~ The use of convertibles, in effect, gives the issuer the opportunity to sell common stock at a price higher than it could sell stock otherwise. However, if the common stock increases greatly in price, the company probably would have been better off if it had used straight debt, in spite of its higher interest rate, and then later sold common stock to refund the debt.
~ Convertibles typically have a low coupon interest rate, an advantage that will be lost when conversion occurs.

☐ In designing securities the financial manager must consider the investor's point of view.
~ Both debt and preferred stock provide investors with a steadier income than common stock, and debtholders and preferred stockholders have preference over common stockholders in the event of liquidation.
~ The firm is legally obligated to make interest payments, and, if payments are missed, debtholders have legal recourse.
~ 70 percent of preferred dividends received by corporations are not taxable.
~ For individual investors as opposed to corporations, after-tax bond yields generally are higher than those on preferred stock, even though preferred stock is riskier.
~ From a social viewpoint, common stock is a desirable form of financing because it makes businesses less vulnerable to declines in sales and earnings.
~ Derivatives are used by investors either to manage risk associated with their portfolios or to speculate which direction prices will change in the future.
  • Options and futures are created by investors; they are not used by firms to raise funds.
  • In aggregate, options and futures do not create wealth in the financial markets.

For the most part, the financial securities of companies and institutions in other countries are similar to those in the U.S. Certain financial securities have been created to permit investors easier access to international investments.

☐ Foreign companies can be traded internationally through depository receipts, which represent shares of the underlying stocks of foreign companies. In the U.S., most foreign stock is traded through *American Depository Receipts (ADRs)*.
~ ADRs are "certificates" that represent ownership in stocks of foreign companies. They are held in trust by a bank located in the country in which the stock is traded.
~ Each ADR certificate represents a certain number of shares of stock of a foreign company, and it entitles the owner to receive any dividends paid by the company in U.S. dollars.
~ ADRs are traded in the stock markets in the U.S. All financial information, including values, is denominated in dollars and stated in English.
~ ADRs provide investors the ability to participate in the international financial markets without having to bear risks greater than those associated with the corporations in which the investments are made. The market values of ADRs move in tandem with the market values of the underlying stocks that are held in trust.

☐ The international debt markets offer a variety of instruments with many different features.

~ Any debt sold outside of the country of the borrower is called an *international debt*. There are two types of international debt: foreign debt and Eurodebt.

- *Foreign debt* is debt sold by a foreign borrower but denominated in the currency of the country in which the issue is sold. Foreign bonds generally are labeled according to the country in which they are issued: Yankee bonds (issued in the U.S.), Samurai bonds (issued in Japan), and Bulldog bonds (issued in England).

- The term *Eurodebt* is used to designate any debt sold in a country other than the one in whose currency the debt is denominated.

~ A far lower level of disclosure is required for Eurobonds than normally is found for bonds issued in domestic markets, particularly in the U.S.

- These bonds' purchasers generally are more sophisticated.

- Lower disclosure requirements result in lower total transaction costs for Eurobonds.

- Eurobonds appeal to investors for several reasons: (1) Generally they are issued in bearer form, so anonymity is provided. (2) Most governments do not withhold taxes on interest payments associated with Eurobonds.

~ There are other types of Eurodebt.

- *Eurocredits* are bank loans denominated in the currency of a country other than where the lending bank is located. Interest rates on Eurocredits typically are tied to a standard rate known as LIBOR, London InterBank Offer Rate. This is the interest rate offered by the largest and strongest London banks on deposits of other large banks of the highest credit standing.

- *Euro-commercial paper (Euro-CP),* similar to commercial paper issued in the U.S., is a short-term debt instrument issued by corporations with typical maturities of one, three, and six months.

- *Euronotes,* which represent medium-term debt, typically have maturities from one to ten years, and have general features much like those of longer-term debt instruments.

☐ The equities of foreign companies are like those of U.S. corporations. The primary difference between stocks of foreign companies and American companies is that U.S. regulations provide greater protection of stockholders' rights than those of most other countries.

~ In international markets, equity generally is referred to as Euro stock or Yankee stock.

- *Euro stock* refers to stock that is traded in countries other than the "home" country of the company, not including the U.S.

- *Yankee stock* is issued by foreign companies and traded in the U.S.

☐ As the financial markets become more "global" and more sophisticated, the financial instruments offered both domestically and internationally will change. As technology improves and regulations that bar or discourage foreign investing are repealed, the financial markets of other developed countries will become more prominent. Subsequently, new, innovative financial products will emerge.

SELF-TEST QUESTIONS

Definitional

1. Ownership interest in a corporation is reflected on the balance sheet by the _____ _____ accounts.

2. Amounts paid by stockholders in excess of the par value are shown as "additional _____-____ _____."

3. _____ _____ is the minimum amount for which new shares of common stock can be issued.

4. _____ _____ is the balance sheet account that indicates the total amount of earnings the firm has not paid out as dividends throughout its history and instead have been reinvested in the firm.

5. One of the fundamental rights of common stockholders is to elect a firm's _____, who, in turn, elect the firm's operating management.

6. If a stockholder cannot vote in person, participation in the annual meeting is still possible through a(n) _____.

7. The preemptive right protects stockholders against loss of _____ of the corporation as well as _____ of market value from the sale of new shares below market value.

8. A(n) _____ _____ is an attempt by a person or group of people to gain control of a firm by getting its stockholders to grant that person or group the authority to vote their shares in order to elect a new management team.

9. A(n) _____ is an action whereby a person or group succeeds in ousting a firm's management and taking control of the company.

10. Firms may find it desirable to separate the common stock into different _____. Generally, this classification is designed to differentiate stock in terms of the right to receive _____ and the right to _____.

11. A(n) _____ _____ or _____ _____ corporation is owned by a few individuals who are typically associated with the firm's management.

12. A(n) _____ loan is a contract to pay _____ and _____ on specific dates to a lender, and is usually negotiated directly between the borrowing firm and a financial institution.

13. A(n) _____ is a long-term contract under which the _____ agrees to make payments of interest and principal on specific dates to the holder.

14. Term loans have three major advantages over public offerings: _____, _____, and _____ _____ _____.

15. The legal document that spells out any legal restrictions associated with a bond, as well as the rights of both the bondholders and the issuing corporation is known as the _____.

16. The _____ represents the bondholders and sees that the terms of the indenture are carried out.

17. A bond secured by specific assets is known as a(n) _____ bond.

18. A(n) _____ is an unsecured bond, and as such, it provides no lien against specific property as security for the obligation.

19. _____ bonds pay interest only when the firm has sufficient income to cover the interest payments.

20. _____ bonds may be turned in and exchanged for cash at the holder's option.

21. _____, or _____ _____, bonds have their interest rate payment tied to an inflation index protecting bondholders against inflation.

22. Failure to make a sinking fund payment places the company in _____, and could ultimately lead to _____.

23. In meeting its sinking fund requirements, a firm can _____ the bonds or purchase them on the _____ _____.

24. Except when the call is for sinking fund purposes, when a bond issue is called, the firm must pay a(n) _____ _____, or an amount in excess of the _____ value of the bond.

25. A(n) _____ _____ is a provision in a debt contract that requires the issuer to meet certain stated conditions.

26. _____ _____ bonds pay no interest but are offered at a substantial discount below their par values and hence provide capital appreciation rather than interest income.

27. A(n) _____ bond is a high-risk, high-yield bond issued to finance mergers, leveraged buyouts, or troubled companies.

28. Firms issue various securities because investors have different _____ / _____ tradeoff preferences.

29. Preferred stock is referred to as a hybrid because it is similar to _____ in some respects and to _____ in others.

30. _____ stockholders have priority over _____ stockholders with regard to earnings and assets.

31. Most preferred stock dividends are _____ and thus must be paid before any dividends can be paid to common stockholders.

32. Preferred stocks are attractive to _____ investors because 70 percent of preferred dividends received are not taxable.

33. Issuing preferred stock decreases the danger of _____ if operating income is too low to pay the preferred dividend.

34. A(n) _____ is a contract that gives its holder the right to buy (or sell) an asset at some predetermined price within a specified period of time.

35. _____ options convey the right to buy a share of stock at a set price, while _____ options give the holder the right to sell the stock at a set price.

36. Convertible securities are bonds or preferred stocks that may be converted into _____ _____ at the option of the _____.

37. The _____ _____ specifies the number of shares of common stock that will be received for each bond or share of preferred stock that is converted.

38. The _____ _____ is the effective price paid for the common stock when conversion occurs.

39. A(n) _____ asset is intangible: It represents an expectation, or promise, that future cash flows will be paid to the owner.

40. _____ _____ represent overnight loans from one bank to another.

41. _____ _____ is a type of promissory note, or legal IOU, issued by large, financially sound firms.

42. A(n) _____ ____ _____ represents a time deposit at a bank or other financial intermediary.

43. A(n) _____ _____ is a deposit in a bank outside the U.S. that is not converted into the currency of the foreign country; instead it is denominated in U.S. dollars.

44. _____ bonds are similar to Treasury bonds, except they are issued by state and local governments.

45. _____ _____ bonds are backed by the government's ability to impose taxes.

46. A(n) _____ asset is typically a tangible, or physically observable item.

47. Total _____ represent funds borrowed from such creditors as banks, materials suppliers, and bond investors.

48. Some debt instruments, called _____ loans, require the principal amount to be repaid in several payments during the life of the loan.

49. A bond's _____ _____ represents the total interest paid each year stated as a percentage of the bond's face value.

50. _____ _____ allow firms to refinance existing high-cost debt and replace it with lower-cost debt.

51. _____ _____ provisions allow stockholders of a firm that is taken over by another firm to buy shares in the second firm at a reduced price; thus, making any acquisition unattractive and warding off any hostile takeover attempts.

52. _____ shares typically have sole voting rights but generally have restricted dividends for a specified number of years.

53. A(n) _____ is an agreement to exchange cash flows or assets at some time in the future.

54. _____ _____ _____ are certificates that represent ownership in stocks of foreign companies.

55. _____ _____ is any debt sold outside of the country of the borrower.

Conceptual

56. There is a direct relationship between bond ratings and the required rate of return on bonds; that is, the higher the rating, the higher is the required rate of return.

   a. True   b. False

57. The "penalty" for having a low bond rating is less severe when the Security Market Line is relatively steep than when it is not so steep.

    a. True   **b.** False

58. The conversion of a convertible bond replaces debt with common equity on a firm's balance sheet, but it does not bring in any additional capital.

    a. True   **b.** False

59. Shares of common stock are authorized by management and issued by the owners of the business.

    a. True   **b.** False

60. When there is a fear of an increase in inflation, there is a "flight to quality;" Treasuries are in great demand, and the premium on low-quality over high-quality bonds increases.

    a. True   **b.** False

61. Preferred stock legally obligates the firm to make payments to stockholders, and it typically has a maturity date.

    a. True   **b.** False

62. Debt sold by a foreign borrower but denominated in the currency of the country in which the issue is sold is called

    a. Eurodebt.   **d.** American Depository Receipts.
    b. International debt.   **e.** None of the above.
    c. Foreign debt.

63. Discounted short-term securities (with typical maturities of less than one year) issued by the U.S. government are called

    a. Certificates of deposit.   **d.** Treasury bills.
    b. Commercial paper.   **e.** Federal funds.
    c. Money market mutual funds.

64. When stockholders assign their right to vote to another party, this is called

    a. A privilege.   **d.** A proxy.
    b. A preemptive right.   **e.** A prospectus.
    c. An ex right.

65. Which of the following would tend to increase the coupon interest rate on a bond that is to be issued?

a. Adding a sinking fund.
b. Adding a restrictive covenant.
c. Adding a call provision.
d. A change in the bond's rating from Aa to Aaa.
e. Both statements a and c above.

66. Which of the following statements is most correct?

a. A banker's acceptance is an arrangement in which one firm sells some of its financial assets to another firm with a promise to repurchase the securities at a higher price at a later date.
b. Bonds usually are not callable until several years (generally five to ten) after they are issued; bonds with these deferred calls are said to have call protection.
c. A conversion feature is a provision that facilitates the orderly retirement of a bond issue (or an issue of preferred stock).
d. Statements a, b, and c are correct.
e. Statements b and c are correct.

67. Which of the following statements is most correct?

a. Founders' shares are stock owned by the firm's founders that have sole voting rights but generally have restricted dividends for a specified number of years.
b. Corporations on whose stock options are written raise money in this market and have direct transactions in it.
c. A futures contract represents an arrangement for delivery of an item at some date in the future, where the details of the delivery, including the amount to be delivered and the price that will be paid at delivery, are specified when the futures contract is created.
d. Statements a, b, and c are correct.
e. Statements a and c are correct.

68. Which of the following is _not_ considered short-term debt?

a. Federal funds.
b. Debentures.
c. Commercial paper.
d. Term loans.
e. Both statements b and d; they are considered long-term debt.

69. Which of the following statements is most correct?

a. Cumulative dividends is a protective feature on common stock that requires common dividends previously unpaid to be paid before any preferred dividends can be paid.
b. Growth stocks are stocks that traditionally pay large, relatively constant dividends each year.
c. Pure options are instruments created by outsiders; they are bought and sold primarily by investors (or speculators).

    d. Both statements b and c are correct.

    e. None of the statements above is correct.

70. Which of the following statements is _not_ an advantage to the corporation when financing with common stock?

    a. Common stock does not legally obligate the firm to make fixed payments to stockholders.

    b. Common stock increases the creditworthiness of the firm, because common stock cushions creditors against losses.

    c. Issuing common stock extends voting rights, and perhaps even control, to new stockholders.

    d. The costs of underwriting and distributing common stock usually are higher than those for debt or preferred stock.

    e. Both statements c and d are disadvantages to the corporation when financing with common stock.

SELF-TEST PROBLEMS

(The following information applies to the next two Self-Test Problems.)

Central Food Brokers (CFB) is considering issuing a 20-year convertible bond that will be priced at its par value of $1,000 per bond. The bonds have a 12 percent annual coupon interest rate, and each bond could be converted into 40 shares of common stock.

1. What is the conversion price?

    a. $20   **b.** $25   **c.** $33   **d.** $40   **e.** $50

2. If CFB's bond conversion price were $20, what would its conversion ratio be?

    a. 20   **b.** 25   **c.** 33   **d.** 40   **e.** 50

3. Suppose you purchased a call option that permits you to purchase 100 shares of the stock of Happy Valley Printing Company for $25 per share any time in the next 3 months. Happy Valley has a current market price of $20 per share. Assume the stock's price increases to $30. What would be your gain or loss if you exercised the option and then immediately sold the stock? Ignore the amount paid for the purchase of the call option.

    a. -$250   **b.** $250   **c.** $500   **d.** $750   **e.** $1,000

4. Suppose you purchased a put option that permits you to sell 150 shares of the stock of XYZ Technology Inc. for $50 per share any time in the next 3 months. XYZ Technology has a current market price of $55 per share. Assume the stock's price decreases to $47.50. What would be your gain or loss if you exercised the put option? Ignore the amount paid for the purchase of the put option.

a. -$375   b. -$125   c. $250   d. $375   e. $500

(The following information applies to the next four Self-Test Problems.)

Energy Dynamics Inc. had the following balance sheet at December 31, 2006:

Energy Dynamics Inc.
Balance Sheet as of December 31, 2006

		Accounts payable	$ 144,900
		Notes payable	160,650
		Long-term debt	340,200
		Preferred stock	100,000
		Common stock (60,000 authorized,	
		42,000 shares outstanding)	769,000
		Retained earnings	706,000
Total assets		$2,220,750	Total liabilities and equity	$2,220,750

5. What is the amount of total liabilities on Energy Dynamics' balance sheet at year-end 2006?

a. $305,550   b. $340,200   c. $645,750   d. $745,750   e. $2,220,750

6. What is the amount of common equity on Energy Dynamics' balance sheet at year-end 2006?

a. $100,000   b. $706,000   c. $769,000   d. $1,475,000   e. $1,575,000

7. What is the book value per share of Energy Dynamics' common stock?

a. $22.23   b. $24.58   c. $26.25   d. $37.50   e. $35.12

8. Suppose the firm sold the remaining authorized shares and netted $33.55 per share from the sale. What would be the new book value per share?

a. $33.55   b. $34.65   c. $35.12   d. $36.32   e. $37.50

ANSWERS TO SELF-TEST QUESTIONS

1.	common equity	3.	Par value
2.	paid-in capital	4.	Retained earnings

5.	directors	31.	cumulative
6.	proxy	32.	corporate
7.	control; dilution	33.	bankruptcy
8.	proxy fight	34.	option
9.	takeover	35.	Call; put
10.	classes; dividends; vote	36.	common stock; holder
11.	closely held; privately owned	37.	conversion ratio
12.	term; interest; principal	38.	conversion price
13.	bond; borrower	39.	financial
14.	speed; flexibility; low issuance costs	40.	Federal funds
15.	indenture	41.	Commercial paper
16.	trustee	42.	certificate of deposit
17.	mortgage	43.	Eurodollar deposit
18.	debenture	44.	Municipal
19.	Income	45.	General obligation
20.	Putable	46.	real
21.	Indexed; purchasing power	47.	liabilities
22.	default; bankruptcy	48.	installment
23.	call; open market	49.	coupon rate
24.	call premium; par	50.	Call provisions
25.	restrictive covenant	51.	Poison pill
26.	Zero coupon	52.	Founders'
27.	junk	53.	swap
28.	risk/return	54.	American Depository Receipts
29.	debt; equity	55.	International debt
30.	Preferred; common		

56. b. The relationship is inverse. The higher the rating, the lower the default risk and hence the lower the required rate of return. Aaa/AAA is the highest rating, and as we go down the alphabet, the ratings are lower.

57. b. A steeper SML implies a higher risk premium on risky securities and thus a greater "penalty" on lower-rated bonds.

58. a. The bond is turned in to the company and replaced with common stock. No cash is exchanged.

59. b. Shares of common stock are authorized by the business' owners and issued by management.

60. a. This statement is correct.

61. b. Preferred stock doesn't legally obligate the firm to make preferred dividend payments, and it typically has no maturity date.

62.   c.   The correct answer is foreign debt. Eurodebt is debt sold in a country other than the one in whose country the debt is denominated. International debt is any debt sold outside of the country of the borrower. American Depository Receipts are certificates that represent ownership in stocks of foreign companies.

63.   d.   The correct answer is Treasury Bills. A certificate of deposit represents a time deposit at a bank or other financial intermediary. Commercial paper is a type of promissory note issued by large, financially sound firms. Money market mutual funds are investment funds pooled and managed by investment companies for the purpose of investing in short-term financial assets. Federal funds represent overnight loans from one bank to another.

64.   d.   Recently, there has been a spate of proxy fights, whereby a dissident group of stockholders solicits proxies in competition with the firm's management. If the dissident group gets a majority of the proxies, then it can gain control of the board of directors and oust existing management.

65.   c.   Sinking funds, restrictive covenants, and an improvement in the bond rating all indicate lower risk for the bond and hence would lower the coupon rate.

66.   b.   Statement a is false; this is the definition of a repurchase agreement. Statement c is false; this is the definition of a sinking fund provision.

67.   e.   Statement b is false; corporations on whose stock options are written do not raise money in this market nor have any direct transactions in it.

68.   e.   Only federal funds and commercial paper included in this list are short-term debt. Both debentures and term loans have maturities greater than one year and are considered long-term debt.

69.   c.   Only statement c is correct. Cumulative dividends are a protective feature on preferred stock that requires previously unpaid preferred dividends to be paid before any common dividends can be paid. Income stocks are stocks that traditionally pay large, relatively constant dividends each year.

70.   e.   Statements a and b are advantages to the corporation when financing with common stock. Additional advantages to the corporation include: (1) common stock has no fixed maturity date and (2) common stock can often be sold on better terms than debt if the firm's prospects look bright.

SOLUTIONS TO SELF-TEST PROBLEMS

1.   b. P_c = Par value/Shares received = $1,000/40 = $25.00.

2.   e. C_R = $1,000/$20 = 50.

3. c. ($30 – $25) × 100 = $500. You would have a gain of $500.

4. d. ($50 – $47.50) × 150 = $375. You would have a gain of $375.

5. c. The firm's total liabilities is the sum of its current liabilities and long-term debt: $144,900 + $160,650 + $340,200 = $645,750.

6. d. The firm's common equity is the sum of the firm's common stock, paid-in capital, and retained earnings: $769,000 + $0 + $706,000 = $1,475,000. Preferred stock is not common equity.

7. e. The firm's book value per share is calculated as ($769,000 + $706,000)/42,000 = $35.12.

8. b. The firm's new book value per share would be calculated as follows:

Additional common equity = 18,000 shares × $33.55 = $603,900.

Total common equity = $1,475,000 + $603,900 = $2,078,900.

New book value per share = $2,078,900/60,000 = $34.65.

OVERVIEW

Financial markets are extremely important to the economic well-being of our country. Thus, it is important that both investors and financial managers understand the environment and markets within which securities are traded and businesses operate. Therefore, in this chapter, we examine the markets where firms raise funds, securities are traded, and the prices for stocks and bonds are established.

OUTLINE

Businesses, individuals, and government units often need to raise capital (funds). People and organizations that need money are brought together with those having surplus funds in the financial markets.

☐ There are a great many different financial markets, each one consisting of many institutions and individuals, in a developed economy.

☐ *Financial asset markets* deal with stocks, bonds, mortgages, and other claims on real assets with respect to the distribution of future cash flows.

☐ In a general sense, the term *financial market* refers to a conceptual mechanism rather than a physical location or a specific type of organization or structure.
   ~ Financial markets are usually described as a system comprised of individuals and institutions, instruments, and procedures that bring together borrowers and savers, no matter the location.

The primary role of financial markets is to help bring together borrowers and savers (lenders) by facilitating the flow of funds. In developed economies, financial markets help efficiently allocate excess funds of savers to individuals and organizations in need of funds for investment or consumption. Financial markets provide us with the ability to transfer income through time. Funds are transferred by three different processes.

☐ A *direct transfer* of money and securities occurs when a business sells its stock or bonds directly to savers (investors), without going through any type of intermediary, or financial institution.

☐ Transfers through an *investment banking house* occur when a brokerage firm serves as a middleman and facilitates the issuance of securities.

☐ Transfers through a *financial intermediary* occur when a bank or mutual fund obtains funds from savers, issues its own securities in exchange, and then uses these funds to purchase other securities.
   ~ The existence of intermediaries greatly increases the efficiency of the financial markets.

☐ The financial markets provide efficient funds transfers. The types of market efficiency include economic efficiency and informational efficiency.
   ~ The financial markets are said to have *economic efficiency* if funds are allocated to their optimal use at the lowest costs.
      • Commissions and other costs associated with transactions are called *transaction costs*. When these costs are very high, investments will not be as attractive as when transaction costs are low.
   ~ If the prices of investments reflect existing information and adjust very quickly when new information becomes available, then the financial markets have achieved *informational efficiency*. Informational efficiency generally is divided into three categories:
      • *Weak-form efficiency* states that all information contained in past price movements is fully reflected in current market prices.
      • *Semistrong-form efficiency* states that current market prices reflect all publicly available information.
      • *Strong-form efficiency* states that current market prices reflect all pertinent information, whether publicly available or privately held.
   ~ The results of most of the market efficiency studies suggest that the financial markets are highly efficient in the weak form and reasonably efficient in the semistrong form, but strong-form efficiency does not hold.
   ~ Financial markets that are informationally efficient also tend to be economically efficient because investors can expect prices to reflect appropriate information and thus make intelligent choices about which investments are expected to provide the highest returns.

There are a number of different types of financial markets. Financial markets are differentiated according to the types of investments, maturities of investments, types of borrowers and lenders, locations of the markets, and types of transactions.

☐ The markets for short-term financial instruments are termed the *money markets*, while the markets for long-term financial instruments are termed the *capital markets*.

~ Money markets include instruments with maturities equal to one year or less when originally issued.

- Money markets include only debt instruments, because equity instruments have no specific maturity.

- The primary function of the money markets is to provide liquidity to businesses, governments, and individuals to meet short-term needs for cash.

~ Capital markets include instruments with original maturities greater than one year.

- Capital markets include both equity instruments and long-term debt instruments, such as mortgages, corporate bonds, and government bonds.

- The primary function of the capital markets is to provide us with the opportunity to transfer cash surpluses or deficits to future years—to transfer income through time.

☐ The *debt markets* are the markets where loans are traded, while the *equity markets* are the markets where stocks of corporations are traded.

~ Equity markets are also called stock markets.

~ Debt markets generally are described according to the characteristics of the debt that is traded.

- The segmentation of the debt markets is based on the maturity of the instrument, the issuer, and the investor.

- The largest segment of the debt markets is represented by the bond markets, where government, corporate, and foreign bonds are traded.

☐ The *primary markets* are the markets where "new" securities are traded, while the *secondary markets* are the markets where "used" securities are traded.

~ The primary markets are the markets in which corporations raise new capital.

~ Secondary markets are markets in which securities and other financial assets are traded among investors after they have been issued by corporations and public agencies such as municipalities.

- The corporation whose securities are being traded in the secondary market is not involved in the transaction and, thus, does not receive any funds from such a sale.

☐ Options, futures, and swaps are some of the securities traded in the *derivatives markets*. These securities are called derivatives because their values are determined, or "derived," directly from other assets.

~ Although derivatives often are used to speculate about the movements of prices in the financial markets and the markets for commodities, they typically are used to help manage risk.

- Individuals, corporations, and governments use derivatives to hedge risk by offsetting exposures to uncertain price changes in the future.

The stock market is one of the most important markets to financial managers because it is here that the price of each stock, and hence the value of all publicly-owned firms, is established. Stock market transactions can be classified into three distinct types:

☐ Trading in the outstanding, previously issued shares of established, publicly owned companies: the secondary market.

☐ Additional shares sold by established, publicly owned companies: the primary market.

☐ New public offerings by privately held firms: the initial public offering (IPO) market: the primary market.
  ~ Whenever stock in a privately held corporation is offered to the public for the first time, the company is said to be *going public*.
  ~ The market for stock that has recently gone public is called the *initial public offering (IPO) market*.

There are two basic types of stock markets in the United States: physical stock exchanges and organized investment networks (over-the-counter market).

☐ *Physical stock exchanges*, typified by the New York Stock Exchange (NYSE) and the American Stock Exchange (AMEX), are tangible, physical entities.
  ~ Companies whose stock trade on an physical exchange are said to be *listed*.
  ~ Exchange members are charged with different trading responsibilities, depending on the type of seat that is owned.
    • *Commission brokers* are individuals employed by brokerage firms that are members of the exchange.
    • *Independent brokers*, sometimes called floor brokers, are independent, freelance brokers who work for themselves rather than for a brokerage firm.
    • *Competitive traders*, also known as registered floor traders, represent a small group of individuals who trade only for their own accounts.
    • *Specialists* are considered the most important participants in NYSE transactions because their role is to bring buyers and sellers together.
  ~ For a stock to be traded on an exchange, it must be *listed*.
    • Each exchange has established *listing requirements*, the quantitative and qualitative characteristics a firm must possess to be listed.
    • The primary purpose for the listing requirements is to ensure that investors have some interest in the company so its stock will be actively traded on the exchange.

☐ *Organized investment networks (over-the-counter (OTC) market)* are intangible organizations that consist of networks of dealers and brokers that provide for security transactions not conducted on the organized exchanges.
  ~ The stocks of smaller publicly owned firms are traded in the OTC market and are said to be *unlisted*.
  ~ Many of the brokers and dealers who make up the over-the-counter market are members of a self-regulating body known as the *National Association of Security Dealers (NASD)*, which licenses brokers and oversees trading practices.

~ Today, the NASDAQ is considered a sophisticated market of its own, separate from the OTC. The NASDAQ has market makers who continuously monitor trading activities in various stocks to ensure stocks are available to traders who want to buy, and vice versa.

~ Electronic Communications Networks (ECN), which are part of the organized investment network system, are systems that transfer information about securities transactions to facilitate the execution of orders by automatically matching buy and sell orders for a large number of investors.

The financial manager must have knowledge of the investment banking process, the process by which new securities are issued. Investment bankers help corporations design securities with the features that are most attractive to investors given existing market conditions, buy these securities from the corporations, and then resell them to investors. Investment banking decisions take place in two stages.

☐ At Stage I, the firm makes some preliminary decisions on its own.
  ~ The dollar amount of new capital required is established.
  ~ The type of securities to be offered is specified.
  ~ The basis on which to deal with the investment bankers, either by a *competitive bid* or a *negotiated deal*, is determined.
    ● Only a handful of the largest firms on the NYSE, whose securities are already well known to the investment banking community, are in a position to use the competitive bid process.
    ● The vast majority of offerings of stocks or bonds are made on a negotiated basis.
  ~ The investment banking firm must be selected.

☐ The Stage II decisions are made jointly by the firm and the selected investment banker.
  ~ First, the two parties will reevaluate the Stage I decisions.
  ~ The firm and its investment banker must decide whether the banker will work on a "best efforts" basis or will "underwrite" the issue.
    ● On a *best efforts sale*, the banker does not guarantee that the securities will be sold or that the company will get the cash it needs. The securities are handled on a contingency basis, and the investment banker is paid a commission based on the amount of the issue that is sold.
    ● On an *underwritten* issue, the company does get a guarantee. Essentially, the banker purchases the issue, then resells the securities at a higher price. The banker bears significant risks in underwritten offerings.
  ~ The costs associated with a new security issue are termed *issuance (flotation) costs*.
    ● These costs include compensation to the investment banker plus legal, accounting, printing and engraving, and other costs borne by the issuer.
    ● The *underwriter's spread* is the difference between the price at which the investment banking firm buys an issue from a company and the price at which the securities are sold in the primary market.
    ● Flotation costs depend on the type of security issued and the size of the issue.
  ~ Several factors must be considered when setting the offering price.

- • If the firm is already publicly owned, the offering price will be based on the existing market price of the stock or the yield on the bonds.
- • The investment banker will have an easier job if the issue is priced relatively low, while the issuer naturally wants as high a price as possible.
- • It is important that the equilibrium price be approximated as closely as possible.

☐ The *registration statement* provides financial, legal, and technical information about the company, while the *prospectus* summarizes the information in the registration statement and is provided to prospective investors for use in selling the securities.

☐ Because of potential losses from price declines caused by a falling market, underwriters do not generally handle issues single-handedly.
- ~ Groups of investment bankers form an *underwriting syndicate* to spread the risk and minimize individual losses. Syndicates are also useful because an individual banker's clients may not be able to absorb a large issue.
  - • The investment banking house that sets up the deal is called the lead, or managing, underwriter.
- ~ A *selling group* may handle the distribution of securities to individual investors.
- ~ The underwriters act as wholesalers and bear the risk associated with the issue, whereas the members of the selling group act as retailers.

☐ A *shelf registration* is a procedure used by large, well-established firms to issue new securities on very short notice.
- ~ Large, well-known public companies that issue securities frequently file a master registration statement with the SEC and then update it with a short-form statement just prior to each individual offering.

☐ For new issues, the investment banker will normally maintain a market in the shares after the public offering. This is done in order to provide liquidity for the shares and to maintain a good relationship with both the issuer and the investors who purchased the shares.

Sales of new securities, such as stocks and bonds, as well as operations in the secondary markets, are regulated by the Securities and Exchange Commission (SEC) and, to a lesser extent, by each of the 50 states.

☐ The SEC regulations are intended to ensure investors receive fair financial disclosure from publicly traded companies and to discourage fraudulent and misleading behavior by firms' investors, owners, and employees to manipulate stock prices.

☐ The SEC has jurisdiction over all interstate offerings of new securities to the public in amounts of $1.5 million or more.

☐ A company wishing to issue new stock must file both a registration statement and a prospectus with the SEC.

~ When the SEC approves the registration statement and prospectus, it only validates that the required information has been furnished. The SEC doesn't provide judgment concerning the quality or value of the issue.

☐ The SEC regulates all national securities exchanges, and companies whose securities are listed on an exchange must file annual reports with both the SEC and the exchange.

☐ The SEC has control over stock trades by corporate *insiders*. Officers, directors, and major stockholders must file monthly reports of changes in their holdings of the corporation's stock.

☐ The SEC has the power to prohibit manipulation of securities' prices by such devices as pools or wash sales.

Financial markets have become much more global during the last few decades.

☐ Even with the expansion of stock markets internationally, exchanges in the U.S. still conduct the greatest number of trades, both with respect to volume and value.

☐ The international market for bonds has experienced growth similar to the international stock markets.

☐ On January 1, 1999, the European Monetary Union (EMU) began. The EMU started with 11 countries that created a common currency, called the euro, and a common debt instrument that is denominated in the euro and is traded in a unified financial market called the Euro market.

☐ While the globalization of financial markets continues and international markets offer investors greater opportunities, investing overseas can be difficult due to restrictions or barriers erected by foreign countries.
~ Most individuals interested in investing internationally do so indirectly by purchasing financial instruments that represent foreign stocks, bonds, and other investments but that are offered by institutions in the United States.
~ Investors can participate internationally by purchasing (1) American Depository Receipts (ADRs), (2) mutual funds that hold international stocks, or (3) foreign securities certificates issued in dollar denominations.

SELF-TEST QUESTIONS

Definitional

1. Markets for short-term debt securities are called _____ markets, while markets for long-term debt and equity are called _____ markets.

2. Firms raise capital by selling newly issued securities in the _____ markets, while

existing, outstanding securities are traded in the _____ markets.

3. An institution that issues its own securities in exchange for funds and then uses these funds to purchase other securities is called a financial _____.

4. A(n) _____ _____ firm facilitates the transfer of capital between savers and borrowers by acting as a middleman.

5. The two basic types of stock markets are the _____ _____, such as the NYSE, and the _____-_____-_____ market, which consists of a network of dealers and brokers.

6. Securities traded on the organized exchanges are known as _____ securities.

7. Before an interstate issue of stock amounting to $1.5 million or more can be sold to the public, it must be _____ with and approved by the _____.

8. Setting the _____ price for a stock issue may present a conflict of interest between the issuer and the _____ _____.

9. In order to spread the risk of underwriting a sizable common stock issue, investment bankers will form a(n) _____ _____.

10. On a(n) _____ _____ arrangement, the investment banker does not guarantee that the securities will be sold or that the company will get the cash it needs.

11. On a(n) _____ issue the investment banker essentially purchases the issue and then resells the securities at a higher price bearing significant risks.

12. A(n) _____ _____ is a procedure used by large, well-established firms to issue new securities on very short notice.

13. The financial markets are said to have _____ _____ if funds are allocated to their optimal use at the lowest costs.

14. If the prices of investments reflect existing information and adjust very quickly when new information becomes available, then the financial markets have achieved _____ _____.

15. _____-_____ efficiency states that current market prices reflect all publicly available information.

16. Options, futures, and swaps are some of the securities traded in the _____ markets.

17. The market for stock that has recently gone public is called the _____ _____ _____ market.

18. The primary purpose for _____ _____ is to ensure that investors have some interest in the company so its stock will be actively traded on the exchange.

19. _____ _____ markets deal with stocks, bonds, mortgages, and other claims on real assets with respect to the distribution of future cash flows.

20. A(n) _____ _____ of money and securities occurs when a business sells its stocks or bonds to savers (investors), without going through any type of intermediary, or financial institution.

21. _____-_____ efficiency states that all information contained in past price movements is fully reflected in current market prices.

22. The segmentation of the _____ markets is based on the maturity of the instrument, the issuer, and the investor.

23. Individuals, corporations, and governments use derivatives to _____ risk by offsetting exposures to uncertain price changes in the future.

24. The _____ market is important to financial managers because it is here that the price of each stock, and hence the value of all publicly owned firms, is established.

25. Additional shares sold by established, publicly owned companies occur in the _____ market.

26. Whenever stock in a privately held corporation is offered to the public for the first time, the company is said to be _____ _____.

27. Exchange members are charged with different trading responsibilities, depending on the type of _____ that is owned.

28. _____ are considered the most important participants in NYSE transactions because their role is to bring buyers and sellers together.

29. The stocks of smaller publicly owned firms are traded in the OTC market and are said to be _____.

30. One of the Stage I investment banking decisions is the basis on which to deal with the investment banker. It can be done either by a(n) _____ _____ or as a(n) _____ _____.

Conceptual

43

31. Flotation costs are generally higher for bond issues than for stock issues.

 a. True   **b.** False

32. The primary role of financial markets is to help bring together borrowers and savers by facilitating the flow of funds.

 a. True   **b.** False

33. The results of most of the market efficiency studies suggest that the financial markets are highly efficient in the semistrong form and reasonably efficient in the strong form.

 a. True   **b.** False

34. Financial markets that are informationally efficient also tend to be economically efficient because investors can expect prices to reflect appropriate information and thus make intelligent choices about which investments are expected to provide the highest returns.

 a. True   **b.** False

35. Which of the following statements is correct?

 a. When the SEC approves the registration statement and prospectus, it provides judgment concerning the quality or value of the issue.
 b. An investment banker will normally maintain a market in the shares after a public offering to provide liquidity for the shares and to maintain a good relationship with both the issuer and the investors who purchased the shares.
 c. The registration statement summarizes the information in a prospectus and is provided to investors for use in selling securities.
 d. Both statements a and c are correct.
 e. Both statements b and c are correct.

36. Which of the following statements is correct?

 a. Large companies such as IBM and Exxon are exempt from SEC listing requirements, but small companies (assets below $10 million) are not. Hence, small companies have listed stock, while large companies have unlisted stock.
 b. If a company's stock is publicly owned, and if its price has been established in the market and is quoted in a source such as *The Wall Street Journal*, then the price of any new issue of stock will be based on the current market price. However, if the stock is not traded, and if the company is issuing shares in an "initial public offering," or IPO, then the Securities and Exchange Commission (SEC) must approve the price at which the stock is to be offered to the public.
 c. In the United States, *most* new issues of stock are sold through the investment banking departments of large commercial banks.

d. The SEC must normally approve the prospectuses relating to new stock offerings by companies whose securities are listed on the New York Stock Exchange before the new stock can be sold to the public.

e. Statements b and d are correct.

SELF-TEST PROBLEMS

1. GJC Inc., whose stock price now is $67.50, needs to raise $35 million in common stock. Underwriters have informed the firm's management that it must price the new issue to the public at $62.00 per share to ensure the shares will be sold. The underwriters' compensation will be 7 percent of the issue price, so GJC will net $57.66 per share. GJC will also incur expenses in the amount of $810,000. How many shares must GJC sell to net $35 million after underwriting and flotation expenses?

    a. 549,825   **b.** 600,250   **c.** 621,055   **d.** 654,975   **e.** 700,000

2. Mansell Industries needs to raise $125 million in debt. To issue the debt, Mansell must pay its underwriter a fee equal to 2.5 percent of the issue. Mansell estimates that other expenses associated with the issue will total $750,625. If the face value of each bond is $1,000, how many bonds must be issued to net the firm the $125 million it needs? Assume that the firm cannot issue a fraction of a bond (i.e., 1/2 a bond)—only "whole bonds" can be issued.

    a. 125,000   **b.** 126,225   **c.** 127,775   **d.** 128,975   **e.** 130,000

3. Better Brokers Inc. specializes in underwriting new issues by small firms. On a recent offering of Reynolds & Zaun Inc. (RZI), the terms were as follows:

Number of shares	5 million
Proceeds to RZI	$27 million

    The out-of-pocket expenses incurred by Better Brokers in the design and distribution of the issue were $625,000. What profit or loss would Better Brokers incur if the issue were sold to the public at an average price of $6.50 per share?

    a. -$3,775,000   **b.** +$4,875,000   **c.** +$5,500,000   **d.** +$32,500,000   **e.** - $5,000,000

ANSWERS TO SELF-TEST QUESTIONS

1.	money; capital		counter (OTC)
2.	primary; secondary	6.	listed
3.	intermediary	7.	registered; SEC
4.	investment banking	8.	offering; investment banker
5.	physical stock exchanges; over-the-	9.	underwriting syndicate

10.	best efforts	**21.**	Weak-form
11.	underwritten	**22.**	debt
12.	shelf registration	**23.**	hedge
13.	economic efficiency	**24.**	stock
14.	informational efficiency	**25.**	primary
15.	Semistrong-form	**26.**	going public
16.	derivatives	**27.**	seat
17.	initial public offering	**28.**	Specialists
18.	listing requirements	**29.**	unlisted
19.	Financial asset	**30.**	competitive bid; negotiated deal
20.	direct transfer		

31. b. The investment banker normally expends greater effort in selling stocks, thus must charge a higher fee.

32. a. This statement is correct.

33. b. Most studies suggest that the financial markets are highly efficient in the weak form and reasonably efficient in the semistrong form, but strong-form efficiency doesn't hold.

34. a. This statement is correct.

35. b. When the SEC approves the registration statement and prospectus, it only validates that the required information has been furnished. So, statement a is false. Statement b is correct. Statement c is false; the registration statement provides financial, legal, and technical information about the company.

36. d. All companies are subject to the SEC's listing requirements, which makes statement a false. The SEC does not have to approve offering prices for IPOs. Therefore, statement b is false. Finally, statement c is false because commercial banks traditionally have not been able to participate in investment banking activities. But at the present time, laws barring commercial banks from investment banking activities are being changed.

SOLUTIONS TO SELF-TEST PROBLEMS

1. c. $(\$62.00X)0.93 - \$810,000 = \$35,000,000$
$\$57.66X = \$35,810,000$
$X = 621,055$ shares.

2. d. $0.975(\$1,000X) = \$125,000,000 + \$750,625$
$\$975X = \$125,750,625$
$X = 128,975$ bonds.

3. b. Better Brokers' profit = Market value of shares – Expenses – Company's net proceeds
= ($6.50)5,000,000 – $625,000 – $27,000,000
= $32,500,000 – $27,625,000
= $4,875,000.

OVERVIEW

Most people do not provide funds directly to borrowers; rather they transfer funds through firms known as financial intermediaries. In this chapter, we describe the functions and types of financial intermediaries as well as the banking system and the role of the Federal Reserve as the central bank of the United States. Finally, we illustrate how the U.S. banking system differs from banking systems in other countries.

OUTLINE

Financial intermediaries include financial service organizations such as commercial banks, savings and loan associations, pension funds, and insurance companies.

☐ *Financial intermediaries* facilitate the transfer of funds from those who have funds (savers) to those who need funds (borrowers).
   ~ Financial intermediaries literally manufacture a variety of financial products, including mortgages, automobile loans, NOW accounts, money market mutual funds, and pension funds.
   ~ When intermediaries take funds from savers, they issue securities that represent claims, or liabilities, against the intermediaries. These funds are lent to businesses and individuals via debt instruments created by intermediaries.
      • The process by which financial intermediaries transform funds provided by savers into funds used by borrowers is called *financial intermediation*.
   ~ The presence of intermediaries improves economic well-being. In fact, financial intermediaries were created to fulfill specific needs of both savers and borrowers, and thus reduce inefficiencies that would exist if users of funds could get loans only by borrowing directly from savers.

☐ Additional benefits associated with intermediaries include:
   ~ *Reduced costs.* Intermediaries are more cost efficient than individuals because they create combinations of financial products that better match funds provided by savers with the needs of borrowers, and are able to achieve economies of scale by spreading costs over large numbers of transactions.
   ~ *Risk/diversification.* The loan portfolios of intermediaries generally are well

48

diversified because they provide funds to a large number and variety of borrowers by offering many different types of loans, thereby spreading their risk.

~ *Funds divisibility/pooling.* Intermediaries can pool funds provided by individuals to offer loans or other financial products with different denominations to borrowers.

~ *Financial flexibility.* Because intermediaries offer a variety of financial products, both savers and borrowers have greater choices, or financial flexibility, than can be achieved with direct placements.

~ *Related services.* Many intermediaries provide financial services in areas in which they achieve comparative advantages, such as expertise or economies of scale, over individuals.

☐ In general, financial intermediaries increase the standard of living in the economy. Thus, intermediaries are good for the economy.

~ The financial products offered by intermediaries help both individuals and businesses invest in opportunities that otherwise might be unreachable.

• Without the mortgages offered by savings and loan associations, individuals would find it much more difficult to purchase houses.

• Intermediaries offer loans to businesses that increase growth, hence improve manufacturing abilities and increase employment.

In the United States, a large set of specialized, highly efficient financial intermediaries has evolved. Competition and government policy have created a rapidly changing arena, however, such that different types of institutions currently create financial products and perform services that previously were reserved for others. This trend has caused institutional distinctions to become blurred. Still, there remains a degree of institutional identity among various financial intermediaries.

☐ Each type of intermediary originated because there existed a particular need in the financial markets that was not satisfied at the time.

~ Historically, it generally has been easy to distinguish among various types of intermediaries with respect to the characteristics of assets and liabilities.

~ Even though various organizations are more alike today than any time in modern history, there still exist differences in the specific asset/liability structures among the intermediaries.

• The assets of financial institutions primarily consist of loans and other instruments that are comparable to the account receivable held by businesses.

• The liabilities of financial institutions primarily result from savers providing funds in the form of deposits or shares, which are similar to the accounts payable or notes payable used by businesses to raise funds.

~ While there exist many similarities, the types of loans, deposits, and other products offered by intermediaries differ among the various intermediaries.

☐ *Commercial banks* are the traditional "department stores of finance" because they offer a wide variety of products and services to a variety of customers.

~ Originally, banks were established to serve the needs of commerce, or business, hence the name commercial banks.

~ Today, commercial banks represent one of the largest depository intermediaries, and their operations impact nearly everyone either directly or indirectly.

~ The loans created by banks are funded by liabilities that consist primarily of deposits; deposits from businesses and individuals represent about two thirds of banks' liabilities.

☐ A *credit union* is a depository institution that is owned by its depositors, who are members of a common organization or association.

~ Credit unions operate as non-profit businesses and are managed by member depositors elected by other members.

~ Today, credit unions differ significantly from their earliest forms—they are much larger, hence less personal. But the spirit of credit unions remains unchanged—to serve depositor members.

- Because of the common bond members possess, loans from credit unions often are the cheapest source of funds available to individual borrowers.

~ Almost 70 percent of federally insured credit unions' assets are loans.

- More than 50 percent of the loans are classified as either individual or automobile.

- The funds used to make these loans primarily come from members' deposits, which generally are either checkable deposits called *share drafts*, regular savings accounts called *share accounts*, or such other types of savings as certificates of deposit and IRA accounts.

☐ *Thrifts* are financial institutions that cater to savers, especially individuals who have relatively small savings or need long-term loans to purchase houses.

~ Thrifts originally were established because the services offered by commercial banks were designed for businesses rather than individuals, whose needs differed greatly.

~ Two basic types of thrifts are *savings and loan associations (S&Ls)* and *mutual savings banks.*

~ Historically, S&Ls have been viewed as the ideal source for real estate mortgages.

~ Today, S&Ls take the funds of many small savers and then lend this money to home buyers and other types of borrowers.

- Without institutions such as S&Ls, savers would not be able to invest in mortgages unless they were willing to lend directly to borrowers, which would require funds to be "tied up" for long time periods.

- Savings accounts provide savers with greater flexibility, because funds do not have to be committed for long periods, and, in many cases, savings can be easily liquidated (withdrawn) with little or no restriction.

- Perhaps the most significant economic function of the S&Ls is to "create liquidity" that otherwise would be lacking.

~ Mutual savings banks, which operate mainly in the northeastern U.S., are similar to S&Ls, except they are owned and managed by their depositors, thus operating like credit unions.

~ About 70 percent of thrifts are savings associations, which have more than 90 percent of thrift deposits.

~ Thrifts still are viewed primarily as mortgage lending institutions.

☐ *Mutual funds* are investment companies that accept money from savers and then use these funds to buy various types of financial assets.
  ~ These organizations pool funds and thus reduce risks through diversification.
  ~ They also achieve economies of scale, which lower the costs of analyzing securities, managing portfolios, and buying and selling securities.
  ~ There are literally hundreds of different types of mutual funds with a variety of goals and purposes that meet the objectives of different types of savers.
    • Investors who prefer current income can invest in mutual funds referred to as *income funds*.
    • In contrast, investors who are willing to accept higher risks in hopes of higher returns can invest in mutual funds referred to as *growth funds*.
  ~ One of the newest savings mediums available in the financial markets is the *money market mutual fund*. This fund includes short-term, low-risk securities and generally allows investors to write checks against their accounts.
    • With more than $7.2 trillion in assets at the beginning of 2005, mutual fund investment companies represented the largest financial institution in the U.S.—with commercial banks a close second.
    • Today there are more than 8,186 individual mutual funds offered by various investment companies. Ninety-percent of the mutual funds are owned by more than 80 million individuals. The primary reason individuals invest in mutual funds is for retirement.
  ~ The assets of investment companies principally include stocks, bonds, and other similar financial instruments the companies purchase, whereas the major liability is represented by investors' (savers') shares that provide the funds used to purchase the financial assets.
  ~ The actual composition of the investment held by mutual funds changes as economic and financial market conditions change.
  ~ In general, when the economy is doing well and stock markets are moving upward, mutual funds tend to invest greater amounts in stocks; when the economy is stagnant and movements in stock markets are very uncertain or exhibit a downward trend, funds then tend to invest greater amounts in short-term, liquid assets (money market instruments).

☐ *Whole life insurance companies* differ from other financial institutions because they provide two services to individuals: insurance and savings. Whole life insurance companies receive premiums from individuals—a portion of the funds is invested and a portion is used to cover the insured.
  ~ In recent years, many life insurance companies have also offered a variety of tax-deferred saving plans designed to provide benefits to the participants when they retire.
  ~ The purpose of life insurance is to provide a beneficiary with protection against financial distress or insecurity that might result from the premature death of a wage earner.
  ~ Life insurance can be labeled either as term or whole life insurance.

- *Term life insurance* is a relatively short-term contract that provides protection for a temporary period, and it must be renewed each period to continue such protection.
- *Whole life insurance* is a long-term contract that provides lifetime protection.
~ The cost of term insurance, called the premium, generally increases with each renewal, because the risk of premature death increases as the insured ages.
~ The premiums associated with whole life insurance policies are fixed payments computed as an average of the premiums required over the expected life of the person insured.
  - The invested amounts provide savings features that create cash values for the whole life insurance policies.
  - Term life insurance policies do not provide savings features, because the premiums are fixed only for a short time period; thus, the premiums are based on the existing risks only and are changed at renewal if risks change.
~ Life insurance companies use statistical tables, called actuarial tables, to estimate the amounts of cash that will be needed each year to satisfy insurance claims.
~ Because whole life policies are long-term contracts, the companies invest significant portions of their funds in long-term assets, such as corporate bonds, stocks, and government bonds.
  - The principal source of funds is represented by the reserves associated with the whole life insurance policies and pension plans sold by the companies.
  - Reserves represent obligations of the companies associated with future commitments derived from currently outstanding policies.
~ To some extent, life insurance companies compete with commercial banks to provide funds to corporations. However, life insurance companies operate in different financial markets than banks.
  - While banks primarily help corporations meet their needs for short-term funds, insurance companies help to support long-term funding needs.

☐ *Pension funds* are retirement plans funded by corporations or government agencies for their workers and administered primarily by the trust departments of commercial banks or by life insurance companies.
~ The most famous pension plan is Social Security, which is a government-sponsored plan funded by tax revenues.
~ Most state and municipal governments and large corporations offer pension plans to their employees.
  - Many of these plans accept both employer and employee contributions, which often are shielded from taxes until the assets are withdrawn from the plan.
~ "Pay-as-you-go" plans are termed *unfunded pensions*.
  - Social Security, which was established in 1935 to supplement the retirement income provided by private pensions, is the largest unfunded pension.
~ Like life insurance companies, pension funds are long-term contracts for fairly predictable payments. Therefore, pension plan assets are similar to those of life insurance companies; funds are invested primarily in long-term assets such as

stocks, mutual funds, and government securities.

Because intermediaries play such a critical role in the welfare of the economy, the financial services industry has been heavily regulated in an effort to ensure stability and safety in the nation's financial markets.

☐ Proponents of regulation argue that the parties involved in the financial intermediation process—savers, borrowers, and intermediaries—do not possess equal levels of expertise or have access to the same information, so legislation is needed to provide a more "even playing field" and to help maintain public confidence in the financial system.
  ~ Most of the financial panics we have experienced in the past can be traced to actions of intermediaries, such as engaging in unscrupulous behavior or taking on too much risk, that contributed to a public loss of faith in the country's financial system.

☐ The primary reason financial institutions are regulated is because it is generally accepted that the public needs protection from financial environments that can result in economic disasters caused by a "domino effect" triggered by the failures of financial intermediaries.
  ~ Much of the regulation that currently exists restricts the activities of financial institutions, presumably to maintain public confidence by helping to assure some degree of safety in the financial system.
  ~ To help maintain confidence, the funds provided to most financial institutions are insured by agencies established through federal or state legislation.
    • The primary purpose of such insurance is to assure savers their funds will be safe even if the financial intermediary fails.

☐ The most familiar insuring agency is the Federal Deposit Insurance Corporation (FDIC), which insures the deposits at most banks and thrift institutions.
  ~ Its primary objective is to maintain safety and depositor confidence by shifting the risk of losing deposited funds from the saver/depositor to the FDIC.
  ~ The federal deposit insurance available for credit unions is through the National Credit Union Share Insurance funds (NCUSIF).
  ~ Both the FDIC and the NCUSIF insure deposits for amounts up to $100,000 per individual.
  ~ The Federal Reserve (Fed) traditionally has been considered the regulatory agency of commercial banking.
    • The Fed actually has the power to impose reserve requirements on other financial institutions that accept deposits from savers or make conventional loans to borrowers.
    • While Fed regulations affect thrifts and credit unions, federally chartered thrifts are also regulated/supervised by the Office of Thrift Supervision (OTS), and federally chartered credit unions are regulated/supervised by the National Credit Union Administration (NCUA).

☐ Insurance companies are primarily regulated by the states in which they operate.
  ~ The purpose of regulations in the insurance industry is to help assure the financial stability of insurance companies.
  ~ The National Association of Insurance Commissioners (NAIC) is a group of state insurance commissioners that meets on a regular basis to discuss concerns in the insurance industry and to try to coordinate legislative efforts in each state to attain more uniform regulations nationwide.

☐ The major legislation affecting pension plans is the Employee Retirement Income Security Act (ERISA), which became law in 1974.
  ~ Although the law does not require firms to have pension plans, it does specify the conditions necessary for a retirement program to receive favorable tax benefits, such as tax-deferred contributions.
  ~ ERISA and its subsequent improvements have been instrumental in reforming the management of pension plans, thus ensuring greater safety of workers' retirement funds.
  ~ The federal insurance organization established by ERISA is the Pension Benefit Guarantee Corporation (PBGC), which insures benefits up to about $2,000 per month, with the maximum amount adjusted for inflation in future periods.

☐ The regulation of mutual funds is the responsibility of the Securities and Exchange Commission (SEC), except in a few instances where state regulations apply.
  ~ Regulations that apply to mutual funds are included in the Investment Company Act of 1940 and its subsequent changes.
  ~ The regulations provide that certain information is disclosed to investors, that the funds be diversified, and that managers and employees of funds avoid conflicts of interest associated with the investments held by the funds.
  ~ Because mutual funds represent investment pools that include risky assets such as stocks, bonds, and options, there is no federal insurance agency to assure the safety of savers funds.
    • Instead, each fund is required to inform investors/savers concerning the investment goal (e.g., income or growth) and an indication of the risk associated with pursuing that goal.

The banking system plays an important role in our business environment and our personal lives. It is important to have a basic knowledge of how the banking system works to understand how the nation's monetary policy is managed and the role of financial intermediaries in this process.

☐ The beginning of banking as we know it today probably did not start until the Middle Ages.
  ~ Widespread unrest and wars during these times resulted in a great deal of anarchy, and wealthy individuals felt compelled to protect their fortunes by storing their valuables with merchants—usually metalsmiths—who maintained facilities that were considered safe havens for property.
  ~ When the valuables were deposited, the merchants would issue a receipt that

verified the deposit and ownership of the property. When individuals wanted to purchase goods and services, they would redeem their depository receipts for the needed gold or silver.

~ In time, individuals found the depository receipts of the better known and more trusted metalsmiths could be used for trade.

~ The "safekeepers" realized a profit could be made by lending some of their idle inventories to other merchants and individuals who found themselves temporarily short of funds needed for trade.

~ It was not long before metalsmiths discovered that they always had positive inventories of gold and silver because only a portion of the receipts were redeemed at any point in time. These safekeepers realized they needed to maintain metal reserves equal to only a fraction of the total deposits.

~ The metalsmiths discovered that "money" could be created by lending some of the deposits of others, as long as there were assurances that less than 100 percent of deposits was required to meet depositors' withdrawals. This was the origination of the fractional reserve system, which forms the basis of our current banking system.

☐ In a *fractional reserve system*, the amount of reserves maintained to satisfy requests for withdrawals of deposits is less than 100 percent of the total deposits.

~ *Excess reserves* are reserves at a bank or other institution affected by reserve requirements in excess of the amount of funds required to be held on deposit. They are equal to total reserves minus required reserves.

~ The amount of additional money produced by the original deposit is dependent on the fraction that must be held in reserves—if the reserve requirement is 100 percent, there is no magnification; if there is no reserve requirement, the magnification is unlimited.

~ The maximum change in the money supply created by a fractional reserve system is computed as:

$$\text{Maximum change in the money supply} = \frac{\text{Excess reserves}}{\text{Reserve requirement}}.$$

- Thus, if all the excess reserves are loaned to individuals and subsequently redeposited in the bank, an initial $100 deposit would create $900 = [($100 − $10)/0.10] new money through additional deposits.

- At the same time, the amount of loans, or credit, created in the banking system also would be $900 because the additional money was created through the loans produced by the bank.

- When the bank has loaned the maximum amount based on a 10 percent reserve requirement, there are no excess reserves, the total deposits in the banking system equal $1,000, and the total required reserves are $100, the amount of the initial deposit.

~ If deposits are withdrawn from the bank, the process reverses, so money would contract according to the equation.

☐ The U.S. banking system is a fractional reserve system consisting of various depository institutions, such as banks and thrifts, chartered either by the federal government or by the state in which they are located.

~ Because the U.S. banking system includes both national and state charters, it is referred to as a *dual banking system*.

~ In the early years of its existence, the U.S. economy was agriculturally oriented with the populace located in fragmented farming communities, thus banking structure and financial markets were quite segmented, or territorial, in nature.

~ Over time, the federal government made several attempts to form a unified banking system by creating a central, or national, bank, with the Federal Reserve being established in 1913.

~ Although banking changed dramatically as the country became more industrialized, the influence of early banking systems is very evident in contemporary banking.

~ Even though legislation passed since 1930 has relaxed some of the branching restrictions, the banking system in the U.S. is still dominated by a large number of individual banks that generally are allowed to branch within the states they are located *(intrastate branching)*, but are somewhat limited when it comes to branching across state lines *(interstate branching)*.

  • During the past couple of decades, interest in unrestricted branch banking has increased greatly. Congress recently passed, and will continue to examine, legislation that promotes elimination of the barriers that currently restrict interstate banking.

~ Even with the barriers to interstate banking, some banking organizations attained quasi-branch banking via bank holding companies, developed in the 1950s.

  • A *bank holding company* is a corporation that owns controlling interest in one or more banks.

  • Bank holding companies often were allowed to own multiple banks in the same state, and, in some cases, unusual circumstances led to ownership of banks in other states. Thus, a bank holding company could effectively achieve branching by operating separate banks in different states.

~ Since the Banking Act of 1933, also known as the Glass-Steagall Act, banks have been prohibited from engaging in activities that are not related to banking services.

  • This law effectively prohibited banks from combining commerce and banking activities.

  • Recent legislation has removed some restrictions, as banks can now establish non-bank subsidiaries that engage in bank-related activities. Well-run bank holding companies face fewer barriers to integrating banking operations with nonbank activities.

☐ There has been a great deal of recent interest in mergers and acquisitions of large banks.

~ Banking experts expect such mergers and acquisitions to continue.

~ The trend is toward fewer, but much larger banks.

☐ The *Federal Reserve System*, established in 1913, is the central banking system charged with managing the monetary policy of the United States.

~ The Fed was established by the Federal Reserve Act to reform the U.S. banking system following the Wall Street panic of 1907, which resulted in financial ruin for much of the country.

~ When originally created, the primary purpose of the Fed was to supervise banking activities such that bank operations were more stable and economic conditions would not cause widespread ruin in the banking industry.

- While it still views banking stability as an important goal, the responsibilities of the Fed have expanded as time has passed.

☐ To ensure control of the banking system was not consolidated in the hands of a few, the central bank of the U.S. was created with a decentralized network of regional, or district, banks.

~ The Fed is comprised of 12 independent district banks located in major cities throughout the country.

~ The district banks, which have branches in larger cities within their Federal Reserve districts, provide loans and deposits to banks and other financial institutions, but not to individuals.

- The Fed often is referred to as a banker's bank.

~ The Fed is also used by the government for its banking needs.

- The U.S. Treasury has a checking account at the Fed, which is used to collect the taxes we pay and to pay government employees and other expenses.

~ The Fed banks are supervised by a central governing body called the *Board of Governors*, the members of which are appointed by the President and approved by the Senate.

- The Board consists of seven members, each appointed to a 14-year term.

~ Other important components of the Federal Reserve include the commercial banks and other financial institutions that are members of the Fed, advisory committees that provide recommendations to the Board of Governors and the district banks, and the Federal Open Market Committee that oversees the principal instrument used by the Fed to manage monetary policy.

☐ According to the Federal Reserve Act, the Fed should direct the *monetary policy* of the U.S. "to promote effectively the goals of maximum employment, stable prices, and moderate long-term interest rates."

~ The primary means by which the Fed attempts to achieve these goals is by changing the nation's money supply through the reserves held at banks and other financial institutions.

~ The Fed affects reserves in the banking system through its lending policy, with changes in reserve requirements, and by buying and selling U.S. government securities.

~ The most important tool used by the Fed to manage the supply of money is *open market operations*, which involves buying or selling U.S. Treasury securities to change bank reserves.

~ The potential by which the money supply can change depends on the existing reserve requirement.

- Currently, a reserve requirement exists only for checking (transactions) deposits of 10 percent.
  ~ The Fed can also affect the money supply by changing the reserve requirement. This method is not used to manage the money supply on a day-to-day basis; reserve requirements are changed infrequently. When the Fed changes the reserve requirement, there is an immediate impact on the ability of banks to lend funds because excess reserves are affected.
  ~ Another tool the Fed uses to direct monetary policy is the *discount rate*, which is the interest rate banks and other financial institutions have to pay when they borrow from one of the Fed district banks to meet temporary shortages in required reserves.
    - Changes in the discount rate affect the amounts banks are willing to borrow and thus ultimately affect the money supply.
    - A discount rate change generally is the result, rather than the cause, of movement in other rates, and this instrument is neither as effective nor as prominent as open market operations for managing monetary policy.

☐ The Federal Reserve also is charged with regulating and supervising depository financial institutions operating in the U.S.
  ~ The Fed monitors such institutions through audits and "bank examinations" to ensure that the U.S. banking system remains sound. In addition, the Fed authorizes bank mergers and any nonbanking activities bank holding companies undertake.

☐ A very important service offered by the Fed is the check-clearing operations provided by its payment system, which clears millions of paper checks and electronic payments each day.

☐ Decisions made by the Fed generally cause significant movements in the financial markets.

☐ A great deal of deregulation has occurred in the financial services industry during the past couple of decades. Banking deregulation is expected to remain steady during the decade from 2001 to 2010. The most influential banking legislation since 1980 can be traced to the three acts below.
  ~ The general purpose of the Depository Institutions Deregulation and Monetary Control Act (DIDMCA) of 1980 was to improve competition among financial institutions for the benefit of customers and to extend the monetary control of the Federal Reserve.
    - Various financial institutions were allowed to offer a greater variety of deposit and credit products than before.
    - Ceilings on interest rates were phased out.
    - Ceilings on insured deposits were increased from $40,000 to $100,000.
    - The power of the Fed to control monetary policy was strengthened because the DIDMCA required all banks and thrifts to maintain reserves established by the Fed.
  ~ The Reigle-Neal Interstate Banking and Branching Efficiency Act of 1984

effectively eliminated barriers that restricted banks and other financial services organizations from expanding geographically.

~ The Gramm-Leach-Bliley Act of 1999 repealed many of the restrictions on banking activities that were enacted with the Glass-Steagall Act of 1933, which prohibited banks from engaging in activities that were not traditionally considered "normal" banking activities.

- The act permits qualified banks to engage in (1) investment banking and related activities, (2) insurance sales and underwriting, and (3) non-financial activities that do not substantially increase the risks of the institutions.

☐ The U.S. banking system has changed significantly during the last couple of decades, and additional changes are certain to continue in the future.

~ Many of the banking regulations have tended to impede the free flow of funds around the country and thus have been detrimental to the efficiency of our financial markets.

~ Recent legislative changes have removed some of the competitive obstacles created by previous regulations, and more changes are forthcoming.

~ During the past several decades, deregulation of depository intermediaries has erased many of the differences between financial institutions.

~ The trend in the U.S. today is toward huge financial service corporations, which own banks, S&Ls, investment banking houses, insurance companies, pension plan operations, and mutual funds, and which have branches across the country and even around the world.

~ In the future, we should see many finance-related companies that have traditionally been focused in a single area such as insurance or real estate branching into related businesses.

~ In recent times, Congress has shown a willingness to permit financial services organizations greater latitude in the products they offer, and it appears such sentiment will continue.

Two notable factors that distinguish the U.S. banking system from banking structures in other countries can be traced to the regulatory climate that has existed historically in the U.S. Generally speaking, financial institutions in the U.S. have been much more heavily regulated and have faced greater limitations with regard to branching activity and nonbanking business relationships than their foreign counterparts.

☐ The U.S. banking system traditionally has been characterized by a large number of independent banks of various sizes rather than a few very large banks that might exist with unrestricted branch banking.

~ The banking companies of nearly every other country in the world have been allowed to branch with few, if any, limitations; thus, their banking systems include far fewer individual, or unit, institutions than exist in the U.S.

☐ The second major difference between U.S. banks and their foreign counterparts is that most foreign banks are allowed to engage in nonbanking business activities while U.S. banks' nonbanking activities have been severely restricted until recently.

~ Regulations that restrict the nonbanking activities of U.S. banks have positioned these institutions such that they are at a competitive disadvantage internationally.

- As Congress has demonstrated recently, the legislative trend is to remove existing "competitive restraints" so U.S. institutions can better compete in the global financial arena.

~ With less restrictive regulations and other limitations on banking activities than in the U.S., foreign banking organizations have tended to develop huge one-stop financial service institutions.

~ Only one of the 10 largest banks in the world is located in the U.S.

~ Foreign banks dominate international banking activities.

- Fewer restrictions have helped foreign banks attain such dominance, but, in addition, foreign banks have been involved in international banking much longer than U.S. banks.

- While the Federal Reserve Act originally allowed banks with certain qualifications to engage in banking outside the U.S., the Edge Act, approved in 1919, allowed U.S. banks to operate subsidiary organizations in other countries.

~ In 1981 the Fed established another tool to help U.S. banks compete for international funds by allowing banks to create International Banking Facilities (IBFs), which take foreign deposits that are not subject to the same restrictions as domestic deposits, such as reserve requirements and deposit insurance.

- An IBF is not a separate banking organization; it is a method of accounting for international deposits separately from domestic deposits.

- Although American banks generally face fewer restrictions in their overseas operations than their domestic operations, for the most part, the overseas organizations are not allowed to engage in all the business activities available to the "native" banks they are competing against.

~ The presence of foreign banks in the U.S. has grown significantly in the past couple of decades. To ensure foreign banking organizations do not have an unfair competitive edge, Congress established regulations that specifically apply to foreign banks operating in the U.S.

- The International Banking Act (IBA), passed in 1978, essentially obligates foreign banking organizations to follow the same rules that are applicable to American banks.

- The Foreign Bank Supervision Enhancement Act (FBSEA), passed in 1991, requires foreign banks to get the Fed's approval before establishing offices in the U.S.

~ Even with the restrictions on American banking operations overseas, the presence of U.S. banks in international banking has increased rapidly in recent years.

- At the same time, the limitations overseas banking operations face in the U.S. have not discouraged the presence of foreign banks.

☐ As the world becomes more globally oriented, so will the banking industry—American banks will become more important internationally, while foreign banks will increase their presence in the U.S.

SELF-TEST QUESTIONS

Definitional

1. _____ _____ facilitate the transfer of funds from those who have funds to those who need funds.

2. _____ _____ are the traditional "department stores of finance" because they offer a wide variety of products and services to a variety of customers.

3. A(n) _____ _____ is a depository institution that is owned by its depositors, who are members of a common organization or association.

4. Two basic types of thrifts are _____ _____ _____ _____ and _____ _____ _____.

5. _____ _____ are investment companies that accept money from savers and then use these funds to buy various types of financial assets.

6. _____ _____ _____ _____ differ from other financial institutions because they provide two services to individuals: insurance and savings.

7. _____ _____ _____ is a relatively short-term contract that provides protection for a temporary period, and it must be renewed each period to continue such protection.

8. Life insurance companies use statistical tables, called _____ _____, to estimate the amounts of cash that will be needed each year to satisfy insurance claims.

9. _____ _____ are retirement plans funded by corporations or government agencies for their workers and administered primarily by the trust departments of commercial banks or by life insurance companies.

10. "Pay-as-you-go" plans are termed _____ _____.

11. The _____ _____ traditionally has been considered the regulatory agency of commercial banking and has the power to impose regulations such as reserve requirements on other financial institutions that accept deposits from savers or make conventional loans to borrowers.

12. The regulation of mutual funds is the responsibility of the _____ _____ _____ _____, except in a few instances where state regulations apply.

13. In a(n) _____ _____ _____, the amount of reserves maintained to satisfy requests for withdrawals of deposits is less than 100 percent of the total deposits.

14. _____ _____ are equal to total reserves minus required reserves.

15. Because the U.S. banking system includes both national and state charters, it is referred

to as a(n) _____ _____ _____.

16. The Fed banks are supervised by a central governing body called the _____ _____ _____, the members of which are appointed by the President and approved by the Senate.

17. The most important tool used by the Fed to manage the supply of money is _____ _____ _____, which involve buying or selling U.S. Treasury securities to change bank reserves.

18. Another tool the Fed uses to direct monetary policy is the _____ _____, which is the interest rate banks and other financial institutions have to pay when they borrow from one of the Fed district banks to meet temporary shortages in required reserves.

19. In 1981 the Fed established another tool to help U.S. banks compete for international funds by allowing banks to create _____ _____ _____, which take foreign deposits that are not subject to the same restrictions as domestic deposits, such as reserve requirements and deposit insurance.

20. _____ originally were established because the services offered by commercial banks were designed for businesses rather than individuals, whose needs differed greatly.

21. _____ _____ _____, which operate mainly in the northeastern U.S., are similar to S&Ls, except they are owned and managed by their depositors, thus operating like credit unions.

22. One of the newest savings mediums available in the financial markets is the _____ _____ _____ _____, which includes short-term, low-risk securities and generally allows investors to write checks against their accounts.

23. _____ _____ _____ is a long-term contract that provides lifetime protection.

24. The most famous pension plan is _____ _____, which is a government-sponsored plan funded by tax revenues.

25. The process by which financial intermediaries transform funds provided by savers into funds used by borrowers is called _____ _____.

26. The most significant economic function of the S&Ls is to create _____ that otherwise would be lacking.

27. Investors who prefer current income can invest in mutual funds referred to as _____ funds.

28. Investors who are willing to accept higher risks in hopes of higher returns can invest in

mutual funds referred to as _____ funds.

29. The primary reason individuals invest in mutual funds is for _____.

30. _____ represent obligations of the insurance companies associated with future commitments derived from currently outstanding policies.

31. The _____ _____ _____ _____ insures the deposits at most banks and thrift institutions.

32. The major legislation affecting pension plans is the _____ _____ _____ _____ _____, which became law in 1974.

33. According to the Federal Reserve Act, the Fed should direct the _____ _____ of the U.S. to promote effectively the goals of maximum employment, stable prices, and moderate long-term interest rates.

34. When the Fed changes the _____ _____, there is an immediate impact on the ability of banks to lend funds because excess reserves are affected.

35. The trend in the U.S. today is toward huge _____ _____ _____, which own banks, S&Ls, investment banking houses, insurance companies, pension plan operations, and mutual funds, and which have branches across the country and even around the world.

Conceptual

36. The maximum change in the money supply created by a fractional reserve system is computed as $\dfrac{\text{Reserve requirement}}{\text{Excess reserves}}$.

   a. True   b. False

37. A bank holding company is a corporation that owns controlling interest in one or more banks.

   a. True   b. False

38. A major difference between U.S. banks and their foreign counterparts is that most U.S. banks are allowed to engage in nonbanking business activities while foreign banks are not.

   a. True   b. False

39. Which of the following pieces of legislation repealed many of the restrictions on banking activities that were enacted with the Glass-Steagall Act of 1933?

    a. Employee Retirement Income Security Act (ERISA) of 1974.

    b. Federal Reserve Act.

    c. Depository Institutions Deregulation and Monetary Control Act (DIDMCA) of 1980.

    d. Gramm-Leach-Bliley Act of 1999.

    e. Reigle-Neal Interstate Banking and Branching Efficiency Act of 1984.

40. Which of the following pieces of legislation had as its general purpose to improve competition among financial institutions for the benefit of customers and to extend the monetary control of the Federal Reserve?

    a. Employee Retirement Income Security Act (ERISA) of 1974.

    b. Federal Reserve Act.

    c. Depository Institutions Deregulation and Monetary Control Act (DIDMCA) of 1980.

    d. Gramm-Leach-Bliley Act of 1999.

    e. Reigle-Neal Interstate Banking and Branching Efficiency Act of 1984.

41. Which of the following activities are qualified banks permitted to engage in under the Gramm-Leach-Bliley Act of 1999?

    a. Investment banking and related activities.

    b. Insurance sales and underwriting.

    c. Non-financial activities that do not substantially increase the risks of the institutions.

    d. All of the statements above.

    e. None of the statements above.

42. Which of the following statements is a benefit associated with intermediaries?

    a. Financial market are more efficient.

    b. Intermediaries provide funds to a large number and variety of borrowers by offering many different types of loans, thereby spreading their risk.

    c. Because intermediaries offer a variety of financial products, both savers and borrowers have greater choices, or financial flexibility, than can be achieved with direct placements.

    d. Without intermediaries, the net cost of borrowing would be greater, and the net return earned by savers would be less.

    e. All of the above statements are benefits of intermediaries.

43. Which of the following statements is most correct?

    a. Commercial banks represent one of the largest depository intermediaries, and their operations impact nearly everyone either directly or indirectly.

    b. Credit unions are investment companies that accept money form savers and then use these funds to buy various types of financial assets.

    c. Whole life insurance is a relatively short-term contract that provides protections for

a temporary period, and it must be renewed each period to continue such protection.
d. Because of the common bond members possess, loans from credit unions often are the cheapest source of funds available to individual borrowers.
e. Statements a and d are true.

44. Which of the following statements is *false*?

a. In general, financial intermediaries increase the standard of living in the economy.
b. "Pay-as-you-go" pension plans are termed funded pensions.
c. Because intermediaries play such a critical role in the welfare of the economy, the financial services industry has been heavily regulated in an effort to ensure stability and safety in the nation's financial markets.
d. The Federal Reserve System is the central banking system charged with managing the monetary policy of the United States.
e. The trend in the U.S. today is toward huge financial service corporations.

45. Which of the following statements is most correct?

a. Decisions made by the Fed generally cause insignificant movements in the financial markets.
b. Originally, banks were established to serve the needs of commerce, or business, hence the name commercial banks.
c. Term life insurance policies provide savings features because the premiums are fixed payments computed as an average of the premiums required over the expected life of the person insured.
d. Statements a, b, and c are correct.
e. Statements b and c are correct.

SELF-TEST PROBLEMS

1. Through its open market operations, the Federal Reserve recently increased deposits at financial institutions by $120 billion. If the reserve requirement for all deposits is 9 percent, what is the maximum impact the Fed's actions can have on total deposits (in billions of dollars).

a. $1,000.00   **b.** $1,213.33   **c.** $1,322.53   **d.** $1,380.00   **e.** $1,415.25

2. What is the maximum change in total deposits that would result if deposits at financial institutions were immediately increased by $100 billion, and the reserve requirements applicable to all deposits are 5 percent?

a. $875   **b.** $1,000   **c.** $1,500   **d.** $1,900   **e.** $2,200

3.   The Federal Reserve has decided interest rates need to be increased to maintain relatively low inflation in the economy. To accomplish this, it has been determined that the money supply needs to be decreased by $75 billion. The Fed wants to affect the decrease in the money supply through reserves at financial institutions. Assume the current reserve requirement is 8 percent, and it applies to all deposits. By how much must reserves be decreased (in billions of dollars) for the Fed to accomplish its goal? Assume that presently there are no excess reserves.

     a. $6.5217   **b.** $6.0000   **c.** $5.5200   **d.** $5.0000   **e.** $3.7500

4.   Assume the reserve requirement for transaction deposits is 10 percent, and it is 6 percent for nontransaction deposits. What is the reserve requirement (in millions of dollars) for a bank that has $200 million deposited in transaction accounts and $60 million deposited in nontransaction accounts?

     a. $3.60   **b.** $7.50   **c.** $15.75   **d.** $20.00   **e.** $23.60

ANSWERS TO SELF-TEST QUESTIONS

1.	Financial intermediaries	19.	International Banking Facilities
2.	Commercial banks	20.	Thrifts
3.	credit union	21.	Mutual savings banks
4.	savings and loan associations; mutual savings banks	22.	money market mutual fund
		23.	Whole life insurance
5.	Mutual funds	24.	Social Security
6.	Whole life insurance companies	25.	financial intermediation
7.	Term life insurance	26.	liquidity
8.	actuarial tables	27.	income
9.	Pension funds	28.	growth
10.	unfunded pensions	29.	retirement
11.	Federal Reserve	30.	Reserves
12.	Securities and Exchange Commission	31.	Federal Deposit Insurance Corporation (FDIC)
13.	fractional reserve system	32.	Employee Retirement Income Security Act (ERISA)
14.	Excess reserves		
15.	dual banking system	33.	monetary policy
16.	Board of Governors	34.	reserve requirement
17.	open market operations	35.	financial service corporations
18.	discount rate		

36.   b.   The maximum change in the money supply equals $\dfrac{\text{Excess reserves}}{\text{Reserve requirement}}$.

37.   a.   This statement is correct.

38.   b.   This statement is just the reverse. U.S. banks have been severely restricted in

nonbanking business activities until recently, while foreign banks are permitted to engage in these nonbanking activities.

39.　d.　The Gramm-Leach-Bliley Act of 1999 repealed many of the restrictions on banking activities that were enacted with the Glass-Steagall Act of 1933. ERISA relates to pension plan regulations, while the Federal Reserve Act established the Fed. DIDMCA of 1980 was enacted to improve competition among financial institutions and to extend the Federal Reserve's monetary control. The Reigle-Neal Act of 1984 effectively eliminated barriers that restricted banks from expanding geographically.

40.　c.　DIDMCA of 1980 had as its general purpose to improve competition among financial institutions and to extend the Federal Reserve's monetary control. ERISA relates to pension plan regulations, while the Federal Reserve Act established the Fed. The Gramm-Leach-Bliley Act of 1999 repealed many of the banking activity restrictions that were enacted with the Glass-Steagall Act of 1933. The Reigle-Neal Act of 1984 effectively eliminated barriers that restricted banks from expanding geographically.

41.　d.　Statements a, b, and c are all activities permitted under the Gramm-Leach-Bliley Act of 1999.

42.　e.　Statements a, b, c, and d are all benefits associated with intermediaries.

43.　e.　Statement b is false; the definition applies to mutual funds. Statement c is false; whole life insurance is a long-term contract that provides lifetime protection.

44.　b.　Statement b is false; "pay-as-you-go" pension plans are termed unfunded pensions.

45.　b.　Statement a is false; decisions made by the Fed generally cause significant movements in the financial markets. Statement c is false; term life insurance policies do not provide savings features.

SOLUTIONS TO SELF-TEST PROBLEMS

1.　b.　Excess reserves = $120 × (1 − 0.09) = $109.2 billion.

$$\text{Maximum change in the money supply} = \frac{\text{Excess reserves}}{\text{Reserve requirement}}$$

$$= \frac{\$109.2}{0.09}$$

$$= \$1,213.33 \text{ billion.}$$

2. d. Excess reserves = $100 × (1 − 0.05) = $95 billion.

$$\text{Maximum change in the money supply} = \frac{\$95}{0.05} = \$1,900 \text{ billion.}$$

3. a. Desired decrease in money supply = $75 billion.
    Reserve requirement = 8%.

    Assuming there are no excess reserves, the amount by which required reserves must be decreased is

$$\frac{\text{Maximum change in deposits}}{} = \frac{\text{Change in required reserves}}{\text{Reserve requirement}}$$

$$\$75 = \frac{\Delta \text{Required reserves} \times (1 - 0.08)}{0.08}$$

$$\Delta \text{Required reserves} = \frac{\$75 \text{ billion} \times (0.08)}{(1 - 0.08)}$$

$$\Delta \text{Required reserves} = \$6.5217.$$

4. e. Transaction deposits = $200 million; Reserve requirement = 10%.
    Required reserves = 0.10 × $200 = $20 million.

    Nontransaction deposits = $60 million; Reserve requirement = 6%.
    Required reserves = 0.06 × $60 = $3.6 million.

    Total required reserves = $20 + $3.6 = $23.6 million.

CHAPTER 5
THE COST OF MONEY (INTEREST RATES)

OVERVIEW

The primary role of the financial markets is to help bring together borrowers and lenders by facilitating the flow of funds from those who have surplus funds (investors) to those who need funds in excess of their current income (borrowers). In a free economy such as ours, the excess funds of lenders are allocated to borrowers in the financial markets through a pricing system that is based on the supply of, and the demand for funds. The pricing system is represented by interest rates, or the cost of money, such that those borrowers who are willing to pay the rates that prevail in the financial markets are those who are able to use the excess funds provided by others. In this chapter, we explain the basic concepts of interest rates, including factors that affect interest rates and how interest rates are forecasted.

OUTLINE

It is important to understand how investors earn returns when supplying funds to borrowers.

☐ Whether the investment is debt or equity, the dollar return earned by an investor can be divided into two categories: (1) income paid by the issuer of the financial asset and (2) the change in value of the financial asset in the financial market.
~ The dollar return on a financial asset can be stated as

$$\text{Dollar return} = \text{Dollar income} + \text{Capital gains}.$$

- Income from debt is the interest paid by the borrower.
- Income from equity is the dividend paid by a corporation.

~ To determine an investment's yield, the dollar return must be stated as a percent of the dollar amount that was originally invested. The yield is computed as:

$$\frac{\text{Dollar income} + (\text{Ending value} - \text{Beginning value})}{\text{Beginning value}}.$$

- The yield represents the average rate investors required during the year to provide their funds to the company that issued the bond.

In a free economy, funds are allocated in the financial markets through a pricing system. Interest rates represent the prices paid to borrow funds, whereas in the case of equity capital, investors expect to receive dividends and capital gains.

☐   The four most fundamental factors affecting the cost of money are (1) production opportunities, (2) time preferences for consumption, (3) risk, and (4) inflation.

    ~   *Production opportunities* are the returns available within an economy from investment in productive (cash-generating) assets.

    ~   *Time preferences for consumption* are the preferences of consumers for current consumption as opposed to saving for future consumption.

    ~   *Risk*, in a financial market context, is the chance that a financial asset will not earn the return promised. The higher the perceived risk, the higher the required rate of return.

    ~   *Inflation* is the tendency of prices to increase over time.

☐   The returns borrowers expect to earn by investing the funds they borrow set an upper limit on how much they can pay for savings, while consumers' time preferences for consumption establish how much consumption they are willing to defer, hence how much they will save at different levels of interest offered by borrowers.

Funds are allocated among borrowers by interest rates: Firms with the most profitable investment opportunities are willing and able to pay the most for capital, so they tend to attract it away from less efficient firms or from those whose products are not in demand.

☐   Supply and demand interact to determine interest rates in capital markets.

    ~   If the demand for funds declines, as it typically does during a business recession, the market-clearing, or equilibrium, interest rate declines.

    ~   If the supply of funds tightens, this would raise interest rates and lower the level of borrowing in the economy.

☐   Financial markets are interdependent.

    ~   For example, when rates on Treasury securities increase, the rates on corporate bonds and mortgages generally follow.

☐   There are many financial markets in the U.S. and throughout the world.

    ~   For each type of funds, there is a price, and each of these prices changes over time as shifts occur in supply and demand conditions.

      •   Short-term interest rates are especially prone to rise during booms and then fall during recessions.

      •   When the economy is expanding, firms need capital, and this demand for capital pushes interest rates up.

      •   Inflationary pressures are strongest during business booms, and that also exerts upward pressure on interest rates.

The quoted (or nominal) interest rate on a debt security, k, is composed of a real risk-free rate of interest, k*, plus several premiums that reflect inflation, the riskiness of the security, and the security's marketability (or liquidity): k = k* + IP + DRP + LP + MRP.

☐ The *real risk-free rate of interest (k*)* is the interest rate that would exist on a security with a guaranteed payoff (termed a riskless, or risk-free, security) if inflation was expected to be zero during the investment period. It can be thought of as the rate of interest that would exist on short-term U.S. Treasury securities in an inflation-free world.

~ The real risk-free rate changes over time depending on economic conditions, especially (1) on the rate of return corporations and other borrowers expect to earn by investing borrowed funds and (2) on people's time preferences for current versus future consumption.

~ It is difficult to measure the real risk-free rate precisely, but most experts think that in the United States k* has fluctuated in the range of 2 percent to 4 percent in recent years.

☐ The *nominal, or quoted, risk-free rate of interest (k_{RF})* is the real risk-free rate plus a premium for expected inflation: $k_{RF} = k^* + IP$.

~ The T-bill rate is used to approximate the short-term risk-free rate, and the T-bond rate is used to approximate the long-term risk-free rate.

☐ The *inflation premium (IP)*, which is equal to the average inflation rate expected over the life of the security, compensates investors for the expected loss of purchasing power.

~ The rate of inflation built into interest rates is the rate of inflation expected in the future, not the rate experienced in the past.

~ Expectations for future inflation are closely correlated with rates experienced in the recent past.

☐ The *default risk premium (DRP)* compensates investors for the risk that a borrower will default and hence not pay the interest or principal on a loan.

~ U.S. Treasury securities have no default risk.

~ The greater a security's default risk, the higher the interest rate lenders charge.

~ The difference between the quoted interest rate on a T-bond and that on a corporate bond with similar maturity, liquidity, and other features is the default risk premium.

~ Default risk premiums vary over time.

☐ *Liquidity* is generally defined as the ability to convert an asset to cash on short notice and "reasonably" capture the amount initially invested.

~ The more easily an asset can be converted to cash at a price that substantially recovers the initial amount invested, the more liquid it is considered.

~ A *liquidity premium (LP)* is also added to the real rate for securities that are not liquid.

~ A differential of at least two and probably four or five percentage points exists between the least liquid and the most liquid financial assets of similar default risk and maturity.

☐ Long-term securities are more price sensitive to interest rate changes than are short-term securities. Therefore, a *maturity risk premium (MRP)* is added to longer-term securities to compensate investors for *interest rate risk*.

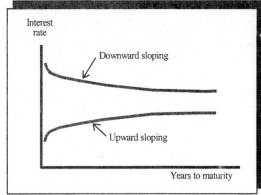

~ The effect of maturity risk premiums is to raise interest rates on long-term bonds relative to those on short-term bonds.

- The maturity risk premium is extremely difficult to measure, but (1) it seems to vary over time, rising when interest rates are more volatile and uncertain, then falling when interest rates are more stable, and (2) in recent years, the maturity risk premium on 30-year T-bonds appears to have generally been in the range of one to two percentage points.

~ Although long-term bonds are heavily exposed to interest rate risk, short-term investments are heavily exposed to *reinvestment rate risk*, the risk that a decline in interest rates will lead to lower income when bonds mature and funds are reinvested.

- Although "investing short" preserves one's principal, the interest income provided by short-term investments varies from year to year, depending on reinvestment rates.

The term structure of interest rates is the relationship between yields and maturities of securities.

☐ It is important to understand (1) how long- and short-term rates are related to each other and (2) what causes shifts in their relative positions.

☐ When plotted, this relationship produces a *yield curve*.
~ The yield curve changes both in position and in slope over time.

☐ Yield curves have different shapes depending on expected inflation rates and supply and demand conditions.
~ The "normal" yield curve is *upward sloping* because investors charge higher rates on longer-term bonds, even when inflation is expected to remain constant.
~ An inverted, or *downward sloping (abnormal)*, yield curve signifies that investors expect inflation to decrease.
~ Corporate yields plot above the Treasury yields on the same date because the corporate yields would include default risk premiums.
~ Yield curves for both the corporate bonds and the Treasury securities would have the same general shape.
~ Riskier corporations have higher yield curves because their bonds have greater default risk premiums.

☐ Three theories have been proposed to explain the shape of the yield curve, or the term structure of interest rates.

~ The *expectations theory* states that the yield curve depends on expectations concerning future inflation rates.

● If the rate of inflation is expected to decline, the curve will be downward sloping, and if the rate of inflation is expected to increase, the curve will be upward sloping.

● Under the expectations theory, the maturity risk premium is assumed to be zero, and, for Treasury securities, the default risk premium and liquidity premium also are zero.

~ The *liquidity preference theory* states that the yield curve tends to be upward sloping.

● Investors prefer short-term to long-term securities, because short-term securities are more liquid in the sense that they can be converted to cash with little danger of loss of principal and due to the interest rate risk associated with long-term securities. Investors will, therefore, generally accept lower yields on short-term securities, and this leads to relatively low short-term rates.

● Borrowers prefer long-term debt because short-term debt exposes them to the risk of having to repay the debt under adverse conditions. Accordingly, borrowers want to lock into long-term funds.

● Thus, both lender and borrower preferences operate to cause short-term rates to be lower than long-term rates.

● These two sets of preferences imply that under normal conditions a positive maturity risk premium exists, and the MRP increases with years to maturity, causing the yield curve to be upward sloping.

~ The *market segmentation theory* states that each borrower and lender has a preferred maturity, and that the slope of the yield curve depends on supply of and demand for funds in the long-term market relative to the short-term markets.

● Under this theory, the yield curve could, at any time, be either flat, upward sloping, or downward sloping.

● An upward-sloping yield curve would occur when there was a large supply of short-term funds relative to demand, but a shortage of long-term funds.

● A downward-sloping curve would indicate relatively strong demand for funds in the short-term market compared with that in the long-term market.

☐ All three theories have merit; that is, actual yield curves are influenced by all three sets of factors.

There are other factors that influence both the general level of interest rates and the shape of the yield curve. The four most important factors are (1) Federal Reserve policy, (2) the level of the federal budget deficit, (3) the foreign trade balance, and (4) the level of business activity.

☐ Expansionary monetary policy (growth in monetary supply) by the Federal Reserve initially lowers the interest rate but inflationary pressures could cause a rise in interest rates in the long term. Contractionary monetary policy has the opposite effect.

~ The reason the Fed intervenes in the financial markets is to help stabilize economic conditions.

~ During periods when the Fed is actively intervening in the markets, the yield curve will be distorted. Short-term rates will be temporarily "too low" if the Fed is easing credit, and "too high" if it is tightening credit. Long-term rates are not affected as much by Fed intervention.

☐ Federal budget deficits drive interest rates up due to (1) increased demand for loanable funds (if the government borrows money) or (2) expectations for future inflation (if the government prints money), while surpluses drive rates down due to increased supply of loanable funds.

~ The larger the federal deficit, the higher the level of interest rates.

☐ Foreign trade deficits push interest rates up because deficits must be financed and this drives up interest rates. Also, foreigners are willing to hold U. S. debt only if the interest on this debt is competitive with interest rates in other countries.

~ The larger the federal deficit, other things held constant, the higher the level of interest rates.

~ The existence of a deficit trade balance hinders the Fed's ability to combat a recession by lowering interest rates.

☐ In relation to the business cycle, there is a general tendency for interest rates to decline during a recession.

~ During recessions, short-term rates decline more sharply than long-term rates because (1) the Fed operates mainly in the short-term sector, so its intervention has the strongest effect here, and (2) long-term rates reflect the average expected inflation rate over the next 20 to 30 years, and this expectation generally does not change much, even when the current rate of inflation is low because of a recession.

Interest rates have two effects on corporate profits.

☐ Because interest is a cost, the higher the rate of interest, the lower a firm's profits, other things held constant.

☐ Interest rates affect the level of economic activity, and economic activity affects corporate profits.

~ Interest rates obviously affect stock prices because of their effects on profits, but, perhaps even more important, they have an effect due to competition in the marketplace between stocks and bonds.

• If interest rates rise sharply, investors can get higher returns in the bond market, which induces them to sell stocks and to transfer funds from the stock market to the bond market.

• A massive sale of stock in response to rising interest rates obviously would depress stock prices.

• The reverse occurs if interest rates decline.

SELF-TEST QUESTIONS

Definitional

1. The risk that a borrower will not pay the interest or principal on a loan is _____ risk.

2. _____ _____ _____ bonds have zero default risk.

3. A(n) _____ premium is added to the real risk-free rate to protect investors against loss of purchasing power.

4. The nominal interest rate on a debt security is determined by adding a(n) _____ premium plus a(n) _____ risk premium plus a(n) _____ premium plus a(n) _____ risk premium to the real risk-free rate of return.

5. The relationship between yields and maturities of securities is called the _____ _____ of interest rates, while the resulting plotted curve is the _____ curve.

6. The "normal" yield curve has a(n) _____ slope.

7. Three theories have been proposed to explain the term structure of interest rates. They are the _____ theory, the _____ preference theory, and the market _____ theory.

8. The four most fundamental factors affecting the cost of money are _____ _____, _____ _____ for consumption, _____, and _____.

9. If the demand for funds declines, the market-clearing, or equilibrium, interest rate _____.

10. Financial markets are _____. An illustration of this occurs when rates on Treasury securities increase and the rates on corporate bonds and mortgages generally follow.

11. If the supply of funds tightens, this would _____ interest rates and _____ the level of borrowing in the economy.

12. The dollar return earned by an investor can be divided into two categories: (1) _____ paid by the issuer of the financial asset and (2) the _____ in value of the financial asset in the financial market.

13. Income from debt is the _____ paid by the borrower.

14. Income from equity is the _____ paid by a corporation.

15. The _____ represents the average rate investors required during the year to provide their funds to the company that issued the bond.

16. The _____ _____-_____ _____ ____ _____ is the interest rate that would exist on a security with a guaranteed payoff if inflation was expected to be zero during the investment period.

17. The _____, or _____, risk-free rate of interest is the real risk-free rate plus a premium for expected inflation.

18. The difference between the quoted interest rate on a T-bond and that on a corporate bond with similar maturity, liquidity, and other features is the _____ _____ _____.

19. _____ is generally defined as the ability to convert an asset to cash on short notice and reasonably capture the amount initially invested.

20. A(n) _____ _____ _____ is added to longer-term securities to compensate investors for interest rate risk.

21. The effect of maturity risk premiums is to _____ interest rates on long-term bonds relative to those on short-term bonds.

22. Although long-term bonds are heavily exposed to interest rate risk, short-term investments are heavily exposed to _____ _____ _____, the risk that a decline in interest rates will lead to lower income when bonds mature and funds are reinvested.

23. Although investing short preserves one's _____, the _____ _____ provided by short-term investments varies from year to year, depending on reinvestment rates.

24. Corporate yields plot _____ the Treasury yields on the same date because the corporate yields would include _____ _____ _____.

25. There are other factors that influence both the general level of interest rates and the shape of the yield curve. The four most important factors are (1) _____ _____ policy, (2) the level of the _____ _____ _____, (3) the _____ _____ _____, and (4) the level of business activity.

Conceptual

26. If a management is sure that the economy is at the peak of a boom and is about to enter

a recession, a firm that needs to borrow money should probably use short-term rather than long-term debt.

a. True   **b.** False

27. Long-term interest rates reflect expectations about future inflation. Inflation has varied greatly from year to year over the last 10 years, and, as a result, long-term rates have fluctuated more than short-term rates.

a. True   **b.** False

28. Suppose the Fed takes actions that lower expectations for inflation this year by 1 percentage point, but these same actions raise expectations for inflation in Years 2 and thereafter by 2 percentage points. Other things held constant, the yield curve becomes steeper.

a. True   **b.** False

29. Assume interest rates on 30-year government and corporate bonds were as follows: T-bond = 7.72%; AAA = 8.72%; A = 9.64%; BBB = 10.18%. The differences in rates among these issues are caused primarily by:

a. Tax effects.   **d.** Inflation differences.
b. Default risk differences.   **e.** Both b and d.
c. Maturity risk differences.

30. Which of the following statements is correct?

a. The introduction of a new technology, such as computers, might be expected to improve labor productivity, making businesses more able and willing to pay a higher price for capital. This would put upward pressure on interest rates. However, the productivity improvements might give rise to lower inflationary expectations, which would put downward pressure on interest rates. Thus, the net effect of the new technology on interest rates might be uncertain.
b. If future inflation were expected to remain constant at 6 percent for all future years, then for all bonds (government and corporate combined) we could measure the maturity risk premium as the difference between the yields on 30-year and 1-year bonds.
c. If investors expect the inflation rate to *decrease* over time, e.g., the expected inflation rate in Year t exceeds the expected rate in Year t+1 for all values of t, then we can be *certain* that the yield curve for U.S. Treasury securities will be downward sloping.
d. Each of the statements above is correct.
e. Statements a and c are correct.

31. Which of the following statements is correct?

    a. Suppose financial institutions, such as savings and loans, were required by law to make long-term, fixed interest rate mortgages, but, at the same time, they were largely restricted, in terms of their capital sources, to taking deposits that could be withdrawn on demand. Under these conditions, these financial institutions should prefer a "normal" yield curve to an inverted curve.

    b. You are considering establishing a new firm, the University Assistance Company (UAC). UAC would obtain funds in the short-term money market and write long-term mortgage loans to students so that they might buy condominiums rather than rent. A downward sloping yield curve, if it persisted over time, would be best for UAC.

    c. The yield curve is upward sloping, or normal, if short-term rates are higher than long-term rates.

    d. All of the statements above are correct.

    e. Statements a and b are correct.

SELF-TEST PROBLEMS

1. You have determined the following data for a given bond: Real risk-free rate (k^*) = 3%; inflation premium = 8%; default risk premium = 2%; liquidity premium = 2%; and maturity risk premium = 1%. What is the nominal risk-free rate, k_{RF}?

    a. 10%   b. 11%   c. 12%   d. 13%   e. 14%

2. Refer to Self-Test Problem 1. What is the interest rate on long-term Treasury securities, or T-bonds, of the relevant maturity?

    a. 10%   b. 11%   c. 12%   d. 13%   e. 14%

3. Assume that a 3-year Treasury note has no maturity risk nor liquidity risk and that the real risk-free rate of interest falls to 2 percent. A 3-year T-note carries a yield to maturity of 12 percent. If the expected inflation rate is 12 percent for the coming year and 10 percent the year after, what is the implied expected inflation rate for the third year?

    a. 8%   b. 9%   c. 10%   d. 11%   e. 12%

4. Assume that the real risk-free rate is 2 percent, that the expected inflation rate during Year 2 is 3 percent, and that 2-year T-bonds yield 5.5 percent. If the maturity risk premium is zero, what is the inflation rate during Year 1?

    a. 3.0%   b. 5.0%   c. 3.5%   d. 4.0%   e. 2.5%

5. Refer to Self-Test Problem 4. Given the same information, what is the rate of return on 1-year T-bonds?

    a. 5.5%   b. 6.0%   c. 5.0%   d. 6.5%   e. 4.5%

6. Assume that the real risk-free rate, k*, is 4 percent and that inflation is expected to be 7 percent in Year 1, 4 percent in Year 2, and 3 percent thereafter. Assume also that all Treasury bonds are highly liquid and free of default risk. If 2-year and 5-year Treasury bonds both yield 11 percent, what is the difference in the maturity risk premiums (MRPs) on the two bonds; that is, what is $MRP_5 - MRP_2$?

    a. 0.5%   **b.** 1.0%   **c.** 2.25%   **d.** 1.5%   **e.** 1.25%

7. Due to the recession, the rate of inflation expected for the coming year is only 3.5 percent. However, the rate of inflation in Year 2 and thereafter is expected to be constant at some level above 3.5 percent. Assume that the real risk-free rate is k* = 2% for all maturities and that the expectations theory fully explains the yield curve, so there are no maturity risk premiums. If 3-year Treasury bonds yield 3 percentage points (0.03) more than 1-year bonds, what rate of inflation is expected after Year 1?

    a. 4%   **b.** 5%   **c.** 7%   **d.** 6%   **e.** 8%

8. A bond issued by Travis Corporation currently has a market price equal to $1,040. The bond pays $110 interest annually. If the price of the bond increases to $1,150 during the year, what is the total dollar return that you would earn on your investment?

    a. $40   **b.** $110   **c.** $150   **d.** $200   **e.** $220

9. Refer to Self-Test problem 8. Given the same information, what is the yield for the year on the bond?

    a. 5.25%   **b.** 10.58%   **c.** 15.75%   **d.** 21.15%   **e.** 24.00%

10. A year ago you purchased 150 shares of common stock for $30 per share. During the year, the value of the stock decreased to $22.50 per share. If the stock paid a dividend of $0.80 during the year ($0.20 per quarter), what yield did you earn on your investment?

    a. -22.33%   **b.** -15.25%   **c.** -5.33%   **d.** 0%   **e.** 2.67%

ANSWERS TO SELF-TEST QUESTIONS

1. default
2. U.S. Treasury
3. inflation
4. inflation; default; liquidity; maturity
5. term structure; yield
6. upward
7. expectations; liquidity; segmentation
8. production opportunities; time preferences; risk; inflation
9. declines
10. interdependent
11. raise; lower

12.	income; change	20.	maturity risk premium
13.	interest	21.	raise
14.	dividend	22.	reinvestment rate risk
15.	yield	23.	principal; interest income
16.	real risk-free rate of interest	24.	above; default risk premiums
17.	nominal; quoted	25.	Federal Reserve; federal budget
18.	default risk premium		deficit; foreign trade balance
19.	Liquidity		

26. a. The firm should borrow short-term until interest rates drop due to the recession, then go long-term. Predicting interest rates is extremely difficult, for managers can rarely be sure about what is going to happen to the economy.

27. b. Fluctuations in long-term rates are smaller because the long-term inflation premium is an average of inflation expectations over many years, and hence the IP on long-term bonds is quite stable relative to the IP on short-term bonds. Also, short-term rates fluctuate as a result of Federal Reserve policy (the Fed intervenes in the short-term rather than the long-term market).

28. a. The yield curve becomes steeper. Although interest rates in Year 1 decrease by 1 percent, interest rates in the following years increase by 2 percent, making the yield curve steeper.

29. b. $k = k^* + IP + DRP + LP + MRP$. Since each of these bonds has a 30-year maturity, the MRP and IP would all be equal. Thus, the differences in the interest rates among these issues are the default risk and liquidity premiums.

30. a. Statement b is false because $k = k^* + IP + DRP + LP + MRP$. $k^* + IP$ would be the same for the two bonds; however, the default risk premium and liquidity premium would not be the same for the two bonds. Thus, you could not simply subtract the two yields to determine the MRP. Statement c is false because the expectations theory is not the only theory proposed to explain the shape of the yield curve. The market segmentation theory states that the slope depends on supply/demand conditions, and the liquidity preference theory states that under normal conditions a positive maturity risk premium exists. So, we cannot be certain that the yield curve would be downward sloping.

31. a. Statement b is incorrect. If a downward-sloping yield curve existed, long-term interest rates would be lower than short-term rates. This would be very serious for UAC: UAC receives as income the interest it charges on its long-term mortgage loans, but it has to pay out interest for obtaining funds in the short-term money market. Therefore, UAC would be receiving low interest income, but it would be paying out even higher interest. Statement c is incorrect. An upward-sloping yield curve would indicate higher interest rates for long-term securities than for short-term securities.

SOLUTIONS TO SELF-TEST PROBLEMS

1. b. $k_{RF} = k* + IP = 3\% + 8\% = 11\%.$

2. c. There is virtually no risk of default on a U.S. Treasury security, and they trade in active markets, which provide liquidity, so

$$k = k* + IP + DRP + LP + MRP$$
$$= 3\% + 8\% + 0\% + 0\% + 1\%$$
$$= 12\%.$$

3. a. $$k = k* + IP + DRP + LP + MRP$$
$$12\% = 2\% + IP + 0\% + 0\% + 0\%$$
$$IP = 10\%.$$

    Thus, the average expected inflation rate over the next 3 years (IP) is 10 percent. Given that the average expected inflation rate over the next three years is 10%, we can find the implied expected inflation rate for the third year by solving the equation that sets the two known plus the one unknown expected inflation rates equal to 10%:

$$\frac{12\% + 10\% + Infl_3}{3} = 10\%$$

$$Infl_3 = 8\%.$$

4. d.

Year	$k*$	Inflation	Average Inflation	k_t
1	2%	?	$Infl_1/1 = ?$	?
2	2%	3	$(Infl_1 + 3\%)/2$	5.5%

    $k_2 = 2\% + (Infl_1 + 3\%)/2 = 5.5\%.$ Solving for $Infl_1$, we find $Infl_1$ = Year 1 inflation = 4%.

5. b. $Infl_1 = IP = 4\%.$ $k_1 = k* + IP = 2\% + 4\% = 6\%.$

6. d. First, note that we will use the equation $k_t = 4\% + IP_t + MRP_t$. We have the data needed to find the IPs:

    $IP_5 = (7\% + 4\% + 3\% + 3\% + 3\%)/5 = 20\%/5 = 4\%.$

    $IP_2 = (7\% + 4\%)/2 = 5.5\%.$

    Now we can substitute into the equation:

    $k_2 = 4\% + 5.5\% + MRP_2 = 11\%.$

$k_5 = 4\% + 4\% + MRP_5 = 11\%$.

Now we can solve for the MRPs, and find the difference:

$MRP_5 = 11\% - 8\% = 3\%$.

$MRP_2 = 11\% - 9.5\% = 1.5\%$.

Difference $= 3\% - 1.5\% = 1.5\%$.

7. e. Basic relevant equations:

$k_t = k^* + IP_t + DRP_t + MRP_t + LP_t$. But $DRP_t = MRP_t = LP_t = 0$, so

$k_t = k^* + IP_t$.

$$IP_t = \text{Average inflation} = \frac{Infl_1 + Infl_2 + \ldots}{N}.$$

We know that $Infl_1 = IP_1 = 3.5\%$, and $k^* = 2\%$. Therefore,

$k_1 = 2\% + 3.5\% = 5.5\%$.

$k_3 = k_1 + 3\% = 5.5\% + 3\% = 8.5\%$.

But $k_3 = k^* + IP_3 = 2\% + IP_3 = 8.5\%$, so

$IP_3 = 8.5\% - 2\% = 6.5\%$.

We also know that $Infl_t = \text{Constant after } t = 1$.

Avg. $Infl = IP_3 = (3.5\% + 2Infl)/3 = 6.5\%$; $2Infl = 16\%$, so $Infl = 8\%$.

We can set up this table:

Year	k^*	$Infl_t$	Avg. $Infl = IP_t$	$k = k^* + IP_t$
1	2%	3.5%	$3.5\%/1 = 3.5\%$	5.5%
2	2%	Infl	$(3.5\% + Infl)/2 = IP_2$	
3	2%	Infl	$(3.5\% + Infl + Infl)/3 = IP_3$	8.5%, so $IP_3 =$ $8.5\% - 2\% = 6.5\%$.

8. e. Dollar return $= \text{Dollar income} + \text{Capital gains}$
$= \$110 + (\$1,150 - \$1,040)$
$= \$110 + \$110$
$= \$220$.

9. d. $\text{Yield} = \dfrac{\text{Dollar income} + (\text{Ending value} - \text{Beginning value})}{\text{Beginning value}}$

$= \dfrac{\$110 + \$110}{\$1,040} = 21.15\%$.

10.   a. $\text{Yield} = \dfrac{\text{Dollar income} + (\text{Ending value} - \text{Beginning value})}{\text{Beginning value}}$

$$= \frac{(\$0.80 \times 150\,\text{shares}) + (\$22.50 - \$30)150\,\text{shares}}{\$30 \times 150\,\text{shares}}$$

$$= \frac{\$120 - \$1{,}125}{\$4{,}500}$$

$$= -22.33\%.$$

The yield can also be computed on a per share basis to arrive at the same answer.

CHAPTER 6
BUSINESS ORGANIZATIONS
AND THE TAX ENVIRONMENT

OVERVIEW

We need to understand the goals of the firm and the way financial managers can contribute to achieving these goals. The purpose of this chapter is to give you an overview of business organizations, including appropriate goals that should be pursued by financial managers and how finance fits in a firm's organizational structure. In addition, because taxes affect every financial decision, whether related to individuals or businesses, some key features of the U.S. tax laws are discussed.

OUTLINE

The three main forms of business organization are proprietorships, partnerships, and corporations. About 73 percent of businesses operate as proprietorships, but when based on dollar value of sales, almost 85 percent of all business is conducted by corporations.

☐ A *proprietorship* is an unincorporated business owned by one individual, in which the sole owner has unlimited personal liability for any debts incurred by the business.
   ~ Advantages are: (a) it is easily and inexpensively formed, (b) it is subject to few government regulations, and (c) it is taxed like an individual, not a corporation.
   ~ Disadvantages are: (a) the proprietor has unlimited personal liability for business debts, (b) it is difficult for a proprietorship to obtain large sums of capital, (c) it is somewhat difficult for a proprietor to transfer ownership, and (d) the proprietorship has a life limited to the life of the individual who created it.
      • For these reasons, individual proprietorships are confined primarily to small business operations.

☐ A *partnership* exists when two or more persons associate to conduct a noncorporate business. Partnerships can operate under different degrees of formality.
   ~ Advantages are: (a) formation is easy and relatively inexpensive, (b) it is subject to few government regulations, and (c) the business is taxed like an individual, not a corporation.

~ Disadvantages are: (a) unlimited liability, (b) limited life, (c) difficulty in trans-
ferring ownership, and (d) difficulty of raising large amounts of capital.

- The partners can potentially lose all of their personal assets, even those assets
not invested in the business, because under partnership law each partner is liable
for the business's debt.

- It is possible to limit the liabilities of some of the partners by establishing a
limited partnership, wherein one (or more) partner is designated the general
partner and the others limited partners. The liability of the limited partners
generally is restricted to the amount of funds they have invested in the company,
while the general partners have unlimited liability.

☐ A *corporation* is a legal entity created by a state, and it is separate and distinct from its
owners and managers.
~ Advantages are: (a) unlimited life, (b) ownership that is easily transferred through
the exchange of stock, and (c) limited liability. Because of these three factors, it is
much easier for corporations to raise money in the capital markets than it is for
proprietorships and partnerships.
~ Disadvantages are: (a) corporate earnings are subject to double taxation and (b) setting up a corporation and filing required state and federal reports are more complex
than for a proprietorship or a partnership.

- A *corporate charter* must be filed with the state where the firm is incorporated,
and *bylaws* that govern the management of the company must be prepared.

☐ The value of any business, other than a very small one, probably will be maximized if it
is organized as a corporation.
~ Most firms are managed with value maximization in mind, which in turn has caused
most large businesses to be organized as corporations.

Organizational structures vary from firm to firm.

☐ The chief financial officer, who has the title of vice-president: finance, reports to the
president.
~ The financial vice-president's key subordinates are the treasurer and the controller.

- In most firms the *treasurer* has direct responsibility for managing the firm's cash
and marketable securities, for planning how funds are raised, for selling stocks
and bonds to raise funds, and for overseeing the corporate pension fund.

- The *controller* is responsible for the activities of the accounting and tax
departments.

**Management's primary goal is stockholder wealth maximization, which translates into
maximizing the value of the firm, which is measured by the price of the firm's common
stock.**

☐ Other objectives, such as personal satisfaction, employees' welfare, and the good of the community and of society at large, also have an influence, but for publicly owned companies, they are less important than stock price maximization.

☐ The stockholders own the firm and elect the management team, and in turn, management is supposed to operate in the best interests of the stockholders.

☐ Managers of a firm operating in a competitive market will be forced to undertake actions that are reasonably consistent with shareholder wealth maximization. If they depart from this goal, they run the risk of being removed from their jobs.

☐ *Social responsibility* raises the question of whether businesses should operate strictly in their stockholders' best interests or also be responsible for the welfare of their employees, customers, and the communities in which they operate.
  ~ Any voluntary, socially responsible acts that raise costs will be difficult, if not impossible, in industries that are subject to keen competition.
  ~ Even firms with above-average profits will be constrained in exercising social responsibility by capital market forces because investors will normally prefer a firm that concentrates on profits over one excessively devoted to social action.
  ~ Socially responsible actions that increase costs may have to be put on a mandatory, rather than a voluntary, basis to insure that the burden falls uniformly on all businesses.

☐ The same actions that maximize stock prices also benefit society.
  ~ To maximize stock price, a firm must provide a low-cost, high-quality product to consumers.
  ~ Stock price maximization requires the development of products that consumers want and need, so the profit motive leads to new technology, to new products, and to new jobs.
  ~ Stock price maximization necessitates efficient and courteous service, adequate stocks of merchandise, and well-located business establishments.
  ~ This is why profit-motivated, free-enterprise economies have been so much more successful than socialistic and communistic economic systems. Because managerial finance plays a crucial role in the operation of successful firms, and because successful firms are absolutely necessary for a healthy, productive economy, it is easy to see why finance is important from a social standpoint.

The financial manager can affect the firm's stock price by influencing the following factors: (1) projected earnings per share (EPS), (2) timing of the earnings stream, (3) riskiness of these projected earnings, (4) use of debt financing, and (5) dividend policy.

☐ Every significant corporate decision should be analyzed in terms of its effects on these factors and hence on the firm's stock price.

An agency relationship exists when one or more people that have principal ownership rights hire another person, or agent, to perform a service and then delegate decision-

making authority to that agent. **The agent acts on behalf of the principal. Important agency relationships exist (1) between stockholders and managers and (2) between stockholders and creditors (debtholders).**

☐ A potential *agency problem* exists whenever a manager of a firm owns less than 100 percent of the firm's common stock.

~ Since the firm's earnings do not go solely to the manager, he or she may not concentrate exclusively on maximizing shareholder wealth.

☐ Several mechanisms are used to motivate managers to act in shareholders' best interests: (1) managerial compensation (incentives), (2) the threat of firing, (3) shareholder intervention, and (4) the threat of takeover.

~ Increasingly, firms are tying managers' compensation to the company's performance, and this motivates managers to operate in a manner consistent with stock price maximization.

  • *Executive stock options* allowed managers to purchase stock at some future time at a given price. This type of managerial incentive lost favor in the 1970s because the general stock market declined, and stock prices didn't necessarily reflect companies' earnings growth.

  • *Performance shares* are shares of stock given to executives on the basis of performance as measured by earnings per share, return on assets, return on equity, and so on.

  • All incentive compensation plans—executive stock options, performance shares, profit-based bonuses, and so forth—are designed to (1) provide inducements to executives to act on those factors under their control in a manner that will contribute to stock price maximization and (2) help companies attract and retain top-level executives. Well-designed plans can accomplish both goals.

~ Much of the stock of an average large corporation is owned by a relatively few large institutions rather than by thousands of individual investors, and the institutional money managers have the clout to influence a firm's operations. Consequently, management teams of major corporations have been ousted.

~ Large stockholders are "flexing their muscles" to ensure that firms pursue goals that are in the best interests of shareholders rather than managers.

~ *Hostile takeovers* are most likely to occur when a firm's stock is undervalued relative to its potential. Managers of the acquired firm generally are fired, and any who are able to stay on lose the power they had prior to the acquisition.

  • Actions to increase the firm's stock price and to keep it from being a bargain are good from the standpoint of the stockholders, but other tactics that managers can use to ward off a hostile takeover might not be.

☐ Another agency problem involves conflicts between stockholders and creditors (debtholders). Creditors lend funds to the firm at rates that are based on (1) the riskiness of the firm's existing assets, (2) expectations concerning the riskiness of future asset additions, (3) the firm's existing capital structure, and (4) expectations concerning future capital structure changes.

~ Conflicts arise if (a) management, acting for its stockholders, takes on projects that have greater risk than was anticipated by creditors or (b) the firm increases debt to a level higher than was anticipated.

- Both of these actions decrease the value of the debt outstanding.

~ It is in the firm's best interest to deal fairly with its creditors in order to assure future access to debt markets at reasonable interest costs.

- Losing access to the debt markets and/or higher interest rates decrease the long-run value of the stock.

~ Managers, as agents of both the creditors and the stockholders, must act in a manner that is fairly balanced between the interests of these two classes of security holders.

~ Management actions that would expropriate wealth from any of the firm's *stakeholders* (employees, customers, suppliers, and the like) will ultimately be to the detriment of shareholders. Consequently, maximizing shareholder wealth requires the fair treatment of all stakeholders.

Business ethics can be thought of as a company's attitude and conduct toward its employees, customers, community, and stockholders. Most firms today have in place strong codes of ethical behavior; however, it is imperative that top management be openly committed to ethical behavior, and that they communicate this commitment through their own personal actions as well as through company policies, directives, and punishment/reward systems.

☐ A firm's commitment to business ethics can be measured by the tendency of the firm and its employees to adhere to laws and regulations relating to such factors as product safety and quality, fair employment practices, fair marketing and selling practices, the use of confidential information for personal gain, community involvement, bribery, and illegal payments to foreign governments to obtain business.

☐ Most executives believe that there is a positive correlation between ethics and long-run profitability because ethical behavior (1) avoids fines and legal expenses, (2) builds public trust, (3) attracts business from customers who appreciate and support its policies, (4) attracts and keeps employees of the highest caliber, and (5) supports the economic viability of the communities in which it operates.

Large corporations in the United States can best be described as "open" companies because they are publicly traded organizations that, for the most part, are independent of each other as well as the government. While most developed countries with free economies have similar types of business organizations as U.S. corporations, there exist some differences relating to ownership structure and management of operations.

☐ Firms in most developed economies offer equities with limited liability to stockholders that can be traded in domestic financial markets.

☐ The primary reason non-U.S. firms are likely to be more "closed," thus have more concentrated ownership, than U.S. firms results from the "universal" banking relationships that exist outside the United States.

~ Non-U.S. firms tend to have a close relationship with individual banking organizations, which also might have ownership positions in the firms.
  • Banks in countries such as Germany can meet the financing needs of family-owned businesses, even if they are very large, so such companies do not have to "go public," and thus relinquish some control, to finance additional growth.
~ Because large U.S. firms do not have "one-stop" financing outlets, growth generally has to be financed by bringing in outside owners, which results in more widely dispersed ownership.

☐ In some parts of the world, firms are part of *industrial groups*, which are organizations comprised of companies in different industries with common ownership interests and, in some instances, shared management.
  ~ The objective of an industrial group is to include firms that provide materials and services required to manufacture and sell products; that is, to create an organization that ties together all the functions of production and sales from start to finish.
    • Industrial groups are most prominent in Asian countries.

☐ The differences in ownership concentration of non-U.S. firms might cause the behavior of managers, thus the goals they pursue, to differ.

☐ Whether the ownership structure of non-U.S. firms is an advantage or a disadvantage is debatable. However, the greater concentration of ownership in non-U.S. firms permits greater control by individuals or groups than the more dispersed ownership structures of U.S. firms.

A multinational corporation is one that operates in two or more countries. The growth of multinationals has greatly increased the degree of worldwide economic and political interdependence. Multinational firms now make direct investments in fully integrated operations and multinational corporate networks control a large and growing share of the world's technological, marketing, and productive resources.

☐ Companies, both U.S. and foreign, go "international" for five principal reasons:
  ~ After a company has saturated its home market, growth opportunities are often better in foreign markets.
  ~ Many of the present multinational firms began their international operations because raw materials were located abroad.
  ~ Because no single nation holds a commanding advantage in all technologies, companies are scouring the globe for leading scientific and design ideas.
  ~ Still other firms have moved their manufacturing facilities overseas to take advantage of cheaper production costs in low-cost countries.
  ~ Finally, firms can avoid political and regulatory hurdles by moving production to other countries.

☐ Since the 1980s, investments in the U.S. by foreign corporations have increased significantly. This "reverse" investment is of increasing concern to U.S. government officials because of its implication for eroding the traditional doctrine of independence and self-reliance that always has been a hallmark of U.S. policy. These developments suggest an increasing degree of mutual influence and interdependence among business enterprises and nations.

In theory, financial concepts and procedures are valid for both domestic and multi-national operations. However, there are six major factors that distinguish managerial finance as practiced by firms operating in several different countries from management by firms that operate entirely within a single country. These six factors complicate managerial finance within multinational firms, and they increase the risks faced by the firms involved. Prospects for high profits often make it worthwhile for firms to accept these risks, and to learn how to minimize or at least live with them.

☐ Cash flows will be denominated in different currencies, making exchange rate analysis necessary for all types of financial decisions.

☐ Economic and legal differences among countries can cause significant problems when a corporation tries to coordinate and control worldwide operations of its subsidiaries.

☐ The ability to communicate is critical in all business transactions. U.S. citizens are often at a disadvantage because we are generally fluent only in English. Thus, it is easier for internationals to invade U.S. markets than it is for Americans to penetrate international markets.

☐ Values and the role of business in society reflect the cultural differences that may vary dramatically from one country to the next.

☐ Financial models based on the traditional assumption of a competitive marketplace must often be modified to include political (governmental) and other non-economic facets of the decision.

☐ Political risk, which is seldom negotiable and may be as extreme as expropriation, varies from country to country, and it must be explicitly addressed in any financial analysis.

Individuals pay taxes on wages and salaries, on investment income (dividends, interest, and profits from the sale of securities), and on the profits of proprietorships and partnerships.

☐ U.S. income tax rates are *progressive*; that is, the higher one's income, the larger the percentage paid in taxes. Marginal tax rates begin at 10 percent and can go up to 35 percent.
   ~ *Taxable income* is defined as gross income less a set of exemptions and deductions that are spelled out in the instructions to the tax forms individuals must file.
   ~ The *marginal tax rate* is defined as the tax on the last unit of income.
   ~ The *average tax rate* equals the percent of taxable income that is paid in taxes.

☐ Because corporations pay dividends from income that has already been taxed, there is *double taxation* of corporate income.

~ Interest on most state and local government bonds, which are called "municipals," is not subject to federal income taxes. This creates a strong incentive for individuals in high tax brackets to purchase such securities.

~ Thus, a lower-yielding muni can provide the same after-tax return as a higher-yielding corporate bond.

$$\text{Equivalent pretax yield} \atop \text{on a taxable investment} = \frac{\text{Yield on tax-free investment}}{1 - \text{Marginal tax rate}}.$$

~ The exemption from federal taxes stems from the separation of federal and state powers, and its primary effect is to help state and local governments borrow at lower rates than otherwise would be available to them.

☐ For the most part, the interest paid by individuals on loans is not tax deductible. The principal exception to this is the interest paid on mortgage financing used to purchase a house for personal residence, which is tax deductible.

~ The effect of tax-deductible interest payments is to lower the actual cost of the mortgage to the taxpayer.

☐ Gains and losses on the sale of *capital assets* such as stocks, bonds, and real estate have historically received special tax treatment.

~ A capital asset sold within one year of the time it was purchased produces a *short-term capital gain or loss*, whereas one held for more than one year produces a *long-term capital gain or loss*.

~ While short-term capital gains are taxed at the same rate as other income, long-term capital gains traditionally have received favorable treatment.

● In 2005, the maximum tax rate on long-term capital gains was 15 percent for assets held greater than 12 months.

● It has been argued that lower tax rates on capital gains (1) stimulate the flow of venture capital to new, start-up businesses and (2) cause companies to retain and reinvest a high percentage of their earnings in order to provide their stockholders with lightly taxed capital gains as opposed to highly taxed dividend income.

☐ Individuals pay taxes on the income generated by proprietorships and partnerships they own—the income "passes through" to the owners of these types of businesses.

~ Business expenses are tax deductible, while personal expenses are not.

~ An allowable business expense is a cost incurred to generate business revenues, while an expense incurred for personal benefit (use) is considered a personal expense.

Corporations pay taxes on profits.

☐ Interest income and dividend income received by a corporation are taxed.

~ Interest is taxed as ordinary income at regular corporate tax rates.

~ However, 70 percent of the dividends received by one corporation from another corporation is excluded from taxable income. The remaining 30 percent is taxed at the ordinary tax rate. Thus, the effective tax rate on intercorporate dividends received by a 35 percent marginal tax bracket corporation is 0.30(35%) = 10.5%.

~ If the corporation that receives dividends pays its own after-tax income out to its stockholders as dividends, the income is ultimately subjected to triple taxation: (1) the original corporation is taxed first, (2) then the second corporation is taxed on the dividends it receives, and (3) the individuals who receive the final dividends are taxed again. This is the reason for the 70 percent exclusion on intercorporate dividends.

☐ Our tax system favors debt financing over equity financing.

~ Interest paid is a tax-deductible business expense.

~ Dividends on common and preferred stock are not deductible. Thus, a 35 percent marginal tax bracket corporation must earn $1/(1.0 − 0.35) = $1/0.65 = $1.54 before taxes to pay $1 of dividends, but only $1 of pretax income is required to pay $1 of interest.

☐ Before 1987, corporate long-term capital gains were taxed at lower rates than ordinary income. However, at present, corporate long-term capital gains are taxed as ordinary income.

☐ Ordinary corporate operating losses can be carried back to each of the preceding 2 years and carried forward for the next 20 years in the future to offset taxable income in those years.

~ The purpose of permitting this loss treatment is to avoid penalizing corporations whose incomes fluctuate substantially from year to year.

☐ Depreciation, the means by which the price of a long-term asset is written off over time, plays an important role in income tax calculations.

~ Depreciation has an important effect on taxes paid and cash flows from operations.

☐ Small businesses that meet certain restrictions may be set up as *S corporations,* which receive benefits of the corporate form—especially limited liability—yet are taxed as proprietorships or partnerships rather than as corporations.

~ This treatment would be preferred by owners of small corporations in which all or most of the income earned each year is distributed as dividends because the income would be taxed only once at the individual level.

Businesses in other countries do not face complicated tax laws such as those we have in the United States.

☐ On average, the tax rates of countries with developed markets are 5 to 10 percent higher than the rates of countries with emerging markets.

Appendix 6A provides the 2005 tax rate schedules for individuals and corporations.

SELF-TEST QUESTIONS

Definitional

1. Proprietorships are easily formed, but often have difficulty raising large sums of _____, they subject proprietors to unlimited _____ for business debts, and they have a limited _____.

2. Partnership profits are taxed as _____ income in proportion to each partner's proportionate ownership.

3. A partnership is dissolved upon the withdrawal or _____ of any one of the partners. In addition, the difficulty in _____ ownership is a major disadvantage of the partnership form of business organization.

4. A(n) _____ is a legal entity created by a state, and it is separate from its owners and managers.

5. The concept of _____ _____ means that a firm's stockholders are not personally liable for the debts of the business.

6. Management's primary goal is the _____ of shareholder _____. This goal is accomplished if the firm's _____ _____ is maximized.

7. Socially responsible activities that increase a firm's costs will be most difficult in those industries where _____ is most intense.

8. Firms with above-average profit levels will find social actions _____ by capital market forces.

9. A firm's stock price depends on several factors. Among the most important of these are the level of projected _____ _____ _____ and the riskiness of these projections.

10. A(n) _____ relationship exists when one or more people that have principal ownership rights hire another person, or agent, to perform a service and then delegate decision-making authority to that agent.

11. Potential agency problems exist between a firm's shareholders and its _____ and also between shareholders and _____.

12. _____ _____ are most likely to occur when a firm's stock is undervalued relative to its potential.

13. _____ _____ are shares of stock given to executives on the basis of performance as measured by earnings per share, return on assets, and return on equity.

14. Maximizing shareholder wealth requires the fair treatment of all _____.

15. External factors that influence stock prices include _____ constraints, the general level of _____ activity, the _____ laws, and conditions in the _____ _____.

16. _____ _____ can be thought of as a company's attitude and conduct toward its employees, customers, community, and stockholders.

17. A(n) _____ corporation is one that operates in two or more countries.

18. Large corporations in the United States can best be described as _____ companies because they are publicly traded organizations that, for the most part, are independent of each other as well as the government.

19. In some parts of the world, firms are part of _____ _____, which are organizations comprised of companies in different industries with common ownership interests and, in some instances, shared management.

20. A(n) _____ tax system is one in which tax rates are higher at higher levels of income.

21. Interest received on _____ bonds is generally not subject to federal income taxes. This feature makes them particularly attractive to investors in _____ tax brackets.

22. In order to qualify as a long-term capital gain or loss, an asset must be held for more than ____ months.

23. Gains or losses on capital assets held less than one year are referred to as _____-_____ transactions.

24. An allowable business expense is a cost incurred to generate _____ _____.

25. Interest income received by a corporation is taxed as _____ income. However, only ____ percent of dividends received from another corporation is subject to taxation.

26. Another important distinction exists between interest and dividends paid by a corporation. Interest payments are _____ _____, while dividend payments are not.

27. Ordinary corporate operating losses can first be carried back ____ years and then carried forward ____ years.

28. The Tax Code permits a corporation (that meets certain restrictions) to be taxed at the

CHAPTER 6—AN OVERVIEW OF MANAGERIAL FINANCE

owners' personal tax rates and to avoid the impact of _____ taxation of dividends. This type of corporation is called a(n) ___ corporation.

29. A(n) _____ exists when two or more persons associate to conduct a noncorporate business.

30. A(n) _____ _____ must be filed with the state where the firm is incorporated, and _____ that govern the management of the company must be prepared.

31. In most firms the _____ has direct responsibility for managing the firm's cash and marketable securities, for planning how funds are raised, for selling stocks and bonds to raise funds, and for overseeing the corporate pension fund.

32. The _____ is responsible for the activities of the accounting and tax departments.

33. _____ _____ raises the question of whether businesses should operate strictly in their stockholders' best interests or also be responsible for the welfare of their employees, customers, and the communities in which they operate.

34. _____ _____ is defined as gross income less a set of exemptions and deductions that are spelled out in the instructions to the tax forms individuals must file.

35. The _____ _____ _____ is defined as the tax on the last unit of income.

36. Our tax system favors _____ financing over _____ financing.

37. _____ is the means by which the price of a long-term asset is written off over time, and it has an important effect on taxes paid and cash flows from operations.

38. _____ _____ _____ allow managers to purchase stock at some future time at a given price. This type of managerial incentive lost favor in the 1970s because the general stock market declined.

Conceptual

39. The primary objective of the firm is to maximize EPS.

    a. True   **b.** False

40. The types of actions that help a firm maximize stock price are generally not directly beneficial to society at large.

    a. True   **b.** False

41. There are factors that influence stock price over which managers have virtually no control.

a. True   b. False

42. Financial analysis is not able to take into account political risk.

a. True   b. False

43. ` The fact that 70 percent of intercorporate dividends received by a corporation is excluded from taxable income has encouraged debt financing over equity financing.

a. True   b. False

44. The value of any business, other than a very small one, probably will be maximized if it is organized as a corporation.

a. True   b. False

45. Socially responsible actions that increase costs may have to be put on a voluntary, rather than a mandatory, basis to insure that the burden falls uniformly on all businesses.

a. True   b. False

46. Which of the following is *not* a reason that companies go international?

    a. To seek production efficiency.
    b. To avoid political and regulatory hurdles.
    c. Language differences.
    d. Cultural differences.
    e. Both statements c and d are not reasons for a company to go international.

47. Which of the following is a major factor distinguishing domestic managerial finance from multinational managerial finance?

    a. Political risk.
    b. Cultural differences.
    c. Different currency denominations.
    d. Economic and legal ramifications.
    e. All of the statements above are major factors.

48. Which of the following does *not* represent a significant disadvantage to the proprietorship form of organization?

    a. It is difficult and expensive to form.
    b. It is difficult to obtain large sums of capital.
    c. It is taxed as a corporation, rather than as an individual.
    d. Statements a and c.
    e. Statements a and b.

49.   Which of the following factors affect stock price?

    a.   Level of projected earnings per share.
    b.   Riskiness of projected earnings per share.
    c.   Timing of the earnings stream.
    d.   The manner of financing the firm.
    e.   All of the above factors.

50.   Which of the following factors tend to encourage management to pursue stock price maximization as a goal?

    a.   Shareholders link management's compensation to company performance.
    b.   Managers' reactions to the threats of firing and takeover.
    c.   Managers do not have goals other than stock price maximization.
    d.   Statements a and b are correct.
    e.   Statements a, b, and c are correct.

51.   Which of the following represents a significant *disadvantage* to the corporate form of organization?

    a.   Difficulty in transferring ownership.
    b.   Exposure to taxation of corporate earnings and stockholder dividend income.
    c.   Degree of liability to which corporate owners and managers are exposed.
    d.   Level of difficulty corporations face in obtaining large amounts of capital in financial markets.
    e.   Limited life of the corporation.

52.   An individual with substantial personal wealth and income is considering the possibility of opening a new business. The business will have a relatively high degree of risk, and losses may be incurred for the first several years. Which legal form of business organization would probably be best?

    a.   Proprietorship.
    b.   Corporation.
    c.   Partnership.
    d.   S corporation.
    e.   Limited partnership.

53. Which of the following statements is correct?

   a. To avoid double taxation and to escape the frequently higher tax rate applied to capital gains, stockholders generally prefer to have corporations pay dividends rather than to retain their earnings and reinvest the money in the business. Thus, earnings should be retained only if the firm needs capital very badly and would have difficulty raising it from external sources.

   b. Under our current tax laws, when investors pay taxes on their dividend income, they are being subjected to a form of double taxation.

   c. The fact that a percentage of the interest received by one corporation, which is paid by another corporation, is excluded from taxable income has encouraged firms to use more debt financing relative to equity financing.

   d. If the tax laws stated that $0.50 out of every $1.00 of interest paid by a corporation was allowed as a tax-deductible expense, this would probably encourage companies to use more debt financing than they presently do, other things held constant.

   e. Statements b and d are correct.

SELF-TEST PROBLEMS

1. Wayne Corporation had income from operations of $385,000, it received interest payments of $15,000, it paid interest of $20,000, it received dividends from another corporation of $10,000, and it paid $40,000 in dividends to its common stockholders. What is Wayne's federal income tax?

   a. $122,760   **b.** $130,220   **c.** $141,700   **d.** $155,200   **e.** $163,500

2. A firm purchases $10 million of corporate bonds that paid a 16 percent interest rate, or $1.6 million in interest. If the firm's marginal tax rate is 35 percent, what is the after-tax interest yield?

   a. 7.36%   **b.** 8.64%   **c.** 10.40%   **d.** 13.89%   **e.** 14.32%

3. Refer to Self-Test Problem 2. The firm also invests in the common stock of another company having a 16 percent before-tax dividend yield. What is the after-tax dividend yield?

   a. 7.36%   **b.** 8.64%   **c.** 10.40%   **d.** 13.89%   **e.** 14.32%

4. The Carter Company's taxable income and income tax payments are shown below for 2003 through 2006:

Year	Taxable Income	Tax Payment
2003	$10,000	$1,500
2004	5,000	750
2005	12,000	1,800
2006	8,000	1,200

Assume that Carter's tax rate for all 4 years was a flat 15 percent; that is each dollar of taxable income was taxed at 15 percent. In 2007, Carter incurred a loss of $17,000. Using corporate loss carry-back, what is Carter's adjusted tax payment for 2006?

   a. $850   **b.** $750   **c.** $610   **d.** $550   **e.** $450

5. A firm can undertake a new project that will generate a before-tax return of 20 percent or it can invest the same funds in the preferred stock of another company that yields 13 percent before taxes. If the only consideration is which alternative provides the highest relevant (after-tax) return and the applicable tax rate is 35 percent, should the firm invest in the project or the preferred stock?

   a. Preferred stock; its relevant return is 12 percent.
   b. Project; its relevant return is 1.36 percentage points higher.
   c. Preferred stock; its relevant return is 0.22 percentage points higher.
   d. Project; its before-tax return is 20 percent.
   e. Either alternative can be chosen; they have the same relevant return.

6. Cooley Corporation has $20,000 that it plans to invest in marketable securities. It is choosing between MCI bonds that yield 10 percent, state of Colorado municipal bonds that yield 7 percent, and MCI preferred stock with a dividend yield of 8 percent. Cooley's corporate tax rate is 25 percent, and 70 percent of its dividends received are tax exempt. What is the after-tax rate of return on the highest yielding security?

   a. 7.4%   **b.** 7.0%   **c.** 7.5%   **d.** 6.5%   **e.** 6.0%

ANSWERS TO SELF-TEST QUESTIONS

1.	capital; liability; life	18.	open
2.	personal	19.	industrial groups
3.	death; transferring	20.	progressive
4.	corporation	21.	municipal; high
5.	limited liability	22.	12
6.	maximization; wealth; stock price	23.	short-term
7.	competition	24.	business revenues
8.	constrained	25.	ordinary; 30
9.	earnings per share	26.	tax deductible
10.	agency	27.	2; 20
11.	managers; creditors (or debtholders)	28.	double; S
12.	Hostile takeovers	29.	partnership
13.	Performance shares	30.	corporate charter; bylaws
14.	stakeholders	31.	treasurer
15.	legal; economic; tax; stock market	32.	controller
16.	Business ethics	33.	Social responsibility
17.	multinational	34.	Taxable income

35.	marginal tax rate	**37.**	Depreciation
36.	debt; equity	**38.**	Executive stock options

39.   b.   An increase in earnings per share will not necessarily increase stock price. For example, if the increase in earnings per share is accompanied by an increase in the riskiness of the firm, stock price might fall. *The primary objective is the maximization of stock price.*

40.   b.   The actions that maximize stock price generally also benefit society by promoting efficient, low-cost operations; encouraging the development of new technology, products, and jobs; and requiring efficient and courteous service.

41.   a.   Managers have no control over factors such as (1) external constraints (for example, antitrust laws and environmental regulations), (2) the general level of economic activity, (3) taxes, and (4) conditions in the stock market, all of which affect the firm's stock price.

42.   b.   Political risk must be explicitly addressed by international financial managers.

43.   b.   Debt financing is encouraged by the fact that interest payments are tax deductible while dividend payments are not.

44.   a.   This statement is correct. Most large businesses are organized as corporations.

45.   b.   This statement is reversed. Socially responsible actions may have to be put on a mandatory basis to insure that the burden falls uniformly on all businesses.

46.   e.   The five principal reasons for companies to go international are: (1) To seek new markets; (2) To seek raw materials; (3) To seek new technology; (4) To seek production efficiency; and (5) To avoid political and regulatory hurdles.

47.   e.   In addition to the four factors listed, language differences and the role of governments are major factors distinguishing domestic and multinational managerial finance.

48.   d.   A proprietorship is easily and inexpensively formed, and it is taxed like an individual, not a corporation—both of which are two of its advantages.

49.   e.   The firm's stock price is dependent on all the factors mentioned. One additional factor not mentioned is dividend policy.

50.   d.   Mechanisms that tend to force managers to act in the shareholders' best interests include (1) the threat of firing, (2) the threat of takeover, and (3) the proper structuring of managerial incentives.

51.   b.   The double taxation of corporate earnings is a significant disadvantage of the corporate form of organization. The corporation's earnings are taxed, and then any earnings paid out as dividends are taxed again as income to the stockholders.

52. d. The S corporation limits the liability of the individual, but permits losses to be deducted against personal income.

53. b. Statement a is incorrect. To avoid double taxation, stockholders would prefer that corporations retain more of their earnings because long-term capital gains are taxed at lower rates than ordinary income. Statement c is incorrect. Debt financing has been encouraged by the fact that interest on debt is tax deductible. Statement d is incorrect. Currently, interest on debt is fully tax deductible; allowing 50 percent of interest to be tax deductible would discourage debt financing.

SOLUTIONS TO SELF-TEST PROBLEMS

1. b. The first step is to determine taxable income:

Income from operations	$385,000
Interest income (fully taxable)	15,000
Interest expense (fully deductible)	(20,000)
Dividend income (30% taxable)	3,000
Taxable income	$383,000

(Note that dividends are paid from after-tax income and do not affect taxable income.)

Based on the current corporate tax table, the tax calculation is as follows:

Tax = $113,900 + 0.34($383,000 – $335,000) = $113,900 + $16,320 = $130,220.

2. c. The after-tax yield (or dollar return) equals the before-tax yield (or dollar return) multiplied by one minus the effective tax rate, or AT = BT(1 – Effective T). Therefore, AT = 16%(1 – 0.35) = 16%(0.65) = 10.40%.

3. e. Since the dividends are received by a corporation, only 30 percent are taxable, and the Effective T = Tax rate × 30%:

AT = BT(1 – Effective T)
    = 16%[1 – 0.35(0.30)]
    = 16%(1 – 0.105)
    = 16%(0.895)
    = 14.32%.

4. e.

Year	Taxable Income	Tax Payment	Adjusted Taxable Income	Adjusted Tax Payment
2003	$10,000	$1,500	$10,000	$1,500
2004	5,000	750	5,000	750
2005	12,000	1,800	0	0
2006	8,000	1,200	3,000	450

The carry-back can only go back 2 years. Thus, there were no adjustments made in 2003 and 2004. After a $12,000 adjustment in 2005 and a $5,000 adjustment in 2006, the 2006 adjusted tax payment is $3,000(0.15) = $450. Thus, Carter received a total of $2,550 in tax refunds after the adjustment.

5. b. The project is fully taxable; thus its after-tax return is as follows:

$$AT = 20\%(1 - 0.35) = 20\%(0.65) = 13.0\%.$$

Only 30 percent of the preferred stock dividends are taxable; thus its after-tax yield is $AT = 13\%[1 - 0.35(0.30)] = 13\%(1 - 0.105) = 13\%(0.895) = 11.64\%$. Therefore, the new project should be chosen since its after-tax return is 1.36 percentage points higher.

6. c. AT yield on Colorado bond = 7%(1 - 0.0) = 7%.

AT yield on MCI bond = 10% − Taxes = 10% − 10%(0.25) = 7.5%.

Check: Invest $20,000 at 10% = $2,000 interest.

Pay 25% tax, so AT income = $2,000(1 − T) = $2,000(0.75) = $1,500.

AT rate of return = $1,500/$20,000 = 7.5%.

AT yield on MCI preferred stock = 8% − Taxes = 8% − 0.3(8%)(0.25) = 8% − 0.6% = 7.4%.

Therefore, invest in MCI bonds—their after-tax yield is 7.5%.

CHAPTER 7
ANALYSIS OF FINANCIAL STATEMENTS

OVERVIEW

Financial statement analysis involves a comparison of a firm's performance with that of other firms in the same line of business, which is often identified by the firm's industry classification. Generally speaking, the analysis is used to determine the firm's financial position in order to identify its current strengths and weaknesses and to suggest actions the firm might enact to take advantage of its strengths and correct its weaknesses.

Financial statement analysis is not only important for the firm's managers, it also is important for the firm's investors and creditors. Internally, financial managers use the information provided by financial analysis to help make financing and investment decisions to maximize the firm's value. Externally, stockholders and creditors use financial statement analysis to evaluate the attractiveness of the firm as an investment by examining its ability to meet its current and expected future financial obligations. Our focus in this chapter is how financial statements are used by management to improve the firm's performance and by investors (either stockholders or creditors) to examine the firm's financial position when evaluating its attractiveness as an investment.

OUTLINE

A firm's annual report is issued annually by a corporation to its stockholders. It contains basic financial statements as well as management's opinion of the past year's operations and the firm's future prospects. It presents two important types of information. The first is a verbal section that describes the firm's operating results during the past year and then discusses new developments that will affect future operations. The second is a set of basic quantitative financial statements that report what actually happened to the firm's financial position, earnings, and dividends over the past few years.

☐ The information contained in an *annual report* is used by investors to form expectations about future earnings and dividends. Of all its communications with shareholders, a firm's annual report is generally most important.

☐ The *income statement*, often referred to as the profit and loss statement, summarizes the firm's revenues and expenses (the results of business operations) over the accounting period.

~ A report on earnings and dividends per share is given at the bottom of the statement. Earnings per share (EPS) is called "the bottom line," denoting that of all the items on the income statement, EPS is the most important.

~ It is important to remember that not all of the amounts shown on the income statement represent cash flows.

~ For most corporations, the income statement is generated using the accrual method of accounting.

- This means revenues are recognized when they are earned, not when the cash is received, and expenses are realized when they are incurred, not when the cash is paid.

☐ The *balance sheet* portrays the firm's financial position at a specific point in time. It indicates the investments made by the firm in the form of assets and the means by which the assets were financed, whether the funds were raised by borrowing (liabilities) or by selling ownership shares (equity).

~ *Assets*, found on the left-hand side of the balance sheet, are typically shown in the order of their liquidity, or the length of time it typically takes to convert them to cash.

~ *Claims*, found on the right-hand side, are generally listed in the order in which they must be paid.

- Only cash represents actual money. Noncash assets should produce cash flows eventually, but they do not represent cash in hand.

~ Claims against the assets consist of liabilities and stockholders' equity. Thus, Assets – Liabilities – Preferred stock = Common stockholders' equity (Net worth).

- The risk of asset value fluctuations is borne by the stockholders. However, if asset values rise, these benefits will accrue exclusively to the stockholders.

- The change in the firm's net worth is reflected by changes in the retained earnings account.

~ In the event of bankruptcy, the payoff to preferred stock ranks below debt but above common stock.

~ The common equity section of the balance sheet is divided into three accounts: common stock, paid-in capital, and retained earnings. *Common stock and paid-in capital accounts* arise from the issuance of stock to raise capital. *Retained earnings* are built up over time as the firm "saves," or reinvests, a part of its earnings rather than paying everything out as dividends.

- The breakdown of the common equity accounts shows whether the company actually earned the funds reported in its equity accounts or whether the funds came mainly from selling (issuing) stock.

~ Not every firm uses the same method to determine the account balances shown on the balance sheet. Thus, when evaluating firms, users of financial statements must be aware that more than one accounting alternative is available for constructing financial statements.

~ The balance sheet may be thought of as a snapshot of the firm's financial position *at a point in time* (for example, end of year), while the income statement reports on operations *over a period of time* (for example, one calendar year).

☐ The *statement of retained earnings* reports the change in the firm's retained earnings as a result of the income generated and retained during the year.

~ The balance sheet figure for retained earnings is the sum of the earnings retained for each year the firm has been in business.

~ The balance sheet account "retained earnings" represents a claim against assets, not assets per se.

- Retained earnings as reported on the balance sheet do not represent cash and are not "available" for the payment of dividends or anything else. Retained earnings represent funds that have already been reinvested in operating assets of the firm.

- Even though a company reports record earnings and shows an increase in the retained earnings account, it still might be short of cash.

☐ In finance the emphasis is on *cash flows* because the value of an asset (or a whole firm) is determined by the cash flows it generates. The firm's net income is important, but cash flows are even more important, because cash is needed to continue normal business operations such as the payment of financial obligations, the purchase of assets, and the payment of dividends.

~ A firm's cash flows include cash receipts and cash disbursements.

~ Depreciation results because we want to match revenues and expenses to compute a firm's income, not because we want to match cash inflows and cash outflows.

- *Depreciation* is the means by which the reduction in an asset's value is matched with the revenues that asset helps to produce.

- Depreciation is a noncash charge used to compute net income, so if net income is used to obtain an estimate of the net cash flow from operations, the amount of depreciation must be added back to net income.

~ Cash flows generally are related to accounting profit, which is simply net income reported on the income statement. Although companies with relatively high accounting profits generally have relatively high cash flows, the relationship is not precise.

~ Firms can be thought of as having two separate but related bases of value: *existing assets,* which provide profits and cash flows, and *growth opportunities,* which represent opportunities to make new investments that will increase future profits and cash flows.

~ It is useful to divide cash flows into two classes:

- *Operating cash flows* arise from normal operations, and they are the difference between cash collections and cash expenses, including taxes paid.

- *Other cash flows* arise from borrowing, from the sale of fixed assets, or from the repurchase of common stock.

~ Operating cash flows could be larger or smaller than accounting profits during any given year.

☐ The *statement of cash flows* reports the impact of a firm's operating, investing, and financing activities on cash flows over an accounting period.

~ This statement is designed to show how the firm's operations have affected its cash position by examining the investment (uses of cash) and financing decisions (sources of cash) of the firm.

- Net income plus depreciation is the primary operating cash flow, but changes in accounts payable, accounts receivable, inventories, and accruals are also classified as operating cash flows because these accounts are directly affected by the firm's day-to-day operations.

- Investment cash flows arise from the purchase or sale of plant, property, and equipment.
- Financing cash inflows result from issuing debt or common stock, while financing outflows occur when the firm pays dividends, repays debt, or repurchases stock.

~ In order to adjust the estimate of cash flows obtained from the income statement and to account for cash flows not reflected in the income statement, one needs to examine the impact of changes in the balance sheet accounts during the year.

- *Sources of cash* include an increase in a liability or equity account or a decrease in an asset account.
- *Uses of cash* include a decrease in a liability or equity account or an increase in an asset account.

~ Each balance sheet change is classified as resulting from operations (those activities associated with the production and sale of goods and services), long-term investments (cash flows arising from the purchase or sale of plant, property, and equipment), or financing activities (cash flows arising from debt and/or common stock).

- The cash inflows and outflows from these three activities are summed to determine their impact on the firm's liquidity position, which is measured by the change in the cash and marketable securities accounts.

Financial statements are used to help predict the firm's future earnings and dividends. From an investor's standpoint, predicting the future is what financial statement analysis is all about. From management's standpoint, financial statement analysis is useful both as a way to anticipate future conditions and, more important, as a starting point for planning actions that will influence the future course of events. An analysis of the firm's ratios is the first step in a financial analysis.

☐ Ratios are designed to show relationships between financial statement accounts within firms and between firms.

☐ Ratio analysis is used by three main groups:
  ~ *Managers,* who employ ratios to help analyze, control, and thus improve the firm's operations.
  ~ *Credit analysts,* such as bank loan officers or bond rating analysts, who analyze ratios to help ascertain a company's ability to pay its debts.
  ~ *Security analysts* (or *investors*), including both stock analysts, who are interested in a company's efficiency and growth prospects, and bond analysts, who are concerned with a company's ability to pay interest on its bonds as well as with the liquidating value of the assets in the event the company fails.

☐ A *liquid asset* is one that can be easily converted to cash without significant loss of its original value. *Liquidity ratios* show the relationship of a firm's cash and other current assets to its current liabilities.

- ~ The *current ratio* indicates the extent to which current liabilities are covered by assets expected to be converted to cash in the near future. It is determined by dividing current assets by current liabilities.
  - Because the current ratio provides the best single indicator of the extent to which the claims of short-term creditors are covered by assets that are expected to be converted to cash fairly quickly, it is the most commonly used measure of short-term solvency.
  - A significant deviation from the industry average should signal the analyst (or management) to check further, even if the deviation is considered to be in the "good" direction.
- ~ The *quick*, or *acid test, ratio* is calculated by deducting inventories from current assets and dividing the remainder by current liabilities.
  - Inventories are excluded because it may be difficult to liquidate them at their full book value.
  - The quick ratio is a variation of the current ratio.

☐ *Asset management ratios* measure how effectively the firm is managing its assets and whether or not the level of those assets is properly related to the level of operations as measured by sales.
- ~ The *inventory turnover ratio* is defined as cost of goods sold divided by inventories.
  - It is often necessary to use the average inventory figure rather than the year-end figure, especially if a firm's business is highly seasonal or if there has been a strong upward or downward sales trend during the year.
- ~ The *days sales outstanding (DSO),* also called the average collection period (ACP), is used to evaluate the firm's ability to collect its credit sales in a timely manner. It is calculated by dividing accounts receivable by average sales per day to find the number of days' sales tied up in receivables.
  - The DSO represents the average length of time it takes the firm to collect for credit sales.
  - The DSO also can be evaluated by comparison with the terms on which the firm sells its goods. If the trend in DSO over the past few years has been rising, but the credit policy has not been changed, this would be strong evidence that steps should be taken to improve the time it takes to collect accounts receivable.
- ~ The *fixed assets turnover ratio* is the ratio of sales to net fixed assets. It measures how effectively the firm uses its plant and equipment to help generate sales.
  - Care should be taken when using the fixed assets turnover ratio to compare different firms. If we were comparing an old firm that acquired many of its fixed assets years ago at low prices with a new company that acquired its fixed assets only recently, we probably would find that the old firm had a higher fixed assets turnover.
- ~ The *total assets turnover ratio* is calculated by dividing sales by total assets. It measures the utilization of all the firm's assets.

☐ *Debt management ratios* measure the extent to which a firm is using debt financing, or *financial leverage*, and the degree of safety afforded to creditors.

~ The extent to which a firm uses debt financing has three important implications:
  - By raising funds through debt, stockholder ownership is not diluted.
  - Creditors look to the equity, or owner-supplied funds, to provide a margin of safety.
  - If the firm earns more on investments financed with borrowed funds than it pays in interest, the return on the owners' capital is magnified, or "leveraged."
~ Financial leverage, or borrowing, affects the expected rate of return realized by stockholders for two reasons:
  - The interest on debt is tax deductible while dividends are not, so paying interest lowers the firm's tax bill, all else equal.
  - Usually the rate a firm earns from its investments in assets is different from the rate at which it borrows.
~ Firms with relatively high debt ratios have higher expected returns when business is normal or good, but they are exposed to risk of loss when business is poor. Firms with low debt ratios are less risky, but they also forgo the opportunity to leverage up their return on equity.
  - Decisions about the use of debt require firms to balance higher expected returns against increased risk.
~ Analysts use two procedures to examine the firm's debt in a financial statement analysis:
  - They check balance sheet ratios to determine the extent to which borrowed funds have been used to finance assets.
  - They review income statement ratios to determine how well operating profits can cover fixed charges such as interest.
~ The *debt ratio*, or the ratio of total debt to total assets, measures the percentage of the firm's assets financed by creditors (borrowing).
  - The lower the ratio, the greater the cushion against creditors' losses in the event of liquidation.
  - Total debt includes both current liabilities and long-term debt.
~ The *times-interest-earned (TIE) ratio* is computed by dividing earnings before interest and taxes (EBIT) by the interest charges. The TIE ratio measures the extent to which earnings before interest and taxes, which represents the firm's operating income, can decline before the firm is unable to meet its annual interest costs.
  - Failure to meet interest costs can bring legal action by the firm's creditors, possibly resulting in bankruptcy.
  - EBIT is used in the numerator because the firm's ability to pay current interest is not affected by taxes.
~ The *fixed charge coverage ratio* is similar to the TIE ratio, but it is more inclusive because it recognizes that many firms lease assets and also must make sinking fund payments (required annual payments designed to reduce the balance of a bond or preferred stock issue).

  - $$\text{Fixed charge coverage ratio} = \frac{\text{EBIT} + \text{Lease Payments}}{\text{Interest Charges} + \text{Lease Payments} + \left[\dfrac{\text{Sinking fund payments}}{(1 - \text{Tax rate})}\right]}.$$

- Fixed charges include interest, annual long-term lease obligations, and sinking fund payments.
- In the numerator of the fixed charge coverage ratio, the lease payments are added to EBIT because we want to determine the firm's ability to cover its fixed charges from the income generated before any fixed charges are deducted. The EBIT figure represents the firm's operating income, net of lease payments, so the lease payments must be added back.

☐ Profitability is the net result of a number of policies and decisions. *Profitability ratios* show the combined effects of liquidity, asset management, and debt management on operating results.

~ The *net profit margin on sales* is calculated by dividing net income by sales, and it gives the profit per dollar of sales.

- The operating profit margin is calculated as EBIT divided by sales. The use of this ratio can show whether the low net profit margin is the result of poor operating results or the use of financial leverage.

~ The *return on total assets (ROA)* is the ratio of net income to total assets; it measures the return on all the firm's assets after interest and taxes.

- It provides an idea of the overall return on investment earned by the firm.

~ The *return on common equity (ROE)* measures the rate of return on the stockholders' investment. It is equal to net income available to common stockholders divided by common equity.

☐ *Market value ratios* relate the firm's stock price to its earnings and book value per share. These ratios give management an indication of what investors think of the company's future prospects based on its past performance.

~ If the firm's liquidity, asset management, debt management, and profitability ratios are all good, then its market value ratios will be high, and its stock price will probably be as high as can be expected.

~ The *price/earnings (P/E) ratio*, or market price per share divided by earnings per share, shows how much investors are willing to pay per dollar of reported profits.

- P/E ratios are higher for firms with high growth prospects, other things held constant, but they are lower for riskier firms.

~ The *market/book (M/B) ratio*, defined as market price per share divided by book value per share, gives another indication of how investors regard the company.

- Higher M/B ratios are generally associated with firms that have high rates of return on common equity.

It is important to analyze trends in ratios as well as their absolute levels. Trend analysis provides information about whether the firm's financial position is more likely to improve or deteriorate in the future.

☐ A simple approach to trend analysis is to construct graphs containing both the firm's ratios and the industry averages for the past five years.

~ Using this approach, we can examine both the direction of the movement in, and the relationships between the firm's ratios and the industry averages.

A modified Du Pont chart shows the relationships among return on investment, assets turnover, the profit margin, and leverage.

☐ The left side of the chart develops the profit margin on sales. The right side of the chart develops the company's total assets turnover ratio.

☐ The profit margin times the total assets turnover is called the *Du Pont equation*. This equation gives the rate of return on assets (ROA): ROA = Net profit margin × Total assets turnover.

☐ The *extended Du Pont equation* calculates ROE as follows:

ROE = Profit margin × Total assets turnover × Equity multiplier.

☐ Management can use the Du Pont system to analyze ways of improving the firm's performance.

Comparative ratio analysis is useful in comparing a firm's ratios with those of other firms in the same industry. Sources for such ratios include Dun & Bradstreet, Robert Morris Associates, the U.S. Commerce Department, and trade associations.

☐ Each of the data-supplying organizations uses a somewhat different set of ratios designed for its own purposes. Therefore, when you select a comparative data source, you should be sure that your emphasis is similar to that of the agency whose ratios you plan to use.

☐ Additionally, there are often definitional differences in the ratios presented by different sources, so before using a source, be sure to verify the exact definitions of the ratios to insure consistency with your work.

There are some inherent problems and limitations to ratio analysis that necessitate care and judgment. Ratio analysis conducted in a mechanical, unthinking manner is dangerous, but used intelligently and with good judgment, it can provide useful insights into a firm's operations.

☐ Ratios are often not useful for analyzing the operations of large firms that operate in many different industries because comparative ratios are not meaningful.

☐ The use of industry averages may not provide a very challenging target for high-level performance.

☐ Inflation has badly distorted firms' balance sheets. For this reason, the analysis of a firm over time, or a comparative analysis of firms of different ages, can be misleading.

☐ Ratios may be distorted by seasonal factors, or manipulated by management to give the impression of a sound financial condition ("window dressing").

~ *Window dressing techniques* are techniques employed by firms to make their financial statements look better than they actually are.

☐ Different accounting practices can distort comparisons.

☐ Many ratios can be interpreted in different ways, and whether a particular ratio is good or bad should be based upon a complete financial analysis rather than the level of a single ratio at a single point in time.

☐ A firm might have some ratios that look "good" and others that look "bad," making it difficult to tell whether the company is, on balance, strong or weak.
~ However, statistical procedures can be used to analyze the net effects of a set of ratios.

SELF-TEST QUESTIONS

Definitional

1. Of all its communications with shareholders, a firm's _____ report is generally the most important.

2. The income statement reports the results of operations during the past year, the most important item being _____ _____ _____.

3. The _____ _____ lists the firm's assets as well as claims against those assets.

4. Typically, assets are listed in order of their _____, while liabilities are listed in the order in which they must be paid.

5. Assets – Liabilities – Preferred stock = _____ worth, or _____ _____ equity.

6. The three accounts that normally make up the common equity section of the balance sheet are common stock, additional _____-_____ capital, and _____ _____.

7. _____ _____ as reported on the balance sheet represent income earned by the firm in past years that has not been paid out as dividends.

8. Retained earnings are generally reinvested in _____ _____ and are not held in the form of cash.

9. In finance the emphasis is on the _____ _____ that the company is expected to generate.

10. Depreciation is a _____ charge used to compute net income, so if net income is used to obtain an estimate of the net cash flow from operations, the amount of depreciation must be added back to net income.

11.   _____ _____ _____ arise from normal operations, and they are the difference between cash collections and cash expenses, including taxes paid.

12.   The _____ ____ _____ _____ reports the change in the firm's retained earnings as a result of the income generated and retained during the year.

13.   The statement of cash flows reports the impact of a firm's _____, _____, and _____ activities on cash flows over an accounting period.

14.   The current and acid-test ratios are examples of _____ ratios.

15.   The days sales outstanding (DSO) ratio is found by dividing accounts _____ by average sales per day. The DSO represents the average length of time that it takes the firm to collect for _____ sales.

16.   Debt management ratios are used to evaluate a firm's use of financial _____.

17.   The debt ratio, which is the ratio of total _____ to total _____, measures the percentage of the firm's assets financed by creditors.

18.   The _____-_____-_____ ratio, calculated by dividing earnings before interest and taxes by the interest charges, measures the extent to which operating income can decline before the firm is unable to meet its annual interest costs.

19.   The combined effects of liquidity, asset management, and debt management on operating results are measured by _____ ratios.

20.   Dividing net income by sales gives the _____ _____ _____ on sales.

21.   The _____ ____ _____ _____ measures the return on all the firm's assets after interest and taxes.

22.   The _____ ____ _____ _____ measures the rate of return on the stockholders' investment.

23.   The _____/_____ ratio measures how much investors are willing to pay per dollar of reported profits.

24.   Firms with higher rates of return on stockholders' equity tend to sell at relatively high ratios of _____ price to _____ value.

25.   Individual ratios are of little value in analyzing a company's financial condition. More important are the _____ of a ratio over time and the comparison of the company's ratios to _____ average ratios.

26.   A modified ____ _____ chart shows the relationships among return on investment, assets turnover, the profit margin, and leverage.

27. Return on assets is a function of two variables, the _____ _____ _____ and _____ _____ turnover.

28. Analyzing a particular ratio over time for an individual firm is known as _____ analysis.

29. The _____ _____ may be thought of as a snapshot of the firm's financial position at a point in time, while the _____ _____ reports on operations over a period of time.

30. Firms can be thought of as having two separate but related bases of value: existing _____, which provide profits and cash flows, and _____ opportunities, which represent opportunities to make new investments that will increase future profits and cash flows.

31. Net income plus _____ is the primary operating cash flow.

32. _____ of cash include an increase in a liability or equity account or a decrease in an asset account.

33. A(n) _____ asset is one that can be easily converted to cash without significant loss of its original value.

34. Because the _____ ratio provides the best single indicator to the extent to which the claims of short-term creditors are covered by assets that are expected to be converted to cash fairly quickly, it is the most commonly used measure of short-term solvency.

35. _____ _____ affects the expected rate of return realized by stockholders because interest on debt is tax deductible and the rate a firm earns on its investments in assets is different from the rate at which it borrows.

Conceptual

36. A high quick ratio is *always* a good indication of a well-managed liquidity position.

    a. True   **b.** False

37. Ratios are designed to show relationships between financial statement accounts within firms and between firms.

    a. True   **b.** False

38. Window dressing techniques are techniques employed by firms to make their financial statements look better than they actually are.

    a. True   **b.** False

39. Which of the following is a source of cash?

    a. An increase in a liability account.
    b. A decrease in an equity account.
    c. An increase in an asset account.
    d. Both statements a and c are sources of cash.
    e. Both statements b and c are sources of cash.

40. Which of the following is a use of cash?

    a. A decrease in an asset account.
    b. A decrease in a liability account.
    c. A decrease in an equity account.
    d. Both statements b and c are uses of cash.
    e. Statements a, b, and c are uses of cash.

41. Which of the following groups use ratio analysis?

    a. Managers.   **d.** All of the above.
    b. Credit analysts.   **e.** None of the above.
    c. Security analysts.

42. International Appliances Inc. has a current ratio of 0.5. Which of the following actions would improve (increase) this ratio?

    a. Use cash to pay off current liabilities.
    b. Collect some of the current accounts receivable.
    c. Use cash to pay off some long-term debt.
    d. Purchase additional inventory on credit (accounts payable).
    e. Sell some of the existing inventory at cost.

43. Refer to Self-Test Question 42. Assume that International Appliances has a current ratio of 1.2. Now, which of the following actions would improve (increase) this ratio?

    a. Use cash to pay off current liabilities.
    b. Collect some of the current accounts receivable.
    c. Use cash to pay off some long-term debt.
    d. Purchase additional inventory on credit (accounts payable).
    e. Use cash to pay for some fixed assets.

44. Examining the ratios of a particular firm against the same measures for a group of firms from the same industry, at a point in time, is an example of

    a. Trend analysis.
    b. Comparative ratio analysis.
    c. Du Pont analysis.
    d. Simple ratio analysis.
    e. Industry analysis.

45. Which of the following statements is correct?

    a. Having a high current ratio and a high quick ratio is always a good indication that a firm is managing its liquidity position well.

    b. A decline in the inventory turnover ratio suggests that the firm's liquidity position is improving.

    c. If a firm's times-interest-earned ratio is relatively high, then this is one indication that the firm should be able to meet its debt obligations.

    d. Because ROA measures how effectively a firm utilizes its assets, two firms with the same EBIT must have the same ROA.

    e. If, through specific managerial actions, a firm has been able to increase its ROA, then, because of the fixed mathematical relationship between ROA and ROE, it must also have increased its ROE.

46. Which of the following statements is correct?

    a. Suppose two firms with the same amount of assets pay the same interest rate on their debt and earn the same rate of return on their assets and that ROA is positive. However, one firm has a higher debt ratio. Under these conditions, the firm with the higher debt ratio will also have a higher rate of return on common equity.

    b. One of the problems of ratio analysis is that the relationships are subject to manipulation. For example, we know that if we use some cash to pay off some of our current liabilities, the current ratio will always increase, especially if the current ratio is weak initially, for example, below 1.0.

    c. Generally, firms with high net profit margins have high assets turnover ratios and firms with low net profit margins have low turnover ratios; this result is exactly as predicted by the extended Du Pont equation.

    d. Firms A and B have identical earnings and identical dividend payout ratios. If Firm A's growth rate is higher than Firm B's, then Firm A's P/E ratio must be greater than Firm B's P/E ratio.

    e. Each of the above statements is false.

SELF-TEST PROBLEMS

(The following information applies to the next six Self-Test Problems.)

Roberts Manufacturing Balance Sheet
December 31, 2006
(Dollars in Thousands)

Cash	$ 200	Accounts payable	$ 205
Receivables	245	Notes payable	425
Inventory	625	Other current liabilities	115
Total current assets	$1,070	Total current liabilities	$ 745
Net fixed assets	1,200	Long-term debt	420
		Common equity	1,105
Total assets	$2,270	Total liabilities and equity	$2,270

Roberts Manufacturing
Income Statement for Year Ended December 31, 2006
(Dollars in Thousands)

Sales		$2,400
Cost of goods sold:		
Materials	$1,000	
Labor	600	
Heat, light, and power	89	
Indirect labor	65	
Depreciation	80	1,834
Gross profit		$ 566
Selling expenses		175
General and administrative expenses		216
Earnings before interest and taxes (EBIT)		$ 175
Less interest expense		35
Earnings before taxes (EBT)		$ 140
Less taxes (40%)		56
Net income (NI)		$ 84

1. Calculate the liquidity ratios, that is, the current ratio and the quick ratio.

   a. 1.20; 0.60 **b.** 1.20; 0.80 **c.** 1.44; 0.60 **d.** 1.44; 0.80 **e.** 1.60; 0.60

2. Calculate the asset management ratios, that is, the inventory turnover ratio, fixed assets turnover, total assets turnover, and days sales outstanding.

   a. 2.93; 2.00; 1.06; 36.75 days **d.** 2.93; 2.00; 1.24; 34.10 days
   b. 2.93; 2.00; 1.06; 35.25 days **e.** 2.93; 2.20; 1.48; 34.10 days
   c. 2.93; 2.00; 1.06; 34.10 days

3. Calculate the debt management ratios, that is, the debt and times-interest-earned ratios.

   a. 0.39; 3.16 **b.** 0.39; 5.00 **c.** 0.51; 3.16 **d.** 0.51; 5.00 **e.** 0.73; 3.16

4. Calculate the profitability ratios, that is, the net profit margin on sales, return on total assets, and return on common equity.

   a. 3.50%; 4.25%; 7.60% **d.** 3.70%; 3.50%; 8.00%
   b. 3.50%; 3.70%; 7.60% **e.** 4.25%; 3.70%; 7.60%
   c. 3.70%; 3.50%; 7.60%

5. Calculate the market value ratios, that is, the price/earnings ratio and the market/book value ratio. Roberts had an average of 10,000 shares outstanding during 2006, and the stock price on December 31, 2006, was $40.00.

   a. 4.21; 0.36 **b.** 3.20; 1.54 **c.** 3.20; 0.36 **d.** 4.76; 1.54 **e.** 4.76; 0.36

6. Use the Du Pont equation to determine Roberts' return on assets.

    a. 7.6%   **b.** 7.9%   **c.** 6.2%   **d.** 3.7%   **e.** 4.5%

7. Lewis Inc. has sales of $2 million per year, all of which are credit sales. Its days sales outstanding is 42 days. What is its average accounts receivable balance?

    a. $233,333   **b.** $266,667   **c.** $333,333   **d.** $350,000   **e.** $366,667

8. Southeast Jewelers Inc. sells only on credit. Its days sales outstanding is 60 days, and its average accounts receivable balance is $500,000. What are its sales for the year?

    a. $1,500,000   **b.** $3,000,000   **c.** $2,000,000   **d.** 2,750,000   **e.**
    $3,225,000

9. A firm has total interest charges of $20,000 per year, sales of $2 million, a tax rate of 40 percent, and a net profit margin of 6 percent. What is the firm's times-interest-earned ratio?

    a. 10   **b.** 11   **c.** 12   **d.** 13   **e.** 14

10. Refer to Self-Test Problem 9. What is the firm's TIE, if its net profit margin decreases to 3 percent and its interest charges double to $40,000 per year?

    a. 3.0   **b.** 2.5   **c.** 3.5   **d.** 4.2   **e.** 3.7

11. A fire has destroyed many of the financial records at Anderson Associates. You are assigned to piece together information to prepare a financial report. You have found that the firm's return on equity is 12 percent and its debt ratio is 0.40. What is its return on assets?

    a. 4.90%   **b.** 5.35%   **c.** 6.60%   **d.** 7.20%   **e.** 8.40%

12. Rowe and Company has a debt ratio of 0.50, a total assets turnover of 0.25, and a net profit margin of 10 percent. The president is unhappy with the current return on assets, and he thinks it could be doubled. This could be accomplished (1) by increasing the net profit margin to 14 percent and (2) by increasing asset utilization (turnover). What new total assets turnover ratio, along with the 14 percent net profit margin, is required to double the return on assets?

    a. 0.50   **b.** 0.18   **c.** 0.36   **d.** 0.70   **e.** 0.62

13. Altman Corporation has $1,000,000 of debt outstanding, and it pays an interest rate of 12 percent annually. Altman's annual sales are $4 million, its marginal tax rate is 25 percent, and its net profit margin on sales is 10 percent. If the company does not maintain a TIE ratio of at least 5 times, its bank will refuse to renew the loan, and bankruptcy will result. What is Altman's TIE ratio?

   a. 3.33   **b.** 4.44   **c.** 2.50   **d.** 4.00   **e.** 5.44

14. Refer to Self-Test Problem 13. What is the maximum amount Altman's EBIT could decrease and its bank still renew its loan?

   a. $53,333   **b.** $45,432   **c.** $66,767   **d.** $47,898   **e.** $57,769

15. Pinkerton Packaging's ROE last year was 2.5 percent, but its management has developed a new operating plan designed to improve things. The new plan calls for a total debt ratio of 50 percent, which will result in interest charges of $240 per year. Management projects an EBIT of $800 on sales of $8,000, and it expects to have a total assets turnover ratio of 1.6. Under these conditions, the marginal tax rate will be 40 percent. If the changes are made, what return on assets will Pinkerton earn?

   a. 6.25%   **b.** 6.72%   **c.** 6.50%   **d.** 7.01%   **e.** 7.28%

(The following information applies to the next three Self-Test Problems.)

Baker Corporation Balance Sheet
December 31, 2006

Cash and marketable securities	$ 50	Accounts payable	$ 250
Accounts receivable	200	Accruals	250
Inventory	250	Notes payable	500
Total current assets	$ 500	Total current liabilities	$1,000
Net fixed assets	1,500	Long-term debt	250
		Common stock	400
		Retained earnings	350
Total assets	$2,000	Total liabilities and equity	$2,000

16. What is Baker Corporation's current ratio as of December 31, 2006?

   a. 0.35   **b.** 0.65   **c.** 0.50   **d.** 0.25   **e.** 0.75

17. If Baker uses $50 of cash to pay off $50 of its accounts payable, what is its new current ratio after this action?

   a. 0.47   **b.** 0.44   **c.** 0.54   **d.** 0.33   **e.** 0.62

18. If Baker uses its $50 cash balance to pay off $50 of its long-term debt, what will be its new current ratio?

   a. 0.35   **b.** 0.50   **c.** 0.55   **d.** 0.60   **e.** 0.45

(The following information applies to the next Self-Test Problem.)

Whitney Inc. Balance Sheet
December 31, 2006

		Total current liabilities	$100
		Long-term debt	250
		Common stockholders' equity	400
Total assets	$750	Total liabilities and equity	$750

Whitney Inc. Income Statement
for Year Ended December 31, 2006

Sales		$1,000
Cost of goods sold (excluding depreciation)	$550	
Other operating expenses	100	
Depreciation	50	
Total operating costs		700
Earnings before interest and taxes (EBIT)		$ 300
Less interest expense		25
Earnings before taxes (EBT)		$ 275
Less taxes (40%)		110
Net income		$ 165

19. What is Whitney Inc.'s ROA?

   a. 35%   **b.** 30%   **c.** 15%   **d.** 22%   **e.** 40%

(The following information applies to the next Self-Test Problem.)

Cotner Enterprises Balance Sheet
December 31, 2006

		Total current liabilities	$ 300
		Long-term debt	500
		Common stockholders' equity	450
Total assets	$1,250	Total liabilities and equity	$1,250

**Cotner Enterprises Income Statement
for Year Ended December 31, 2006**

Sales		$1,700
Cost of goods sold (excluding depreciation)	$1,190	
Other operating expenses	135	
Depreciation	75	
Total operating costs		1,400
Earnings before interest and taxes (EBIT)		$ 300
Less interest expense		54
Earnings before taxes (EBT)		$ 246
Less taxes (34%)		84
Net income		$ 162

20. What is Cotner Enterprise's ROA?

    a. 9.85%   **b.** 12.96%   **c.** 15.75%   **d.** 17.50%   **e.** 20.50%

21. Dauten Enterprises is just being formed. It will need $2 million of assets, and it expects to have an EBIT of $400,000. Dauten will own no securities, so all of its income will be operating income. If it chooses to, Dauten can finance up to 50 percent of its assets with debt that will have a 9 percent interest rate. Dauten has no other liabilities. Assuming a 40 percent marginal tax rate on all taxable income, what is the difference between the expected ROE if Dauten finances with 50 percent debt versus the expected ROE if it finances entirely with common stock?

    a. 7.2%   **b.** 6.6%   **c.** 6.0%   **d.** 5.8%   **e.** 9.0%

(The following information applies to the next two Self-Test Problems.)

**American Products Corporation
Balance Sheets
(Dollars in Millions)**

	December 31, 2006	December 31, 2005
Cash	$ 42	$ 90
Marketable securities	0	66
Net receivables	180	132
Inventory	450	318
Total current assets	$ 672	$606
Gross fixed assets	900	450
Less accumulated depreciation	(246)	(156)
Net fixed assets	654	294
Total assets	$1,326	$900

Accounts payable	$ 108	$ 90
Notes payable	18	90
Other current liabilities	90	42
Long-term debt	156	48
Common stock	384	228
Retained earnings	570	402
Total liabilities and equity	$1,326	$900

During 2006, the company earned $228 million after taxes, of which $60 million were paid out as dividends.

22.   Looking **only** at the balance sheet accounts, what are the total sources of funds (which must equal the total uses of funds) for 2006 (dollars in millions)?

    a. $426   **b.** $572   **c.** $702   **d.** $856   **e.** $1,061

23.   What are the cash flows from operations for 2006 (dollars in millions)?

    a. -$246   **b.** $204   **c.** $246   **d.** -$114   **e.** -$204

ANSWERS TO SELF-TEST QUESTIONS

1.   annual
2.   earnings per share
3.   balance sheet
4.   liquidity
5.   Net; Common stockholders'
6.   paid-in; retained earnings
7.   Retained earnings
8.   operating assets
9.   cash flows
10.   noncash
11.   Operating cash flows
12.   statement of retained earnings
13.   operating, investing, financing
14.   liquidity
15.   receivable; credit
16.   leverage
17.   debt; assets
18.   times-interest-earned
19.   profitability
20.   net profit margin
21.   return on total assets
22.   return on common equity
23.   price/earnings
24.   market; book
25.   trend; industry
26.   Du Pont
27.   net profit margin; total assets
28.   trend
29.   balance sheet; income statement
30.   assets; growth
31.   depreciation
32.   Sources
33.   liquid
34.   current
35.   Financial leverage

36.   b.   Excess cash resulting from poor management could produce a high quick ratio. Similarly, if accounts receivable are not collected promptly, this could also lead to a high quick ratio.

37.   a.   This is a correct statement.

38. a. This is a correct statement.

39. a. A decrease in an equity account and an increase in an asset account are both uses of cash.

40. d. A decrease in an asset account is a source of cash.

41. d. Managers use ratios to help analyze, control, and improve the firm's operations. Credit analysts analyze ratios to help ascertain a company's ability to pay its debts. Security analysts are interested in a company's efficiency and growth prospects and a company's ability to pay interest on its bonds, as well as with the liquidating value of the assets in the event the company fails.

42. d. This question is best analyzed using numbers. For example, assume current assets equal $50 and current liabilities equal $100; thus, the current ratio equals 0.5. For answer a, assume $5 in cash is used to pay off $5 in current liabilities. The new current ratio would be $45/$95 = 0.47. For answer d, assume a $10 purchase of inventory on credit (accounts payable). The new current ratio would be $60/$110 = 0.55, which is an increase over the old current ratio of 0.5.

43. a. Again, this question is best analyzed using numbers. For example, assume current assets equal $120 and current liabilities equal $100; thus, the current ratio equals 1.2. For answer a, assume $5 in cash is used to pay off $5 in current liabilities. The new current ratio would be $115/$95 = 1.21, which is an increase over the old current ratio of 1.2. For answer d, assume a $10 purchase of inventory on credit (accounts payable). The new current ratio would be $130/$110 = 1.18, which is a decrease over the old current ratio of 1.2.

44. b. The correct answer is comparative ratio analysis. A trend analysis compares the firm's ratios over time, while a Du Pont analysis shows the relationships among return on investment, assets turnover, net profit margin, and leverage.

45. c. Excess cash resulting from poor management could produce high current and quick ratios; thus statement a is false. A decline in the inventory turnover ratio suggests that either sales have decreased or inventory has increased—which suggests that the firm's liquidity position is *not* improving; thus statement b is false. ROA = Net income/Total assets, and EBIT does not equal net income. Two firms with the same EBIT could have different financing and different tax rates resulting in different net incomes. Also, two firms with the same EBIT do not necessarily have the same total assets; thus statement d is false. ROE = ROA × Assets/Equity. If ROA increases because total assets decrease, then the equity multiplier decreases, and depending on which effect is greater, ROE may or may not increase; thus statement e is false. Statement c is correct; the TIE ratio is used to measure whether the firm can meet its debt obligations, and a high TIE ratio would indicate this is so.

46. a. Ratio analysis is subject to manipulation; however, if the current ratio is less than 1.0 and we use cash to pay off some current liabilities, the current ratio will decrease, *not* increase; thus statement b is false. Statement c is just the reverse of what actually occurs. Firms with high net profit margins have low turnover ratios and vice versa. Statement d is false; it does not necessarily follow that if a firm's growth rate is higher that its stock price will be higher. Statement a is correct. From the information given in statement a, one can determine that the two firms' net incomes are equal; thus, the firm with the higher debt ratio (lower equity ratio) will indeed have a higher ROE.

SOLUTIONS TO SELF-TEST PROBLEMS

1.   c. $\text{Current ratio} = \dfrac{\text{Current assets}}{\text{Current liabilities}} = \dfrac{\$1,070}{\$745} = 1.44.$

         $\text{Quick ratio} = \dfrac{\text{Current assets} - \text{Inventory}}{\text{Current liabilities}} = \dfrac{\$1,070 - \$625}{\$745} = 0.60.$

2.   a. $\text{Inventory turnover} = \dfrac{\text{Cost of goods sold}}{\text{Inventory}} = \dfrac{\$1,834}{\$625} = 2.93.$

         $\text{Fixed assets turnover} = \dfrac{\text{Sales}}{\text{Net fixed assets}} = \dfrac{\$2,400}{\$1,200} = 2.00.$

         $\text{Total assets turnover} = \dfrac{\text{Sales}}{\text{Total assets}} = \dfrac{\$2,400}{\$2,270} = 1.06.$

         $\text{DSO} = \dfrac{\text{Accounts receivable}}{\text{Sales}/360} = \dfrac{\$245}{\$2,400/360} = 36.75 \text{ days}.$

3.   d.   Debt ratio = Total debt/Total assets = $1,165/$2,270 = 0.51.

         TIE ratio = EBIT/Interest = $175/$35 = 5.00.

4.   b. $\text{Net profit margin} = \dfrac{\text{Net income}}{\text{Sales}} = \dfrac{\$84}{\$2,400} = 0.0350 = 3.50\%.$

         $\text{ROA} = \dfrac{\text{Net income}}{\text{Total assets}} = \dfrac{\$84}{\$2,270} = 0.0370 = 3.70\%.$

         $\text{ROE} = \dfrac{\text{Net income}}{\text{Common equity}} = \dfrac{\$84}{\$1,105} = 0.0760 = 7.60\%.$

5. e. $$EPS = \frac{\text{Net income}}{\text{Number of shares outstanding}} = \frac{\$84,000}{10,000} = \$8.40.$$

$$P/E \text{ ratio} = \frac{\text{Price}}{EPS} = \frac{\$40.00}{\$8.40} = 4.76.$$

$$\text{Market/book value} = \frac{\text{Market price}}{\text{Book value}} = \frac{\$40(10,000)}{\$1,105,000} = 0.36.$$

6. d. ROA = Net profit margin × Total assets turnover
$$= \frac{\$84}{\$2,400} \times \frac{\$2,400}{\$2,270} = 0.035 \times 1.057 = 0.037 = 3.7\%.$$

7. a. $$DSO = \frac{\text{Accounts receivable}/(\text{Sales}/360)}{\text{Sales}/360}$$

$$42 \text{ days} = \frac{AR}{\$2,000,000/360}$$
    AR = \$233,333.

8. b.   DSO = Accounts receivable/(Sales/360)
          60 days = \$500,000/(Sales/360)
    60(Sales/360) = \$500,000
          Sales = \$3,000,000.

9. b. Net income = \$2,000,000(0.06) = \$120,000.
    Earnings before taxes = \$120,000/(1 − 0.4) = \$200,000.
    EBIT = \$200,000 + \$20,000 = \$220,000.
    TIE = EBIT/Interest = \$220,000/\$20,000 = 11.

10. c. Net income = \$2,000,000(0.03) = \$60,000.
    Earnings before taxes = \$60,000/(1 − 0.4) = \$100,000.
    EBIT = \$100,000 + \$40,000 = \$140,000.
    TIE = EBIT/Interest = \$140,000/\$40,000 = 3.5.

11. d. ROE = NI/Equity = 0.12. Total debt/Total assets = 0.40,
    so Total equity/Total assets = 0.60, and Total equity = 0.60(Total assets).
    ROE = NI/[0.60(TA)] = 0.12.
    NI = (0.6)(0.12)(TA) = 0.072(TA).
    ROA = NI/TA = [0.072(TA)]/TA = 0.072 = 7.2%.

12. c. If Total debt/Total assets = 0.50, then Total equity/Total assets = 0.50.
    ROA = Net profit margin × Total assets turnover.

Before: ROA $= 10\% \times 0.25 = 2.5\%$.

After: $5.0\% = 14\% \times$ Total assets turnover

$$\text{Total assets turnover} = \frac{5.0\%}{14\%} = 0.36 \times .$$

13. e. TIE = EBIT/Interest, so find EBIT and Interest.
Interest $= \$1,000,000(0.12) = \$120,000$.
Net income $= \$4,000,000(0.10) = \$400,000$.
Taxable income $= $ EBT $= \$400,000/(1 - T) = \$400,000/(0.75) = \$533,333$.
EBIT $= \$533,333 + \$120,000 = \$653,333$.
TIE $= \$653,333/\$120,000 = 5.44\times$.

14. a. TIE = EBIT/INT
$5 = $ EBIT$/\$120,000$
EBIT $= \$600,000$.

From Self-Test Problem 13, EBIT $= \$653,333$, so EBIT could decrease by $\$653,333 - \$600,000 = \$53,333$.

15. b. ROE = Net profit margin × Total assets turnover × Equity multiplier
= NI/Sales × Sales/TA × TA/Equity.

Now we need to determine the inputs for the equation from the data that were given. On the left we set up an income statement, and we put numbers in it on the right:

Sales (given)	$8,000
– Cost	NA
EBIT (given)	$ 800
– Interest (given)	240
EBT	$ 560
– Taxes (40%)	224
Net income	$ 336

Now we can use some ratios to get some more data:
Total assets turnover = 1.6 = S/TA.
D/A = 50%.
Now we can complete the Du Pont equation to determine ROA:
ROA = $336/$8,000 × 1.6 = 4.2% × 1.6 = 6.72%.

16. c. Baker Corporation's current ratio equals Total current assets/Total current liabilities
= $500/$1,000 = 0.50.

17. a. Baker Corporation's new current ratio equals ($500 – $50)/($1,000 – $50) = $450/$950 = 0.47.

18. e. Only the current asset balance is affected by this action. Baker's new current ratio =

($500 − $50)/$1,000 = $450/$1,000 = 0.45.

19.   d.   Whitney's ROA equals Net income/Total assets = $165/$750 = 22%.

20.   b.   Cotner's ROA equals Net income/Total assets = $162/$1,250 = 12.96%.

21.   b.   Known data: Total assets = $2,000,000, EBIT = $400,000, k_d = 9%, T = 40%.

	D/A = 0%	D/A = 50%
EBIT	$400,000	$400,000
Interest	0	90,000*
Taxable income	$400,000	$310,000
Taxes (40%)	160,000	124,000
Net income (NI)	$240,000	$186,000

*If D/A = 50%, then half of assets are financed by debt, so Debt = 0.5($2,000,000) = $1,000,000. At a 9 percent interest rate, INT = 0.09($1,000,000) = $90,000.

For D/A = 0%, ROE = NI/Equity = $240,000/$2,000,000 = 12%. For D/A = 50%, ROE = $186,000/$1,000,000 = 18.6%. Difference = 18.6% − 12.0% = 6.6%.

22.   c.   Total sources and uses of funds = $702 million.

	Change	
(In millions)	Sources	Uses
Cash	$ 48	
Marketable securities	66	
Net receivables		$ 48
Inventories		132
Gross fixed assets		450
Accumulated depreciation	90	
Accounts payable	18	
Notes payable		72
Other current liabilities	48	
Long-term debt	108	
Common stock	156	
Retained earnings	168	
	$702	$702

Note that accumulated depreciation is a contra-asset account, and an increase in this account is a source of funds. Also note that no total lines such as total current assets can be used to determine sources and uses since to do so would be to "double count."

23.   b.   Cash flows from operations (in millions of dollars):

Operating activities:	
Net income	$228
Other additions (sources of cash):	
Depreciation	90
Increase in accounts payable	18
Increase in other current liabilities	48
Subtractions (uses of cash):	
Increase in accounts receivable	(48)
Increase in inventories	(132)
Net cash flows from operations	$204

CHAPTER 8
FINANCIAL PLANNING AND CONTROL

OVERVIEW

In the last chapter, we focused on how to use financial statement analysis to evaluate the existing financial position of a firm. In this chapter, we see how a financial manager can use some of the information obtained through financial statement analysis for financial planning and control of the firm's future operations.

The first part of the chapter is devoted to financial planning using projected financial statements, or forecasts. The second part of the chapter focuses on financial control using budgeting and the analysis of leverage to determine how changes in operations affect financial forecasts.

OUTLINE

Well-run companies generally base their operating plans on a set of forecasted financial statements. The planning process begins with a sales forecast for the next few years. Then the assets required to meet the sales targets are determined, and a decision is made concerning how to finance the required assets. At that point, income statements and balance sheets can be projected. These forecasts represent the "base case" and are a standard by which to judge alternate forecasts.

☐ Forecasting is an essential part of the planning process, and a *sales forecast* is the most important ingredient of financial forecasting.
  ~ The sales forecast is a forecast of a firm's unit and dollar sales for some future period; generally based on recent sales trends plus forecasts of the economic prospects for the nation, region, industry, and so forth.
  ~ The sales forecast generally starts with a review of sales during the past 5 to 10 years.

☐ If the sales forecast is inaccurate, the consequences can be serious. Thus, an accurate sales forecast is critical to the well being of the firm.

Any forecast of financial requirements involves (1) determining how much money the firm will need during a given period, (2) determining how much money the firm will generate internally during the same period, and (3) subtracting the internally generated funds from the total funds needed to support expected operations to determine the external financial requirements. The projected, or pro forma, balance sheet method is a method of forecasting financial requirements based on forecasted financial statements.

☐ The methodology involves projecting the asset requirements for the coming period, then projecting the liabilities and equity that will be generated under normal operations, and subtracting the projected liabilities and equity from the required assets to estimate the *additional funds needed (AFN)* to support the level of forecasted operations.

~ Additional funds needed are the funds that a firm must raise externally through borrowing or by selling new stock.

☐ The first step is to forecast next year's income statement.

~ A sales forecast is needed.

~ Assumptions about the operating cost ratio, the tax rate, interest charges, and dividends paid are made.

~ In the simplest case, costs are assumed to increase at the same rate as sales; in more complicated situations, cost changes are forecasted separately.

~ The objective of this part of the analysis is to determine how much income the company will earn and then retain for reinvestment in the business during the forecasted year.

~ To complete the initial forecast of next year's income, an assumption is made that no change in the financing of the firm will take place.

• At this point it is not known if additional financing is needed.

☐ The second step is to forecast next year's balance sheet.

~ All asset accounts can be assumed to vary directly with sales unless the firm is operating at less than full capacity.

• If the firm is not operating at full capacity, then fixed assets will not vary directly with sales, but the cash, receivables, and inventory accounts will increase in proportion to the increase in sales.

~ Liabilities, equity, or both must also increase if assets increase—asset expansions must be financed in some manner.

~ Certain liability accounts, such as accounts payable and accruals, provide *spontaneously generated funds*, because they increase spontaneously at the same rate as sales due to routine business transactions.

~ Retained earnings will increase, but not proportionately with sales. The new retained earnings will be determined from the projected income statement.

~ Other financing accounts, such as notes payable, long-term debt, preferred and common stock, are not directly related to sales.

• Changes in these accounts result from conscious financing decisions; they do not increase spontaneously as sales increase.

• For the initial forecast, it is assumed that these account balances remain unchanged from their prior year levels.

~ The difference between projected total assets and projected liabilities and equity is the amount of additional funds needed (AFN).

• The additional funds needed (AFN) can be raised by borrowing from the bank as notes payable, by issuing long-term bonds, by selling new common stock, or by some combination of these actions.

- From the initial forecast of financial statements we see that (1) higher sales must be supported by higher asset levels, (2) some of the asset increases can be financed by spontaneous increases in accounts payable and accruals and by retained earnings, and (3) any shortfall must be financed from external sources, either by borrowing or by selling new stock.

☐ The third step is the decision on how to finance the additional funds needed.
  ~ A firm's decision on how to raise the additional funds will be based on several factors, including its ability to handle additional debt, conditions in the financial markets, and restrictions imposed by existing debt agreements.
    - Sometimes contractual agreements, such as a limit on the debt ratio, will restrict the firm's financing decisions.
  ~ If a firm takes on new debt, its interest expenses will rise; and, if additional shares of common stock are sold, total dividend payments will increase if the same dividend per share is paid to all common stockholders (including new stockholders).
    - Each of these changes will affect the amount of additional retained earnings originally forecasted, which, in turn, will affect the amount of additional funds needed.

☐ One complexity that arises in financial forecasting relates to *financing feedbacks*, which are the effects on both the income statement and the balance sheet of actions taken to finance forecasted increases in assets.
  ~ The external funds raised to pay for new assets create additional expenses that must be reflected in the income statement, and this lowers the initially forecasted addition to retained earnings, which means more external funds are needed to make up for the lower amount added to retained earnings.
  ~ Financing feedbacks are incorporated into the pro forma financial statements through additional calculations, or *passes*, of the projected income statement and balance sheet until AFN is equal to zero.

☐ Once the pro forma financial statements have been developed, the projected statements must be analyzed to determine whether the forecast meets the firm's financial targets. If the statements do not meet the targets, then elements of the forecast must be changed.
  ~ Forecasting is an iterative process, both in the way the financial statements are generated and in the way the financial plan is developed.
  ~ For planning purposes, the financial staff develops a preliminary forecast based on a continuation of past policies and trends. This provides the executives with a starting point, or "straw man" forecast.
    - Next, the model is modified to see what effects alternative operating plans would have on the firm's earnings and financial condition. This results in a revised forecast.

The method presented above is a very simple one for constructing pro forma financial statements under rather restrictive conditions. Below are some other conditions that should be considered when creating forecasts.

☐ If *excess capacity* exists in fixed assets, then fixed assets would only have to be increased if the additional sales forecasted exceeded the unused capacity of the existing assets.

~ Full capacity sales is defined as the existing sales level divided by the percentage of capacity at which the fixed assets were used to achieve these sales:

$$\text{Full capacity sales} = \frac{\text{Existing sales level}}{\substack{\text{Percentage of capacity used} \\ \text{to generate sales level}}}.$$

~ In addition to the excess capacity of fixed assets, the firm could have excesses in other assets that can be used for increases in operations.

~ In general, excess capacity means less external financing is required to support increases in operations than would be needed if the firm previously operated at full capacity.

☐ There are *economies of scale* in the use of many types of assets, and when economies occur, a firm's variable cost of goods sold ratio is likely to change as the size of the firm changes substantially.

~ If everything else is the same, changes in the variable cost ratio affect the addition to retained earnings, which, in turn, affects the amount of AFN.

☐ In many industries, technological considerations dictate that if a firm is to be competitive, it must add fixed assets in large, discrete units, often referred to as *lumpy assets*.

~ This automatically creates excess capacity immediately after a plant expansion.

~ Lumpy assets primarily affect the fixed assets turnover.

~ With lumpy assets, it is possible that a small projected increase in sales would require a significant increase in plant and equipment, which would require a very large financial requirement.

Financial managers use planning and control systems when implementing forecasts.

☐ The relationship between sales volume and profitability under different operating conditions provides information that is used by managers to plan for changes in the firm's level of operations, financing needs, and profitability.

☐ The planning process can be enhanced by examining the effects of changing operations on the firm's profitability, both from the standpoint of profits from operations and from the standpoint of profitability after financing effects are considered.

☐ A good control system is essential both to ensure that plans are executed properly and to facilitate a timely modification of plans if the assumptions upon which the initial plans were based turn out to be different than expected.

The relationship between sales volume and operating profitability is explored in cost-volume-profit planning, or operating breakeven analysis.

☐ *Breakeven analysis* is a method of determining the point at which sales will just cover operating costs; that is, the point at which the firm's operations will break even. It also shows the magnitude of the firm's operating profits or losses if sales exceed or fall below that point.

~ If a firm is to avoid accounting losses, its sales must cover all costs—those that vary directly with production and those that remain constant even when production levels change.

~ The breakeven analysis discussed in the text deals only with the upper portion of the income statement—the portion from sales to net operating income (NOI), or earnings before interest and taxes (EBIT).

• This portion generally is referred to as the operating section, because it contains revenues and expenses associated with the normal production operations of the firm.

• At this point, we are concerned with the firm's operating plan and how changes in sales affect its general operating results.

☐ The point at which the total revenue line intersects the total cost line is the *breakeven point*; this is where the revenues generated from sales just cover the *total operating costs* of the firm.

~ Prior to the breakeven point, the total cost line is above the total revenue line, which shows the firm will suffer operating losses because the total costs cannot be covered by the sales revenues.

~ After the breakeven point, the total revenue line is above the total cost line because revenues are more than sufficient to cover total operating costs, so the firm will realize operating profits.

☐ A firm's breakeven point can be calculated algebraically in terms of units or total dollar sales. The breakeven graph shows this relationship.

~ The breakeven quantity in units is defined as the units of output at which total revenues are equal to total operating costs (fixed costs plus variable costs) so that net operating income (NOI) is zero.

• Let P = price per unit, F = total fixed operating costs, and V = variable operating cost per unit. The breakeven quantity, Q_{BE}, is that quantity that solves the following equation and forces total revenues to equal total operating costs: $PQ = F + QV$.

• The equation can be solved for Q_{BE}:

$$Q_{BE} = \frac{F}{P - V} = \frac{F}{\text{Contribution margin}}.$$

~ The breakeven sales volume, S_{BE}, can be calculated as PQ_{BE}:

$$S_{BE} = \frac{F}{1 - \left(\dfrac{V}{P}\right)} = \frac{F}{\text{Gross profit margin}}.$$

• Breakeven analysis based on dollar sales rather than on units of output is useful in determining the breakeven

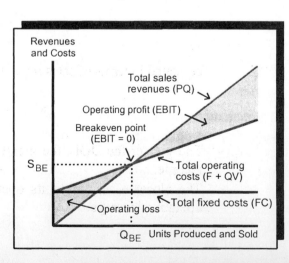

132

volume for a firm that sells many products at varying prices.
- ~ All else equal, one firm will have a lower breakeven point than another firm if its fixed costs are lower, if the selling price of its product is higher, if its variable operating cost per unit is lower, or if some combination of these exists.

☐ Breakeven analysis can shed light on three important types of business decisions:
- ~ It can help determine how large the sales of a new product must be for the firm to achieve profitability.
- ~ It can be used to study the effects of a general expansion in the level of the firm's operations.
- ~ It can help management analyze the consequences of modernization and automation projects.

☐ There are some limitations when one attempts to apply breakeven analysis in practice.
- ~ Any linear breakeven chart is based on the assumption that sales price, total fixed costs, and variable cost per unit are constant for all quantities of output. If these items are not constant then computer simulation is required.

Operating leverage is defined as the extent to which fixed costs are used in a firm's operations. High fixed costs arise from employing larger amounts of capital, thus permitting the firm to operate with reduced labor and smaller variable costs.

☐ A high degree of operating leverage, other things held constant, means that a relatively small change in sales will result in a large change in operating income.

☐ The *degree of operating leverage (DOL)* measures the effect of a change in sales volume on net operating income (NOI). It is defined as the percentage change in NOI (or EBIT) associated with a given percentage change in sales:

$$DOL = \frac{\text{Percentage change in NOI}}{\text{Percentage change in sales}} = \frac{\frac{\Delta EBIT}{EBIT}}{\frac{\Delta Q}{Q}}.$$

- ~ The degree of operating leverage can also be calculated as DOL_Q, which is equal to the degree of operating leverage at a particular level of operations, point Q:

$$DOL_Q = \frac{Q(P - V)}{Q(P - V) - F},$$

or, stated in terms of sales revenues:

$$DOL_S = \frac{S - VC}{S - VC - F} = \frac{\text{Gross profit}}{EBIT}.$$

- ~ The greater the DOL, the greater the impact of a change in operations on operating income.
- ~ The closer a firm is to its operating breakeven point, the greater is its degree of operating leverage.

~ It generally can be concluded the higher the DOL for a particular firm, the closer the firm is to its operating breakeven point, and the more sensitive its operating income is to a change in sales volume.

~ Greater sensitivity generally implies greater risk; thus, it can be stated that firms with higher DOLs generally are considered to have riskier operations than firms with lower DOLs.

Financial leverage considers the impact changing operating income has on earnings per share, or earnings available to common stockholders.

☐ *Financial leverage* takes over where operating leverage leaves off, further magnifying the effects on earnings per share of changes in the level of sales.

~ Operating leverage sometimes is referred to as first-stage leverage and financial leverage is referred to as second-stage leverage.

☐ The *degree of financial leverage (DFL)* is defined as the percent change in EPS that results from a given percent change in EBIT, and it is calculated as:

$$DFL = \frac{\%\Delta EPS}{\%\Delta EBIT} = \frac{\dfrac{\Delta EPS}{EPS}}{\dfrac{\Delta EBIT}{EBIT}} = \frac{EBIT}{EBIT - I}.$$

~ To find the effects on income available to common stockholders, multiply the percentage change in EBIT by DFL. The greater the degree of financial leverage, the greater the impact of a given change in EBIT on EPS.

~ The higher the DFL for a particular firm, it generally can be concluded the lower the firm's times-interest-earned ratio and the more sensitive its EPS is to a change in operating income.

~ Greater sensitivity implies greater risk; thus, it can be stated that firms with higher DFLs generally are considered to have greater financial risk than firms with lower DFLs.

Degree of total leverage (DTL) combines DOL and DFL. If a firm has a considerable amount of both operating and financial leverage, then even small changes in sales will lead to wide fluctuations in EPS.

☐ The *degree of total leverage (DTL)* is defined as the percent change in EPS resulting from a change in sales volume.

~ The relationship between DOL and DFL can be written as:

$$DTL = DOL \times DFL.$$

☐ This equation can be rewritten as:

$$DTL = \frac{Gross\ profit}{EBIT} \times \frac{EBIT}{EBIT - I} = \frac{Gross\ profit}{EBIT - I}$$

$$= \frac{S - VC}{EBIT - I} = \frac{Q(P - V)}{[Q(P - V) - F] - I}.$$

☐ DTL can be used to compute the new earnings per share (EPS*) after a change in sales volume:

$$EPS^* = EPS[1 + (\%\Delta Sales)(DTL)].$$

☐ DTL is useful primarily for the insights it provides regarding the joint effects of operating and financial leverage on earnings per share.

The forecasting (planning) and control of the firm is an ongoing activity, a vital function to the long-run survival of any firm.

☐ If the projected operating results are unsatisfactory, management can "go back to the drawing board," reformulate its plans, and develop more reasonable targets for the coming year.

☐ If the funds required to meet the sales forecast cannot be obtained, the projected level of operations can be scaled back.

☐ It is desirable to plan for the acquisition of funds well in advance.

☐ Any deviation from projections needs to be dealt with to improve future forecasts and the predictability of the firm's operations to ensure the goals of the firm are being pursued appropriately.

One of the most important procedures in budgeting and control is construction of a cash budget. The cash budget helps management plan investment and borrowing strategies, and it also is used to provide feedback and control to improve the efficiency of financial management in the future.

☐ The *cash budget* shows the firm's projected cash inflows and outflows over some specified period. It provides much more detailed information concerning a firm's future cash flows than do the forecasted financial statements. It is the most important tool for managing cash.

☐ The cash budget is useful in determining when cash surpluses or shortages will occur. Plans can then be made to borrow to cover shortages or to invest surpluses.

☐ The *target (minimum) cash balance* is the minimum cash balance a firm desires to maintain in order to conduct business. The target cash balance probably will be adjusted over time, rising and falling with seasonal patterns and with long-term changes in the scale of the firm's operations.

☐   The approach used to construct the cash budget generally is termed the *disbursements and receipts method (scheduling)* because the cash disbursements and cash receipts are estimated to determine the net cash flow expected to be generated each period.

☐   If cash inflows and outflows are not uniform during the month, we could seriously understate the firm's peak financing requirements. In this case, we would have to prepare a cash budget identifying requirements on a daily basis.

☐   Because depreciation is a noncash charge, it does not appear on the cash budget other than through its effect on taxable income, hence on taxes paid.

☐   Because the cash budget represents a forecast, all the values in the table are expected values.

☐   Computerized spreadsheet programs are particularly well suited for constructing and analyzing cash budgets, especially with respect to the sensitivity of cash flows to changes in sales levels, collection periods, and the like.

Appendix 8A demonstrates the iterative process of the construction of projected financial statements due to financing feedbacks.

SELF-TEST QUESTIONS

Definitional

1.   The most important ingredient of financial forecasting is the _____ _____.

2.   The difference between projected total assets and projected liabilities and equity is the amount of _____ _____ _____.

3.   Those asset items that typically increase proportionately with higher sales are _____, _____, and _____. _____ assets are frequently not used to full capacity and hence do not increase in proportion to sales.

4.   If various asset categories increase, _____ and/or _____ must also increase.

5.   Typically, certain liability accounts will provide _____ generated funds. These include accounts _____ and _____.

6.   Notes _____, _____-_____ debt, and _____ and _____ stock are examples of accounts that do not increase automatically with higher levels of sales. Changes in these accounts result from conscious financing decisions.

7.   _____ _____ are the effects on the income statement and balance sheet of actions taken to finance forecasted increases in assets.

8. If _____ _____ exists in fixed assets, then fixed assets would only have to be increased if the additional sales forecasted exceeded the unused capacity of the existing assets.

9. When _____ ____ _____ occur, a firm's variable cost of goods sold ratio is likely to change as the size of the firm changes substantially.

10. In many industries, technological considerations dictate that if a firm is to be competitive, it must add fixed assets in large, discrete units, often referred to as _____ _____.

11. _____ analysis is a method of determining the point at which sales will just cover operating costs.

12. The _____ ____ _____ _____ is defined as the percentage change in EBIT associated with a given percentage change in sales.

13. Financing feedbacks are incorporated into the pro forma financial statements through additional calculations, or _____, of the projected income statement and balance sheet until AFN is equal to _____.

14. The _____ ____ _____ _____ is defined as the percent change in EPS that results from a given percent change in EBIT.

15. The _____ ____ _____ _____ is defined as the percent change in EPS resulting from a change in sales volume.

16. The _____ _____ shows the firm's projected cash inflows and outflows over some specified period.

17. The _____ cash balance is the minimum cash balance that a firm desires to maintain in order to conduct business.

18. The approach used to construct the cash budget generally is termed the _____ _____ _____ method.

19. Well-run companies generally base their operating plans on a set of _____ _____ _____.

20. In general, excess capacity means _____ external financing is required to support increases in operations than would be needed if the firm previously operated at _____ _____.

21. Additional funds needed are the funds that a firm must raise externally through _____ or by selling new _____.

22. A firm's decision on how to raise the additional funds will be based on several factors, including its ability to handle additional _____, conditions in the _____ _____, and restrictions imposed by existing _____ _____.

23. Lumpy assets primarily affect the _____ _____ _____.

24. _____ _____ _____ is defined as the existing sales level divided by the percentage of capacity at which the fixed assets were used to achieve these sales.

25. A good _____ _____ is essential both to ensure that plans are executed properly and to facilitate a timely modification of plans if the assumptions upon which the initial plans were based turn out to be different than expected.

Conceptual

26. An increase in a firm's inventories will call for additional financing unless the increase is offset by an equal or larger *decrease* in some other asset account.

   a. True   **b.** False

27. If the dividend payout ratio is 100 percent, all ratios are held constant, and the firm is operating at full capacity, then any increase in sales will require additional financing.

   a. True   **b.** False

28. One of the first steps in the projected balance sheet method of forecasting is to identify those asset and liability accounts that increase spontaneously with retained earnings.

   a. True   **b.** False

29. All else equal, one firm will have a higher breakeven point than another firm if its fixed costs are lower, if the selling price of its product is higher, if its variable operating cost per unit is lower, or if some combination of these exists.

   a. True   **b.** False

30. The point at which the total revenue line intersects the total cost line is the breakeven point, because this is where the revenues generated from sales just cover the firm's total operating costs.

   a. True   **b.** False

31. A high degree of operating leverage lowers risk by stabilizing a firm's earnings stream.

   a. True   **b.** False

32. Which of the following assumptions is *not* a limitation of breakeven analysis?

   a. Constant price for all levels of sales.
   b. Constant variable cost per unit for all levels of output.
   c. Constant total fixed costs over the range of output being evaluated.

    d. Constant product mix over time.
    e. Constant sales volume over time.

33.   Which of the following would _reduce_ the additional funds needed (AFN) if all other things are held constant?

    a. An increase in the dividend payout ratio.
    b. A decrease in the profit margin.
    c. An increase in the expected sales growth rate.
    d. A decrease in the firm's tax rate.
    e. Both c and d reduce additional funds needed.

34.   Which of the following statements is correct?

    a. The degree of financial leverage is defined as the percentage change in NOI associated with a given percentage change in sales.
    b. The degree of operating leverage is defined as the percent change in EPS resulting from a change in sales volume.
    c. The degree of total leverage is defined as the percent change in EPS that results from a given percent change in EBIT.
    d. It generally can be concluded the higher the DOL for a particular firm, the closer the firm is to its breakeven point, and the more sensitive its operating income is to a change in sales volume.
    e. All of the above statements are false.

35.   Which of the following statements is correct?

    a. Breakeven analysis can help determine how large the sales of a new product must be for the firm to achieve profitability.
    b. Breakeven analysis can be used to study the effects of a general expansion in the level of the firm's operations.
    c. Breakeven analysis can help management analyze the consequences of modernization and automation projects.
    d. All of the statements above are correct.
    e. None of the statements above is correct.

SELF-TEST PROBLEMS

1.   United Products Inc. has the following balance sheet:

Current assets	$ 5,000	Accounts payable	$ 1,000
		Notes payable	1,000
Net fixed assets	5,000	Long-term debt	4,000
		Common equity	4,000
Total assets	$10,000	Total liabilities and equity	$10,000

Business has been slow; therefore, fixed assets are vastly underutilized. Management believes it can double sales next year with the introduction of a new product. No new fixed assets will be required, and management expects that there will be no earnings retained next year. What is next year's additional funding requirement?

a. $0   **b.** $4,000   **c.** $6,000   **d.** $13,000   **e.** $19,000

2.   The 2006 balance sheet for American Pulp and Paper is shown below ($ millions):

Cash	$ 3.0	Accounts payable	$ 2.0
Accounts receivable	3.0	Notes payable	1.5
Inventory	5.0		
Current assets	$11.0	Current liabilities	$ 3.5
Fixed assets	3.0	Long-term debt	3.0
		Common equity	7.5
Total assets	$14.0	Total liabilities and equity	$14.0

In 2006, sales were $60 million. In 2007, management believes that sales will increase by 20 percent to a total of $72 million. Net income is expected to be $3.6 million, and the dividend payout ratio is targeted at 40 percent. No excess capacity exists. What is the additional funding requirement (in millions) for 2007?

a. $0.36   **b.** $0.24   **c.** $0   **d.** -$0.24   **e.** -$0.36

(The following information applies to the next two Self-Test Problems.)

Crossley Products Company's 2006 financial statements are shown below:

Crossley Products Company
Balance Sheet as of December 31, 2006
(Thousands of Dollars)

Cash	$ 600	Accounts payable	$ 2,400
Receivables	3,600	Notes payable	1,157
Inventories	4,200	Accruals	840
Total current assets	$ 8,400	Total current liabilities	$ 4,397
		Mortgage bonds	1,667
		Common stock	667
Net fixed assets	7,200	Retained earnings	8,869
Total assets	$15,600	Total liabilities and equity	$15,600

Crossley Products Company
Incomes Statement for December 31, 2006
(Thousands of Dollars)

Sales	$12,000
Operating costs	10,261

Earnings before interest and taxes	$ 1,739
Interest	339
Earnings before taxes	$ 1,400
Taxes (40%)	560
Net income	$ 840
Dividends (60%)	$504
Addition to retained earnings	$336

3. Assume that the company was operating at full capacity in 2006 with regard to all items except fixed assets; fixed assets in 2006 were being utilized to only 75 percent of capacity. By what percentage could 2007 sales increase over 2006 sales without the need for an increase in fixed assets?

   a. 33%   **b.** 25%   **c.** 20%   **d.** 44%   **e.** 50%

4. Now suppose 2007 sales increase by 25% over 2006 sales. How much additional external capital (in thousands) will be required? Assume that Crossley cannot sell any fixed assets. Use the projected balance sheet method to develop a pro forma balance sheet and income statement. Assume that any required financing is borrowed as notes payable. Do not include any financing feedbacks, and use a pro forma income statement to determine the addition to retained earnings.

   a. $825   **b.** $925   **c.** $750   **d.** $900   **e.** $850

(The following information applies to the next Self-Test Problem.)

Taylor Technologies Inc.'s 2006 financial statements are shown below:

Taylor Technologies Inc.
Balance Sheet as of December 31, 2006

Cash	$ 90,000	Accounts payable	$ 180,000
Receivables	180,000	Notes payable	78,000
Inventories	360,000	Accruals	90,000
Total current assets	$ 630,000	Total current liabilities	$ 348,000
		Common stock	900,000
Net fixed assets	720,000	Retained earnings	102,000
Total assets	$1,350,000	Total liabilities and equity	$1,350,000

Taylor Technologies Inc.
Income Statement for December 31, 2006

Sales	$1,800,000
Operating costs	1,639,860
EBIT	$ 160,140

Interest	10,140
EBT	$ 150,000
Taxes (40%)	60,000
Net income	$ 90,000
Dividends (60%)	$54,000
Addition to retained earnings	$36,000

5. Suppose that in 2007 sales increase by 10 percent over 2006 sales. Construct Taylor's pro forma financial statements using the projected balance sheet method. How much additional capital will be required? Assume the firm operated at full capacity in 2006. Do not include financing feedbacks.

   a. $72,459   **b.** $70,211   **c.** $68,157   **d.** $66,445   **e.** $63,989

6. The Bouchard Company's sales are forecasted to increase from $500 in 2006 to $1,000 in 2007. Here is the December 31, 2006, balance sheet:

Cash	$ 50	Accounts payable	$ 25
Receivables	100	Notes payable	75
Inventories	100	Accruals	25
Total current assets	$250	Total current liabilities	$125
		Long-term debt	200
		Common stock	50
Net fixed assets	250	Retained earnings	125
Total assets	$500	Total liabilities and equity	$500

   Bouchard's fixed assets were used to only 50 percent of capacity during 2006, but its current assets were at their proper levels. All assets except fixed assets should be a constant percentage of sales, and fixed assets would also increase at the same rate if the current excess capacity did not exist. Bouchard's net profit margin is forecasted to be 8 percent, and its payout ratio will be 40 percent. What is Bouchard's additional funds needed (AFN) for the coming year? Ignore financing feedbacks.

   a. $102   **b.** $152   **c.** $197   **d.** $167   **e.** $183

7. Aquarium Suppliers, Inc., produces 10-gallon aquariums. The firm's variable costs equal 40 percent of dollar sales, while fixed costs total $150,000. The firm plans to sell the aquariums for $10 each. What is Aquarium Suppliers' breakeven quantity of sales?

   a. 22,000   **b.** 25,000   **c.** 28,000   **d.** 30,000   **e.** 40,000

8. Refer to Self-Test Problem 7. What is Aquarium Suppliers' breakeven sales volume?

   a. $100,000   **b.** $150,000   **c.** $200,000   **d.** $250,000   **e.** $300,000

9. Refer to Self-Test Problem 7. What price must Aquarium Suppliers charge to break even at sales of 40,000 units? (Assume variable costs still equal 40 percent of dollar sales.)

   a. $5.28   **b.** $5.60   **c.** $5.95   **d.** $6.25   **e.** $7.00

10. The Spade Company has identified two methods of producing playing cards. One method involves using a machine having a fixed cost of $20,000 and variable costs of $1.00 per deck. The other method would use a less expensive machine having a fixed cost of $5,000, but it would require variable costs of $2.00 per deck. If the selling price will be

the same under each method, at what level of output would the two methods produce the same earnings before interest and taxes (EBIT)?

    a. 5,000   **b.** 10,000   **c.** 15,000   **d.** 20,000   **e.** 25,000

11.   Outfitters, Inc., is a new firm just starting operations. The firm will produce backpacks that will sell for $22.00 a piece. Fixed costs are $500,000 per year, and variable costs are $2.00 per unit of production. The company expects to sell 50,000 backpacks per year, and its marginal rate is 40 percent. What is Outfitters' degree of operating leverage at the expected level of sales?

    a. 1.00   **b.** 1.08   **c.** 2.00   **d.** 2.16   **e.** 3.00

12.   Refer to Self-Test Problem 11. What is Outfitters' breakeven quantity of sales?

    a. 5,000   **b.** 10,000   **c.** 15,000   **d.** 20,000   **e.** 25,000

13.   Refer to Self-Test Problem 11. If Outfitters has $250,000 of 10 percent debt, what is the firm's degree of financial leverage?

    a. 0.95   **b.** 1.00   **c.** 1.05   **d.** 1.10   **e.** 1.25

14.   Refer to Self-Test Problems 11 and 13. What is Outfitters' degree of total leverage?

    a. 2.11   **b.** 2.50   **c.** 2.85   **d.** 3.33   **e.** 3.66

15.   Matthew and Sarah Weisner recently leased space in the Plaza Shopping Center and opened a new business, Weisner's Ice Cream Shop. Business has been good but the Weisners frequently run out of cash. This has necessitated late payment of certain ice cream orders, which in turn is beginning to cause a problem with suppliers. The Weisners plan to borrow from a bank to have cash ready as needed, but first they need to forecast how much cash will be needed. Therefore, they have decided to prepare a cash budget for June, July, and August to determine their cash needs. Ice cream sales are made on a cash basis only. The Weisners must pay for their ice cream orders 1 month after the purchase. Rent is $1,000 per month, and they pay themselves a combined salary of $2,400 per month. In addition, they must make a tax payment of $6,000 in June. The current cash on hand (June 1) is $200, but the Weisners have decided to maintain a target cash balance of $3,000. Estimated ice cream sales and purchases for June, July, and August are given below. May purchases amounted to $70,000.

	Sales	Purchases
June	$80,000	$20,000
July	20,000	20,000
August	30,000	20,000

What amount of money will the Weisners need to borrow or have in surplus in each of the months in the budget period (June, July, and August)?

a. $2,200; $5,600; ($1,000)*
b. $2,700; $5,600; ($1,000)*
c. $2,200; $9,400; ($1,000)*
d. ($1,000)*; $4,700; $500
e. $2,200; $5,600; $2,000

*The firm projects a cash surplus in this month.

Appendix 8A

A-1. Use the Crossley financial statements developed in the answer to Self-Test Problem 4 to incorporate the financing feedback that results from the addition of notes payable. (That is, do the next financial statement iteration.) For purposes of this part, assume that the notes payable interest rate is 12 percent. What is the AFN (in thousands) for this iteration?

a. $28   b. $30   c. $20   d. $24   e. $36

A-2. Refer to the first pass financial statements developed in the answer to Self-Test Problem 5. Now assume that 50 percent of the additional capital required will be financed by selling common stock and the remainder by borrowing as notes payable. Assume that the interest rate on notes payable is 13 percent. Do the next iteration of Taylor's financial statements incorporating financing feedbacks. What is the AFN for this iteration?

a. $1,063   b. $957   c. $1,124   d. $927   e. $1,185

ANSWERS TO SELF-TEST QUESTIONS

1. sales forecast
2. additional funds needed
3. cash; receivables; inventories; Fixed
4. liabilities; equity
5. spontaneously; payable; accruals
6. payable; long-term; preferred; common
7. Financing feedbacks
8. excess capacity
9. economies of scale
10. lumpy assets
11. Breakeven
12. degree of operating leverage
13. passes; zero
14. degree of financial leverage
15. degree of total leverage
16. cash budget
17. target
18. disbursements and receipts
19. forecasted financial statements
20. less; full capacity
21. borrowing; stock
22. debt; financial markets; debt agreements
23. fixed assets turnover
24. Full capacity sales
25. control system

26. a. When an increase in one asset account is not offset by an equivalent decrease in another asset account, then financing is needed to reestablish equilibrium on the

balance sheet. Note, though, that this additional financing may come from a spontaneous increase in accounts payable or from retained earnings.

27. a. With a 100 percent payout ratio, there will be no retained earnings. When operating at full capacity, *all* assets are spontaneous, but *all* liabilities cannot be spontaneous since a firm must have common equity. Thus, the growth in assets cannot be matched by a growth in spontaneous liabilities, so additional financing will be required in order to keep the financial ratios (the debt ratio in particular) constant.

28. b. The first step is to identify those accounts that increase spontaneously with sales.

29. b. One firm will have a lower breakeven point than another firm if these conditions exist.

30. a. This is the definition for breakeven point.

31. b. A high degree of operating leverage increases a firm's risk by causing earnings to fluctuate more with changes in sales.

32. e. Breakeven analysis does not assume a constant level of sales.

33. d. Answers a through c would increase the additional funds needed (AFN), but a decrease in the tax rate would raise the profit margin and thus increase the amount of available retained earnings.

34. d. Statement a is incorrect; this is the definition for the degree of operating leverage. Statement b is incorrect; this is the definition for the degree of total leverage. Statement c is incorrect; this is the definition for the degree of financial leverage.

35. d. Statements a, b, and c all show the important types of business decisions on which breakeven analysis can shed light.

SOLUTIONS TO SELF-TEST PROBLEMS

1. b. Look at next year's balance sheet:

Current assets	$10,000	Accounts payable	$ 2,000
Net fixed assets	5,000	Notes payable	1,000
		Current liabilities	$ 3,000
		Long-term debt	4,000
		Common equity	4,000
			$11,000
		AFN	4,000
Total assets	$15,000	Total liabilities and equity	$15,000

With no retained earnings next year, the common equity account remains at $4,000. Thus, the additional financing requirement is $15,000 - $11,000 = $4,000.

2. b. Look at next year's balance sheet for American Pulp and Paper (in millions of dollars):

Cash	$ 3.60	Accounts payable	$ 2.40
Accounts receivable	3.60	Notes payable	1.50
Inventory	6.00		
Current assets	$13.20	Current liabilities	$ 3.90
		Long-term debt	3.00
Fixed assets	3.60	Common equity	9.66
			16.56
		AFN	0.24
Total assets	$16.80	Total liabilities and equity	$16.80

Note that common equity has been increased by the addition to retained earnings, which is calculated as $3.60(0.6) = \$2.16$. Therefore, common equity $= \$7.50 + \$2.16 = \$9.66$.

3. a.

$$\text{Full capacity sales} = \frac{\text{Existing sales level}}{\begin{array}{c}\text{\% of capacity used}\\ \text{to generate sales level}\end{array}} = \frac{\$12,000}{0.75} = \$16,000.$$

$$\text{Percent increase} = \frac{\text{New sales} - \text{Old sales}}{\text{Old sales}} = \frac{\$16,000 - \$12,000}{\$12,000} = 0.33 = 33\%.$$

Therefore, sales could expand by 33 percent before Crossley Products would need to add fixed assets.

4. e.

Crossley Products Company
Pro Forma Income Statement
December 31, 2007
(Thousands of Dollars)

	2006	(1 + g)	1st Pass 2007
Sales	$12,000	(1.25)	$15,000
Operating costs	10,261	(1.25)	12,826
EBIT	$ 1,739		$ 2,174
Interest	339		339
EBT	$ 1,400		$ 1,835
Taxes (40%)	560		734
Net income	$ 840		$ 1,101
Dividends (60%)	$504		$661
Addition to RE	$336		$440

Crossley Products Company
Pro Forma Balance Sheet
December 31, 2007
(Thousands of Dollars)

	2006	(1 + g)	2007	AFN	2007 After AFN
Cash	$ 600	(1.25)	$ 750		$ 750
Receivables	3,600	(1.25)	4,500		4,500
Inventories	4,200	(1.25)	5,250		5,250
Total current assets	$ 8,400		$10,500		$10,500
Net fixed assets	7,200		7,200[b]		7,200
Total assets	$15,600		$17,700		$17,700
Accounts payable	$ 2,400	(1.25)	$ 3,000		$ 3,000
Notes payable	1,157		1,157	+850	2,007
Accruals	840	(1.25)	1,050		1,050
Total current liabilities	$ 4,397		$ 5,207		$ 6,057
Mortgage bonds	1,667		1,667		1,667
Common stock	667		667		667
Retained earnings	8,869	440[a]	9,309		9,309
Total liabilities and equity	$15,600		$16,850		$17,700
AFN =			$850		

Notes:
[a]See income statement on previous page.
[b]From Self-Test Problem 3 we know that sales can increase by 33 percent before additions to fixed assets are needed.

5. c. The first pass balance sheet indicates that the AFN = $68,157. This AFN ignores financing feedbacks.

Taylor Technologies Inc.
Pro Forma Income Statement
December 31, 2007

	2006	(1 + g)	1st Pass 2007
Sales	$1,800,000	(1.10)	$1,980,000
Operating costs	1,639,860	(1.10)	1,803,846
EBIT	$ 160,140		$ 176,154
Interest	10,140		10,140
EBT	$ 150,000		$ 166,014
Taxes (40%)	60,000		66,406
Net income	$ 90,000		$ 99,608
Dividends (60%)	$54,000		$59,765
Addition to RE	$36,000		$39,843

Taylor Technologies Inc.
Pro Forma Balance Sheet
December 31, 2007

	2006	(1 + g)	1st Pass 2007
Cash	$ 90,000	(1.10)	$ 99,000
Receivables	180,000	(1.10)	198,000
Inventories	360,000	(1.10)	396,000
Total current assets	$ 630,000		$ 693,000
Fixed assets	720,000	(1.10)	792,000
Total assets	$1,350,000		$1,485,000
Accounts payable	$ 180,000	(1.10)	$ 198,000
Notes payable	78,000		78,000
Accruals	90,000	(1.10)	99,000
Total current liabilities	$ 348,000		$ 375,000
Common stock	900,000		900,000
Retained earnings	102,000	39,843[a]	141,843
Total liabilities and equity	$1,350,000		$1,416,843
AFN =			$68,157

Notes: [a]See 1st pass income statement.

6. b.

	2006		(1 + g)	1st Pass 2007
Cash	$ 50	×	2	$100
Receivables	100	×	2	200
Inventories	100	×	2	200
Total current assets	$250			500
Net fixed assets	250	+	0[a]	250
Total assets	$500			$750
Accounts payable	$ 25	×	2	$ 50
Notes payable	75			75
Accruals	25	×	2	50
Total current liabilities	$125			$175
Long-term debt	200			200
Common stock	50			50
Retained earnings	125	+	48[b]	173
Total claims	$500			$598
AFN =				$152

Notes:
[a]Capacity sales = Existing sales/Capacity factor = $500/0.5 = $1,000.
Since 2007 sales = $1,000, no new fixed assets will be needed.
[b]Addition to RE = 0.08($1,000)(0.6) = $48.

7. b. $P - V = \$10.00 - 0.40(\$10.00) = \$10.00 - 4.00 = \$6.00.$

$Q_{BE} = F/(P - V) = \$150,000/\$6.00 = 25,000.$

8. d. $S_{BE} = P(Q_{BE}) = \$10(25,000) = \$250,000.$

9. d. Given that $V = 0.4P$,

$$Q_{BE} = F/(P - V)$$
$$40,000 = \$150,000/(P - V)$$
$$40,000 = \$150,000/(P - 0.4P)$$
$$40,000 = \$150,000/0.6P$$
$$24,000P = \$150,000$$
$$P = \$6.25.$$

10. c. First method: $EBIT = PQ - \$1.00Q - \$20,000.$

Second method: $EBIT = PQ - \$2.00Q - \$5,000.$

Now, equate the EBITs:

$$PQ - \$1.00Q - \$20,000 = PQ - \$2.00Q - \$5,000$$
$$\$1.00Q = \$15,000$$
$$Q = 15,000.$$

11. c. The DOL at 50,000 units can be calculated as follows:

$$
\begin{aligned}
DOL_{50,000} &= \frac{Q(P - V)}{Q(P - V) - F} \\[6pt]
&= \frac{50,000(\$22 - \$2)}{50,000(\$22 - \$2) - \$500,000} \\[6pt]
&= \frac{\$1,000,000}{\$1,000,000 - \$500,000} = 2.0.
\end{aligned}
$$

12. e. $Q_{BE} = F/(P - V) = \$500,000/(\$22 - \$2) = \$500,000/\$20 = 25,000.$

13. c. From Self-Test Problem 11 we know that $EBIT = PQ - VQ - F = \$500,000.$ So,

$$DFL = \frac{EBIT}{EBIT - I} = \frac{\$500,000}{\$500,000 - (0.10)(\$250,000)} = 1.05.$$

14. a. $DTL = DOL \times DFL = 2 \times 1.053 = 2.106 \approx 2.11.$

$$\text{Alternatively, } DTL = \frac{\$50,000(\$22 - \$2)}{50,000(\$22 - \$2) - \$500,000 - \$25,000} = \frac{\$1,000,000}{\$475,000} = 2.11.$$

15. a.

Worksheet	June	July	August
Sales	$80,000	$20,000	$30,000
Purchases	20,000	20,000	20,000
Payments for purchases	70,000	20,000	20,000
Cash budget			
Receipts from sales	$80,000	$20,000	$30,000
Payments:			
Purchases	$70,000	$20,000	$20,000
Salaries	2,400	2,400	2,400
Rent	1,000	1,000	1,000
Taxes	6,000		
Total payments	$79,400	$23,400	$23,400
Net cash gain (loss)	$ 600	($ 3,400)	$ 6,600
Beginning cash balance	200	800	(2,600)
Ending cash balance	$ 800	($ 2,600)	$ 4,000
Less: Target cash balance	3,000	3,000	3,000
Surplus cash or total loans to maintain $3,000 target cash balance	($ 2,200)	($ 5,600)	$ 1,000

Appendix 8A

A-1. d.

Crossley Products Company
Pro Forma Income Statement
December 31, 2007
(Thousands of Dollars)

	1st Pass 2007	Financing Feedback	2nd Pass 2007
Sales	$15,000		$15,000
Operating costs	12,826		12,826
EBIT	$ 2,174		$ 2,174
Interest	339	+102*	441
EBT	$ 1,835		$ 1,733
Taxes (40%)	734		693
Net income	$ 1,101		$ 1,040
Dividends (60%)	$661		$624
Addition to RE	$440		$416

*Change in interest = $850(0.12) = $102.

Crossley Products Company
Pro Forma Balance Sheet
December 31, 2007
(Thousands of Dollars)

	1st Pass 2007	Financing Feedback	2nd Pass 2007
Total assets	$17,700		$17,700
Accounts payable	$ 3,000		$ 3,000
Notes payable	2,007		2,007
Accruals	1,050		1,050
Total current liabilities	$ 6,057		$ 6,057
Mortgage bonds	1,667		1,667
Common stock	667		667
Retained earnings	9,309	-24**	9,285
Total liabilities and equity	$17,700		$17,676
AFN =			$24

**Change in RE addition = $416 – $440 = -$24.

A-2. a.

Taylor Technologies Inc.
Pro Forma Income Statement
December 31, 2007

	1st Pass 2007	AFN Effects	2nd Pass 2007
Sales	$1,980,000		$1,980,000
Operating costs	1,803,846		1,803,846
EBIT	$ 176,154		$ 176,154
Interest	10,140	+4,430[a]	14,570
EBT	$ 166,014		$ 161,584
Taxes (40%)	66,406		64,634
Net income	$ 99,608		$ 96,950
Dividends (60%)	$59,765		$58,170
Addition to RE	$39,843		$38,780

[a]Change in interest = $34,079(0.13) = $4,430.

Taylor Technologies Inc.
Pro Forma Balance Sheet
December 31, 2007

	1st Pass 2007	AFN Effects	2nd Pass 2007
Cash	$ 99,000		$ 99,000
Receivables	198,000		198,000
Inventories	396,000		396,000
Total current assets	$ 693,000		$ 693,000
Fixed assets	792,000		792,000
Total assets	$1,485,000		$1,485,000
Accounts payable	$ 198,000		$ 198,000
Notes payable	78,000	+34,079	112,079
Accruals	99,000		99,000
Total current liabilities	$ 375,000		$ 409,079
Common stock	900,000	+34,078	934,078
Retained earnings	141,843	-1,063[b]	140,780
Total liabilities and equity	$1,416,843		$1,483,937
AFN =	$68,157		$1,063

[b]Change in addition to RE = $38,780 − $39,843 = -$1,063.

CHAPTER 9
THE TIME VALUE OF MONEY

OVERVIEW

A dollar in the hand today is worth more than a dollar to be received in the future because, if you had it now, you could invest that dollar and earn interest. Of all the techniques used in finance, none is more important than the concept of the time value of money, or discounted cash flow (DCF) analysis. It is essential that both financial managers and investors have a clear understanding of the time value of money and its impact on the value of an asset. The principles of time value analysis that are developed in this chapter have many applications, ranging from setting up schedules for paying off loans to decisions about whether to acquire new equipment.

Future value and present value techniques can be applied to a single cash flow (lump sum), ordinary annuities, annuities due, and uneven cash flow streams. Future and present values can be calculated using interest factor tables, a regular calculator, or a calculator with financial functions. When compounding occurs more frequently than once a year, the effective rate of interest is greater than the quoted rate.

OUTLINE

The cash flow time line is an essential tool in time value of money analysis. Cash flow time lines help to visualize when the cash flows associated with a particular situation occur. Cash flows are placed directly below the tick marks, and interest rates are shown directly above the time line; unknown cash flows are indicated by question marks. Thus, to find the future value of $100 after 5 years at 5 percent interest, the following cash flow time line can be set up:

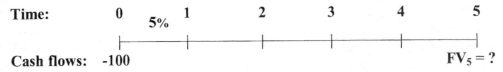

- ☐ A *cash outflow* is a payment, or disbursement, of cash for expenses, investments, and so on.

- ☐ A *cash inflow* is a receipt of cash from an investment, an employer, or other sources.

Compounding is the process of determining the value of a cash flow or series of cash flows some time in the future when compound interest is applied. Compounded interest is interest earned on interest. The future value is the amount to which a cash flow or series of cash flows will grow over a given period of time when compounded at a given interest rate. The future value can be calculated as

$$FV_n = PV(1 + k)^n,$$

where PV = present value, or beginning amount; k = interest rate per year; and n = number of periods involved in the analysis. This equation can be solved in one of three ways: numerically, with interest tables, or with a financial calculator. For calculations, assume the following data that were presented in the time line above: present value (PV) = $100, interest rate (k) = 5%, and number of years (n) = 5.

☐   To solve numerically, use a regular calculator to find 1 + k = 1.05 raised to the fifth power, which equals 1.2763. Multiply this figure by PV = $100 to get the final answer of FV_s = $127.63.

    ~   The term $(1 + k)^n$ is the multiple by which an initial investment grows because of interest earned [termed the *future value interest factor for k and n (FVIF$_{i,n}$)*],.

☐   With a financial calculator, the future value can be found by using the time value of money input keys, where N = number of periods, I = interest rate per period, PV = present value, PMT = annuity payment, and FV = future value. By entering N = 5, I = 5, PV = -100, and PMT = 0, and then pressing the FV key, the answer 127.63 is displayed.

    ~   On some financial calculators, these keys actually are buttons on the face of the calculator, while on others they are shown on a screen after going into the time value of money (TVM) menu.

    ~   Some financial calculators require that all cash flows be designated as either inflows or outflows, thus an outflow must be entered as a negative number (for example, PV = -100 instead of PV = 100).

    ~   Some calculators require you to press a "Compute" key before pressing the FV key.

☐   A graph of the compounding process shows how any sum grows over time at various interest rates. The higher the rate of interest, the faster the rate of growth.

    ~   The interest rate is, in fact, a growth rate.

The process of finding the present value of a cash flow or series of cash flows is called discounting, and it is simply the reverse of compounding. In general, the present value is the value today of a future cash flow or series of cash flows. By solving for PV in the future value equation, the present value, or discounting, equation can be developed and written in several forms:

$$PV = \frac{FV_n}{(1+k)^n} = FV_n \left[\frac{1}{(1+k)^n} \right]$$

☐   To solve for the present value of $127.63 discounted back 5 years at a 5% opportunity cost rate, one can utilize any of the three solution methods:

~ Numerical solution:

$$PV = 127.63 \left[\frac{1}{(1.05)^5} \right] = 100.00$$

~ Financial calculator solution: Enter N = 5, I = 5, PMT = 0, and FV = 127.63, and then press the PV key to get PV = -100.

☐ The *opportunity cost rate* is the rate of return you could earn on alternative investments of similar risk.

☐ A graph of the discounting process shows (1) that the present value of a sum to be received at some future date decreases and approaches zero as the payment date is extended further into the future, (2) that the rate of decrease is greater the higher the interest (discount) rate. At relatively high interest rates, funds due in the future are worth very little today, and even at a relatively low discount rate, the present value of a sum due in the very distant future is quite small.

The compounding and discounting processes are reciprocals, or inverses, of one another. In addition, there are four variables in the time value of money equations: PV, FV, k, and n. If values for three of the four variables are known, you can find the value of the fourth.

☐ If we are given PV, FV, and n, we can determine k by substituting the known values into either the present value or future value equations, and then solving for k. Thus, if you can buy a security at a price of $78.35 that will pay you $100 after 5 years, what is the interest rate earned on the investment?

~ Numerical solution: Use a trial and error process to reach the 5% value for k. This is a tedious and inefficient process. Alternatively, you could use algebra to solve the time value equation:

$$k = \left(\frac{FV}{PV} \right)^{1/n} - 1 = \left(\frac{100.00}{78.35} \right)^{1/5} - 1 = 0.05 = 5.0\%$$

~ Financial calculator solution: Enter N = 5, PV = -78.35, PMT = 0, and FV = 100, then press the I key, and I = 5 is displayed.

☐ Likewise, if we are given PV, FV, and k, we can determine n by substituting the known values into either the present value or future value equations, and then solving for n. Thus, if you can buy a security with a 5 percent interest rate at a price of $78.35 today, how long will it take for your investment to return $100?

~ Numerical solution: Use a trial and error process to reach the value of 5 for n. This is a tedious and inefficient process. The equation can also be solved algebraically.

~ Financial calculator solution: Enter I = 5, PV = -78.35, PMT = 0, and FV = 100, then press the N key, and N = 5 is displayed.

An annuity is a series of equal payments made at fixed intervals for a specified number of periods. If the payments occur at the end of each period, as they typically do in business transactions, the annuity is an ordinary (or deferred) annuity. If the payments occur at

the beginning of each period, it is called an annuity due. Because ordinary annuities are more common in finance, when the term annuity is used in this text, you should assume that the payments occur at the end of each period unless otherwise noted.

☐ The future value of an annuity is the total amount one would have at the end of the annuity period if each payment were invested at a given interest rate and held to the end of the annuity period.

~ Defining FVA_n as the future value of an ordinary annuity over n periods, and PMT as the periodic payment, we can write

$$FVA_n = PMT \sum_{t=1}^{n}(1+k)^{n-t} = PMT \sum_{t=0}^{n-1}(1+k)^t = PMT\left[\frac{(1+k)^n - 1}{k}\right]$$

~ For example, the future value of a 3-year, 5 percent ordinary annuity of $100 per year would be $100(3.1525) = $315.25.

$$FVA_3 = 100\left[\frac{(1.05)^3 - 1}{0.05}\right] = 100(3.1525) = 315.25$$

~ The same calculation can be made using the financial function keys of a calculator. Enter N = 3, I = 5, PV = 0, and PMT = -100. Then press the FV key, and 315.25 is displayed.

~ For an annuity due, each payment is compounded for one additional period, so the future value of the entire annuity is equal to the future value of an ordinary annuity compounded for one additional period. Thus:

$$FVA(DUE)_n = PMT\left\{\left[\frac{(1+k)^n - 1}{k}\right] \times (1+k)\right\}$$

~ For example, the future value of a 3-year, 5 percent annuity due of $100 per year is $100[(3.1525)(1.05)] = $331.01.

~ Most financial calculators have a switch, or key, marked "DUE" or "BEG" that permits you to switch from end-of-period payments (an ordinary annuity) to beginning-of-period payments (an annuity due). Switch your calculator to "BEG" mode, and calculate as you would for an ordinary annuity. Do not forget to switch your calculator back to "END" mode when you are finished.

☐ The present value of an annuity is the single (lump sum) payment today that would be equivalent to the annuity payments spread over the annuity period. It is the amount today that would permit withdrawals of an equal amount (PMT) at the end (or beginning for an annuity due) of each period for n periods.

~ Defining PVA_n as the present value of an ordinary annuity over n periods and PMT as the periodic payment, we can write

$$PVA_n = PMT \sum_{t=1}^{n}\left(\frac{1}{1+k}\right)^t = PMT\left[\frac{1 - \dfrac{1}{(1+k)^n}}{k}\right]$$

~ For example, an annuity of $100 per year for 3 years at 5 percent would have a present value of $100(2.7232) = \$272.32$.

$$PVA_3 = 100 \left[\frac{1 - \dfrac{1}{(1.05)^3}}{0.05} \right] = 100(2.7232) = 272.32$$

~ Using a financial calculator, enter N = 3, I = 5, PMT = -100, and FV = 0, and then press the PV key, for an answer of $272.32.

~ One especially important application of the annuity concept relates to loans with constant payments, such as mortgages and auto loans. With these loans, called *amortized loans*, the amount borrowed is the present value of an ordinary annuity, and the payments constitute the annuity stream.

~ The present value for an annuity due is

$$PVA(DUE)_n = PMT \left[\left\{ \frac{1 - \dfrac{1}{(1+k)^n}}{k} \right\} \times (1+k) \right]$$

~ The difference between the PV of the annuity due and the PV of an ordinary annuity is that each of the payments of the annuity due is discounted one less year.

~ The present value of a 3-year, 5 percent annuity due of $100 is $100[(2.7232)(1.05)] = $285.94.

~ Using a financial calculator, switch to the "BEG" mode, and then enter N = 3, I = 5, PMT = -100, and FV = 0, and then press PV to get the answer, $285.94. Again, do not forget to switch your calculator back to "END" mode when you are finished.

☐ You can solve for both time and the interest rate (rate of return) earned on an annuity.

~ To solve numerically for the interest rate (or the number of annuity payments), you must use the trial-and-error process and plug in different values for k (or n) in the annuity equation to solve for the interest rate.

~ You can use the financial calculator by entering the appropriate values for N (or I), PMT, and either FV or PV, and then pressing I (or N) to solve for the interest rate.

A perpetuity is a stream of equal payments expected to continue forever.

☐ Perpetuities are illustrated by consols. *Consols* are perpetual bonds issued by the British government to consolidate past debts. In general, they are any perpetual bonds.

☐ The present value of a perpetuity is:

PVP = Payment/Interest rate = PMT/k.

☐ For example, if the interest rate were 12 percent, a perpetuity of $1,000 a year would have a present value of $1,000/0.12 = $8,333.33.

☐ The value of a perpetuity changes dramatically when interest rates change. All else equal, when interest rates increase the value of an investment decreases. This is a fundamental valuation concept.

Many financial decisions require the analysis of uneven, or nonconstant, cash flows rather than a stream of fixed payments such as an annuity. An uneven cash flow stream is a series of cash flows in which the amount varies from one period to the next.

☐ The term PMT designates constant cash flows, while the term CF designates cash flows in general, including uneven cash flows.
~ Financial calculators are set up to follow this convention.

☐ The present value of an uneven cash flow stream is the sum of the PVs of the individual cash flows of the stream.
~ The PV is found by applying the following general present value equation:

$$PV = \sum_{t=1}^{n} CF_t \left[\frac{1}{(1+k)^t} \right]$$

☐ With a financial calculator, enter each cash flow (beginning with the t = 0 cash flow) into the cash flow register, CF_j, enter the appropriate interest rate, and then press the NPV key to obtain the PV of the cash flow stream.
~ Annuities can be entered into the cash flow register more efficiently by using the Nj, or frequency, key.
~ Note that amounts entered into the cash flow register remain in the register until they are cleared. Be sure to clear the cash flow register before starting a new problem.

☐ Similarly, the future value of an uneven cash flow stream (sometimes called the *terminal value*) is the sum of the FVs of the individual cash flows of the stream.
~ The FV can be found by applying the following general future value equation:

$$FV_n = \sum_{t=1}^{n} CF_t (1+k)^{n-t}$$

~ Some calculators have a net future value (NFV) key that allows you to obtain the FV of an uneven cash flow stream.
~ Once we know the present value of an uneven cash flow stream, we can find its future value by compounding the present value amount to the future period.

☐ If one knows the relevant cash flows, the effective interest rate can be calculated efficiently with a financial calculator. Enter each cash flow (beginning with the t = 0 cash flow) into the cash flow register, CF_j, and then press the IRR key to obtain the interest rate of an uneven cash flow stream.
~ IRR stands for *internal rate of return*, which is the return on an investment.

Annual compounding is the arithmetic process of determining the final value of a cash flow or series of cash flows when interest is added once a year. Semiannual, quarterly, and other compounding periods more frequent than on an annual basis are often used in

financial transactions. Compounding on a nonannual basis requires an adjustment to both the compounding and discounting procedures discussed previously. Moreover, when comparing securities with different compounding periods, they need to be put on a common basis. This requires distinguishing between the simple, or quoted, interest rate and the effective annual rate.

☐ The *simple*, or *quoted, interest rate* is the contracted, or quoted, interest rate that is used to compute the interest paid per period.

☐ The *effective annual rate* is the annual rate of interest actually being earned, as opposed to the quoted rate, considering the compounding of interest. The effective annual rate (EAR) is defined as that rate that would produce the same ending (future) value if annual compounding had been used. The effective annual percentage rate is given by the following formula:

$$\text{Effective annual rate} = \text{EAR} = (1 + k_{\text{SIMPLE}}/m)^m - 1.0,$$

where k_{SIMPLE} is the simple, or quoted, interest rate and m is the number of compounding periods per year. The EAR is useful in comparing securities with different compounding periods.

☐ To find the effective annual rate if the simple rate is 6 percent and semiannual compounding is used, we have:

$$\text{EAR} = (1 + 0.06/2)^2 - 1.0 = 6.09\%.$$

☐ For annual compounding use the formula to find the future value of a single payment (lump sum):

$$FV_n = PV(1 + k)^n.$$

When compounding occurs more frequently than once a year, use this formula:

$$FV_n = PV(1 + k_{\text{SIMPLE}}/m)^{m \times n}.$$

Here m is the number of times per year compounding occurs, and n is the number of years.

☐ The amount to which $1,000 will grow after 5 years if quarterly compounding is applied to a simple 8 percent interest rate is found as follows:

$$FV_n = \$1,000(1 + 0.08/4)^{(4)(5)} = \$1,000(1.02)^{20} = \$1,485.95.$$

~ Financial calculator solution: Divide the interest rate by 4, so k = 8%/4 = 2%, and multiply the number of years by 4, so n = 5 H 4 = 20. Enter N = 20, I = 2, PV = -1000, and PMT = 0, and then press the FV key to find FV = $1,485.95.

☐ The present value of a 5-year future investment equal to $1,485.95, with an 8 percent simple interest rate, compounded quarterly, is found as follows:

$$\$1,485.95 = PV(1 + 0.08/4)^{(4)(5)}$$
$$PV = \frac{\$1,485.95}{(1.02)^{20}} = \$1,000.$$

~ Financial calculator solution: Enter N = 20, I = 2, PMT = 0, and FV = 1485.95, and then press the PV key to find PV = -$1,000.00.

☐ In general, nonannual compounding can be handled one of two ways.
~ State everything on a periodic rather than on an annual basis. Thus, n = 6 periods rather than n = 3 years and k = 3% instead of k = 6% with semiannual compounding.
~ Find the effective annual rate (EAR) with the equation below and then use the EAR as the rate over the given number of years.

$$EAR = \left(1 + \frac{k_{SIMPLE}}{m}\right)^{m} - 1.0.$$

☐ The *annual percentage rate* is the periodic rate multiplied by the number of periods per year. It is often used in bank loan advertisements because it meets the minimum requirements contained in "truth in lending" laws.
~ The annual percentage rate represents the periodic rate stated on an annual basis without considering compounding.
~ The APR is never used in actual calculations; it is simply reported to borrowers.

One of the most important applications of compound interest involves amortized loans, which are paid off in equal installments over the life of the loan.

☐ The amount of each payment, PMT, is found as follows:

$$PMT = \frac{PVA_n}{\left[\dfrac{1 - \dfrac{1}{(1+k)^n}}{k}\right]}$$

☐ With a financial calculator, enter N (number of years), I (interest rate), PV (amount borrowed), and FV = 0, and then press the PMT key to find the periodic payment.

☐ Each payment consists partly of interest and partly of the repayment of principal. This breakdown is often developed in a *loan amortization schedule.*
~ The interest component is largest in the first period, and it declines as the outstanding loan balance decreases.
~ For tax purposes, a business borrower reports the interest component as a deductible cost each year, while the lender reports the same amount as taxable income.

☐ Most financial calculators are programmed to calculate amortization tables.

The text discussion has involved three different interest rates. It is important to understand their differences.

☐ The *simple*, or *quoted, rate* is the interest rate quoted by borrowers and lenders. This quotation must include the number of compounding periods per year.

~ This rate is never shown on a time line, and it is never used as an input in a financial calculator unless compounding occurs only once a year.

~ k_{SIMPLE} = Periodic rate × m = Annual percentage rate = APR.

☐ The *periodic rate, k_{PER},* is the rate charged by a lender or paid by a borrower each interest period. Periodic rate = k_{PER} = k_{SIMPLE}/m.

~ The periodic rate is used for calculations in problems where two conditions hold: (1) payments occur on a regular basis more frequently than once a year and (2) a payment is made on each compounding (or discounting) date.

☐ The *effective annual rate* is the rate with which, under annual compounding, we would obtain the same result as if we had used a given periodic rate with m compounding periods per year.

~ EAR is found as follows:

$$\text{EAR} = \left(1 + \frac{k_{SIMPLE}}{m}\right)^m - 1.0 = (1 - k_{PER})^m - 1.$$

Appendix 9A shows how to use spreadsheets to solve time value of money problems.

Appendix 9B shows how to use the interest tables in Appendix A at the end of the text to solve time value of money problems.

Appendix 9C explains how to generate an amortization schedule for a loan using a financial calculator.

Appendix 9D explains how to calculate the PV of an uneven cash flow stream using a financial calculator.

SELF-TEST QUESTIONS

Definitional

1. A(n) _____ _____ is a payment, or disbursement, of cash for expenses, investments, and so on.

2. A(n) _____ _____ is a receipt of cash from an investment, an employer, or other sources.

3.   _____ is the process of determining the value of a cash flow or series of cash flows some time in the future.

4.   The _____ is the amount to which a cash flow or series of cash flows will grow over a given period of time when compounded at a given interest rate.

5.   The _____ is the value today of a future cash flow or series of cash flows.

6.   _____ _____ is interest earned on interest.

7.   Using a savings account as an example, the difference between the account's present value and its future value at the end of the period is due to _____ earned during the period.

8.   The equation $FV_n = PV(1 + k)^n$ determines the _____ _____ of a sum at the end of n periods.

9.   The process of finding the present value of a cash flow or series of cash flows is called _____, and it is simply the reverse of _____.

10.   The _____ _____ _____ is the rate of return you could earn on alternative investments of similar risk.

11.   A series of equal payments made at fixed intervals for a specified number of periods is a(n) _____. If the payments occur at the end of each period it is a(n) _____ annuity, while if the payments occur at the beginning of each period it is an annuity _____.

12.   A(n) _____ is a stream of equal payments expected to continue forever.

13.   The term PMT designates _____ cash flows, while the term CF designates cash flows in general, including _____ cash flows.

14.   The present value of an uneven cash flow stream is the _____ of the PVs of the individual cash flows of the stream.

15.   Because different types of investments use different compounding periods, it is important to distinguish between the quoted, or _____, interest rate and the _____ annual interest rate, the annual rate of interest actually being earned considering the compounding of interest.

16.   _____ loans are paid off in equal installments over the life of the loan.

17.   The _____ rate is equal to the simple interest rate divided by the number of compounding periods per year.

18.   The _____ _____ _____ is the periodic rate multiplied by the number of periods per year, and it is often used in bank loan advertisements because it meets the minimum requirements contained in "truth in lending" laws.

19.   The cash flow _____ _____ is an essential tool in time value of money analysis.

20.   _____ are perpetual bonds issued by the British government to consolidate past debts. In general, they are any perpetual bonds.

21.   A fundamental valuation concept is that, all else equal, when interest rates increase the value of an investment _____ .

22.   The future value of an uneven cash flow stream (sometimes called the _____ _____) is the sum of the FVs of the individual cash flows of the stream.

23.   The breakdown of loan payments into interest and the repayment of principal is known as a loan _____ _____ .

Conceptual

24.   If a bank uses quarterly compounding for savings accounts, the simple interest rate will be greater than the effective annual rate (EAR).

       a. True   b. False

25.   If money has time value (that is, k > 0), the future value of some amount of money will always be more than the amount invested. The present value of some amount to be received in the future is always less than the amount to be received.

       a. True   b. False

26.   The value of a perpetuity remains constant when interest rates change.

       a. True   b. False

27.   Once we know the present value of an uneven cash flow stream, we can find its future value by compounding the present value amount to the future period.

       a. True   b. False

28.   Which of the following statements is correct?

       a. The internal rate of return is the rate of return you could earn on alternative investments of similar risk.

    b. Discounting is the process of determining the value of a cash flow or series of cash flows some time in the future when compound interest is applied.

    c. An amortized loan is a loan with constant payments, the amount borrowed is the present value of an ordinary annuity and the payments constitute the annuity stream.

    d. The simple interest rate is the annual rate of interest actually being earned considering the compounding of interest.

    e. All of the statements above are false.

29. Which of the following statements is *false*?

    a. The annual percentage rate represents the periodic rate stated on an annual basis without considering interest compounding.

    b. The future value of an ordinary annuity is greater than the future value of an annuity due because the ordinary annuity's payments are received sooner than payments for the annuity due.

    c. The simple interest rate is never shown on a time line, and it is never used as an input in a financial calculator unless compounding occurs only once a year.

    d. In general, consols are any perpetual bonds.

    e. The future value of an uneven cash flow stream is sometimes called the terminal value.

30. You have determined the profitability of a planned project by finding the present value of all the cash flows from that project. Which of the following would cause the project to look less appealing, that is, have a lower present value?

    a. The discount rate decreases.

    b. The cash flows are received in later years (further into the future).

    c. The discount rate increases.

    d. Statements b and c are correct.

    e. Statements a and b are correct.

31. As the discount rate increases without limit, the present value of a future cash inflow

    a. Gets larger without limit.

    b. Stays unchanged.

    c. Approaches zero.

    d. Gets smaller without limit; that is, approaches minus infinity.

    e. Goes to $e^{k \times n}$.

32. Which of the following statements is correct?

    a. Except in situations where compounding occurs annually, the periodic interest rate exceeds the simple interest rate.

    b. The effective annual rate always exceeds the simple interest rate, no matter how few or many compounding periods occur each year.

    c. The periodic rate, k_{PER}, is the rate charged by a lender or paid by a borrower each interest period. It is calculated as the effective annual rate divided by the number of compounding periods per year.

    d. The annual percentage rate is the periodic rate multiplied by the number of periods per year.

    e. Statements a, b, c, and d are false.

SELF-TEST PROBLEMS

(Note: In working these problems, you may get an answer that differs from ours by a few cents due to differences in rounding. This should not concern you; just pick the closest answer.)

1. Assume that you purchase a 6-year, 8 percent savings certificate for $1,000. If interest is compounded annually, what will be the value of the certificate when it matures?

    a. $630.17   b. $1,469.33   c. $1,677.10   d. $1,586.87   e. $1,766.33

2. A savings certificate similar to the one in the previous problem is available with the exception that interest is compounded semiannually. What is the difference between the ending value of the savings certificate compounded semiannually and the one compounded annually?

    a. The semiannual certificate is worth $14.16 more than the annual one.
    b. The semiannual certificate is worth $14.16 less than the annual one.
    c. The semiannual certificate is worth $21.54 more than the annual one.
    d. The semiannual certificate is worth $21.54 less than the annual one.
    e. The semiannual certificate is worth the same as the annual one.

3. A friend promises to pay you $600 two years from now if you loan him $500 today. What annual interest rate is your friend offering?

    a. 7.38%   b. 8.42%   c. 9.54%   d. 10.59%   e. 11.49%

4. At an inflation rate of 9 percent, the purchasing power of $1 would be cut in half in just over 8 years (some calculators round to 9 years). How long, to the nearest year, would it take for the purchasing power of $1 to be cut in half if the inflation rate were only 4 percent?

    a. 12 years   b. 15 years   c. 18 years   d. 20 years   e. 23 years

5. You are offered an investment opportunity with the "guarantee" that your investment will double in 5 years. Assuming annual compounding, what annual rate of return would this investment provide?

a. 40.35%   **b.** 100.00%   **c.** 14.87%   **d.** 20.25%   **e.** 18.74%

6. You decide to begin saving toward the purchase of a new car in 5 years. If you put $1,000 at the end of each of the next 5 years in a savings account paying 6 percent compounded annually, how much will you accumulate after 5 years?

    a. $6,691.13   **b.** $5,637.09   **c.** $1,338.23   **d.** $5,975.32   **e.** $5,731.94

7. Refer to Self-Test Problem 6. What would be the ending amount if the payments were made at the beginning of each year?

    a. $6,691.13   **b.** $5,637.09   **c.** $1,338.23   **d.** $5,975.32   **e.**
    $5,731.94

8. Refer to Self-Test Problem 6. What would be the ending amount if $500 payments were made at the end of each 6-month period for 5 years and the account paid 6 percent compounded semiannually?

    a. $6,691.13   **b.** $5,637.09   **c.** $1,338.23   **d.** $5,975.32   **e.**
    $5,731.94

9. Calculate the present value of $1,000 to be received at the end of 8 years. Assume an interest rate of 7 percent.

    a. $582.01   **b.** $1,718.19   **c.** $531.82   **d.** $5,971.30   **e.** $649.37

10. How much would you be willing to pay today for an investment that would return $800 each year at the end of each of the next 6 years? Assume a discount rate of 5 percent.

    a. $5,441.53   **b.** $4,800.00   **c.** $3,369.89   **d.** $4,060.55   **e.**
    $4,632.37

11. You have applied for a mortgage of $60,000 to finance the purchase of a new home. The bank will require you to make annual payments of $7,047.55 at the end of each of the next 20 years. Determine the interest rate in effect on this mortgage.

    a. 8.0%   **b.** 9.8%   **c.** 10.0%   **d.** 5.1%   **e.** 11.2%

12. If you would like to accumulate $7,500 over the next 5 years, how much must you deposit each six months, starting six months from now, given a 6 percent interest rate and semiannual compounding?

    a. $1,330.47   **b.** $879.23   **c.** $654.23   **d.** $569.00   **e.** $732.67

13. A company is offering bonds that pay $100 per year indefinitely. If you require a 12 percent return on these bonds)) that is, the discount rate is 12 percent)) what is the value of each bond?

   a. $1,000.00   **b.** $962.00   **c.** $904.67   **d.** $866.67   **e.** $833.33

14. What is the present value (t = 0) of the following cash flows if the discount rate is 12 percent?

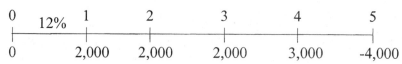

   a. $4,782.43   **b.** $4,440.51   **c.** $4,221.79   **d.** $4,041.23   **e.** $3,997.98

15. What is the effective annual percentage rate (EAR) of 12 percent compounded monthly?

   a. 12.00%   **b.** 12.55%   **c.** 12.68%   **d.** 12.75%   **e.** 13.00%

16. Martha Mills, manager of Plaza Gold Emporium, wants to sell on credit, giving customers 3 months in which to pay. However, Martha will have to borrow from her bank to carry the accounts receivable. The bank will charge a simple 16 percent, but with monthly compounding. Martha wants to quote a simple interest rate to her customers (all of whom are expected to pay on time at the end of 3 months) *that will exactly cover her financing costs*. What simple annual rate should she quote to her credit customers?

   a. 15.44%   **b.** 19.56%   **c.** 17.11%   **d.** 16.21%   **e.** 16.88%

17. Self-Test Problem 11 refers to a 20-year mortgage of $60,000. This is an amortized loan. How much principal will be repaid in the second year?

   a. $1,152.30   **b.** $1,725.70   **c.** $5,895.25   **d.** $7,047.55   **e.** $1,047.55

18. You have $1,000 invested in an account that pays 16 percent compounded annually. A commission agent (called a "finder") can locate for you an equally safe deposit that will pay 16 percent, compounded quarterly, for 2 years. What is the maximum amount you should be willing to pay him now as a fee for locating the new account?

   a. $10.92   **b.** $13.78   **c.** $16.14   **d.** $16.78   **e.** $21.13

19. The present value (t = 0) of the following cash flow stream is $11,958.20 when discounted at 12 percent annually. What is the value of the missing t = 2 cash flow?

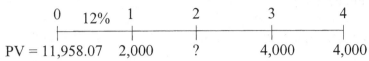

a. $4,000.00   b. $4,500.00   c. $5,000.00   d. $5,500.00   e. $6,000.00

20. Today is your birthday, and you decide to start saving for your college education. You will begin college on your 18th birthday and will need $4,000 per year at the *end* of each of the following 4 years. You will make a deposit 1 year from today in an account paying 12 percent annually and continue to make an identical deposit each year up to and including the year you begin college. If a deposit amount of $2,542.05 will allow you to reach your goal, what birthday are you celebrating today?

a. 13   b. 14   c. 15   d. 16   e. 17

21. Assume that your aunt sold her house on December 31 and that she took a mortgage in the amount of $10,000 as part of the payment. The mortgage has a simple interest rate of 10 percent, but it calls for payments every 6 months, beginning on June 30, and the mortgage is to be amortized over 10 years. Now, one year later, your aunt must file Schedule B of her tax return with the IRS informing them of the interest that was included in the two payments made during the year. (This interest will be income to your aunt and a deduction to the buyer of the house.) What is the total amount of interest that was paid during the first year?

a. $1,604.86   b. $619.98   c. $984.88   d. $1,205.76   e. $750.02

22. Assume that you inherited some money. A friend of yours is working as an unpaid intern at a local brokerage firm, and her boss is selling some securities that call for four payments, $50 at the end of each of the next 3 years, plus a payment of $1,050 at the end of Year 4. Your friend says she can get you some of these securities at a cost of $900 each. Your money is now invested in a bank that pays an 8 percent simple interest rate, but with quarterly compounding. You regard the securities as being just as safe, and as liquid, as your bank deposit, so your required effective annual rate of return on the securities is the same as that on your bank deposit. You must calculate the value of the securities to decide whether they are a good investment. What is their present value to you?

a. $957.75   b. $888.66   c. $923.44   d. $1,015.25   e. $893.26

23. Your company is planning to borrow $1,000,000 on a 5-year, 15 percent, annual payment, fully amortized term loan. What fraction of the payment made at the end of the second year will represent repayment of principal?

a. 57.18%   b. 42.82%   c. 50.28%   d. 49.72%   e. 60.27%

24. Your firm can borrow from its bank for one month. The loan will have to be "rolled over" at the end of the month, but you are sure the rollover will be allowed. The simple interest rate is 14 percent, but interest will have to be paid at the end of each month, so the bank interest rate is 14 percent, monthly compounding. Alternatively, your firm can borrow from an insurance company at a simple interest rate that would involve quarterly compounding. What simple quarterly rate would be equivalent to the rate charged by the bank?

   a. 12.44%   **b.** 14.16%   **c.** 13.55%   **d.** 13.12%   **e.** 12.88%

25. Assume that you have $15,000 in a bank account that pays 5 percent annual interest. You plan to go back to school for a combination MBA/law degree 5 years from today. It will take you an additional 5 years to complete your graduate studies. You figure you will need a fixed income of $25,000 in today's dollars; that is, you will need $25,000 of today's dollars during your first year and each subsequent year. (*Thus, your real income will decline while you are in school.*) You will withdraw funds for your annual expenses at the beginning of each year. Inflation is expected to occur at the rate of 3 percent per year. How much must you save during each of the next 5 years in order to achieve your goal? The first increment of savings will be deposited one year from today.

   a. $20,241.66 **b.** $19,224.55 **c.** $18,792.11 **d.** $19,559.42 **e.** $20,378.82

26. You plan to buy a new HDTV. The dealer offers to sell the set to you on credit. You will have 3 months in which to pay, but the dealer says you will be charged a 15 percent interest rate; that is, the simple interest rate is 15 percent, quarterly compounding. As an alternative to buying on credit, you can borrow the funds from your bank, but the bank will make you pay interest each month. At what simple bank interest rate should you be indifferent between the two types of credit?

   a. 13.7643% **b.** 14.2107% **c.** 14.8163% **d.** 15.5397% **e.** 15.3984%

27. Assume that your father is now 50 years old, that he plans to retire in 10 years, and that he expects to live for 25 years after he retires, that is, until he is 85. He wants a fixed retirement income that has the same purchasing power at the time he retires as $60,000 has today (he realizes that the real value of his retirement income will decline year-by-year after he retires). His retirement income will begin the day he retires, 10 years from today, and he will then get 24 additional annual payments. Inflation is expected to be 5 percent per year from today forward; he currently has $150,000 saved up; and he expects to earn a return on his savings of 7 percent per year, annual compounding. To the nearest dollar, how much must he save during each of the next 10 years (with deposits being made at the end of each year) to meet his retirement goal?

   a. $66,847.95 **b.** $77,201.21 **c.** $54,332.88 **d.** $41,987.33 **e.** $62,191.25

ANSWERS TO SELF-TEST QUESTIONS

1.	cash outflow	13.	constant; uneven (nonconstant)
2.	cash inflow	14.	sum
3.	Compounding	15.	simple; effective
4.	future value	16.	Amortized
5.	present value	17.	periodic
6.	Compounded interest	18.	annual percentage rate
7.	interest	19.	time line
8.	future value	20.	Consols
9.	discounting; compounding	21.	decreases
10.	opportunity cost rate	22.	terminal value
11.	annuity; ordinary; due	23.	amortization schedule
12.	perpetuity		

24. b. The EAR is always greater than or equal to the simple interest rate.

25. a. Both these statements are correct.

26. b. Obviously, the value of the perpetuity changes as interest rates change—the higher the interest rate the lower the value of the perpetuity.

27. a. This statement is correct.

28. c. Statement a is the definition of the opportunity cost rate. Statement b describes the process of compounding. Statement c is true. Statement d describes the effective annual rate.

29. b. The future value of an ordinary annuity is less than the future value of an annuity due because the ordinary annuity's payments are received later than payments for the annuity due.

30. d. The slower the cash flows come in and the higher the interest rate, the lower the present value.

31. c. As the discount rate increases, the present value of a future sum decreases and eventually approaches zero.

32. d. APR, the annual percentage rate, is equal to k_{PER} times the number of periods per year. Statement a is false because the periodic interest rate is equal to the simple interest rate divided by the number of compounding periods, so it will be equal to or smaller than the simple interest rate. Statement b is false because the EAR will equal the simple interest rate if there is one compounding period per year (annual compounding). Statement c is false because the periodic interest rate is equal to the simple interest rate divided by the number of compounding periods.

SOLUTIONS TO SELF-TEST PROBLEMS

1. **d.**

```
0    1    2    3    4    5    6
  8%
├────┼────┼────┼────┼────┼────┤
-1,000                  FV₆ = ?
```

$FV_n = \$1,000(1.08)^6 = \$1,000(1.58687) = \$1,586.87.$

With a financial calculator, input N = 6, I = 8, PV = -1000, PMT = 0, and solve for FV = $1,586.87.

2. **a.**

```
0         1         2         3         4         5       6 Years
0    1    2    3    4    5    6    7    8    9   10   11  12 Periods
  4%
├────┼────┼────┼────┼────┼────┼────┼────┼────┼────┼────┤
-1,000                                          FV₁₂ = ?
```

Thus, $FV_{12} = \$1,000(1.04)^{12} = \$1,601.03.$ The difference, $\$1,601.03 - \$1,586.87 = \$14.16$, is the additional interest.

With a financial calculator, input N = 12, I = 4, PV = -1000, and PMT = 0, and then solve for FV = $1,601.03. The difference, $1,601.03 – $1,586.87 = $14.16.

3. **c.**

```
0            1            2
   k = ?
├──────────┼──────────┤
-500                 600
```

With a financial calculator, input N = 2, PV = -500, PMT = 0, FV = 600, and solve for I = 9.54%.

4. **c.**

```
0         N = ?
  4%
├─────────┤
1.00     0.50
```

With a financial calculator, input I = 4, PV = -1.00, PMT = 0, and FV = 0.50. Solve for N = 17.67 . 18 years.

5. **c.**

```
0    1    2    3    4    5
 k = ?
├────┼────┼────┼────┼────┤
-1                      2
```

Assume any value for the present value and double it.

With a financial calculator, input N = 5, PV = -1, PMT = 0, FV = 2, and solve for I = 14.87%.

6. **b.**

```
0    1    2    3    4    5
  6%
├────┼────┼────┼────┼────┤
```

$$-1,000 \quad -1,000 \quad -1,000 \quad -1,000 \quad -1,000$$
$$FVA_5 = ?$$

$$FVA_5 = PMT\left[\frac{(1.06)^5 - 1}{0.06}\right] = \$1,000(5.63709) = \$5,637.09.$$

With a financial calculator, input N = 5, I = 6, PV = 0, PMT = -1000, and solve for FV = \$5,637.09.

7. d.

$$
\begin{array}{ccccccc}
0 & & 1 & 2 & 3 & 4 & 5 \\
& 6\% & & & & & \\
\end{array}
$$

$$-1,000 \qquad -1,000 \qquad -1,000 \qquad -1,000 \qquad -1,000 \quad FVA_5 = ?$$

$$FVA(DUE)_5 = \$1,000(5.63709)(1.06) = \$5,975.32.$$

With a financial calculator, switch to "BEG" mode, then input N = 5, I = 6, PV = 0, PMT = -1000, and solve for FV = \$5,975.32. Be sure to switch back to "END" mode.

8. e.

$$
\begin{array}{cccccccccccc}
0 & & 1 & & 2 & & 3 & & 4 & & 5 & \text{Years} \\
0 & 1 & 2 & 3 & 4 & 5 & 6 & 7 & 8 & 9 & 10 & \text{Periods} \\
& 3\% & & & & & & & & & & \\
\end{array}
$$

$$-500 \;\; -500 \;\; -500 \;\; -500 \;\; -500 \;\; -500 \;\; -500 \;\; -500 \;\; -500 \;\; -500$$
$$FVA_{10} = ?$$

$$FVA_{10} = PMT\left[\frac{(1.03)^{10} - 1}{0.03}\right] = \$500(11.46388) = \$5,731.94.$$

With a financial calculator, input N = 10, I = 3, PV = 0, PMT = -500, and solve for FV = \$5,731.94.

9. a.

$$
\begin{array}{ccccccccc}
0 & & 1 & 2 & 3 & 4 & 5 & 6 & 7 & 8 \\
& 7\% & & & & & & & & \\
\end{array}
$$

$$PV = ? \qquad\qquad\qquad\qquad\qquad\qquad\qquad 1,000$$

$$PV = FV_8\left[\frac{1}{(1.07)^8}\right] = \$1,000(0.58201) = \$582.01.$$

With a financial calculator, input N = 8, I = 7, PMT = 0, FV = 1000, and solve for PV = -\$582.01.

10. d.

$$
\begin{array}{ccccccc}
0 & & 1 & 2 & 3 & 4 & 5 & 6 \\
& 5\% & & & & & & \\
\end{array}
$$

$$PVA = ? \quad 800 \quad\;\; 800 \quad\;\; 800 \quad\;\; 800 \quad\;\; 800 \quad\;\; 800$$

173

$$PVA_6 = PMT\left[\frac{1-(1.05)^{-6}}{0.05}\right] = \$800(5.07569) = \$4,060.55.$$

With a financial calculator, input N = 6, I = 5, PMT = 800, FV = 0, and solve for PV = -\$4,060.55.

11.　c.

The amount of the mortgage (\$60,000) is the present value of a 20-year ordinary annuity with payments of \$7,047.55.

With a financial calculator, input N = 20, PV = 60000, PMT = -7047.55, FV = 0, and solve for I = 10.00%.

12.　c.

$$FVA_{10} = PMT\left[\frac{(1.03)^{10}-1}{0.03}\right]$$

$\$7,500 = PMT(11.46388)$

$\quad PMT = \$654.23.$

With a financial calculator, input N = 10, I = 3, PV = 0, FV = 7500, and solve for PMT = -\$654.23.

13.　e.　$PVP = PMT/k = \$100/0.12 = \$833.33.$

14.　b.　With a financial calculator, using the cash flow register, CF_j, input 0; 2000; 2000; 2000; 3000; and -4000. Enter I = 12 and solve for NPV = \$4,440.51.

15.　c.　$EAR = (1 + k_{SIMPLE}/m)^m) \ 1.0$

$\qquad = (1 + 0.12/12)^{12}) \ 1.0$

$\qquad = (1.01)^{12}) \ 1.0$

$\qquad = 1.1268) \ 1.0$

$\qquad = 0.1268 = 12.68\%.$

16.　d.　Here we want to have the same effective annual rate on the credit extended as on the bank loan that will be used to finance the credit extension.

First, we must find the EAR on the bank loan. With a financial calculator, enter

P/YR = 12, NOM% = 16, and press EFF% to get EAR = 17.23%.

Now recognize that giving 3 months of credit is equivalent to quarterly compounding; interest is earned at the end of the quarter, so it is available to earn interest during the next quarter. Therefore, enter on your calculator P/YR = 4, EFF% = EAR = 17.23%, and press NOM% to find the simple interest rate of 16.21%. Therefore, if Martha charges a 16.21% simple interest rate and gives credit for 3 months, she will cover the cost of her bank loan.

Alternative solution: First, we need to find the effective annual rate charged by the bank:

$$EAR = (1 + k_{SIMPLE}/m)^m) 1$$
$$= (1 + 0.16/12)^{12}) 1$$
$$= (1.0133)^{12}) 1 = 17.23\%.$$

Now, we can find the simple rate Martha must quote her customers so that her financing costs are exactly covered:

$$17.23\% = (1 + k_{SIMPLE}/4)^4) 1$$
$$1.1723 = (1 + k_{SIMPLE}/4)^4$$
$$1.0405 = 1 + k_{SIMPLE}/4$$
$$0.0405 = k_{SIMPLE}/4$$
$$k_{SIMPLE} = 16.21\%.$$

17. a.

Year	Payment	Interest	Repayment on Principal	Remaining Principal Balance
1	$7,047.55	$6,000.00	$1,047.55	$58,952.45
2	7,047.55	5,895.25	1,152.30	57,800.15

18. d. Currently: $FV_n = \$1,000(1.16)^2 = \$1,000(1.3456) = \$1,345.60.$

With a financial calculator, input N = 2, I = 16, PV = -1000, PMT = 0, and solve for FV = $1,345.60.

New account: $FV_n = \$1,000(1 + k_{SIMPLE}/m)^{mn} = \$1,000\left(1 + \dfrac{0.16}{4}\right)^{4(2)}$

$$= \$1,000(1.36857) = \$1,368.57.$$

With a financial calculator, input N = 8, I = 4, PV = -1000, PMT = 0, and solve for FV = $1,368.57.

Thus, the new account will be worth $1,368.57 - $1,345.60 = $22.97 more after 2 years.

PV of difference $= \$22.97\left[\dfrac{1}{(1.04)^8}\right] = \$22.97(0.73069) = \$16.78.$ With a financial calculator, input N = 8, I = 4, PMT = 0, FV = 22.97, and solve for PV = -$16.78. Therefore, the most you should be willing to pay the finder for locating the new account is $16.78.

19. e. With a financial calculator, input cash flows into the cash flow register, using 0 as the value for the unknown cash flow, input I = 12, and then press the NPV key to solve for the present value of the unknown cash flow, $4,783.16. This value should be compounded by $(1.12)^2$, so that $4,783.16(1.2544) = $6,000.

20. b. First, how much must you accumulate on your 18th birthday?

Present birthday = ?

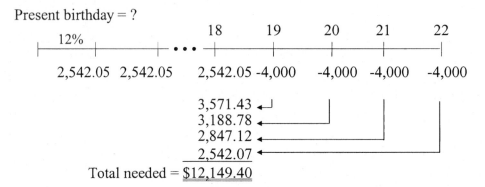

2,542.05 2,542.05 2,542.05 -4,000 -4,000 -4,000 -4,000

3,571.43
3,188.78
2,847.12
2,542.07
Total needed = $12,149.40

Using a financial calculator (with the calculator set for an ordinary annuity), enter N = 4, I = 12, PMT = -4000, FV = 0, and solve for PV = $12,149.40. This is the amount (or lump sum) that must be present in your bank account on your 18th birthday in order for you to withdraw $4,000 at the end of each year for the next 4 years.

Now, how many payments must you make to accumulate $12,149.40?

Using a financial calculator, enter I = 12, PV = 0, PMT = -2542.05, FV = 12149.40, and solve for N = 4. Therefore, if you make payments at 18, 17, 16, and 15, you are now 14.

21. c. This can be done with a calculator by specifying an interest rate of 5 percent per period for 20 periods.

N = 10 × 2 = 20.
I = 10/2 = 5.
PV = -10000.
FV = 0.
PMT = $802.43.

Set up an amortization table:

Period	Beginning Balance	Payment	Interest	Payment of Principal	Ending Balance
1	$10,000.00	$802.43	$500.00	$302.43	$9,697.57
2	9,697.57	802.43	484.88		9,697.57
			$984.88		

You can really just work the problem with a financial calculator using the amortization function. Find the interest in each 6-month period, sum them, and you have the answer. Even simpler, with some calculators such as the HP-17B, just input 2 for periods and press INT to get the interest during the first year, $984.88.

22. e.

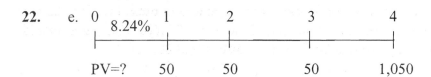

Discount rate: Effective annual rate on bank deposit: $EAR = (1 + 0.08/4)^4 - 1 = 8.24\%$.

Input the cash flows in the cash flow register, input I = 8.24, and solve for NPV = $893.26. Or, get PV = -$893.26 by inputting N = 4, I = 8.24, PMT = 50, and FV = 1000. Alternatively, each cash flow could be discounted to t = 0 and summed.

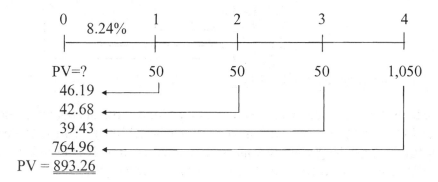

$$PV = \frac{\$50}{1.0824} + \frac{\$50}{(1.0824)^2} + \frac{\$50}{(1.0824)^3} + \frac{\$1,050}{(1.0824)^4} = \$893.26.$$

23. a. Input N = 5, I = 15, PV = -1000000, and FV = 0 to solve for PMT = $298,315.55.

Year	Beginning Balance	Payment	Interest	Payment of Principal	Ending Balance
1	$1,000,000.00	$298,315.55	$150,000.00	$148,315.55	$851,684.45
2	851,684.45	298,315.55	127,752.67	170,562.88	681,121.57

The fraction that is principal is $170,562.88/$298,315.55 = 57.18%.

24. b. Start with a time line to picture the situation:

Bank: Simple = 14%; EAR = 14.93%.

Insurance company: EAR = 14.93%; Simple = 14.16%.

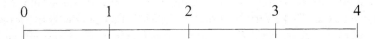

Here we must find the EAR on the bank loan and then find the quarterly simple rate for that EAR. The bank loan amounts to a simple 14 percent, monthly compounding.

Using the interest conversion feature of the calculator, or the EAR formula, we must find the EAR on the bank loan. Enter P/YR = 12 and NOM% = 14, and then press the EFF% key to find EAR bank loan = 14.93%.

Now, we can find the simple interest rate with quarterly compounding that also has an EAR of 14.93 percent. Enter P/YR = 4 and EFF% = 14.93, and then press the NOM% key to get 14.16%. If the insurance company quotes a simple rate of 14.16%, with quarterly compounding, then the bank and insurance company loans would be equivalent in the sense that they both have the same effective annual rate, 14.93%.

Alternative solution:

$$EAR = (1 + k_{SIMPLE}/12)^{12}) \ 1$$
$$= (1 + 0.14/12)^{12}) \ 1$$
$$= 14.93\%.$$

$$0.1493 = (1 + k_{SIMPLE}/4)^4) \ 1$$
$$1.1493 = (1 + k_{SIMPLE}/4)^4$$
$$1.0354 = 1 + k_{SIMPLE}/4$$
$$0.0354 = k_{SIMPLE}/4$$
$$k_{SIMPLE} = 14.16\%.$$

25. e. Inflation = 3%.

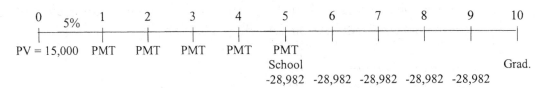

Fixed income = $25,000(1.03)^5 = $28,981.85.

1. Find the FV of $25,000 compounded for 5 years at 3 percent; that FV, $28,981.85, is the amount you will need each year while you are in school. (Note: Your real income will decline.)

2. You must have enough in 5 years to make the $28,981.85 payments to yourself. These payments will begin as soon as you start school, so we are dealing with a 5-year,
5 percent interest rate *annuity due.* Set the calculator to "BEG" mode, because we

are dealing with an annuity due, and then enter N = 5, I = 5, PMT = -28981.85, and FV = 0. Then press the PV key to find the PV, $131,750.06. This is the amount you must have in your account 5 years from today. (Do not forget to switch the calculator back to "END" mode.)

3. You now have $15,000. It will grow at 5 percent to $19,144.22 after 5 years. Enter N = 5, I = 5, PV = -15000, and PMT = 0, to solve for FV = $19,144.22. You can subtract this amount to determine the FV of the amount you must save: $131,750.06) $19,144.22 = $112,605.84.

4. Therefore, you must accumulate an additional $112,605.84 by saving PMT per year for 5 years, with the first PMT being deposited at the end of this year and earning a 5 percent interest rate. Now we have an ordinary annuity, so be sure you returned your calculator to "END" mode. Enter N = 5, I = 5, PV = 0, FV = 112605.84, and then press PMT to find the required payments, -$20,378.82.

26.   c. Find the EAR on the TV dealer's credit. Use the interest conversion feature of your calculator. First, though, note that if you are charged a 15 percent simple interest rate, you will have to pay interest of 15%/4 = 3.75% after 3 months. The dealer then has the use of the interest, so he can earn 3.75 percent on it for the next three months, and so forth. Thus, we are dealing with quarterly compounding. The nominal rate is 15 percent, quarterly compounding.

Enter NOM% = 15, P/YR = 4, and then press EFF% to get EAR = 15.8650%.

You should be indifferent between the dealer credit and the bank loan if the bank loan has an EAR of 15.8650 percent. The bank is using monthly compounding, or 12 periods per year. To find the simple interest rate at which you should be indifferent, enter P/YR = 12, EFF% = 15.8650, and then press NOM% to get NOM% = 14.8163%.

Conclusion: A loan that has a 14.8163 percent nominal rate with monthly compounding is equivalent to a 15 percent nominal rate loan with quarterly compounding. Both have an EAR of 15.8650 percent.

Alternative Solution:

$$\text{EAR} = (1 + k_{SIMPLE}/4)^4) \ 1 = (1 + 0.15/4)^4) \ 1 = (1.0375)^4) \ 1 = 15.8650\%.$$

$$15.8650\% = (1 + k_{SIMPLE}/12)^{12}) \ 1$$
$$1.15865 = (1 + k_{SIMPLE}/12)^{12}$$
$$k_{SIMPLE} = 14.8163\%.$$

27.   a. Information given:

1. Will save for 10 years, then receive payments for 25 years.

179

2. Wants payments of $60,000 per year in today's dollars for first payment only. Real income will decline. Inflation will be 5 percent. Therefore, to find the inflated fixed payments, we have this time line:

    Enter N = 10, I = 5, PV = -60000, PMT = 0, and press FV to get FV = $97,733.68.

3. He now has $150,000 in an account that pays 7 percent, annual compounding. We need to find the FV of $150,000 after 10 years. Enter N = 10, I = 7, PV = -150000, PMT = 0, and press FV to get FV = $295,072.70.

4. He wants to withdraw, or have payments of, $97,733.68 per year for 25 years, with the first payment made at the beginning of the first retirement year. So, we have a 25-year annuity due with PMT = $97,733.68, at an interest rate of 7 percent. (The interest rate is 7 percent annually, so no adjustment is required.) Set the calculator to "BEG" mode, then enter N = 25, I = 7, PMT = -97733.68, FV = 0, and press PV to get PV = $1,218,673.90. This amount must be on hand to make the 25 payments.

5. Since the original $150,000, which grows to $295,072.70, will be available, he must save enough to accumulate $1,218,673.90 – $295,072.70 = $923,601.20.

6. The $923,601.20 is the FV of a 10-year ordinary annuity. The payments will be deposited in the bank and earn 7 percent interest. Therefore, set the calculator to "END" mode and enter N = 10, I = 7, PV = 0, FV = 923601.20, and press PMT to find PMT = -$66,847.95.

CHAPTER 10
VALUATION CONCEPTS

OVERVIEW

This chapter uses time value of money techniques to explain how the values of assets are determined. The material covered in the chapter is important to investors who want to establish the values of their investments. But, knowledge of valuation is also important to financial managers because all important corporate decisions should be analyzed in terms of how they will affect the value of the firm. It is critical that we understand the valuation process so we can determine what affects the value of the firm.

The value of any asset is the present value of the cash flows the asset is expected to produce in the future. Therefore, once the cash flows have been estimated, and a discount rate determined, the value of the asset can be calculated.

A bond is valued as the present value of the stream of interest payments (an annuity) plus the present value of the par value that is received by the investor on the bond's maturity date. Depending on the relationship between the current interest rate and the bond's coupon rate, a bond can sell at its par value, at a discount, or at a premium. The expected rate of return on a bond is comprised of two components: an interest yield and a capital gains yield.

The value of a share of preferred stock that is expected to pay a constant dividend forever is found as the dividend divided by the discount rate. A common stock is valued as the present value of the expected future dividend stream. The expected rate of return on a stock is comprised of a dividend yield plus a capital gains yield. For both stocks and bonds, the expected rate of return must equal the average investor's required rate of return.

OUTLINE

The value of any asset is based on the present value of the cash flows the asset is expected to produce in the future.

☐ The value of any asset can be expressed in general form as:

$$\text{Asset value} = \sum_{t=1}^{n} \frac{\hat{CF}_t}{(1+k)^t}.$$

Here, $\hat{CF}_t$ = the cash flow expected to be generated by the asset in period t, and k = the return investors consider appropriate for holding such an asset.

☐   The higher the expected cash flows, the greater the asset's value; also, the lower the required return, the greater the asset's value.

Capital is raised in two forms—debt and equity. As the principal type of long-term debt, a bond is a long-term promissory note issued by a business or governmental unit. The conditions of the bond are contractually specified, such that the principal amount, the coupon interest rate, the maturity date, and any other features are known by investors.

☐   A bond's market price is determined primarily by the cash flows it generates, or the interest it pays, which depends on the coupon interest rate.
   ~   The higher the coupon rate, other things held constant, the higher the bond's market price.
   ~   At the time a bond is issued, the coupon is generally set at a level that will cause the bond's market price to equal its par value.

☐   A bond that has just been issued is known as a *new issue*.
   ~   *The Wall Street Journal* classifies a bond as a new issue for about one month after it has first been issued.
   ~   Once the bond has been on the market for a while, it is classified as an *outstanding bond*, also called a *seasoned issue*.
      •   Newly issued bonds generally sell very close to par, but the prices of outstanding bonds vary widely from par.

☐   The value of a financial asset is based on the cash flows expected to be generated by the asset in the future. In the case of a bond, the cash flows consist of interest payments during the life of the bond plus a return of the principal amount borrowed, generally the par value, when the bond matures. Its value is found as the present value of this payment stream:

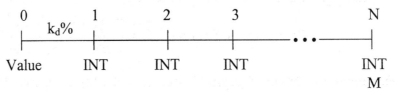

$$\text{Bond value} = V_d = \sum_{t=1}^{N} \frac{\text{INT}}{(1+k_d)^t} + \frac{M}{(1+k_d)^N},$$

where INT = dollars of interest paid each year, M = par, or maturity, value, which is typically $1,000, k_d = rate of interest on the bond, and N = number of years before the bond matures.

☐   For example, consider a 15-year, $1,000 bond paying $150 annually, when the appropriate interest rate, k_d, is 15 percent. Using a financial calculator, enter N = 15, k_d = I = 15, PMT = 150, and FV = 1000, and then press the PV key for an answer of -$1,000. Because the PV is an outflow to the investor, it is shown with a negative sign.
   ~   The value of the bond can also be found numerically as follows:

$$V_d = \$150\left[\dfrac{1 - \dfrac{1}{(1.15)^{15}}}{0.15}\right] + \$1,000\left(\dfrac{1}{1.15}\right)^{15}$$

$$= \$150(5.84737) + \$1,000(0.12289)$$

$$= \$877.11 + \$122.89 = \$1,000.$$

☐ Bond prices and interest rates are inversely related; that is, they tend to move in the opposite direction from one another.
  ~ A bond will sell at its par value when its coupon interest rate is equal to the market rate of interest, k_d.
  ~ When the market rate of interest is above the coupon rate, the bond will sell at a "discount" below its par value.
  ~ If current interest rates are below the coupon rate, the bond will sell at a "premium" above its par value.
  ~ The market value of a bond always will approach its par value as its maturity date approaches, provided the firm does not go bankrupt.
  ~ The bond's rate of return consists of an interest yield (or current yield) plus a capital gains yield.
    • The *current yield* is the annual interest payment on a bond divided by its current market value:

$$\text{Current yield} = \dfrac{INT}{V_d}.$$

    • The *capital gains yield* is calculated as:

$$\text{Capital gains yield} = \dfrac{\text{Ending bond value} - \text{Beg. bond value}}{\text{Beg. bond value}}.$$

  ~ Bondholders can suffer capital losses or make capital gains, depending on whether market interest rates rise or fall after the bond is purchased.

☐ The annual rate of return earned on a bond if it is held to maturity is the *yield to maturity (YTM)*, and it is the interest rate discussed by bond traders when they talk about rates of return.
  ~ The YTM for a bond that sells at par consists entirely of an interest yield, but if the bond sells at a price other than its par value, the YTM consists of the interest yield plus a positive or negative capital gains yield.
  ~ One who purchases a bond and holds it until it matures will receive the YTM that existed on the purchase date, but the bond's calculated YTM will change frequently between the purchase date and the maturity date.
  ~ The YTM is easily found with a calculator. It can also be found through "trial and error."

☐ An approximate yield to maturity can be calculated by the following formula:

$$\text{Approximate yield to maturity} = \frac{\text{Annual interest} + \text{Accrued capital gains}}{\text{Average value of bond}}$$

$$= \frac{\text{INT} + \left(\dfrac{M - V_d}{N} \right)}{\left[\dfrac{2(V_d) + M}{3} \right]}.$$

☐ The bond valuation model must be adjusted when interest is paid semiannually:

$$V_d = \sum_{t=1}^{2N} \frac{\text{INT}/2}{(1 + k_d/2)^t} + \frac{M}{(1 + k_d/2)^{2N}}.$$

~ The value of a bond that pays interest semiannually can be solved either numerically or with a calculator.

~ All cash flows in a given contract must be discounted at the same periodic rate because this is the opportunity rate for the investor. For consistency, bond traders must use the same discount rate for all cash flows, including the cash flow at maturity; and they do.

~ The value of a bond with semiannual interest payments is slightly larger than the value when interest is paid annually. This higher value occurs because interest payments are received, and therefore can be reinvested, somewhat faster under semiannual compounding.

☐ Interest rates fluctuate over time, and people or firms who invest in bonds are exposed to risk of changes in bond prices from changing interest rates, or *interest rate price risk*. However, the shorter the maturity of the bond, the greater the exposure to *interest rate reinvestment rate risk*, the risk that income from a bond portfolio will vary because cash flows have to be reinvested at current market rates.

~ These two risks tend to offset one another. For example, an increase in interest rates will lower the current value of a bond portfolio, but because the future cash flows produced by the portfolio will then be reinvested at a higher rate of return, the future value of the portfolio will be increased.

~ For bonds with similar coupons, the longer the maturity of the bond, the greater its price changes in response to a given change in interest rates.

~ When interest rates fall, many firms refinance by issuing new, lower-cost debt and using the proceeds to repay higher-cost debt.

Corporations can issue two forms of equity—preferred stock and common stock.

☐ Preferred stock is generally considered a hybrid because it is similar to bonds in some respects and to common stock in other respects.

~ Preferred dividends are similar to interest payments on bonds in that they are fixed in amount and generally must be paid before common stock dividends can be paid.

~ Like common dividends, preferred dividends can be omitted without bankrupting the firm, and preferred issues generally have no specific maturity date.

184

~ Preferred stock does not represent an ownership interest and cash distributions (dividends) to preferred stockholders do not vary with the firm's success.

Stocks provide an expected future cash flow stream, and a stock's value is found in the same manner as the values of other assets. Stocks are valued by finding the present value of the expected future cash flow stream.

☐ The expected cash flows consist of two elements: (1) the dividends expected in each year and (2) the price investors expect to receive when they sell the stock. The expected final stock price includes the return of the original investment plus a capital gain or loss.
  ~ The *expected dividend yield* on a stock during the coming year is equal to the expected dividend, $\hat{D}_1$, divided by the current stock price, P_0.

  ~ $(\hat{P}_1 - P_0)/P_0$ is the *expected capital gains yield*.

  ~ The expected dividend yield plus the expected capital gains yield equals the *expected rate of return*.

☐ The value of the stock today is calculated as the present value of an infinite stream of dividends. For any investor, cash flows consist of dividends plus the expected future sales price of the stock. This sales price, however, depends on dividends expected by future investors:

$$\text{Value of stock} = V_s = \hat{P}_0 = \text{PV of expected future dividends}$$

$$= \frac{\hat{D}_1}{(1 + k_s)^1} + \frac{\hat{D}_2}{(1 + k_s)^2} + \cdots + \frac{\hat{D}_\infty}{(1 + k_s)^\infty}$$

$$= \sum_{t=1}^{\infty} \frac{\hat{D}_t}{(1 + k_s)^t}.$$

Here k_s is the discount rate used to find the present value of the dividends.
  ~ This is a generalized stock valuation model in the sense that the time pattern of $\hat{D}_t$ can be anything: $\hat{D}_t$ can be rising, falling, or constant, or it can even be fluctuating randomly.
  ~ Often, the projected stream of dividends follows a systematic pattern, in which case we can develop a simplified version of the stock valuation model.

☐ If expected dividend growth is zero $(g = 0)$, the stock's value is found as follows: $\hat{P}_0 = D/k_s$.
  ~ A *zero growth stock* is expected to pay a constant dividend, so it can be thought of as a *perpetuity*.
  ~ The expected rate of return is simply the dividend yield: $\hat{k}_s = D/P_0$.
  ~ This equation can be used to value preferred stock.

☐ For many companies, earnings and dividends are expected to grow at some normal, or constant, rate.

~ Dividends in any future Year t may be forecasted as $D_t = D_0(1 + g)^t$, where D_0 is the last dividend paid and g is the expected growth rate.

~ For a company that last paid a $2.00 dividend and that has an expected 6 percent constant growth rate, the estimated dividend one year from now would be $D_1 = \$2.00(1.06) = \$2.12$; D_2 would be $\$2.00(1.06)^2 = \$2.25$, and the estimated dividend 4 years hence would be $D_t = D_0(1 + g)^t = \$2.00(1.06)^4 = \$2.525$.

~ The current price, $\hat{P}_0$, is determined as follows:

$$\hat{P}_0 = \frac{D_0(1+g)}{k_s - g} = \frac{\hat{D}_1}{k_s - g}.$$

This *constant growth model* for valuing a constant growth stock is often called the Gordon Model, after Myron J. Gordon, who did much to develop and popularize it.

● A necessary condition for this equation is that k_s be greater than g. If the equation is used in situations where k_s is not greater than g, the results will be meaningless.

~ Growth in dividends occurs primarily as a result of growth in earnings per share.

● Earnings growth, in turn, results from a number of factors, including (1) inflation, (2) the amount of earnings the company retains and reinvests, and (3) the rate of return the company earns on its equity (ROE).

☐ For all stocks, the expected rate of return is composed of an expected dividend yield plus an expected capital gains yield. For a constant growth stock, the formula for the expected rate of return can be written as:

$$\hat{k}_s = \frac{D_1}{P_0} + g.$$

~ For a constant growth stock, the following conditions must hold:

● The dividend is expected to grow forever at a constant rate, g.

● The stock price is expected to grow at this same rate.

● The expected dividend yield is a constant.

● The expected capital gains yield is also a constant, and it is equal to g.

● The expected total rate of return, $\hat{k}_s$, is equal to the expected dividend yield plus the expected growth rate: $\hat{k}_s$ = Dividend yield + g.

☐ Firms typically go through periods of nonconstant growth, after which time their growth rate settles to a rate close to that of the economy as a whole. The value of such a firm is equal to the present value of its expected future dividends. To find the value of such a stock, we proceed in three steps:

~ Find the present value of the dividends during the period of nonconstant growth.

~ Find the price of the stock at the end of the nonconstant growth period, at which point it has become a constant growth stock, and discount this price back to the present.

~ Add these two components to find the intrinsic value of the stock, P_0.

Stock prices are not constant—they sometimes change significantly, as well as very quickly.

☐ Changes in stock prices occur because (1) investors change the rates of return required to invest in stocks or (2) expectations about the cash flows associated with stocks change.

☐ Stock prices move opposite changes in rates of return, but they move the same as changes in future cash flows expected from the stock.
  ~ If investors demand higher (lower) returns to invest in stocks, prices should fall (increase); if investors expect their investments to generate lower (higher) future cash flows, prices should also fall (increase).

Valuing real assets is no different from valuing financial assets.

☐ One must calculate the present value of the expected cash flows associated with the asset.
  ~ The value of a real asset can be found numerically and with a financial calculator.

☐ The valuation of real assets is a critical concern for financial managers because they need to know whether the plant and equipment and other long-term assets they purchase will help achieve the goal of wealth maximization.
  ~ The financial manager must be able to determine whether the asset is worth its purchase price and if the asset will increase the firm's wealth.
  ~ The process of evaluating projects and deciding which projects should be purchased is called *capital budgeting*.
    • The capital budgeting decision-making process is crucial to the firm's success, and it is especially important if the firm is to achieve the goal of wealth maximization.

SELF-TEST QUESTIONS

Definitional

1.   The value of any asset is based on the present value of the _____ _____ the asset is expected to produce in the future.

2.   Capital is raised in two forms: _____ and _____.

3.   A(n) _____ is a long-term promissory note issued by a business or governmental unit.

4.   A(n) _____ _____ is the term applied to a bond that has just been issued, whereas if the bond has been on the market for a while it is classified as an outstanding bond, or a(n) _____ _____.

5.   A bond with annual coupon payments represents an annuity of INT dollars per year for N years, plus a lump sum of M dollars at the end of N years, and its value, V_d, is the _____ _____ of this payment stream.

6. At the time a bond is issued, the coupon interest rate is generally set at a level that will cause the _____ _____ and the _____ _____ of the bond to be approximately equal.

7. Market interest rates and bond prices move in _____ directions from one another.

8. The annual rate of return earned by purchasing a bond and holding it until maturity is known as the bond's _____ ____ _____.

9. When the market rate of interest is above the coupon rate, the bond will sell at a(n) _____.

10. If current interest rates are below the coupon rate, the bond will sell at a(n) _____.

11. The _____ _____ is the annual interest payment on a bond divided by its current market value.

12. To adjust the bond valuation formula for semiannual coupon payments, the _____ _____ and _____ _____ must be divided by 2, and the number of _____ must be multiplied by 2.

13. _____ _____ is a hybrid—it is similar to bonds in some respects and to common stock in other respects.

14. Like other assets, the value of common stock is the _____ value of the expected future cash flow stream.

15. For all stocks, the expected rate of return is composed of an expected _____ yield and an expected _____ _____ yield.

16. If the future growth rate of dividends is expected to be _____, the rate of return is simply the dividend yield.

17. Growth in dividends occurs primarily as a result of growth in _____ _____ _____.

18. Stock prices move _____ changes in rates of return, but they move the _____ as changes in future cash flows expected from the stock.

19. The _____ the expected cash flows, the greater the asset's value; also the _____ the required return, the greater the asset's value.

20. A bond's market price is determined primarily by the _____ it pays, which depends on the _____ _____ _____.

21. Newly issued bonds generally sell _____ to par, but the prices of outstanding bonds _____ from par.

22. A bond will sell at its _____ _____ when its coupon interest rate is equal to the market rate of interest.

23. The market value of a bond always will approach its par value as its _____ _____ approaches, provided the firm does not go _____.

24. The YTM for a bond that sells at par consists entirely of a(n) _____ _____.

25. If a bond sells at a price other than its par value, the YTM consists of the _____ _____ plus a positive or negative _____ _____ _____.

26. Interest rates fluctuate over time, and people or firms who invest in bonds are exposed to risk of changes in bond prices from changing interest rates, or _____ _____ _____ _____.

27. The shorter the maturity of a bond, the greater the exposure to _____ _____ _____ _____ _____, the risk that income from a bond portfolio will vary because cash flows have to be reinvested at current market rates.

28. An increase in interest rates will _____ the current value of a bond portfolio, but because the future cash flows produced by the portfolio will then be reinvested at a _____ rate of return, the future value of the portfolio will be _____.

29. For bonds with similar coupons, the _____ the maturity of the bond, the greater its price changes in response to a given change in interest rates.

30. The value of a bond with semiannual interest payments is _____ than the value when interest is paid annually. This occurs because interest payments are received, and therefore can be reinvested, somewhat faster under _____ _____.

31. A(n) _____ _____ stock is expected to pay a constant dividend, so it can be thought of as a perpetuity.

Conceptual

32. Changes in economic conditions cause interest rates and bond prices to vary over time.

    a. True   **b.** False

33. If the market rate of interest on a bond is greater than its coupon interest rate, the market value of that bond will be above par value.

    a. True   **b.** False

34. A 20-year, annual coupon bond with one year left to maturity has the same interest rate price risk as a 10-year, annual coupon bond with one year left to maturity. Both bonds are of equal risk, have the same coupon interest rate, and the prices of the two bonds are equal.

    a. True   **b.** False

35. According to the valuation model developed in this chapter, the value that an investor assigns to a share of stock is independent of the length of time the investor plans to hold the stock.

    a. True   **b.** False

36. Which of the following assumptions would cause the constant growth stock valuation model to be invalid? The constant growth model is given below:

$$\hat{P}_0 = \frac{D_0(1 + g)}{k_s - g}.$$

    a. The growth rate is negative.
    b. The growth rate is zero.
    c. The growth rate is less than the required rate of return.
    d. The required rate of return is above 30 percent.
    e. None of the above assumptions would invalidate the model.

37. Which of the following statements is correct?

    a. Ignoring interest accrued between payment dates, if the required rate of return on a bond is less than its coupon interest rate, and k_d remains below the coupon rate until maturity, then the market value of that bond will be below its par value until the bond matures, at which time its market value will equal its par value.
    b. Assuming equal coupon rates, a 20-year original maturity bond with one year left to maturity has more interest rate price risk than a 10-year original maturity bond with one year left to maturity.
    c. Regardless of the size of the coupon payment, the price of a bond moves in the same direction as interest rates; for example, if market interest rates rise, bond prices also rise.
    d. For bonds, price sensitivity to a given change in market interest rates generally increases as years remaining to maturity increases.
    e. Because short-term interest rates are much more volatile than long-term rates, you would, in the real world, be subject to more interest rate price risk if you purchased a 30-*day* bond than if you bought a 30-*year* bond.

38. Assume that a company's dividends are expected to grow at a rate of 25 percent per year for 5 years and then to slow down and to grow at a constant rate of 5 percent thereafter. The required (and expected) total return, k_s, is expected to remain constant at 12 percent. Which of the following statements is correct?

    a. The dividend yield will be higher in the early years and then will decline as the annual capital gains yield gets larger and larger, other things held constant.

    b. Right now, it would be easier (require fewer calculations) to find the dividend yield expected in Year 7 than the dividend yield expected in Year 3.

    c. The stock price will grow each year at the same rate as the dividends.

    d. The stock price will grow at a different rate each year during the first 5 years, but its average growth rate over this period will be the same as the average growth rate in dividends; that is, the average stock price growth rate will be (25 + 5)/2.

    e. Statements a, b, c, and d are all false.

39. Which of the following statements is correct?

    a. According to the text, the constant growth stock valuation model is especially useful in situations where g is greater than 15 percent and k_s is 10 percent or less.

    b. According to the text, the constant growth model can be used as one part of the process of finding the value of a stock that is expected to experience a very rapid rate of growth for a few years and then to grow at a constant ("normal") rate.

    c. According to the text, the constant growth model cannot be used unless g is greater than zero.

    d. According to the text, the constant growth model cannot be used unless the constant g is greater than k.

    e. Statements a, b, c, and d are all true.

SELF-TEST PROBLEMS

1. Delta Corporation has a bond issue outstanding with an annual coupon interest rate of 7 percent and 4 years remaining until maturity. The par value of the bond is $1,000. Determine the current value of the bond if present market conditions justify a 14 percent required rate of return. The bond pays interest annually.

    a. $1,126.42   b. $1,000.00   c. $796.04   d. $791.00   e. $536.38

2. Refer to Self-Test Problem 1. Suppose the bond had a semiannual coupon. Now what would be its current value?

    a. $1,126.42   b. $1,000.00   c. $796.04   d. $791.00   e. $536.38

3. Refer to Self-Test Problem 1. Assume an annual coupon but 20 years remaining to maturity. What is the current value under these conditions?

    a. $1,126.42   **b.** $1,000.00   **c.** $796.04   **d.** $791.00   **e.** $536.38

4.   Acme Products has a bond issue outstanding with 8 years remaining to maturity, a coupon interest rate of 10 percent paid annually, and a par value of $1,000. If the current market price of the bond issue is $814.45, what is the yield to maturity, k_d?

    a. 12%   **b.** 13%   **c.** 14%   **d.** 15%   **e.** 16%

5.   Stability Inc. has maintained a dividend rate of $4 per share for many years. The same rate is expected to be paid in future years. If investors require a 12 percent rate of return on similar investments, determine the present value of the company's stock.

    a. $15.00   **b.** $30.00   **c.** $33.33   **d.** $35.00   **e.** $40.00

6.   Your sister-in-law, a stockbroker at Invest Inc., is trying to sell you a stock with a current market price of $25. The stock's last dividend (D_0) was $2.00, and earnings and dividends are expected to increase at a constant growth rate of 10 percent. Your required return on this stock is 20 percent. From a strict valuation standpoint, you should:

    a. Buy the stock; it is fairly valued.
    b. Buy the stock; it is undervalued by $3.00.
    c. Buy the stock; it is undervalued by $2.00.
    d. Not buy the stock; it is overvalued by $2.00.
    e. Not buy the stock; it is overvalued by $3.00.

7.   Lucas Laboratories' last dividend was $1.50. Its current equilibrium stock price is $15.75, and its expected growth rate is a constant 5 percent. If the stockholders' required rate of return is 15 percent, what is the expected dividend yield and expected capital gains yield for the coming year?

    a. 0%; 15%   **b.** 5%; 10%   **c.** 10%; 5%   **d.** 15%; 0%   **e.** 15%; 15%

8.   The Canning Company has been hard hit by increased competition. Analysts predict that earnings (and dividends) will decline at a rate of 5 percent annually into the foreseeable future. If Canning's last dividend (D_0) was $2.00, and investors' required rate of return is 15 percent, what will be Canning's stock price *in 3 years*?

    a. $8.15   **b.** $9.50   **c.** $10.00   **d.** $10.42   **e.** $10.96

(The following information applies to the next three Self-Test Problems.)

The Club Auto Parts Company has just recently been organized. It is expected to experience no growth for the next 2 years as it identifies its market and acquires its inventory. However, Club will grow at an annual rate of 5 percent in the third year and, beginning with the fourth year, should attain a 10 percent growth rate that it will sustain thereafter. The first dividend (D_1) to be paid at the end of the first year is expected to be $0.50 per share. Investors require a 15 percent rate of return on Club's stock.

9.   What is Club's current stock price?

   a. $5.00   **b.** $8.75   **c.** $9.56   **d.** $12.43   **e.** $15.00

10.   What will Club's stock price be at the end of the first year (P_1)?

   a. $5.00   **b.** $8.75   **c.** $9.56   **d.** $12.43   **e.** $15.00

11.   What dividend yield and capital gains yield should an investor in Club expect for the first year?

   a. 7.5%; 7.5%   **b.** 4.7%; 10.3% **c.** 5.7%; 9.3%   **d.** 10.5%; 4.5% **e.** 11.5%;3.5%

12.   You have just been offered a bond for $863.73. The coupon interest rate is 8 percent, payable annually, and market interest rates on new issues with the same degree of risk are 10 percent. You want to know how many more interest payments you will receive, but the party selling the bond cannot remember. If the par value is $1,000, how many interest payments remain?

   a. 10   **b.** 11   **c.** 12   **d.** 13   **e.** 14

13.   Johnson Corporation's stock is currently selling at $45.83 per share. The last dividend paid (D_0) was $2.50. Johnson is a constant growth firm. If investors require a return of 16 percent on Johnson's stock, what do they think Johnson's growth rate will be?

   a. 6%   **b.** 7%   **c.** 8%   **d.** 9%   **e.** 10%

14.   Assume that the average firm in your company's industry is expected to grow at a constant rate of 7 percent and its dividend yield is 8 percent. Your company is about as risky as the average firm in the industry, but it has just successfully completed some R&D work that leads you to expect that its earnings and dividends will grow at a rate of 40 percent [$D_1 = D_0(1 + g) = D_0(1.40)$] this year and 20 percent the following year, after which growth should match the 7 percent industry average rate. The last dividend paid (D_0) was $1. What is the value per share of your firm's stock?

   a. $22.47   **b.** $24.15   **c.** $21.00   **d.** $19.48   **e.** $22.00

15. Chadmark Corporation is expanding rapidly, and it currently needs to retain all of its earnings, hence it does not pay any dividends. However, investors expect Chadmark to begin paying dividends, with the first dividend of $0.75 coming 2 years from today. The dividend should grow rapidly, at a rate of 40 percent per year, during Years 3 and 4. After Year 4, the company should grow at a constant rate of 10 percent per year. If the required return on the stock is 16 percent, what is the value of the stock today?

    a. $16.93   **b.** $17.54   **c.** $15.78   **d.** $18.87   **e.** $16.05

16. Some investors expect Endicott Industries to have an irregular dividend pattern for several years, and then to grow at a constant rate. Suppose Endicott has $D_0 = \$2.00$; no growth is expected for 2 years $(g_1 = 0)$; then the expected growth rate is 8 percent for 2 years; and finally the growth rate is expected to be constant at 15 percent thereafter. If the required return is 20 percent, what will be the value of the stock today?

    a. $28.53   **b.** $25.14   **c.** $31.31   **d.** $21.24   **e.** $23.84

ANSWERS TO SELF-TEST QUESTIONS

1.	cash flows	17.	earnings per share
2.	debt; equity	18.	opposite; same
3.	bond	19.	higher; lower
4.	new issue; seasoned issue	20.	interest; coupon interest rate
5.	present value	21.	close; vary
6.	market price; par value	22.	par value
7.	opposite	23.	maturity date; bankrupt
8.	yield to maturity	24.	interest yield
9.	discount	25.	interest yield; capital gains yield
10.	premium	26.	interest rate price risk
11.	current yield	27.	interest rate reinvestment rate risk
12.	coupon payment; interest rate; years	28.	lower; higher; increased
13.	Preferred stock	29.	longer
14.	present	30.	larger; semiannual compounding
15.	dividend; capital gains	31.	zero growth
16.	zero		

32. a. For example, if inflation increases, the interest rate (or required return) will increase, and since interest rates and bond prices move in opposite directions, bond prices will decline.

33. b. The bond will sell at a discount (below par).

34. a. Both bonds are valued as 1-year bonds regardless of their original issue dates, and since they are of equal risk and have the same coupon interest rate, their prices must be equal.

35. a. The model considers all future dividends. This produces a current value that is appropriate for all investors independent of their expected holding period.

36. e. The model would be invalid, however, if the growth rate *exceeded* the required rate of return.

37. d. Statement a is false because the bond sells at a premium and thus sells above par value. Statement b is false because both bonds would have the same interest rate price risk because they both have one year left to maturity. Statement c is false because the price of a bond moves in the opposite direction as interest rates. Statement e is false because the 30-year bond would have more interest rate price risk than the 30-day bond. Statement d is correct. As years to maturity increases for a bond, the number of discount periods used in finding the current bond value also increases. Therefore, bonds with longer maturities will have more price sensitivity to a given change in interest rates.

38. b. Statement b is correct. We know that after Year 5, the stock will have a constant growth rate, and the capital gains yield will be equal to that growth rate. We also know that the total return is expected to be constant. Therefore, we could find the expected dividend yield in Year 7 simply by subtracting the growth rate from the total return: yield = 12% – 5% = 7% in Year 7. The other statements are all false. This could be confirmed by thinking about how the dividend growth rate starts high, ends up at the constant growth rate, and must lie between these two rates and be declining between Years 1 and 5. The average growth rate in dividends during Years 1 through 5 will be (25 + 5)/2 = 15%, which is above k_s = 12%, so statements c and d must be false.

39. b. Statement b is correct. In the case of a nonconstant growth stock that is expected to grow at a constant rate after Year N, we would find the value of D_{N+1} and use it in the constant growth model to find P_N. The other statements are all false. Note that the constant growth model can be used for g = 0 or g < 0, but not for g > k.

SOLUTIONS TO SELF-TEST PROBLEMS

1. c. Calculator solution: Input N = 4, I = 14, PMT = 70, FV = 1000, and solve for PV = -$796.04.

2. d. Calculator solution: Input N = 8, I = 7, PMT = 35, FV = 1000, and solve for PV = -$791.00.

3. e. Calculator solution: Input N = 20, I = 14, PMT = 70, FV = 1000, and solve for PV = -$536.38.

4. c. The approximate yield to maturity can be calculated as:

$$\frac{\text{Approximate}}{\text{yield to maturity}} = \frac{\$100 + \dfrac{\$1,000 - \$814.45}{8}}{\left[\dfrac{2(\$814.45) + \$1,000}{3}\right]} = \frac{\$123.19}{\$876.30} = 14.06\% \approx 14\%.$$

Calculator solution: Input $N = 8$, $PV = -814.45$, $PMT = 100$, $FV = 1000$, and solve for I $= k_d = 14.00\%$.

5. c. This is a zero-growth stock, or perpetuity: $\hat{P}_0 = D/k_s = \$4.00/0.12 = \$33.33.$

6. e. $\hat{P}_0 = \dfrac{D_0(1+g)}{k_s - g} = \dfrac{\$2.00(1.10)}{0.20 - 0.10} = \$22.00.$

Because the stock is currently selling for $25.00, the stock is overvalued by $3.00.

7. c. $\dfrac{\text{Dividend}}{\text{yield}} = \dfrac{D_1}{P_0} = \dfrac{D_0(1+g)}{P_0} = \dfrac{\$1.50(1.05)}{\$15.75} = 0.10 = 10\%.$

$$\frac{\text{Capital}}{\text{gains yield}} = \frac{\hat{P}_1 - P_0}{P_0} = \frac{P_0(1+g) - P_0}{P_0} = \frac{\$16.54 - \$15.75}{\$15.75} = g = 5\%.$$

For a constant growth stock, the capital gains yield is equal to g.

8. a. $\hat{P}_0 = \dfrac{D_0(1+g)}{k_s - g} = \dfrac{\$2.00(0.95)}{0.15 - (-0.05)} = \dfrac{\$1.90}{0.20} = \$9.50.$

$\hat{P}_3 = \hat{P}_0(1+g)^3 = \$9.50(0.95)^3 = \$9.50(0.8574) = \$8.15.$

The Gordon model can also be used:

$$\hat{P}_3 = \frac{D_4}{k_s - g} = \frac{D_0(1+g)^4}{0.15 - (-0.05)} = \frac{\$2.00(0.95)^4}{0.20} = \frac{\$2.00(0.8145)}{0.20} = \$8.15.$$

9. b. To calculate the current value of a nonconstant growth stock, follow these steps:

1. Determine the expected stream of dividends during the nonconstant growth period. Also, calculate the expected dividend at the end of the first year of constant growth that will be used later to calculate stock price.

$D_1 = \$0.50.$
$D_2 = D_1(1 + g) = \$0.50(1 + 0.0) = \$0.50.$
$D_3 = D_2(1 + g) = \$0.50(1.05) = \$0.525.$
$D_4 = D_3(1 + g) = \$0.525(1.10) = \$0.5775.$

2. Discount the expected dividends during the nonconstant growth period at the investor's required rate of return to find their present value.

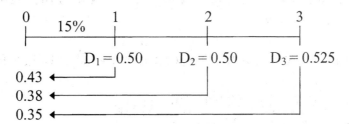

3. Calculate the expected stock price at the end of the final year of nonconstant growth. This occurs at the end of Year 3. Use the Gordon model for this calculation.

$$\hat{P}_3 = \frac{D_4}{k_s - g} = \frac{\$0.5775}{0.15 - 0.10} = \$11.55.$$

Then discount this stock price back 3 periods at the investor's required rate of return to find its present value.

$$PV = \$11.55\left(\frac{1}{1.15^3}\right) = \$11.55(0.6575) = \$7.59.$$

4. Add the present value of the stock price expected at the end of Year 3 plus the dividends expected in Years 1, 2, and 3 to find the present value of the stock, P_0.

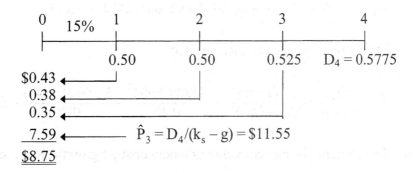

Alternatively, input 0, 0.5, 0.5, 12.075 (0.525 + 11.55) into the cash flow register, input I = 15, and then solve for NPV = $8.75.

10.   c.   To calculate the expected stock price at the end of Year 1, P_1, follow the same procedure you did to find the value of the nonconstant growth stock in Self-Test Problem 9. However, discount values to Year 1 instead of Year 0. Also, remember that the dividend in Year 1, D_1, is not included in the valuation because it has already been

paid and therefore adds nothing to the wealth of the investor buying the stock at the end of Year 1.

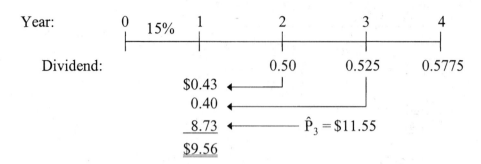

Alternatively, input 0, 0.5, 12.075 (0.525 + 11.55) into the cash flow register, input I = 15, and then solve for NPV = $9.57.

11. c. $\dfrac{\text{Dividend}}{\text{yield}} = \dfrac{D_1}{P_0} = \dfrac{\$0.50}{\$8.75} = 5.7\%.$

$\dfrac{\text{Capital}}{\text{gains yield}} = \dfrac{\hat{P}_1 - P_0}{P_0} = \dfrac{\$9.56 - \$8.75}{\$8.75} = 9.3\%.$

The expected rate of return = Dividend yield + Capital gains yield = 5.7% + 9.3% = 15%. The expected rate of return must equal the required rate of return. Also, the capital gains yield is not equal to the growth rate during the nonconstant growth phase of a nonconstant growth stock. Finally, the dividend and capital gains yields are not constant until the constant growth state is reached.

12. c. Using a financial calculator, input I = 10, PV = -863.73, PMT = 80, FV = 1000, and solve for N = 12.

13. e.

$$P_0 = \frac{D_0(1 + g)}{k_s - g}$$

$$\$45.83 = \frac{\$2.50(1 + g)}{0.16 - g}$$

$$\$7.33 - \$45.83g = \$2.50 + \$2.50g$$
$$\$48.33g = \$4.83$$
$$g = 0.0999 \approx 10\%.$$

14. d. $D_0 = \$1.00$; $k_s = 8\% + 7\% = 15\%$; $g_1 = 40\%$; $g_2 = 20\%$; $g_n = 7\%$.

```
 0  k  = 15%  1        2        3
     s
 |————————————|————————|————————|

             1.40      1.68     1.7976
  $ 1.22 ◄——————┘      22.47* ◄——————┘
                       24.15
    18.26 ◄—————————————————┘
   $19.48
```

$$*\hat{P}_2 = \frac{\$1.7976}{0.15 - 0.07} = \$22.47.$$

15. a. To calculate Chadmark's current stock price, follow the following steps: (1) Determine the expected stream of dividends during the nonconstant growth period. You will need to calculate the expected dividend at the end of Year 5, which is the first year of constant growth. This dividend will be used in the next step to calculate the stock price.

(2) Calculate the expected stock price at the end of the final year of nonconstant growth. This occurs at the end of Year 4. Use the Gordon model for this calculation. (3) Add the value obtained in Step 2 to the dividend expected in Year 4. (4) Put the values obtained in the prior steps on a cash flow time line and discount them at the required rate of return to find the present value of Chadmark's stock. These steps are shown below.

$D_0 = \$0$; $D_1 = \$0$; $D_2 = \$0.75$; $D_3 = \$0.75(1.4) = \$1.05$; $D_4 = \$0.75(1.4)^2 = \$1.47$; $D_5 = \$0.75(1.4)^2(1.10) = \$1.617$

```
 0  k  = 16%  1       2          3        4          5
     s
 |————————————|———————|——————————|————————|——————————|
              0      0.75 g=40%  1.05    1.47 g=10%  1.617
   0.00 ◄——————┘
   0.56 ◄———————————————┘                26.95* ◄——————┘
   0.67 ◄——————————————————————————┘     28.42
   15.70 ◄——————————————————————————————————┘
 P  = $16.93
  0
```

$$*\hat{P}_4 = \$1.617/(0.16 - 0.10) = \$26.95.$$

$CF_0 = 0$; $CF_1 = 0$; $CF_2 = 0.75$; $CF_3 = 1.05$; $CF_4 = 28.42$.

Alternatively, using a financial calculator you could input the cash flows as shown above into the cash flow register, input $I = 16$, and press NPV to obtain the stock's value today of $16.93.

16.   c.   First, set up the cash flow time line as follows. Note that D_5 is used to find $\hat{P}_4$, which is treated as part of the cash flow at $t = 4$:

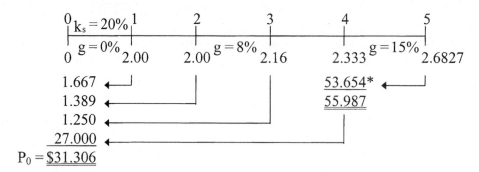

$$* \hat{P}_4 = \$2.6827/(0.20 - 0.15) = \$53.654.$$

Enter the time line values into the cash flow register, with $I = 20$, to find $NPV = \$31.31$. Be sure to enter $CF_0 = 0$. Note that $\hat{P}_4$ is the PV, at $t = 4$, of dividends from $t = 5$ to infinity; that is, the PV of the dividends after the stock is expected to become a constant growth stock.

OVERVIEW

Risk is an important concept in financial analysis, especially in terms of how it affects security prices and rates of return. Investment risk is associated with the likelihood an investment will not yield the return investors expect.

Each investment has two different types of risks: diversifiable and nondiversifiable risk, the sum of which is the investment's total risk. Diversifiable risk is not important to rational, informed investors because they will eliminate its effects by diversifying it away. The significant risk is nondiversifiable risk—this risk cannot be eliminated, and if you invest in anything other than riskless assets, you will be exposed to it.

An attempt has been made to quantify nondiversifiable, or market, risk with a measure called beta. Beta is a measurement of how a particular firm's stock returns move relative to overall movements of stock market returns. The Capital Asset Pricing Model (CAPM), using the concept of beta and investors' aversion to risk, specifies the relationship between market risk and the required rate of return. This relationship can be visualized graphically with the Security Market Line (SML). The slope of the SML can change, or the line can shift upward or downward, in response to changes in risk or required rates of return.

OUTLINE

Risk refers to the chance that some unfavorable event will occur. Risk occurs when we cannot be certain about the outcome of a particular activity or event, so we are not sure what will occur in the future.

☐ *Investment risk* is related to the possibility of actually earning a return other than expected; thus, the greater the variability of the possible outcomes, the riskier the investment.

☐ A *probability distribution* is the listing of all possible outcomes, or events, with a probability (chance of occurrence) assigned to each outcome.
  ~ The sum of the probabilities must equal 1.0.

☐ Probabilities can also be assigned to the possible outcomes from an investment.
  ~ If you buy a bond, you expect to receive interest on the bond, and those interest payments will provide you with a rate of return on your investment.

~ The possible outcomes from this investment are (1) that the issuer will make the interest payments or (2) that the issuer will fail to make the interest payments.
~ The higher the probability of default on the interest payments, the riskier the bond; and the higher the risk, the higher the rate of return you would require to invest in the bond.
~ If instead of buying a bond you invest in a stock, you will again expect to earn a return on your money. The riskier the stock, which means the greater the variability of the possible payoffs, the higher the stock's expected return must be to induce you to invest in it.

☐ The *expected rate of return (k̂)* is the weighted average of the various possible outcomes, where the weights are their probabilities of occurrence:

$$\text{Expected rate of return} = \hat{k} = \sum_{i=1}^{n} Pr_i k_i.$$

~ Here k_i is the *i*th possible outcome, Pr_i is the probability the *i*th outcome will occur, and n is the number of possible outcomes.
~ A graph can be developed that gives a picture of the variability of possible outcomes.

☐ In *continuous probability distributions* the number of possible outcomes is unlimited, whereas *in discrete probability distributions* the number of outcomes is limited, or finite.
~ The tighter, or more peaked, a probability distribution, the less variability there is, and the more likely it is that the actual outcome will be close to the expected value, consequently, the less likely it is that the actual return will be much different from the expected return.
~ The tighter the probability distribution, the lower the risk assigned to a stock.

☐ One measure for determining the tightness of a distribution is the *standard deviation, σ.*

$$\text{Standard deviation} = \sigma = \sqrt{\sigma^2} = \sqrt{\sum_{i=1}^{n} (k_i - \hat{k})^2 Pr_i}.$$

~ The smaller the standard deviation, the tighter the probability distribution, and, accordingly, the lower the riskiness of the investment.
~ The standard deviation is a weighted average deviation from the expected value, and it gives you an idea of how far above or below the expected value the actual value is likely to be.
~ This is based on data that are in the form of a known probability distribution.

☐ To calculate the standard deviation for data over some past period the following formula is used:

$$\text{Estimated } \sigma = S = \sqrt{\frac{\sum_{t=1}^{n} (k_t - \bar{k})^2}{n-1}}.$$

where k_t is the past realized annual rate of return in Period t, and $\bar{k}$ is the arithmetic average of the annual returns.

~ The historical standard deviation often is used as an estimate of the future σ.

~ Because past variability is likely to be repeated, S might be a good estimate of future risk, but it is much less reasonable to expect that the past level of return is the best expectation of what investors think will happen in the future.

☐ Another useful measure of risk is the *coefficient of variation (CV)*, which is the standard deviation divided by the expected return. It shows the risk per unit of return, and it provides a more meaningful basis for comparison when the expected returns on two alternatives are not the same:

$$\text{Coefficient of variation (CV)} = \frac{\text{Risk}}{\text{Return}} = \frac{\sigma}{\hat{k}}.$$

~ Because the coefficient of variation captures the effects of both risk and return, it is a better measure for evaluating risk in situations where investments differ with respect to both their amounts of total risk and their expected returns.

☐ Most investors are *risk averse*. This means that for two alternatives with the same expected rate of return, investors will choose the one with the lower risk.

~ The implications of risk aversion for security prices and rates of return are that, other things held constant, the higher a security's risk, the higher the return investors demand, thus the less they are willing to pay for the investment.

~ In a market dominated by risk-averse investors, riskier securities must have higher expected returns, as estimated by the average investor, than less risky securities because if this situation does not hold, investors will buy and sell investments and prices will continue to change until the higher risk investments have higher expected returns than the lower risk investments.

Holding an investment, whether a stock, bond, or other asset as part of a portfolio is generally less risky than holding the same investment all by itself. Most institutions and individual investors hold portfolios of securities rather than one stock. This fact has been incorporated into a procedure called the Capital Asset Pricing Model (CAPM), used to analyze the relationship between risk and rates of return.

☐ Theoretically, the CAPM can be applied to any asset, including such financial assets as stocks and bonds, and such real assets as real estate and manufacturing equipment.

☐ The CAPM is a model based on the proposition that any stock's required rate of return is equal to the risk-free rate of return plus a risk premium, where risk reflects diversification.

☐ From an investor's standpoint, what is important is the return on his or her portfolio, and the portfolio's risk—not the fact that a particular stock goes up or down. Thus, the risk and return of an individual security should be analyzed in terms of how that security affects the risk and return of the portfolio in which it is held.

~ The *expected return on a portfolio*, $\hat{k}_p$, is the weighted average of the expected returns on the individual stocks in the portfolio, with the weights being the fraction of the total portfolio invested in each stock:

$$\hat{k}_p = \sum_{j=1}^{N} w_j \hat{k}_j .$$

~ Of course, the actual *realized rate of return*, k_j, the return that is actually earned is usually different from the expected return.

☐ The *riskiness of a portfolio*, σ_p, is generally *not* a weighted average of the standard deviations of the individual securities in the portfolio. The portfolio's risk usually is smaller than the weighted average of the stocks' σs.

~ The riskiness of a portfolio depends not only on the standard deviations of the individual stocks, but also on the *correlation* between the stocks.

- The *correlation coefficient, r,* measures the degree of the relationship between two variables. With stocks, these variables are the individual stock returns.

- Theoretically, it is possible to combine two stocks that, by themselves, are quite risky as measured by their standard deviations and to form a portfolio that is completely riskless. Two stocks that are *perfectly negatively correlated* can be combined to form a riskless portfolio because their returns move opposite to each other.

- Diversification does nothing to reduce risk if the portfolio consists of *perfectly positively correlated* stocks. Such a portfolio would be exactly as risky as the individual stocks.

- In the typical case, where the correlations among the individual stocks are positive, but less than +1.0, some, but not all, risk can be eliminated.

- As a rule, the riskiness of a portfolio is reduced as the number of stocks in the portfolio increases.

- The smaller the positive correlation coefficient, the lower the risk in a large portfolio.

☐ Even very large portfolios end up with a substantial amount of risk, but the risk is generally less than if all the money was invested in only one stock. Almost half of the riskiness inherent in an average individual stock can be eliminated if the stock is held in a reasonably well-diversified portfolio, which is one containing 40 or more stocks. Some risk always remains, however, so it is virtually impossible to diversify away the effects of broad stock market movements that affect almost all stocks.

~ *Firm-specific* (also known as *diversifiable* or *unsystematic) risk* is that part of the risk of a stock that can be eliminated. It is caused by events unique to a particular firm.

~ *Market* (also known as *nondiversifiable* or *systematic) risk* is that part of the risk that cannot be eliminated, and it stems from factors that systematically affect most firms, such as war, inflation, recessions, and high interest rates.

~ The relevant riskiness of an individual stock is its contribution to the riskiness of a well-diversified portfolio. The *relevant risk* is the risk of a security that cannot be diversified away, or its market risk. This reflects a security's contribution to the risk of a portfolio.

~ The risk that remains after diversifying is market risk, or risk that is inherent in the market, and it can be measured by evaluating the degree to which a given stock tends to move up and down with the market.

The measure of a stock's sensitivity to market fluctuations is called its beta coefficient, β, the measure of the extent to which the returns on a given stock move with the stock market. Beta is a key element of the CAPM.

☐ An *average-risk stock* is defined as one that tends to move up and down in step with the general market as measured by some index. By definition it has a beta of 1.0.

☐ A stock that is twice as volatile as the market will have a beta of 2.0, while a stock that is half as volatile as the market will have a beta coefficient of 0.5. The average beta for all stocks is 1.0 by definition.

☐ Because a stock's beta measures its contribution to the riskiness of a portfolio, theoretically beta is the correct measure of the stock's riskiness.

☐ Risk premiums in a market populated with rational investors will reflect only market risk.

☐ Because a stock's beta coefficient determines how the stock affects the riskiness of a diversified portfolio, beta is the most relevant measure of a stock's risk.

☐ The beta coefficient of a portfolio of securities is the weighted average of the individual securities' betas:

$$\beta_p = \sum_{j=1}^{N} w_j \beta_j.$$

The Capital Asset Pricing Model (CAPM) employs the concept of beta, which measures risk as the relationship between a particular stock's movements and the movements of the overall stock market. The CAPM uses a stock's beta, in conjunction with the average investor's degree of risk aversion, to calculate the return that investors require, k_s, on that particular stock.

☐ The *Security Market Line (SML)* shows the relationship between risk as measured by beta and the required rate of return for individual securities. The SML equation can be used to find the required rate of return on Stock j:

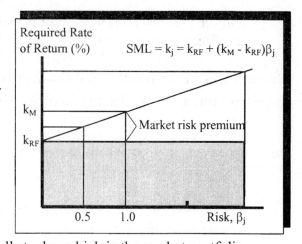

SML: $k_j = k_{RF} + (RP_M)\beta_j$.

SML: $k_j = k_{RF} + (k_M - k_{RF})\beta_j$.

Here k_{RF} is the risk-free rate of return, β_j is the *j*th stock's beta, and k_M is the required rate of return on a portfolio consisting of all stocks, which is the market portfolio.

~ The term $k_M - k_{RF}$ is the market risk premium, RP_M. This is the additional return above the risk-free rate required to compensate an average investor for assuming an average amount of risk.

~ The market risk premium, RP_M, depends on the degree of aversion that investors on average have to risk.

~ Risk premium for Stock j = $RP_j = (RP_M) \beta_j$. The stock's risk premium is less than, equal to, or greater than the premium on an average stock, depending on whether its beta is less than, equal to, or greater than 1.0.

☐ Both the Security Market Line and a company's position on it change over time due to changes in interest rates, investors' risk aversion, and individual companies' betas.

☐ The risk-free rate of interest is called the *nominal*, or *quoted*, *rate*, and it consists of two elements: (1) a *real inflation-free rate of return, k**, and (2) *an inflation premium, IP*, equal to the anticipated rate of inflation.

~ As the expected rate of inflation increases, a higher premium must be added to the real risk-free rate of return to compensate for the loss of purchasing power.

● The increase in k_{RF} causes an equal increase in the rate of return on all risky assets because the inflation premium is built into the required rate of return of both riskless and risky assets.

☐ As risk aversion increases, so does the risk premium and, thus, the slope of the SML.

~ The slope of the SML reflects the degree of risk aversion in the economy; the greater the average investor's aversion to risk, the steeper the slope of the line, the greater the risk premium for any stock, and the higher the required rate of return on stocks.

☐ Many factors can affect a company's beta. When such changes occur, the required rate of return also changes.

~ A firm can affect its beta risk through changes in the composition of its assets as well as through its use of debt financing.

~ A company's beta can also change as a result of external factors, such as increased competition in its industry or the expiration of basic patents.

☐ Any change that affects the required rate of return on a security, such as a change in its beta coefficient or in expected inflation, will have an impact on the price of the security.

Equilibrium is the condition under which the expected return on a security is just equal to its required return, $\hat{k} = k$, and the price is stable.

☐ In *equilibrium* two conditions must hold:
~ The expected rate of return as seen by the marginal investor must equal the required rate of return: $\hat{k}_j = k_j$.
~ The actual market price of the stock must equal its intrinsic value as estimated by the marginal investor: $P_0 = \hat{P}_0$.

☐ If these conditions do not hold, trading will occur until they do hold.

☐ Stock market prices are not constant—they undergo violent changes at times.

☐ Evidence suggests that stocks, especially those of large NYSE companies, adjust rapidly to disequilibrium situations.
~ Equilibrium ordinarily exists for any given stock, and, in general, required and expected returns are equal.
~ Stock prices certainly change, sometimes violently and rapidly, but this simply reflects changing conditions and expectations.

☐ The expected returns as estimated by a marginal investor are always positive, but in some years negative returns have been realized.

For a management whose goal is stock price maximization, the overriding consideration is the riskiness of the firm's stock, and the relevant risk of any physical asset must be measured in terms of its effect on the stock's risk.
A word of caution is in order about betas and the Capital Asset Pricing Model. The entire theory is based on ex ante, or expected, conditions, yet we have available only ex post, or past, data. Thus, the betas we calculate show how volatile a stock has been in the past, but conditions may change, and the stock's future volatility, which is the item of real concern to investors, might be quite different from its past volatility.

☐ Although the CAPM represents a significant step forward in security pricing theory, it does have some potentially serious deficiencies when applied in practice, so estimates of k_j found through use of the SML may be subject to considerable error.

☐ Many investors and analysts use the CAPM and the concept of beta to provide "ballpark" figures for further analysis.

☐ To this point in the book, different types of risk have been discussed. The table on the next page shows the risks that are discussed in the book, classified as components of systematic or unsystematic risks.

Appendix 11A presents a discussion on the calculation of beta coefficients. The discussion concentrates on graphic and least squares regression techniques.

Different Types (Sources) of Risk

		Type of Risk	Brief Description
I.	**Systematic Risk** (nondiversifiable risk; relevant risk)	Interest rate risk	Interest rates changes, (1) the values of investments change (opposite directions) and (2) the rate at which funds can be reinvested also changes (in the same direction).
		Inflation risk	The primary reason interest rates change is because investors change their expectations about future inflation.
		Maturity risk	Long-term investments experience greater price reactions to interest rate changes than do short-term bonds.
		Liquidity risk	Reflects the fact that some investments are more easily converted into cash on a short notice at a "reasonable price."
		Exchange rate risk	The rate at which the currency of one country can be *exchanged* into the currency of another country changes as market conditions change.
		Political risk	Any action by a government that reduces the value of an investment.
II.	**Unsystematic Risk** (diversifiable risk; firm-specific risk)	Business risk	Risk that would be inherent in the firm's operations if it used no debt—factors such as labor conditions, product safety, quality of management, competitive conditions, and so forth, affect firm-specific risk.
		Financial risk	Risk associated with how the firm is financed (its credit risk).
		Default risk	Part of financial risk—the chance that the firm cannot service its existing debt.
III.	**Combined Risks** (some systematic and some unsystematic risk)	Total Risk	The combination of systematic risk and unsystematic risk; also referred to as stand-alone risk, because this is the risk an investor takes if he or she purchases only one investment, which is tantamount to "putting all your eggs into one basket."
		Corporate risk	The riskiness of the firm without considering the effect of stockholder diversification; based on the combination of assets held by the firm (inventory, accounts receivable, plant and equipment, and so forth). Some diversification exists because the firm's assets represent a portfolio of investments in real assets.

SELF-TEST QUESTIONS

Definitional

1. _____ _____ is related to the possibility of actually earning a return other than expected; thus, the greater the variability of the possible outcomes, the riskier the investment.

2. A listing of all possible _____, with a probability assigned to each, is known as a probability _____.

3. Weighting each possible outcome of a distribution by its _____ of occurrence and summing the results give the expected _____ of the distribution.

4. In a(n) _____ probability distribution the number of possible outcomes is unlimited, whereas in a(n) _____ probability distribution the number of outcomes is finite.

5. One measure of the tightness of a probability distribution is the _____ _____, a weighted average deviation from the expected value.

6. The _____ _____ _____ shows the risk per unit of return and provides a meaningful basis for comparison when the expected returns on two alternatives are not the same.

7. Investors who prefer outcomes with a high degree of certainty to those that are less certain are described as being _____ _____.

8. The _____ _____ _____ Model is based on the proposition that any stock's required rate of return is equal to the risk-free rate of return plus a risk premium, where risk reflects diversification.

9. The riskiness of a portfolio depends not only on the standard deviations of individual stocks, but also on the _____ between the stocks.

10. The _____ _____ measures the degree of the relationship between two variables.

11. _____ does nothing to reduce risk if the portfolio consists of _____ _____ _____ stocks. Such a portfolio would be exactly as risky as the individual stocks.

12. That part of a stock's risk that can be eliminated is known as _____-_____ risk, while the portion that cannot be eliminated is called _____ risk.

13.   The _____ coefficient measures the extent to which the returns on a given stock move with the stock market.

14.   A stock that is twice as volatile as the market would have a beta coefficient of _____, while a stock with a beta of 0.5 would be only _____ as volatile as the market.

15.   The beta coefficient of a portfolio of securities is the _____ _____ of the individual securities' betas.

16.   The _____ _____ _____ is the additional return above the risk-free rate required to compensate an average investor for assuming an average amount of risk.

17.   The risk premium for a particular stock may be calculated by multiplying the market risk premium times the stock's _____ _____.

18.   A stock's required rate of return is equal to the _____-_____ rate plus the stock's _____ _____.

19.   The risk-free rate of interest consists of two elements: a real inflation-free rate of return plus a(n) _____ premium.

20.   Changes in investors' risk aversion alter the _____ of the Security Market Line.

21.   _____ refers to the chance that some unfavorable event will occur.

22.   The sum of probabilities must equal _____.

23.   The _____ _____ ____ _____ is the weighted average of the various possible outcomes.

24.   The _____ the standard deviation, the tighter the probability distribution, and the _____ the riskiness of the investment.

25.   The _____ _____ ____ _____ is the return that is actually earned.

26.   _____ is the condition under which the expected return on a security is just equal to its required return and the price is stable.

27.   The expected returns as estimated by a(n) _____ investor are always positive, but in some years negative returns have been realized.

Conceptual

28. The Y-axis intercept of the Security Market Line (SML) indicates the required rate of return on an individual stock with a beta of 1.0.

    a. True **b.** False

29. If a stock has a beta of zero, it will be riskless when held in isolation.

    a. True **b.** False

30. A group of 200 stocks each has a beta of 1.0. We can be certain that each of the stocks was positively correlated with the market.

    a. True **b.** False

31. Refer to Self-Test Question 30. If we combined these same 200 stocks into a portfolio, market risk would be reduced below the average market risk of the stocks in the portfolio.

    a. True **b.** False

32. Refer to Self-Test Question 31. The standard deviation of the portfolio of these 200 stocks would be lower than the standard deviations of the individual stocks.

    a. True **b.** False

33. Suppose $k_{RF} = 7\%$ and $k_M = 12\%$. If investors became more risk averse, k_M would be likely to decrease.

    a. True **b.** False

34. Refer to Self-Test Question 33. The required rate of return for a stock with $\beta = 0.5$ would increase more than for a stock with $\beta = 2.0$.

    a. True **b.** False

35. Refer to Self-Test Questions 33 and 34. If the expected rate of inflation increased, the required rate of return on a $\beta = 2.0$ stock would rise by more than that of a $\beta = 0.5$ stock.

    a. True **b.** False

36. Which is the best measure of risk for an asset held in a well-diversified portfolio?

    a. Variance. **d.** Semi-variance.
    b. Standard deviation. **e.** Expected value.
    c. Beta.

37. In a portfolio of three different stocks, which of the following could *not* be true?

    a. The riskiness of the portfolio is less than the riskiness of each stock held in isolation.
    b. The riskiness of the portfolio is greater than the riskiness of one or two of the stocks.
    c. The beta of the portfolio is less than the beta of each of the individual stocks.
    d. The beta of the portfolio is greater than the beta of one or two of the individual stocks.
    e. The beta of the portfolio is equal to the beta of one of the individual stocks.

38. If investors expected inflation to increase in the future, and they also became more risk averse, what could be said about the change in the Security Market Line (SML)?

    a. The SML would shift up and the slope would increase.
    b. The SML would shift up and the slope would decrease.
    c. The SML would shift down and the slope would increase.
    d. The SML would shift down and the slope would decrease.
    e. The SML would remain unchanged.

39. Which of the following statements is correct?

    a. The SML relates required returns to firms' systematic (or market) risk. The slope and intercept of this line *cannot* be controlled by the financial manager.
    b. The slope of the SML is determined by the value of beta.
    c. If you plotted the returns of a given stock against those of the market, and if you found that the slope of the regression line was negative, then the CAPM would indicate that the required rate of return on the stock should be less than the risk-free rate for a well-diversified investor, assuming that the observed relationship is expected to continue on into the future.
    d. If investors become less risk averse, the slope of the Security Market Line will increase.
    e. Both statements a and c are correct.

40. Which of the following statements is correct?

    a. The expected future rate of return, $\hat{k}$, is always *above* the past realized rate of return, k, except for highly risk-averse investors.
    b. The expected future rate of return, $\hat{k}$, is always *below* the past realized rate of return, k, except for highly risk-averse investors.
    c. The expected future rate of return, $\hat{k}$, is always *below* the required rate of return, k, except for highly risk-averse investors.
    d. There is no logical reason to think that any relationship exists between the expected future rate of return, $\hat{k}$, on a security and the security's required rate of return, k.
    e. Each of the above statements is false.

SELF-TEST PROBLEMS

1. Stock A has the following probability distribution of expected returns:

Probability	Rate of Return
0.1	-15%
0.2	0
0.4	5
0.2	10
0.1	25

What is Stock A's expected rate of return and standard deviation?

a. 8.0%; 9.5%   **b.** 8.0%; 6.5%   **c.** 5.0%; 3.5%   **d.** 5.0%; 6.5%   **e.** 5.0%;9.5%

2. If k_{RF} = 5%, k_M = 11%, and β = 1.3 for Stock X, what is k_X, the required rate of return for Stock X?

a. 18.7%   **b.** 16.7%   **c.** 14.8%   **d.** 12.8%   **e.** 11.9%

3. Refer to Self-Test Problem 2. What would k_X be if investors expected the inflation rate to increase by 2 percentage points?

a. 18.7%   **b.** 16.7%   **c.** 14.8%   **d.** 12.8%   **e.** 11.9%

4. Refer to Self-Test Problem 2. What would k_X be if an increase in investors' risk aversion caused the market risk premium to increase by 3 percentage points? k_{RF} remains at 5 percent.

a. 18.7%   **b.** 16.7%   **c.** 14.8%   **d.** 12.8%   **e.** 11.9%

5. Refer to Self-Test Problem 2. What would k_X be if investors expected the inflation rate to increase by 2 percentage points *and* their risk aversion increased by 3 percentage points?

a. 18.7%   **b.** 16.7%   **c.** 14.8%   **d.** 12.8%   **e.** 11.9%

6. Jan Middleton owns a 3-stock portfolio with a total investment value equal to $300,000.

Stock	Investment	Beta
A	$100,000	0.5
B	100,000	1.0
C	100,000	1.5
Total	$300,000	

What is the weighted average beta of Jan's 3-stock portfolio?

a. 0.9   **b.** 1.3   **c.** 1.0   **d.** 0.4   **e.** 1.2

7. The Apple Investment Fund has a total investment of $450 million in five stocks.

Stock	Investment (Millions)	Beta
1	$130	0.4
2	110	1.5
3	70	3.0
4	90	2.0
5	50	1.0
Total	$450	

What is the fund's overall, or weighted average, beta?

a. 1.14 **b.** 1.22 **c.** 1.35 **d.** 1.46 **e.** 1.53

8. Refer to Self-Test Problem 7. If the risk-free rate is 12 percent and the market risk premium is 6 percent, what is the required rate of return on the Apple Fund?

a. 20.76% **b.** 19.92% **c.** 18.81% **d.** 17.62% **e.** 15.77%

9. Stock A has a beta of 1.2, Stock B has a beta of 0.6, the expected rate of return on an average stock is 12 percent, and the risk-free rate of return is 7 percent. By how much does the required return on the riskier stock exceed the required return on the less risky stock?

a. 4.00% **b.** 3.25% **c.** 3.00% **d.** 2.50% **e.** 3.75%

10. You are managing a portfolio of 10 stocks that are held in equal dollar amounts. The current beta of the portfolio is 1.8, and the beta of Stock A is 2.0. If Stock A is sold and the proceeds are used to purchase a replacement stock, what does the beta of the replacement stock have to be to lower the portfolio beta to 1.7?

a. 1.4 **b.** 1.3 **c.** 1.2 **d.** 1.1 **e.** 1.0

11. Consider the following information for the Alachua Retirement Fund, with a total investment of $4 million.

Stock	Investment	Beta
A	$ 400,000	1.2
B	600,000	-0.4
C	1,000,000	1.5
D	2,000,000	0.8
Total	$4,000,000	

The market required rate of return is 12 percent, and the risk-free rate is 6 percent. What is its required rate of return?

a. 9.98% **b.** 10.45% **c.** 11.01% **d.** 11.50% **e.** 12.56%

12. You are given the following probability distribution of returns:

Probability	Return
0.4	$30
0.5	25
0.1	-20

What is the coefficient of variation of the expected dollar returns?

   a. 206.2500   **b.** 0.6383   **c.** 14.3614   **d.** 0.7500   **e.** 1.2500

13. If the risk-free rate is 8 percent, the expected return on the market is 13 percent, and the expected return on Security J is 15 percent, then what is the beta of Security J?

   a. 1.40   **b.** 0.90   **c.** 1.20   **d.** 1.50   **e.** 0.75

ANSWERS TO SELF-TEST QUESTIONS

1. Investment risk
2. outcomes; distribution
3. probability; return
4. continuous; discrete
5. standard deviation
6. coefficient of variation
7. risk averse
8. Capital Asset Pricing
9. correlation
10. correlation coefficient
11. Diversification; perfectly positively correlated
12. firm-specific (diversifiable or unsystematic); market (nondiversifiable or systematic)

13. beta
14. 2.0; half
15. weighted average
16. market risk premium
17. beta coefficient
18. risk-free; risk premium
19. inflation
20. slope
21. Risk
22. one
23. expected rate of return
24. smaller; lower
25. realized rate of return
26. Equilibrium
27. marginal

28. b. The Y-axis intercept of the SML is k_{RF}, which is the required rate of return of a security with a beta of zero.

29. b. A zero beta stock could be made riskless if it were combined with enough other zero beta stocks, but it would still have firm-specific risk and be risky when held in isolation.

30. a. By definition, if a stock has a beta of 1.0 it moves exactly with the market. In other words, if the market moves up by 7 percent, the stock will also move up by 7 percent, while if the market falls by 7 percent, the stock will fall by 7 percent.

31. b. Market risk is measured by the beta coefficient. The beta for the portfolio would be a weighted average of the betas of the stocks, so β_p would also be 1.0. Thus, the market risk for the portfolio would be the same as the market risk of the stocks in the portfolio.

32. a. Note that with a 200-stock portfolio, the actual returns would all be on or close to the regression line. However, when the portfolio (and the market) returns are quite high, some individual stocks would have higher returns than the portfolio, and some would have much lower returns. Thus, the range of returns, and the standard deviation, would be higher for the individual stocks.

33. b. RP_M, which is equal to $k_M - k_{RF}$, would rise, leading to an increase in k_M.

34. b. The required rate of return for a stock with $\beta = 0.5$ would increase less than for a stock with $\beta = 2.0$.

35. b. If the expected rate of inflation increased, the SML would shift parallel due to an increase in k_{RF}. Thus, the effect on the required rates of return for both the $\beta = 0.5$ and $\beta = 2.0$ stocks would be the same.

36. c. The best measure of risk is the beta coefficient, which is a measure of the extent to which the returns on a given stock move with the stock market.

37. c. The beta of the portfolio is a weighted average of the individual securities' betas, so it could not be less than the betas of all of the stocks.

38. a. The increase in inflation would cause the SML to shift up, and investors becoming more risk averse would cause the slope to increase.

39. e. Statement b is false because the slope of the SML is $k_M - k_{RF}$. Statement d is false because as investors become less risk averse the slope of the SML decreases. Statement a is correct because the financial manager has no control over k_M or k_{RF}. ($k_M - k_{RF} =$ slope and k_{RF} = intercept of the SML.) Statement c is correct because the slope of the regression line is beta and beta would be negative; thus, the required return would be less than the risk-free rate.

40. e. All the statements are false. For equilibrium to exist, the expected return must equal the required return.

ANSWERS TO SELF-TEST PROBLEMS

1. e. $\hat{k}_A = 0.1(-15\%) + 0.2(0\%) + 0.4(5\%) + 0.2(10\%) + 0.1(25\%) = 5.0\%$.

$$\begin{aligned} \text{Variance} = \sigma^2 &= 0.1(-0.15 - 0.05)^2 + 0.2(0.0 - 0.05)^2 + 0.4(0.05 - 0.05)^2 \\ &\quad + 0.2(0.10 - 0.05)^2 + 0.1(0.25 - 0.05)^2 \\ &= 0.009. \end{aligned}$$

Standard deviation $= \sigma = \sqrt{0.009} = 0.0949 \approx 9.5\%$.

2. d. $k_X = k_{RF} + (k_M - k_{RF}) \beta_X = 5\% + (11\% - 5\%)1.3 = 5\% + 6\%(1.3) = 12.8\%$.

3. c. $k_X = k_{RF} + (k_M - k_{RF}) \beta_X = 7\% + (6\%)1.3 = 14.8\%$.

    A change in the inflation premium does _not_ change the market risk premium $(k_M - k_{RF})$ $= 6\%$ since both k_M and k_{RF} are affected.

4. b. $k_X = k_{RF} + (k_M - k_{RF}) \beta_X = 5\% + (9\%)1.3 = 16.7\%$.

5. a. $k_X = k_{RF} + (k_M - k_{RF}) \beta_X = 7\% + (9\%)1.3 = 18.7\%$.

6. c. The calculation of the portfolio's beta is as follows: $\beta_p = (1/3)(0.5) + (1/3)(1.0) + (1/3)(1.5) = 1.0$.

7. d. $\beta_p = \displaystyle\sum_{j=1}^{5} w_j \beta_j$

    $$= \frac{\$130}{\$450}(0.4) + \frac{\$110}{\$450}(1.5) + \frac{\$70}{\$450}(3.0) + \frac{\$90}{\$450}(2.0) + \frac{\$50}{\$450}(1.0) = 1.46.$$

8. a. $k_p = k_{RF} + (k_M - k_{RF}) \beta_p = 12\% + (6\%)1.46 = 20.76\%$.

9. c. We know $\beta_A = 1.20$; $\beta_B = 0.60$; $k_M = 12\%$; and $k_{RF} = 7\%$.
    $k_j = k_{RF} + (k_M - k_{RF}) \beta_j = 7\% + (12\% - 7\%)\beta_j$.
    $k_A = 7\% + 5\%(1.20) = 13.0\%$.
    $k_B = 7\% + 5\%(0.60) = 10.0\%$.
    $k_A - k_B = 13\% - 10\% = 3\%$.

10. e. First find the beta of the remaining 9 stocks:

    $1.8 = 0.9(\beta_R) + 0.1(\beta_A)$
    $1.8 = 0.9(\beta_R) + 0.1(2.0)$
    $1.8 = 0.9(\beta_R) + 0.2$
    $1.6 = 0.9(\beta_R)$
    $\beta_R = 1.78$.

    Now find the beta of the new stock that produces $\beta_p = 1.7$.

    $1.7 = 0.9(1.78) + 0.1(\beta_N)$
    $1.7 = 1.6 + 0.1(\beta_N)$
    $0.1 = 0.1(\beta_N)$
    $\beta_N = 1.0$.

11. c. Determine the weight each stock represents in the portfolio:

Stock	Investment	w_j	Beta	$w_j \times$ Beta
A	$ 400,000	0.10	1.2	0.1200
B	600,000	0.15	-0.4	-0.0600
C	1,000,000	0.25	1.5	0.3750
D	2,000,000	0.50	0.8	0.4000

$$\beta_p = \underline{0.8350} = \text{Portfolio beta}$$

Write out the SML equation, and substitute known values including the portfolio beta. Solve for the required portfolio return.

$$k_p = k_{RF} + (k_M - k_{RF})\,\beta_p = 6\% + (12\% - 6\%)0.8350$$
$$= 6\% + 5.01\% = 11.01\%.$$

12. b. Use the given probability distribution of returns to calculate the expected value, variance, standard deviation, and coefficient of variation.

Pr_i	k_i		$Pr_i k_i$	k_i		$\hat{k}$		$(k_i - \hat{k})$	$(k_i - \hat{k})^2$	$Pr_i(k_i - \hat{k})^2$
0.4 ×	$30	=	$12.0	$30	−	$22.5	=	$ 7.5	56.25	$ 22.500
0.5 ×	25	=	12.5	25	−	22.5	=	2.5	6.25	3.125
0.1 ×	-20	=	-2.0	-20	−	22.5	=	-42.5	1,806.25	180.625
	$\hat{k}$	=	$22.5					σ^2 = Variance =		$206.250

The standard deviation (σ) of $\hat{k}$ is $\sqrt{\$206.25} = \$14.3614$.

Use the standard deviation and the expected return to calculate the coefficient of variation: $14.3614/$22.5 = 0.6383$.

13. a. Use the SML equation, substitute in the known values, and solve for beta.

$$k_{RF} = 8\%;\ k_M = 13\%;\ k_j = 15\%.$$

$$k_j = k_{RF} + (k_M - k_{RF})\beta_j$$
$$15\% = 8\% + (13\% - 8\%)\beta_j$$
$$7\% = (5\%)\beta_j$$
$$\beta_j = 1.4.$$

CHAPTER 12
THE COST OF CAPITAL

OVERVIEW

The cost of capital is a very important element in the capital budgeting process. The cost of capital is the average return required by the firm's investors—it is the firm's average cost of funds. The firm's cost of capital is very important because it represents the minimum rate of return that must be earned from investments to ensure the value of the firm does not decrease. The cost of capital is the firm's required rate of return.

This chapter focuses on the components of the cost of capital and the appropriate way to apply the cost of these components in making investment decisions. First, we discuss the logic behind the weighted average cost of capital (WACC). Next, the component costs of the capital structure are discussed and then used to determine the WACC. Then, the marginal cost of capital (MCC) schedule is developed. The MCC schedule is a step-function that increases as the need for capital surpasses certain limits. These limits occur at certain points known as break points. Finally, the MCC schedule is compared with an invest-ment opportunity schedule (IOS), which is a plot of the firm's potential projects arrayed in descending order of their rates of return. By combining the MCC and IOS schedules, a firm's optimal investment amount can be determined.

OUTLINE

Determining the firm's cost of capital, or the proper discount rate, for use in calculating the present value of the cash inflows for the firm's projects is an important element in making investment decisions. The cost of capital must reflect the average cost of the various sources of long-term funds used.

☐ The cost of capital used in capital budgeting to evaluate investment opportunities should be calculated as a weighted average, or combination, of the various types of funds generally used, regardless of the specific financing used to fund a particular project.

☐ *Capital components* are items on the right-hand side of the balance sheet such as debt, preferred stock, and common equity.
   ~ Any increase in total assets must be financed by an increase in one or more of these capital components.

☐ *Capital* is a necessary factor of production, and, like any other factor, it has a cost.

☐ Each element of capital has a *component cost* that can be identified as follows:
- ~ k_d = interest rate on the firm's new debt, before tax.
- ~ $k_d(1 - T) = k_{dT}$, or the after-tax cost of debt, where T is the firm's marginal tax rate.
- ~ k_{ps} = component cost of preferred stock.
- ~ k_s = component cost of retained earnings (or internal equity); it is equal to the required rate of return on common stock.
- ~ k_e = cost of external equity obtained by issuing new common stock as opposed to retained earnings; it must be distinguished from equity raised through retained earnings due to the flotation costs incurred when new stock is issued.
- ~ WACC = the weighted average cost of capital.

☐ *Capital structure* is the combination or mix of different types of capital used by a firm.

The cost of each capital component used to calculate the WACC can be determined as follows:

☐ The *after-tax cost of debt, k_{dT},* is defined as the interest rate on debt, k_d, less the tax savings that result because interest is tax deductible: $k_d(1 - T)$.
- ~ For example, if a firm has a tax rate of 40 percent and can borrow at a rate of 10 percent, then its after-tax cost of debt is $k_{dT} = 10\%(1 - 0.40) = 10\%(0.60) = 6.0\%$.
- ~ The tax deductibility of interest payments has the effect of causing the federal government to pay part of the interest charges.
- ~ We are concerned with after-tax cash flows, so after-tax rates of return are appropriate.
- ~ k_d is the interest rate on new debt, not that on already outstanding debt. We are interested in the marginal cost of debt.
  - • Our primary concern with the cost of capital is to use it for investment decisions.
  - • The rate at which the firm has borrowed in the past is a sunk cost, and it is irrelevant for cost of capital purposes.

☐ The component *cost of preferred stock, k_{ps},* is the rate of return investors require on the firm's preferred stock.
- ~ It is calculated as the preferred dividend, D_{ps}, divided by the net issuing price, NP, or the price the firm receives after deducting flotation, or issuing, costs: $k_{ps} = D_{ps}/NP = D_{ps}/(P_0 - \text{Flotation costs})$.
- ~ No tax adjustments are made when calculating k_{ps} because preferred dividends, unlike interest expense on debt, are not tax deductible, so there are no tax savings associated with the use of preferred stock.

☐ The *cost of retained earnings, k_s,* is the rate of return stockholders require on equity capital the firm obtains by retaining earnings that otherwise could be distributed to common stockholders as dividends.
- ~ Assigning a cost to retained earnings is based on the *opportunity cost principle.*
- ~ The firm's after-tax earnings belong to its stockholders, and these earnings serve to compensate stockholders for the use of their capital.
- ~ The firm must earn a return on earnings it retains that is at least as great as the

stockholders themselves could earn on alternative investments of comparable risk.
~ If the firm cannot invest retained earnings and earn at least k_s, it should pay these funds to its stockholders and let them invest directly in other assets that do provide this return.

☐ There are three methods commonly used for finding the cost of retained earnings.
~ The *Capital Asset Pricing Model (CAPM)* works as follows:
- Estimate the risk-free rate, k_{RF}, usually based on U.S. Treasury securities.
- Estimate the stock's beta coefficient as an index of risk.
- Estimate the expected rate of return on the market, or on an "average" stock, k_M.
- Substitute the preceding values into the CAPM equation, $k_s = k_{RF} + (k_M - k_{RF})\beta_s$, to estimate the required rate of return on the stock in question.
- If $k_{RF} = 8\%$, $k_M = 13\%$, and the beta is 0.7, then $k_s = 8\% + (13\% - 8\%)0.7 = 11.5\%$.
~ Although the CAPM appears to yield an accurate estimate of k_s, there actually are several problems with it.
- If stockholders are not well diversified, they might be concerned with total risk rather than with market risk; in this case the firm's true investment risk will not be measured by its beta, and the CAPM will understate the correct value of k_s.
- It is difficult to obtain correct estimates of the inputs. There is controversy about whether to use long-term or short-term Treasury yields for k_{RF} and both beta and k_M should be estimated values, which often are difficult to obtain.
~ The required rate of return, k_s, may also be estimated by the *discounted cash flow (DCF) approach*. This approach combines the expected dividend yield, $\hat{D}_1/P_0$, with the expected future growth rate, g, of earnings and dividends, or

$$k_s = \hat{k}_s = \frac{\hat{D}_1}{P_0} + \text{Expected g}.$$

- The DCF approach assumes that stocks are normally in equilibrium and that growth is expected to be at a constant rate. If growth is not constant, then a nonconstant growth model must be used.
- The expected growth rate may be based on projections of past growth rates, if they have been relatively stable, or on expected future growth rates as estimated in some other manner.
- If the firm's next expected dividend is $1.24, its expected growth rate is 8 percent per year, and its stock is selling for $23 per share, then

$$k_s = \hat{k}_s = \frac{\$1.24}{\$23} + 8.0\% = 13.4\%.$$

~ The *bond-yield-plus-risk-premium approach* estimates k_s by adding a risk premium of three to five percentage points to the interest rate on the firm's own long-term debt. Thus, $k_s = \text{Bond yield} + \text{Risk premium}$.
- If the firm uses a risk premium of 4 percentage points, and the interest rate on its

long-term debt is 9 percent, then $k_s = 9\% + 4\% = 13\%$.

- It is logical to think that firms with risky, low-rated, and consequently, high-interest-rate debt will also have risky, high-cost equity.
- Because the risk premium is a judgmental estimate, this method is not likely to produce a precise cost of equity; however, it does get us "into the right ballpark."

~ It is recommended that all three approaches be used in estimating the required rate of return on common stock.

- It is not unusual to get different estimates, because each of the approaches is based on different assumptions—the CAPM assumes investors are well diversified, the constant growth model assumes the firm's dividends and earnings will grow at a constant rate far into the future, and the bond-yield-plus-risk-premium approach assumes the cost of equity is closely related to the firm's cost of debt.
- When the methods produce widely different results, judgment must be used in selecting the best estimate. People experienced in estimating equity capital costs recognize that both careful analysis and sound judgment are required.

☐ The *cost of new common equity, k_e,* or external equity capital, is higher than the cost of retained earnings, k_s, because there is a cost to issuing new stock.

~ *Flotation costs* are the expenses incurred when selling new issues of securities.

~ To allow for flotation costs, F, we must adjust the DCF formula for the required rate of return as follows:

$$k_e = \frac{\hat{D}_1}{NP} + g = \frac{\hat{D}_1}{P_0(1-F)} + g.$$

- $P_0(1 - F)$ is the net price per share received by the company.
~ If the firm has a flotation cost of 10 percent, its cost of new outside equity is computed as follows:

$$k_e = \frac{\$1.24}{\$23(1-0.10)} + 8.0\% = 14.0\%.$$

- In this example, if the firm can earn 14 percent on investments financed by new common stock, then earnings, dividends, and the growth rate will be maintained, and the price per share will not fall. If it earns more than 14 percent, the price will rise; while if it earns less, the price will fall.

The target proportions of debt, preferred stock, and common equity, along with the component costs of capital, are used to calculate the firm's weighted average cost of capital (WACC).

☐ The *target (optimal) capital structure* is the percentage of debt, preferred stock, and common equity that will maximize the price of the firm's stock.

☐ The *weighted average cost of capital (WACC)* is a weighted average of the component costs of debt, preferred stock, and common equity.

~ The WACC represents the minimum return the firm needs to earn with its existing assets to ensure wealth is maintained.

☐ The calculation of the weighted average cost of capital is shown below for a firm that finances 30 percent with debt, 10 percent with preferred stock, and 60 percent with common equity and that has the following after-tax component costs:

Component	Weight	×	After-tax Cost	=	Weighted Cost
Debt	0.30	×	8.4%	=	2.52%
Preferred	0.10	×	12.6	=	1.26
Common	0.60	×	16.0	=	9.60
				WACC =	13.38%

☐ In more general terms, and in equation format,

$$WACC = w_d k_{dT} + w_{ps} k_{ps} + w_s (k_s \text{ or } k_e).$$

☐ If the component costs of capital change when new funds are raised in the future, then WACC changes.

☐ The capital structure that minimizes a firm's weighted average cost of capital also maximizes its stock price.

The marginal cost of capital (MCC) is defined as the cost of the last dollar of new capital that the firm raises, and the marginal cost rises as more and more capital is raised during a given period.

☐ Firms raise capital in accordance with their target capital structures.

☐ As companies raise larger and larger sums during a given time period, the component costs begin to rise. This causes an increase in the weighted average cost of each additional dollar of new capital. Companies cannot raise unlimited amounts of capital at a constant cost. At some point, the cost of each new dollar will increase, no matter what its source.

☐ A graph that relates the firm's weighted average cost of each dollar of capital to the total amount of new capital raised is the *marginal cost of capital (MCC) schedule*.

☐ Suppose that a firm needs $500,000 in new capital. Its capital structure is 60 percent common equity, 30 percent debt, and 10 percent preferred stock, and its marginal tax rate is 40 percent. The before-tax cost of debt is 14 percent, and the cost of preferred stock is 12.6 percent. The firm will need to raise 0.6($500,000) = $300,000 in common equity. It expects retained earnings for the year to be $100,000; therefore, it needs to sell $300,000 − $100,000 = $200,000 of new common stock. The cost of retained earnings is 16.0 percent, but the cost of new equity is 16.8 percent. The average cost of capital, using new equity, is

$$\text{WACC} = w_d k_{dT} + w_{ps} k_{ps} + w_s k_e$$
$$= 0.3(14\%)(0.60) + 0.1(12.6\%) + 0.6(16.8\%) = 13.86\%.$$

☐ The point at which the marginal cost of capital increases is called a *break point (BP)*. A break point is defined as the dollars of new total capital that can be raised before an increase in the firm's weighted average cost of capital occurs.

~ The retained earnings break point is calculated as Retained earnings/Equity proportion.

~ For the firm discussed above, this break point is $100,000/0.6 = $166,667. That is, when $166,667 of new capital is raised, the firm will have used 0.6($166,667) = $100,000 of retained earnings. After that, more costly new common equity must be used.

~ Other break points for the other capital components can be calculated in a similar manner.

☐ In general, a break point will occur in the MCC schedule whenever the cost of one of the capital components increases.

~ The break point is determined by the following equation:

$$\text{Break point} = \frac{\text{Maximum amount of lower - cost capital of a given type}}{\text{Proportion of this type of capital in the capital structure}}.$$

·· If there are no break points, there will be one WACC. If there are n break points, there will be n + 1 different WACCs.

·· Numerous break points can occur.

● At the limit, we can even think of an MCC schedule with so many break points that it rises almost continuously beyond some given level of new financing.

☐ For ease in calculating the MCC schedule, first identify the points where breaks occur, then determine the cost of capital for each component in the intervals between the breaks, and, finally, calculate the weighted averages of these component costs to obtain the WACCs for each interval.

The optimal capital budget and a firm's marginal cost of capital are interrelated.

☐ Investments should be made only if the returns they are expected to generate are greater than the cost of capital (WACC) that is associated with the level of financing needed to make the investments.

☐ The *investment opportunity schedule (IOS)* is a graph of the firm's investment opportunities ranked in order of the projects' rates of return.

~ The IOS schedule shows, in rank order, how much money a firm could invest at different rates of return.

☐ The intersection of the IOS and MCC schedules determines the cost of capital that is used in investment decisions.

~ This discount rate is influenced both by the shape of the MCC curve and by the set of available projects.

~ If the cost of capital at the intersection is used, then the firm will make correct investment decisions, and its level of financing and investment will be optimal.

☐ The discount rate determined by the intersection of the MCC curve and IOS curve should be used to make investment decisions concerning new projects that are as risky as the firm's existing assets, but this corporate cost of capital should be adjusted upward or downward when investments with higher or lower risk than the average project are being evaluated.

Most firms incorporate project risk in investment decisions by adjusting the required rate of return used to evaluate projects that have risks substantially different from the firm's average risk.

☐ Average-risk projects would require an average rate of return, which would be the firm's WACC; above-average risk projects would require a higher-than-average rate; and below-average risk projects would require a lower-than-average rate.

~ Risk adjustments are necessarily judgmental and somewhat arbitrary.

☐ Many companies use a two-step procedure to develop risk-adjusted WACCs to make investment decisions.

~ The WACC is determined, and this rate is considered the required rate of return that should be used to evaluate projects whose risk is similar to the firm's existing assets.

~ All projects generally are classified into three categories—high risk, average risk, and low risk. Adjustments to the WACC are made accordingly.

☐ If project risk is not considered when evaluating investments, incorrect decisions are possible.

☐ The process for adjusting the WACC for risk isn't precise, but it recognizes that different projects have different risks, and projects with different risks should be evaluated using different required rates of return.

SELF-TEST QUESTIONS

Definitional

1. The firm should calculate its cost of capital as a(n) _____ _____ of the after-tax costs of the various types of funds it uses.

2. Capital components are items on the right-hand side of the balance sheet such as the following: (1) _____, (2) _____ _____, and (3) _____ _____.

3. The cost of retained earnings is defined as the _____ ____ _____ stockholders require on equity capital the firm obtains by retaining earnings that otherwise could be distributed to common stockholders as dividends.

4. The component cost of preferred stock is calculated as the _____ _____ divided by the _____ _____ _____.

5. There are _____ methods commonly used for finding the cost of retained earnings.

6. Assigning a cost to retained earnings is based on the _____ _____ principle.

7. The cost of external equity capital is higher than the cost of retained earnings due to _____ _____.

8. Using the Capital Asset Pricing Model (CAPM), the required rate of return on common stock is found as a function of the _____-_____ _____, the firm's _____ _____, and the required rate of return on an average _____.

9. The cost of common equity may also be found by adding a(n) _____ _____ to the interest rate on the firm's own _____-_____ _____.

10. The required rate of return may also be estimated as the expected _____ _____ on the common stock plus the expected future _____ _____ of the earnings and dividends.

11. The proportions of _____, _____ _____, and _____ _____ in the target capital structure should be used to calculate the _____ _____ cost of capital.

12. The _____ cost of capital is defined as the cost of the last dollar of new capital that the firm raises.

13. A graph that relates the firm's weighted average cost of each dollar of capital to the total amount of new capital raised is the _____ _____ ____ _____ _____.

14. A(n) _____ _____ is defined as the dollars of new total capital that can be raised before an increase in the firm's weighted average cost of capital occurs.

15. The _____ _____ _____ graphs a firm's investment opportunities ranked in order of the projects' _____ ____ _____.

16. The intersection of the IOS and MCC schedules determines the _____ ____ _____ that is used in investment decisions.

17. _____ is a necessary factor of production, and, like any other factor, it has a cost.

18.   _____ _____ is the combination or mix of different types of capital used by a firm.

19.   _____ _____ are items on the right-hand side of the balance sheet.

20.   The _____-_____ _____ ____ _____ is defined as the interest rate on debt less the tax savings that result because interest is tax deductible.

21. k_d is the interest rate on _____ debt, not that on already _____ debt.

22.   The rate at which the firm has borrowed in the past is a(n) _____ _____, and it is irrelevant for cost of capital purposes.

23.   No _____ _____ are made when calculating k_{ps} because preferred dividends, unlike interest expense on debt, are not tax deductible, so there are no tax savings associated with the use of preferred stock.

24.   The cost of new common equity, or external equity capital, is _____ than the cost of retained earnings because there is a cost to issuing new stock.

25.   The WACC represents the _____ return the firm needs to earn with its existing assets to ensure wealth is maintained.

Conceptual

26.   If a firm obtains all of its common equity from retained earnings, its MCC schedule would always be flat; that is, there would be no break points.

       a. True   b. False

27.   If there are n break points in the MCC schedule, there will be n + 1 different WACCs.

       a. True   b. False

28.   Funds acquired by the firm through preferred stock have a cost to the firm equal to the preferred dividend divided by the price investors paid for one share.

       a. True   b. False

29.   Which of the following statements could be true concerning the costs of debt and equity?

       a. The cost of debt for Firm A is greater than the cost of equity for Firm A.
       b. The cost of debt for Firm A is greater than the cost of equity for Firm B.
       c. The cost of retained earnings for Firm A is less than its cost of external equity.

    d. The cost of retained earnings for Firm A is less than its cost of debt.

    e. Statements b and c could both be true.

30. Which of the following statements is correct?

    a. If Congress raised the corporate tax rate, this would lower the effective cost of debt but probably would also reduce the amount of retained earnings available to corporations, so the effect on the marginal cost of capital is uncertain.

    b. For corporate investors, 70 percent of the dividends received on both common and preferred stocks is exempt from taxes. However, neither preferred dividends nor common dividends are tax deductible by the issuing company. Therefore, the dividend exclusion has no effect on a company's cost of capital, and its WACC would probably not change at all if the dividend exclusion rule was rescinded by Congress.

    c. Normally, an MCC schedule is drawn with an upward slope, reflecting the fact that as more capital is raised, the cost of capital increases. However, if the firm uses a lot of short-term debt, then its MCC schedule could, according to the text, have a U shape.

    d. Each of the above statements is correct.

    e. Each of the above statements is false.

31. Which of the following statements is correct?

    a. If a firm that has income and pays dividends estimates its MCC schedule on out to a very large amount of new capital, there will always be at least one break in the MCC, due to running out of retained earnings. However, once the IOS is considered, then, for capital budgeting purposes, the MCC may turn out to be constant over the range of funds the company will actually raise; that is, there will be only one relevant WACC.

    b. If there is more than one break in the MCC, we can be absolutely sure that the firm's investment bankers have told it that if it wants to sell more than some given amount of new stock, the flotation costs on new stock issues will rise.

    c. As the situation was explained in the text, the firm's WACC should be calculated using constant weights for debt, preferred, and common equity as long as all equity comes from retained earnings, but if new common stock must be sold, then the weight used for equity must be increased.

    d. The MCC-IOS concept is used by firms as they make plans for some future period. Further, we know that the WACC will eventually increase if the firm uses larger and larger amounts of capital during a given year, which means that the MCC can rise. If this situation occurs, then higher-return projects, which will be financed with the earlier, low-cost capital, should use a lower WACC than that used for later projects.

    e. All of the above statements are false.

32. Which of the following statements is correct?

    a. Dividends must be paid with after-tax dollars, but interest is paid with before-tax dollars. This situation encourages corporations to finance with stock rather than with debt.

    b. If a company accepts a new project that is expected to earn exactly the cost of the capital used to finance it, then the investment decision should not affect the value of the firm's stock.

    c. The cost of retained earnings is higher than the cost of newly issued common equity because of the taxes that must be paid on income before earnings are available for retention.

    d. Since the CAPM cost of common equity is affected by the interest rate on Treasury securities, if interest rates in the economy rise sharply, then the CAPM estimate of the cost of equity should, in theory, rise to a level above the DCF cost estimate if equilibrium is to exist.

    e. Statements a, b, c, and d are all correct.

33. Which of the following statements is correct?

    a. Holding other things constant, an increase in the corporate tax rate would generally increase the WACC for a company that uses no debt.

    b. Holding other things constant, an increase in the corporate tax rate would generally lower the WACC for a company that uses no debt.

    c. Other things held constant, changes in the corporate tax rate would generally have no effect on a company's WACC, regardless of its use of debt.

    d. According to the text, new retained earnings are generated from income after the payment of taxes, but new common stock issues do not require the payment of income taxes. Therefore, an increase in the corporate tax rate would have a greater impact on the cost of retained earnings (k_s) than on the cost of equity obtained by selling new stock (k_e).

    e. Statements a, b, c, and d are all false.

34. The first break point in the WACC:

    a. Always results from using up retained earnings.

    b. Always results from using up cheap debt.

    c. Depends jointly on the capital structure and the amount of each type of low-cost funds that are available.

    d. Assuming net income is held constant, the first break point is directly affected by the tax rate because the cost of debt is reduced due to the deductibility of interest.

    e. Both statements c and d are correct.

SELF-TEST PROBLEMS

1. Roland Corporation's last dividend (D_0), which was paid yesterday, was $2.50. The firm has maintained a constant payout ratio of 50 percent during the past 7 years. Seven years ago its EPS was $1.50. The firm's beta coefficient is 1.2. The required return on an average stock in the market is 13 percent, and the risk-free rate is 7 percent. Roland's A-rated bonds are yielding 10 percent, and its current stock price is $30. Which of the following values is the most reasonable estimate of Roland's cost of retained earnings, k_s?

   a. 10%   **b.** 12%   **c.** 14%   **d.** 20%   **e.** 26%

2. The director of capital budgeting for See-Saw Inc., manufacturers of playground equipment, is considering a plan to expand production facilities in order to meet an increase in demand. He estimates that this expansion will produce a rate of return of 11 percent. The firm's target capital structure calls for a debt/equity ratio of 0.8. See-Saw currently has a bond issue outstanding that will mature in 25 years and has a 7 percent annual coupon rate. The bonds are currently selling for $804. The firm has maintained a constant growth rate of 6 percent. See-Saw's next expected dividend is $2 and its current stock price is $40. Its marginal tax rate is 40 percent. Should it undertake the expansion? (Assume that there is no preferred stock outstanding and that any new debt will have a 25-year maturity.)

   a. No; the expected return is 2.5 percentage points lower than the cost of capital.
   b. No; the expected return is 1.0 percentage points lower than the cost of capital.
   c. Yes; the expected return is 0.5 percentage points higher than the cost of capital.
   d. Yes; the expected return is 1.0 percentage points higher than the cost of capital.
   e. Yes; the expected return is 2.5 percentage points higher than the cost of capital.

3. Midterm Corporation's present capital structure, which is also its target capital structure, calls for 50 percent debt and 50 percent common equity. The firm has only one potential project, an expansion program with a 10.2 percent rate of return and a cost of $20 million but which is completely divisible; that is, Midterm can invest any amount up to $20 million. Midterm expects to retain $3 million of earnings next year. It can raise up to $5 million in new debt at a before-tax cost of 8 percent, and all debt after the first $5 million will have a cost of 10 percent. The cost of retained earnings is 12 percent; Midterm can sell any amount of new common stock desired at a constant cost of new equity of 15 percent. The firm's marginal tax rate is 40 percent. What is Midterm's optimal investment amount?

   a. $0 million   **b.** $5 million   **c.** $6 million   **d.** $10 million   **e.** $20 million

4. The management of Florida Phosphate Industries (FPI) is planning next year's investments. FPI projects net income of $10,500, and its payout ratio is 40 percent. The company's earnings and dividends are growing at a constant rate of 5 percent. The last dividend, D_0, was $0.90; and the current equilibrium stock price is $8.59. FPI can raise up to $10,000 of debt at a 12 percent before-tax cost, the next $10,000 will cost 14

percent, and all debt after $20,000 will cost 16 percent. If FPI issues new common stock, a 10 percent flotation cost will be incurred on the first $16,000 issued, while flotation costs will be 20 percent on all new stock issued after the first $16,000. FPI is at its optimal capital structure, which is 40 percent debt and 60 percent equity, and the firm's marginal tax rate is 40 percent. FPI has the following independent, indivisible, and equally risky investment opportunities:

Project	Cost	Rate of Return
A	$15,000	17%
B	15,000	16
C	12,000	15
D	20,000	14

What is FPI's optimal investment level?

a. $62,000   b. $42,000   c. $30,000   d. $15,000   e. $0

5. Gator Products Company (GPC) is at its optimal capital structure of 70 percent common equity and 30 percent debt. GPC's MCC and IOS schedules for next year intersect at a 14 percent marginal cost of capital. At the intersection, the IOS schedule is vertical and the MCC schedule is horizontal. GPC has a marginal tax rate of 40 percent. Next year's dividend is expected to be $2.00 per share, and GPC has a constant growth in earnings and dividends of 6 percent. The after-tax cost of equity used in the MCC at the intersection is based on new equity with a flotation cost of 10 percent, while the before-tax cost of debt is 12 percent. What is GPC's current equilibrium stock price?

1. $12.73   b. $17.23   c. $20.37   d. $23.70   e. $37.20

(The following information applies to the next two Self-Test Problems.)

Sun Products Company (SPC) uses only debt and equity. It can borrow unlimited amounts at an interest rate of 12 percent as long as it finances at its target capital structure, which calls for 45 percent debt and 55 percent common equity. Its last dividend was $2.40, its expected constant growth rate is 5 percent, its stock sells for $30 per share, and new stock would net the company $24 per share after flotation costs. SPC's marginal tax rate is 40 percent, and it expects to have $120 million of retained earnings this year. Two projects are available: Project A has a cost of $240 million and a rate of return of 13 percent, while Project B has a cost of $150 million and a rate of return of 10 percent. All of the company's potential projects are equally risky.

6. What is SPC's cost of equity from newly issued stock?

a. 15.50%   b. 13.40%   c. 7.20%   d. 12.50%   e. 16.00%

7. What is SPC's marginal cost of capital? In other words, what WACC should it use to evaluate investment projects (these two projects plus any others that might arise during the year, provided the cost of capital schedule remains as it is currently)?

a. 12.05%   b. 13.40%   c. 11.77%   d. 12.50%   e. 10.61%

8. A company's 7 percent coupon rate, semiannual payment, $1,000 par value bond that matures in 40 years sells at a price of $600. The company's marginal tax rate is 34 percent. What is the firm's component cost of debt for purposes of calculating the WACC? (Hint: Base your answer on the simple rate, not the EAR.)

    a. 8.67%   **b.** 7.24%   **c.** 7.76%   **d.** 11.75%   **e.** 11.42%

9. Stacy Paints Corporation has a target capital structure of 50 percent debt and 50 percent common equity. The company expects to have $500 of after-tax income during the coming year, and it plans to retain 60 percent of its earnings. The current stock price is $P_0 = \$32$; the last dividend was $D_0 = \$2.10$; and the dividend is expected to grow at a constant rate of 8 percent. New stock can be sold at a flotation cost of $F = 25\%$. What will Stacy Paint's marginal cost of equity capital (not the WACC) be if it raises a total of $700 of new capital?

    a. 15.09%   **b.** 16.51%   **c.** 17.45%   **d.** 16.25%   **e.** 17.18%

ANSWERS TO SELF-TEST QUESTIONS

1. weighted average
2. debt; preferred stock; common equity
3. rate of return
4. preferred dividend; net issuing price
5. three
6. opportunity cost
7. flotation costs
8. risk-free rate (k_{RF}); beta coefficient (β); stock (k_M)
9. risk premium; long-term debt
10. dividend yield; growth rate
11. debt; preferred stock; common equity; weighted average
12. marginal

13. marginal cost of capital (MCC) schedule
14. break point
15. investment opportunity schedule (IOS); rates of return
16. cost of capital
17. Capital
18. Capital structure
19. Capital components
20. after-tax cost of debt
21. new; outstanding
22. sunk cost
23. tax adjustments
24. higher
25. minimum

26. b. The component cost of debt and/or preferred equity might increase, thus causing break points in the MCC schedule.

27. a. This statement is correct.

28. b. Flotation costs must be subtracted from the investor's cost to get the net issuing price, which is then used to calculate the cost of preferred stock.

29. e. If Firm A has more business risk than Firm B, Firm A's cost of debt could be greater than Firm B's cost of equity. Also, the cost of retained earnings is less than the cost of external equity because of flotation costs.

30. a. Statement a is correct. If Congress were to raise the tax rate, this would lower the cost of debt; however, a bigger chunk of the firm's earnings would go to Uncle Sam. The effect on the MCC would depend on which had the greater effect on the MCC. Statement b is false. Preferred stock generally has a lower before-tax cost than debt due to the dividend exclusion; however, if the dividend exclusion were omitted, preferred stock would have an increased cost. Statement c is false because short-term debt is not considered in the MCC schedule. The MCC schedule is usually drawn as a step function; however, at some point numerous break points would occur and the MCC would rise almost continuously beyond some level of new financing.

31. a. Statement a is true. Statement b is false; breaks in the MCC can occur due to increased costs at different levels of debt and/or preferred stock financing. Statement c is false; the weights used in calculating the WACC depend on the (optimal) capital structure used and do not change because retained earnings are used up and new equity must be used. Statement d is false because the intersection of the MCC and IOS curves determines the WACC that should be used in evaluating all average-risk projects.

32. b. Statement b is correct. If a project's return exceeds its cost of capital, the value of the firm, and the stock price, will rise, and vice versa if the project's return is less than the cost of capital. Therefore, if the project's return is just equal to the cost of the capital used to finance it, accepting the project should have no effect on the value of the stock. The other statements are all false. Note that an increase in interest rates will cause the CAPM cost of equity to rise, but the interest rate increase would also cause the DCF cost to increase. The stock price would decline, causing the dividend yield to increase. Equilibrium requires the two cost of equity estimates to be equal.

33. e. Statement e is true because the other statements are all false. Recall that the component cost of debt for use in the WACC is $k_d(1 - T)$. Therefore, an increase in the tax rate would, other things held constant, decrease the WACC for a company that uses debt.

34. c. Look at the break point formula; it is obvious that the capital structure and the amount of low-cost funds of each type affect the break point. The tax rate affects the after-tax cost of debt, but it does not directly affect the break point, so statement d is incorrect. Therefore, statement c is the correct response.

SOLUTIONS TO SELF-TEST PROBLEMS

1. c. Use all three methods to estimate k_s.

CAPM: $k_s = k_{RF} + (k_M - k_{RF})\beta = 7\% + (13\% - 7\%)1.2 = 14.2\%$.

Risk Premium: k_s = Bond yield + Risk premium = 10% + 4% = 14%.

DCF: $k_s = D_0(1 + g)/P_0 + g = \$2.50(1 + g)/\$30 + g$, where g can be estimated as follows using a financial calculator:
N = 7, PV = -0.75, PMT = 0, FV = 2.50, and solve for I = g = 18.77%.

Thus k, which is the compound growth rate, g, is about 18.8%. Therefore, k_s = $2.50(1.188)/$30 + 0.188 = 0.099 + 0.188 = 28.7%.

Roland Corporation has apparently been experiencing supernormal growth during the past 7 years, and it is not reasonable to assume that this growth will continue. The first two methods yield a k_s of about 14 percent, which appears reasonable.

2. **e.** Cost of equity = k_s = $2/$40 + 0.06 = 0.11 = 11%.

Cost of debt = k_d = Yield to maturity on outstanding bonds based on current market price.

The approximate yield to maturity is:

$$\text{pproximate YTM} = \frac{\$70 + \left(\dfrac{\$1{,}000 - \$804}{25}\right)}{\left[\dfrac{2(\$804) + \$1{,}000}{3}\right]} = \frac{\$77.84}{\$869.33} \approx 9\%.$$

Alternatively, with a financial calculator: Input N = 25, PV = -804, PMT = 70, FV = 1000, and solve for I = k_d = 9%.

In determining the capital structure weights, note that debt/equity = 0.8 or, for example, 4/5. Therefore, debt/assets is

$$\frac{D}{A} = \frac{\text{Debt}}{\text{Debt} + \text{Equity}} = \frac{4}{4+5} = \frac{4}{9},$$

and equity/assets = 5/9. Hence, the weighted average cost of capital is calculated as follows:

$$\begin{aligned} \text{WACC} &= [k_d(1 - T)](D/A) + k_s(1 - D/A) \\ &= [0.09(1 - 0.4)](4/9) + 0.11(5/9) \\ &= 0.024 + 0.061 \\ &= 0.085 = 8.5\%. \end{aligned}$$

The cost of capital is 8.5 percent, while the expansion project's rate of return is 11.0 percent. Since the expected return is 2.5 percentage points higher than the cost, the expansion should be undertaken.

3. d. First, look only at debt (in millions of dollars):

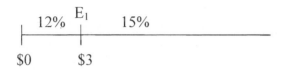

Now, look only at equity (in millions of dollars):

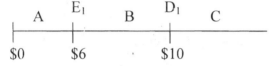

Now combine debt and equity and look at total capital (in millions of dollars):

The break points are calculated as follows:
$E_1 = \$3,000,000/0.5 = \$6,000,000.$
$D_1 = \$5,000,000/0.5 = \$10,000,000.$

Now, determine the weighted average cost of capital for intervals A, B, and C:

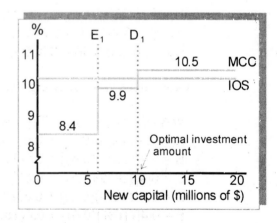

$\text{WACC} = w_d[(k_d)(1 - T)] + w_s(k_s \text{ or } k_e).$
$A = 0.5[(8\%)(0.6)] + 0.5(12\%) = 8.4\%.$
$B = 0.5[(8\%)(0.6)] + 0.5(15\%) = 9.9\%.$
$C = 0.5[(10\%)(0.6)] + 0.5(15\%) = 10.5\%.$

Finally, graph the IOS and MCC schedules.

Thus, the optimal investment amount is $10 million.

4. b. First look only at debt:

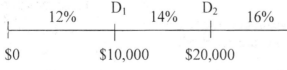

Now, look only at equity:

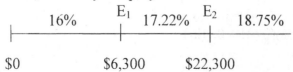

Retained earnings are forecast to be $10,500(0.6) = $6,300. The cost of retained earnings is as follows:

$$k_s = \frac{D_0\,(1+g)}{P_0} + g = \frac{\$0.90(1.05)}{\$8.59} + 0.05 = 0.16 = 16.0\%.$$

The cost of new equity is as follows:

$$k_{e1} = \frac{D_0\,(1+g)}{P_0\,(1-F)} + g = \frac{\$0.90(1.05)}{\$8.59(1-0.10)} + 0.05 = 0.1722 = 17.22\%.$$

$$k_{e2} = \frac{\$0.90(1.05)}{\$8.59(1-0.20)} + 0.05 = 0.1875 = 18.75\%.$$

Now, combine debt and equity and look at total capital:

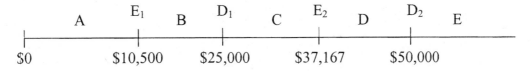

The break points are calculated as follows:
$E_1 = \$6,300/0.60 = \$10,500.$
$D_1 = \$10,000/0.40 = \$25,000.$
$E_2 = \$22,300/0.60 = \$37,167.$
$D_2 = \$20,000/0.40 = \$50,000.$

Now, determine the weighted average cost of capital for intervals A through E:

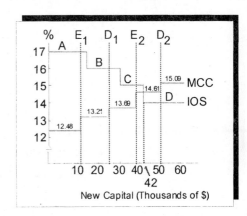

WACC = $w_d[(k_d)(1 - T)] + w_s(k_s$ or $k_e).$
A = $0.4[(12\%)(0.6)] + 0.6(16.00\%) = 12.48\%.$
B = $0.4[(12\%)(0.6)] + 0.6(17.22\%) = 13.21\%.$
C = $0.4[(14\%)(0.6)] + 0.6(17.22\%) = 13.69\%.$
D = $0.4[(14\%)(0.6)] + 0.6(18.75\%) = 14.61\%.$
E = $0.4[(16\%)(0.6)] + 0.6(18.75\%) = 15.09\%.$

Finally, graph the MCC and IOS schedules.

Therefore, the optimal investment amount is $42,000. Projects A, B, and C are accepted.

5.   c.   At the intersection of the IOS and MCC schedules, WACC = 14%. Therefore,

$$\text{WACC} = 14\% = w_d[(k_d)(1 - T)] + w_s(k_e)$$
$$14\% = 0.3[(12\%)(0.6)] + 0.7(k_e)$$
$$k_e = 16.91\%.$$

Now, at equilibrium:

$$\hat{k}_e = k_e = \frac{D_1}{P_0(1-F)} + g$$

$$0.1691 = \frac{\$2.00}{P_0(1-0.10)} + 0.06$$

$$0.1091 = \frac{\$2.222}{P_0}$$

$$P_0 = \$20.37.$$

6.   a. $k_e = [\$2.40(1.05)]/\$24 + 5\% = 0.1050 + 0.05 = 0.1550 = 15.50\%.$

7.   c. $k_d = 12\%; k_d(1 - T) = 12\%(0.6) = 7.2\%.$

$k_s = [\$2.40(1.05)]/\$30 + 5\% = 13.40\%.$

$k_e = 15.50\%.$ (From Self-Test Problem #6.)

RE = \$120 million; D/A = 45\%; E/A = 55\%; $BP_{RE} = \$120/0.55 = \$218.18$ million.

0 − \$218.18 million: $WACC_1 = 0.45(7.2\%) + 0.55(13.40\%) = 10.61\%.$

> \$218.18 million: $WACC_2 = 0.45(7.2\%) + 0.55(15.50\%) = 11.77\%.$

8.   c. Enter these values into a financial calculator: N = 80, PV = -600, PMT = 35, FV = 1000, and press I to get I = 5.8745% = periodic rate. The nominal rate is 5.8745%(2) = 11.75%, and the after-tax component cost of debt is 11.75%(0.66) = 7.76%.

9.   . 50% = Debt, 50% = Equity, NI = \$500, Retain 60%.

$P_0 = \$32$, $D_0 = \$2.10$, g = 8\%, $D_1 = \$2.268$, and F = 25\%. RE = \$500(0.6) = \$300.

RE_{BP} = RE/Equity ratio = \$300/0.5 = \$600.

At total capital of \$700, retained earnings will have been used up, so equity will come from new common stock, with a cost equal to:

$$k_e = \frac{D_1}{P_0(1-F)} + g = \frac{\$2.268}{\$32(1-0.25)} + 8\% = 17.45\%.$$

CHAPTER 13
CAPITAL BUDGETING

OVERVIEW

In this chapter we apply the finance concepts of valuation and the calculation of required rates of return to investment decisions involving the fixed assets of a firm, or capital budgeting. Here the term capital refers to fixed assets used in production, while a budget is a plan that details projected inflows and outflows during some future period. Thus, the capital budget is an outline of planned expenditures on fixed assets, and capital budgeting is the process of analyzing projects and deciding which are acceptable investments and which actually should be purchased.

Our treatment of capital budgeting is divided into two general areas. First, we consider how the cash flows associated with capital budgeting projects are estimated. And then we describe the basic techniques used in capital budgeting analysis and how investment decisions are made.

OUTLINE

Capital budgeting is the process of analyzing fixed asset investment proposals and deciding which are acceptable investments.

☐ A number of factors combine to make capital budgeting decisions perhaps the most important ones financial managers must make.
  ~ Since the results of such decisions continue for many years, capital budgeting decisions have long-term consequences.
  ~ Timing is also important since capital assets must be ready to come on line when they are needed; otherwise, opportunities might be lost.
  ~ Capital budgeting is also important because the acquisition of fixed assets typically involves substantial expenditures. A firm contemplating a major capital expenditure program must arrange its financing well in advance to be sure the funds required are available.

☐ The ideas for capital budgeting projects are generally created by the firm.
  ~ A firm's growth, and even its ability to remain competitive and to survive, depends on a constant flow of ideas for new products, ways to make existing products better, and ways to produce output more efficiently.
  ~ Procedures must be established for evaluating the worth of capital projects to the firm.

☐ Capital budgeting decisions are termed either replacement decisions or expansion decisions.

~ *Replacement decisions* involve determining whether to invest in capital projects to take the place of (replace) existing assets to maintain existing operations.
~ *Expansion decisions* involve determining whether to invest in capital projects and add them to existing assets to increase existing operations.

☐ Capital budgeting decisions involve either independent or mutually exclusive projects.
~ *Independent projects* are projects whose cash flows are not affected by the acceptance or nonacceptance of other projects.
  ● All independent projects can be purchased if they all are acceptable.
~ *Mutually exclusive projects* are a set of projects in which the acceptance of one project means the others cannot be accepted.
  ● Only one mutually exclusive project can be purchased, even if they all are acceptable.

☐ In general, relatively simple calculations and only a few supporting documents are required for replacement decisions, especially maintenance-type investments in profitable plants.
~ More detailed analysis is required for cost-reduction replacements, for expansion of existing product lines, and especially for investments in new products or areas.
~ Also, more expensive projects, whether replacement or expansion, usually require both more detailed analysis and approval at a higher level within the firm.

☐ The capital budgeting decision involves the same steps used in general asset valuation.
~ Determine the cost of the project.
~ Estimate the cash flows from the project.
~ Evaluate the riskiness of the projected cash flows to determine the appropriate rate of return to use for computing the present value of the estimated cash flows.
~ Compute the present value of the expected cash flows.
~ Compare the present value of the benefits with the initial investment, or cost.
  ● If the asset's value exceeds its cost, the project should be accepted; otherwise, it should be rejected.
  ● If a firm invests in a project with a present value greater than its cost, the value of the firm will increase.
  ● The more effective the firm's capital budgeting procedures, the higher the price of its stock.

The most important, and also the most difficult, step in the analysis of a capital project is estimating its cash flows. When estimating cash flows, only identifiable relevant cash flows are to be considered. Two cardinal rules can help financial analysts avoid mistakes: (1) Capital decisions must be based on cash flows after taxes, not accounting income, and (2) only incremental cash flows are relevant to the analysis.

☐ In capital budgeting analysis, after-tax *cash flows*, not accounting profits, are used. It is cash that pays the bills and can be invested in capital projects, not profits.
~ The amount of money received by the firm is represented by the cash flow figure, not the net income figure.

~ Cash flows are relevant for the purposes of valuing an asset—cash flows can be reinvested to create value; profits cannot.

☐ In evaluating a capital project, we are concerned only with those cash flows that occur as a direct result of accepting the project. Cash flows that will change because the project is purchased are *incremental cash flows* that need to be included in the capital budgeting evaluation. Five special problems in determining incremental cash flows follow:

~ A *sunk cost* is a cash outlay that already has been incurred and that cannot be recovered regardless of whether the project is accepted or rejected. Sunk costs are not incremental and, hence, should not be included in the analysis.

~ An *opportunity cost* is defined as the cash flows that could be generated from assets the firm already owns provided they are not used for the project in question. These cash flows must be included in the analysis.

~ *Externalities* are the effects of a project on the cash flows in other parts of the firm, and their effects need to be considered in the incremental cash flows.

~ *Shipping and installation costs* must be taken into account since they are part of the full cost of the equipment and are included in the depreciable basis when depreciation charges are calculated.

  • Although depreciation is a noncash expense, it affects the firm's taxable income; thus, it affects the amount of taxes paid by the firm, which is a cash flow.

~ *Inflation* should be recognized in capital budgeting decisions. Inflationary expectations must be built into the cash flows used in the capital budgeting analysis to avoid inflation bias.

  • If expected inflation is not built into the determination of expected cash flows, then the asset's calculated value and expected rate of return will be artificially low.

  • The required rate of return does not have to be adjusted by the firm for inflation expectations because investors include such expectations when establishing the rate at which they are willing to permit the firm to use their funds.

☐ When we identify the incremental cash flows associated with a capital project, we separate them according to when they occur during the life of the project. In most cases, we can classify a project's incremental cash flows as (1) cash flows that occur only at the start of the project's life, (2) cash flows that continue throughout the project's life, and (3) cash flows that occur only at the end, or the termination, of the project.

~ The *initial investment outlay* refers to the incremental cash flows that occur only at the start of a project's life, CF_0.

  • The initial investment includes such cash flows as the purchase price of the new project and shipping and installation costs.

  • If the capital budgeting decision is a replacement decision, the initial investment also must take into account the cash flows associated with the disposal of the old, or replaced, asset, which include any cash received or paid to scrap the old asset and any tax effects associated with the disposal.

  • The change in net working capital that results from the acceptance of a project is an incremental cash flow that must be considered in the capital budgeting analysis. Because the change in net working capital requirements occurs at the start of the project's life, this cash flow impact is an incremental cash flow that is included as a part of the initial investment outlay.

~ *Incremental operating cash flows* are the changes in day-to-day cash flows that result from the purchase of a capital project and continue until the firm disposes of the asset.

- Incremental operating cash flows can be calculated as follows:

$$\begin{matrix} \text{Incremental operating} \\ \text{cash flow}_t \end{matrix} = \Delta \text{Revenue} - \Delta \text{Cash operating expenses} - \Delta \text{Taxes}$$

$$= \Delta \text{NOI}_t \times (1 - T) + \Delta \text{Depr}_t$$
$$= (\Delta S_t - \Delta OC_t - \Delta \text{Depr}_t) \times (1 - T) + \Delta \text{Depr}_t$$
$$= (\Delta S_t - \Delta OC_t) \times (1 - T) + T(\Delta \text{Depr}_t).$$

- Although depreciation is a noncash expense, the change in depreciation expense needs to be included when computing incremental operating cash flows because, when depreciation changes, taxable income changes, and so does the amount of income taxes paid—the amount of taxes paid is a cash flow.

- When identifying relevant cash flows, the effects of financing the new project are not included, because financing effects, such as interest charges, are reflected in the cost of capital used in the evaluation; thus, financing effects should not be included in the cash flows.

~ The *terminal cash flow* is the net cash flow that occurs at the end of the life of a project, including the cash flows associated with (1) the final disposal of the project and (2) returning the firm's operations to where they were before the project was accepted.

- The terminal cash flow includes the salvage value, the tax impact of the disposition of the project, and any net working capital changes that occurred at the beginning of the project's life that will be reversed at the end of its life.

Two types of capital budgeting decisions are (1) expansion project analysis and (2) replacement project analysis.

☐ An *expansion project* is one that calls for the firm to invest in new assets to increase sales. Steps in the capital budgeting analysis for the project include:

~ Summarize the initial investment outlays required for the project. Changes that increase (decrease) net working capital should be included as an outflow (inflow) here; however, they should be considered as an inflow (outflow) at the end of the project.

~ Estimate the cash flows that will occur once production begins, including the impact of depreciation and its tax effects.

~ Estimate the cash flows that will occur at the end of the project, including salvage value and the tax impact resulting from the sale of equipment.

~ Summarize the data by combining all the net cash flows on a time line and evaluate the project.

~ The project's required rate of return may need to be increased if the project is deemed riskier than the firm's average project.

☐ *Replacement analysis* is the same as for expansion projects, except, to some extent, identifying the incremental cash flows associated with a replacement project is more complicated than for an expansion project, because the cash flows both from the new asset and from the old asset must be considered. The net difference between the new and the old cash flows must be considered because a replacement decision involves comparing two mutually exclusive projects—retaining the old asset vs. buying a new one.

~ The following additional cash flows must be considered at time 0:

• The cash received from the sale of the old equipment is an inflow.

• However, the sale of the old machine will usually have tax effects. If the old equipment is sold below book value, there will be a tax savings; if the equipment is sold at a profit, taxes must be paid. The tax effect is equal to the loss or gain on the sale times the firm's marginal tax rate.

~ The operating cash flow calculation must also be modified.

• First, look at the effects of the new equipment on revenues and costs. An incremental increase in revenues would produce a cash inflow, while an incremental increase in costs would produce a cash outflow, just as before. (Tax effects need to be included.)

• The depreciation expense on the old equipment must be subtracted from the depreciation expense on the new equipment to get the net change in depreciation. (Tax effects need to be included.)

~ Any salvage value on the old machine, including tax effects, must be included as a cash outflow at the end of the project's life. Accepting the new project causes the firm to forgo the old machine's salvage value. Thus, it must be included as an opportunity cost. Of course, any salvage value on the new machine must also be included in the analysis.

The three most popular methods used by businesses to evaluate capital budgeting projects are: (1) payback, (2) net present value (NPV), and (3) internal rate of return (IRR).

☐ The *payback period* is defined as the expected number of years it takes to recover the original investment. It is the simplest and the oldest formal method used to evaluate capital budgeting projects. Payback can be calculated using the following formula:

$$\text{Payback} = \begin{array}{c}\text{Number of years}\\\text{before full recovery}\\\text{of original investment}\end{array} + \left(\frac{\text{Unrecovered cost at start of recovery year}}{\text{Total cash flow during recovery year}}\right).$$

~ As a rule, a project is considered acceptable if its payback is less than the maximum cost recovery time established by the firm.

~ The payback method's main flaws are that it does not take into account the time value of money and cash flows beyond the payback period are ignored.

~ A variant of the payback period is the *discounted payback period*. It is the length of time it takes for a project's discounted cash flows to repay the cost of the investment.

• The discounted payback computation does consider the time value of money.

• Using the discounted payback method, a project should be accepted when the value of its discounted payback is less than its expected life.

☐ The *net present value (NPV)* method of evaluating investment proposals is a *discounted cash flow (DCF)* technique that accounts for the time value of all cash flows from a project. The NPV method evaluates capital investment proposals by finding the present value of future net cash flows, discounted at the rate of return required by the firm.

~ To implement the NPV, proceed as follows: (a) Find the present value of each cash flow, discounted at the firm's required rate of return, (b) sum these discounted cash flows to obtain the project's NPV, and (c) accept the project if the NPV is positive.

~ The NPV is defined as follows:

$$NPV = \sum_{t=0}^{n} \frac{\hat{CF_t}}{(1+k)^t}.$$

Here, CF_t is the expected net cash flow at Period t and k is the firm's required rate of return to invest in this project. Cash outflows (expenditures on the project) are treated as negative cash flows.

• Finding the NPV with a financial calculator is efficient and easy. Simply enter the different cash flows into the "cash flow register" (being sure to observe the signs of the cash flows) along with the value of $k = I$, and then press the NPV key for the solution.

~ If the NPV is positive, the project should be accepted; if negative, it should be rejected.

• If projects with positive NPVs are accepted, the value of the firm will increase; accepting negative NPV projects will lower the value of the firm.

• An NPV of zero signifies that the project's cash flows are just sufficient to repay the invested capital and to provide the required rate of return on that capital.

~ If two projects are mutually exclusive (that is, only one can be accepted), the one with the higher NPV should be chosen, assuming that the NPV is positive. If both projects have negative NPVs, neither should be chosen.

☐ The *internal rate of return (IRR)* is defined as the discount rate that forces the present value of a project's expected cash flows to equal its cost (initial amount invested). IRR is similar to the YTM on a bond.

~ The equation for calculating the IRR is shown below:

$$\sum_{t=0}^{n} \frac{\hat{CF_t}}{(1+IRR)^t} = 0.$$

This equation has one unknown, the IRR, and we can solve for the value of the IRR that will make the equation equal to zero. The solution value of IRR is defined as the internal rate of return.

• To find the IRR with a financial calculator, simply enter the different cash flows into the cash flow register, making sure to input the $t = 0$ cash flow, and then press the IRR key for the solution.

~ The IRR formula is simply the NPV formula solved for the particular discount rate that causes the NPV to equal zero.

~ As long as the rate of return expected from a project, its IRR, is greater than the rate of return required by the firm, or the *hurdle rate*, for such an investment, the project is acceptable.

- Because the IRR on a project is its expected rate of return, if the IRR exceeds the cost of the funds used to finance the project, a surplus remains after paying for the funds—this surplus accrues to the firm's stockholders. Therefore, taking on a project whose IRR exceeds its required rate of return, or cost of funds, increases shareholders' wealth.

We generally measure wealth in dollars, so the NPV method should be used to accomplish the goal of maximizing shareholders' wealth.

☐ In reality, using the IRR method could lead to investment decisions that increase, but do not maximize, wealth.

~ Because many corporate executives are familiar with the meaning of IRR and it is entrenched in the corporate world, it is important to understand the IRR method and be prepared to explain why, at times, a project with a lower IRR might be preferable to one with a higher IRR.

☐ A *net present value (NPV) profile* is a curve showing the relationship between a project's NPV and various discount rates (required rates of return).

~ The NPV profile crosses the Y-axis at the undiscounted NPV (k = 0), while it crosses the X-axis at a project's internal rate of return.

~ The *crossover rate* is the discount rate at which the NPV profiles of two projects cross and, thus, at which the projects' NPVs are equal.

~ If two projects are *independent*, then the NPV and IRR criteria always lead to the same accept/reject decision. If a project's NPV is positive, its IRR will exceed k, while if NPV is negative, k will exceed the IRR.

~ If two *mutually exclusive* projects have NPV profiles that intersect, then there may be a conflict between the NPV and IRR methods. Two basic conditions can lead to conflicts between NPV and IRR:

- *Project size (or scale) differences* exist; that is, the cost of one project is larger than that of the other.

- *Timing differences* exist such that most of the cash flows from one project come in the early years and most of the cash flows from the other project come in the later years.

~ The critical issue in resolving conflicts between mutually exclusive projects is to determine how useful it is to generate cash flows earlier rather than later. Thus, the value of early cash flows depends on the rate at which we can reinvest these cash flows.

- The NPV method implicitly assumes that project cash flows are reinvested at the required rate of return.

- The IRR method implicitly assumes that project cash flows are reinvested at the project's IRR.

- The more realistic *reinvestment rate assumption* is the required rate of return, which is implicit in the NPV method. This, in turn, leads us to prefer the NPV method.

~ In summary, when projects are independent, the NPV and IRR methods both make exactly the same accept/reject decision. However, when evaluating mutually exclusive projects, especially those that differ in scale and/or timing, the NPV method should be used.

☐ Multiple IRRs can result when the IRR criterion is used with a project that has unconventional cash flows. A project with unconventional cash flow patterns has a large cash outflow either sometime during or at the end of its life. In such cases, the NPV criterion can be easily applied, and this method leads to conceptually correct capital budgeting decisions.

In making the accept/reject decision, most large, sophisticated firms calculate and consider multiple measures because each provides decision makers with a somewhat different piece of relevant information.

☐ Payback and discounted payback provide an indication of both the risk and the liquidity of a project.
~ A long payback means (1) that the investment dollars will be locked up for many years, hence the project is relatively illiquid, and (2) that the project's cash flows must be forecast far out into the future, which is difficult, hence the project probably is quite risky.

☐ NPV is important because it gives a direct measure of the dollar benefit (on a present value basis) to the firm's shareholders, so NPV is regarded as the best single measure of profitability.

☐ IRR also measures profitability, but expressed as a percentage rate of return, which many decision makers seem to prefer.
~ IRR contains information regarding a project's "safety margin" that is not inherent in NPV.

☐ In summary, the different methods provide different types of information to decision makers. Because it is easy to calculate them, all three evaluation methods should be considered in the decision process.
~ For any specific decision, more weight might be given to one method than another, but it would be foolish to ignore the information provided by any of the methods.

Three separate and distinct types of project risk can be identified in capital budgeting: (1) stand-alone risk, (2) corporate (within-firm) risk, and (3) beta (market) risk.

☐ *Stand-alone risk* is the risk an asset would have if it were a firm's only asset.
~ It is measured by the variability of the asset's expected returns.
~ One method used by firms to assess a project's stand-alone risk is *scenario analysis*, which is a risk analysis technique that helps decision makers get an idea of the range of outcomes that are possible if a project is accepted.
• *Worst case* and *best case scenarios* are estimated, and the input values from these scenarios are used to find the worst-case NPV and the best-case NPV.

- Probabilities can be assigned to the best, worst, and base case NPVs to obtain the expected NPV.

- The project's coefficient of variation can be compared with the coefficient of variation of the firm's average project to determine the relative stand-alone riskiness of the project.

☐ *Corporate risk* is that risk which does not consider the effects of stockholders' diversification.
  ~ It is measured by a project's effect on the firm's earnings variability.
  ~ To measure corporate, or within-firm, risk, we need to determine how the capital budgeting project is related to the firm's existing assets.
    - Many firms add new projects that are not highly related to existing assets to help reduce corporate risk.
    - Corporate risk is important because the firm's stability is important to its managers, workers, customers, suppliers, and creditors, as well as to the community in which it operates and to undiversified stockholders.

☐ *Beta risk* is that part of a project's risk that cannot be eliminated by diversification.
  ~ It is measured by the project's beta coefficient.
  ~ Beta (market) risk measures risk from the standpoint of an equity investor holding a highly diversified portfolio.
    - The firm can be thought of as a composite of all the projects it has undertaken. Thus, the relevant risk of a project can be viewed as the impact it has on the firm's systematic risk.
    - If the beta coefficient for each project can be determined, then individual projects' costs of equity capital can be found as follows:

$$k_{proj} = k_{RF} + (k_M - k_{RF})\beta_{proj}.$$

    - High-beta, or high-risk, projects will have relatively high required rates of return, while low-beta projects will have correspondingly low required rates of return.
    - The estimation of project betas is even more difficult than that for stocks. However, an approach that has been developed for this purpose is the pure play method.
    - The *pure play method* is an approach used for estimating the beta of a project in which a firm identifies companies whose only business is the product in question, determines the beta for each firm, and then averages the betas to find an approximation of its own project's beta.
    - The single-product companies that are used for comparisons are called *pure play firms*.
    - Generally, the pure play method can only be used for major projects such as whole divisions, and even then it is frequently difficult to implement because pure play proxy firms are scarce.

Most firms use risk-adjusted discount rates to incorporate differential project risk in the capital budgeting process. If project risk is not considered in capital budgeting analysis,

incorrect decisions are possible.

☐   The *risk-adjusted discount rate* is the required rate of return that applies to a particular risky stream of income; it is equal to the risk-free rate of interest plus a risk premium appropriate to the level of risk attached to a particular project's income stream.

☐   Increasing the discount rate for high-risk projects and lowering it for low-risk projects is a somewhat arbitrary and judgmental process, but it does force managers to at least consider a project's riskiness.

☐   The risk-adjusted discount rate approach is far from precise, but it recognizes that different projects have different risks, and projects with different risks should be evaluated using different required rates of return.

Capital rationing occurs when firms place a constraint on the total size of the firm's capital investment.

☐   Elaborate and mathematically sophisticated models have been developed to help firms maximize their values when they are subject to capital rationing.

☐   A firm that subjects itself to capital rationing is deliberately forgoing profitable projects, and hence it is not truly maximizing its value.
       ~   This point is well known, so few sophisticated firms ration capital today.

There are several important differences in capital budgeting analysis of foreign versus domestic operations.

☐   Cash flow analysis is much more complex for overseas investments.
       ~   Usually a firm will organize a separate subsidiary in each foreign country in which it operates.
       ~   Moving funds from a foreign subsidiary to the parent company is called *repatriation of earnings*.
           •   Any dividends or royalties repatriated by the subsidiary must be converted to the currency of the parent company and thus are subject to exchange rate changes.
       ~   Dividends and royalties received are normally taxed by both foreign and domestic governments.
       ~   Some governments place restrictions, or exchange controls, on the amount of cash that may be remitted to the parent company in order to encourage reinvestment of earnings in the foreign country.
       ~   The only relevant cash flows for the analysis of a foreign investment are the cash flows that the subsidiary can legally send back to the parent.

☐   In addition to the complexities of the cash flow analysis, the rate of return required for a foreign project might be different than for an equivalent domestic project because foreign projects might be more or less risky. A higher risk could arise from two primary sources—

exchange rate risk and political risk—while a lower risk might result from international diversification.

~ *Exchange rate risk* is the uncertainty associated with the price at which the currency from one country can be converted into the currency of another country.

~ *Political risk* refers to the risk of expropriation of a foreign subsidiary's assets by the host country, or of unanticipated restrictions on cash flows to the parent company. Political risk refers to any action (or chance of such action) by a host government that reduces the value of a company's investment.

• Generally, political risk premiums are not added to the required rate of return to adjust for political risk. If a company's management has a serious concern that a given country might expropriate foreign assets, it simply will not make significant investments in that country.

• Companies can take steps to reduce the potential loss from expropriation in three major ways: (1) by financing the subsidiary with local capital, (2) by structuring operations so that the subsidiary has value only as a part of the integrated corporate system, and (3) by obtaining insurance against economic losses from expropriation.

Appendix 13A discusses depreciation and gives recovery allowance percentages for various classes of personal property. It also gives a depreciation illustration.

Appendix 13B shows how spreadsheets can be used to compute NPV and IRR.

SELF-TEST QUESTIONS

Definitional

1. A firm's _____ _____ outlines its planned expenditures on fixed assets.

2. _____ _____ involve determining whether to invest in capital projects to take the place of existing assets to maintain existing operations.

3. _____ _____ involve determining whether to invest in capital projects and add them to existing assets to increase existing operations.

4. _____ projects are projects whose cash flows are not affected by the acceptance or nonacceptance of other projects.

5. _____ _____ projects are a set of projects in which the acceptance of one project means the others cannot be accepted.

6. The expected number of years required to recover the original investment in a project is known as the _____ _____.

7. As a rule, a project is considered acceptable if its payback is _____ than the maximum cost recovery time established by the firm.

8. One important weakness of payback analysis is the fact that _____ _____ beyond the payback period are _____.

9. The net present value (NPV) method of evaluating investment proposals is a(n) _____ cash flow technique.

10. A capital investment proposal should be accepted if its NPV is _____.

11. The _____ _____ period is the length of time it takes for a project's discounted cash flows to repay the cost of the investment.

12. If two projects are _____ _____, the one with the _____ positive NPV should be selected.

13. In the IRR approach, a discount rate is sought which makes the NPV equal to _____.

14. As long as the IRR is greater than the rate of return required by the firm, or the _____ rate, an independent project is acceptable.

15. A net present value profile is a curve showing the relationship between a project's _____ and various _____ _____.

16. The _____ rate is the discount rate at which the NPV profiles of two projects cross and at which the projects' NPVs are equal.

17. If two mutually exclusive projects are being evaluated and one project has a higher NPV while the other project has a higher IRR, the project with the higher _____ should be preferred.

18. The NPV method implicitly assumes reinvestment at the firm's _____ _____ ____ _____, while the IRR method implicitly assumes reinvestment at the _____ _____ ____ _____.

19. The internal rate of return (IRR) is the _____ rate that forces the present value of a project's expected _____ _____ to equal its _____.

20. _____ _____ can result when the IRR criterion is used with a project that has unconventional cash flows.

21. Payback and discounted payback provide an indication of both the _____ and the _____ of a project.

22.   _____ gives a direct measure of the dollar benefit to the firm's shareholders, so it is regarded as the best single measure of profitability.

23.   _____ contains information regarding a project's "safety margin."

24.   One of the most important, and also one of the most difficult, steps in capital budgeting analysis is _____ _____ _____.

25.   When estimating cash flows, only identifiable _____ cash flows are to be considered.

26.   An increase in net working capital would show up as a cash _____ at time 0 and then again as a cash _____ at the _____ of the project's life.

27.   A(n) _____ _____ is a cash outlay that already has been incurred and that cannot be recovered regardless of whether the project is accepted or rejected.

28.   A(n) _____ _____ is defined as the cash flows that could be generated from assets the firm already owns provided they are not used for the project in question.

29.   _____ are the effects of a project on the cash flows in other parts of the firm, and their effects need to be considered in the incremental cash flows.

30.   The _____ cash flow is the net cash flow that occurs at the end of a project's life.

31.   In replacement analysis, two cash flows that occur at t = 0 that are not present in expansion projects are the price received from the sale of the _____ equipment and the _____ effects of the sale.

32.   In replacement analysis, the depreciation included in the analysis is based on the _____ in depreciation expense between the old and new asset.

33.   A(n) _____ cash flow represents the change in the firm's total cash flow that occurs as a direct result of project acceptance.

34.   Three types of separate risk have been identified in capital budgeting decisions: beta (market) risk, _____-_____ risk, and _____ risk.

35.   _____-_____ risk is the risk an asset would have if it were a firm's only asset and is measured by the variability of the asset's expected returns.

36.   _____ risk is that risk which does not consider the effects of stockholders' diversification and is measured by a project's effect on the firm's earnings variability.

37.   _____ risk is that part of a project's risk that cannot be eliminated by diversification.

38.   A commonly used method of risk analysis based on constructing optimistic, pessimistic,

and expected value estimates for key variables is called _____ _____.

39. The _____ _____ method is an approach used for estimating the beta of a project in which a firm identifies companies whose only business is the product in question, determines the beta for each firm, and then averages the betas to find an approximation of its own project's beta.

40. Most firms use _____-_____ discount rates to incorporate differential project risk in the capital budgeting process.

41. _____ _____ occurs when firms set an absolute limit on the dollar amount of investment capital.

42. _____ _____ is the process of analyzing projects and deciding which are acceptable investments and which actually should be purchased.

43. The ideas for capital budgeting projects are generally created by the _____.

44. The capital budgeting decision involves the same steps used in _____ _____.

45. Using the discounted payback method, a project should be accepted when the value of its discounted payback is _____ than its expected life.

46. An NPV of _____ signifies that the project's cash flows are just sufficient to repay the invested capital and to provide the required rate of return on that capital.

47. Two basic conditions that can lead to conflicts between NPV and IRR are _____ _____ or _____ differences and _____ differences.

48. Capital decisions must be based on _____-_____ _____ _____, not accounting income.

49. _____ and _____ costs must be taken into account since they are part of the full cost of equipment and are included in the asset's depreciable basis.

50. If expected _____ is not built into the determination of expected cash flows, then the asset's calculated value and expected rate of return will be artificially low.

51. Moving funds from a foreign subsidiary to the parent company is called _____ ____ _____.

52. _____ _____ _____ is the uncertainty associated with the price at which the currency from one country can be converted into the currency of another country.

53. _____ _____ refers to any action (or the chance of such action) by a host government that reduces the value of a company's investment.

Conceptual

54. The NPV of a project with cash flows that accrue relatively slowly is *more sensitive* to changes in the discount rate than is the NPV of a project with cash flows that come in more rapidly.

    a. True   **b.** False

55. The NPV method is preferred over the IRR method because the NPV method's reinvestment rate assumption is better.

    a. True   **b.** False

56. Other things held constant, a decrease in the firm's required rate of return (discount rate) will cause an *increase* in a project's IRR.

    a. True   **b.** False

57. The IRR method can be used in place of the NPV method for all independent projects.

    a.   True   **b.** False

58. In general, the value of land currently owned by a firm is irrelevant to a capital budgeting decision because the cost of that property is a sunk cost.

    a. True   **b.** False

59. McDonald's is planning to open a new store across from the student union. Annual revenues are expected to be $5 million. However, opening the new location will cause annual revenues to drop by $3 million at McDonald's existing stadium location. The relevant, before-tax sales revenues for the capital budgeting analysis are $2 million per year.

    a. True   **b.** False

60. In a replacement decision, the salvage value of the old asset need not be considered since the current market value of the asset is included in the analysis.

    a. True   **b.** False

61. Even if the beta of a project being considered has a value of zero, acceptance of the project will affect the beta (market) risk of the firm.

    a. True   **b.** False

62. When independent projects of different risk are to be considered in capital budgeting, any project will be acceptable to the firm if the project's IRR is greater than the firm's required rate of return.

    a. True   **b.** False

63. Projects A and B each have an initial cost of $5,000, followed by a series of positive cash inflows. Project A has total undiscounted cash inflows of $12,000, while B has total undiscounted inflows of $10,000. Further, at a discount rate of 10 percent, the two projects have identical NPVs. Which project's NPV will be *more sensitive* to changes in the discount rate? (Hint: Projects with steeper NPV profiles are more sensitive to discount rate changes.)

    a. Project A.
    b. Project B.
    c. Both projects are equally sensitive to changes in the discount rate since their NPVs are equal at all costs of capital.
    d. Neither project is sensitive to changes in the discount rate, since both have NPV profiles that are horizontal.
    e. The solution cannot be determined unless the timing of the cash flows is known.

64. Which of the following statements is correct?

    a. The IRR of a project whose cash flows accrue relatively rapidly is more sensitive to changes in the discount rate than is the IRR of a project whose cash flows come in more slowly.
    b. There are many conditions under which a project can have more than one IRR. One such condition is where an otherwise conventional project has a negative cash flow at the end of its life.
    c. The phenomenon called "multiple internal rates of return" arises when two or more mutually exclusive projects that have different lives are being compared.
    d. Both statements b and c are correct.
    e. Each of the above statements is false.

65. Which of the following statements is correct?

   a. If a project has an IRR greater than zero, then taking on the project will increase the value of the company's common stock because the project will make a positive contribution to net income.

   b. If a project has an NPV greater than zero, then taking on the project will increase the value of the firm's stock.

   c. Assume that you plot the NPV profiles of two mutually exclusive projects with conventional cash flows and that the firm's required rate of return is *greater* than the rate at which the profiles cross one another. In this case, the NPV and IRR methods will lead to contradictory evaluations of the two projects.

   d. For independent (as opposed to mutually exclusive) projects with conventional cash flows, the NPV and IRR methods will generally lead to conflicting accept/reject decisions.

   e. Statements b, c, and d are correct.

66. Which of the following statements is correct?

   a. The payback method's main flaws are that it ignores the time value of money and it ignores cash flows beyond the payback period.

   b. Underlying the IRR is the assumption that cash flows can be reinvested at the firm's required rate of return.

   c. Underlying the NPV is the assumption that cash flows can be reinvested at the firm's required rate of return.

   d. The discounted payback method always leads to the same accept/reject decisions as the NPV method when mutually exclusive projects are involved.

   e. Both statements a and c are correct.

67. Two corporations are formed. They are identical in all respects except for their methods of depreciation. Firm A uses MACRS depreciation, while Firm B uses the straight-line method. Both plan to depreciate their assets for tax purposes over a 5-year life (6 calendar years), which is equal to the useful life, and both pay a 34 percent marginal tax rate. (Note: The half-year convention will apply, so the firm using the straight-line method will take 10 percent depreciation in Year 1 and 10 percent in Year 6.) Which of the following statements is *false*?

   a. Firm A will generate higher cash flows from operations in the first year than B.

   b. Firm A will pay more federal corporate income taxes in the first year than B.

   c. If there is no change in tax rates over the 6-year period and if we disregard the time value of money, the total amount of funds generated from operations by these projects for each corporation will be the same over the 6 years.

   d. Firm B will pay the same amount of federal corporate income taxes, over the 6-year period, as A.

   e. Firm A could, if it chose to, use straight-line depreciation for stockholder reporting even if it used MACRS for tax purposes.

68. In capital budgeting decisions, corporate risk will be of least interest to

    a. Employees.
    b. Stockholders with few shares.
    c. Institutional investors.
    d. Creditors.
    e. The local community.

69. A company owns a building, free and clear, which had a cost of $100,000. The building is currently unoccupied, but it can be sold at a net price of $50,000, after taxes. Now the company is thinking of using the building for a new project. Which of the following statements is correct?

    a. The building is unoccupied, and its cost was incurred in the past, and hence, is a sunk cost. Therefore, no cost for the building should be charged to the new project.
    b. A cost should be charged to the new project, and that cost should be $100,000.
    c. A cost should be charged to the new project, and that cost should be $50,000.
    d. The cost charged to the building would vary depending on the expected profitability of the new project and hence on the new project's ability to help carry the corporation's overhead.
    e. A cost for the building should be charged to the new project only if the NPV on the new project without considering the building is less than zero.

70. Which of the following statements is correct?

    a. If a project's returns are negatively correlated with returns on most other assets in the economy, then stand-alone risk is a better proxy for market risk than would be true if the project's returns were positively correlated with most other assets' returns.
    b. In capital budgeting analysis, accounting profits rather than after-tax cash flows are used.
    c. It would be easier to use the pure play method to assess the riskiness of a project such as a corporate aircraft than for a project that involves expanding into a new line of business, such as IBM's analysis of whether or not to go into the personal computer business.
    d. Statements a, b, and c are correct.
    e. All of the above statements are false.

SELF-TEST PROBLEMS

1. Your firm is considering a fast-food concession at the World's Fair. The cash flow pattern is somewhat unusual since you must build the stands, operate them for two years, and then tear the stands down and restore the sites to their original condition. You estimate the net cash flows to be as follows:

Time	Expected Net Cash Flows
0	($800,000)
1	700,000
2	700,000
3	(400,000)

What is the approximate IRR of this venture?

a. 5%   **b.** 15%   **c.** 25%   **d.** 35%   **e.** 45%

(The following information applies to the next three Self-Test Problems.)

Toya Motors needs a new machine for production of its 2007 models. The financial vice president has appointed you to do the capital budgeting analysis. You have identified two different machines that are capable of performing the job. You have completed the cash flow analysis, and the expected net cash flows are as follows:

Year	Expected Net Cash Flow Machine B	Machine O
0	($5,000)	($5,000)
1	2,085	0
2	2,085	0
3	2,085	0
4	2,085	9,677

2.   What is the payback period for Machine B?

a. 1.0 year   **b.** 2.0 years   **c.** 2.4 years   **d.** 2.6 years   **e.** 3.0 years

3.   The firm's required rate of return is uncertain at this time, so you construct NPV profiles to assist in the final decision. The profiles for Machines B and O cross at what discount rate?

a. 6%   **d.** 24%
b. 10%   **e.** They do not cross in the upper right-hand quadrant.
c. 18%

4.   If the required rate of return for both projects is 14 percent at the time the decision is made, which project would you choose?

a. Project B; it has the higher positive NPV.
b. Project 0; it has the higher positive NPV.
c. Neither; both have negative NPVs.
d. Either; both have the same NPV.
e. Project B; it has the higher IRR.

(The following information applies to the next four Self-Test Problems.)

The director of capital budgeting for Giant Inc. has identified two mutually exclusive projects, L and S, with the following expected net cash flows:

	Expected Net Cash Flows	
Year	Project L	Project S
0	($100)	($100)
1	10	70
2	60	50
3	80	20

Both projects have a required rate of return of 10 percent.

5. What is the payback period for Project S?

   a. 1.6 years   b. 1.8 years   c. 2.1 years   d. 2.5 years   e. 2.8 years

6. What is Project L's NPV?

   a. $50.00   b. $34.25   c. $22.64   d. $18.79   e. $10.06

7. What is Project L's IRR?

   a. 18.1%   b. 19.7%   c. 21.4%   d. 23.6%   e. 24.2%

8. Plot the NPV profiles for the two projects. Where is the crossover rate?

   a. 4.8%   b. 5.7%   c. 8.7%   d. 11.0%   e. 12.3%

9. A company is analyzing two mutually exclusive projects, S and L, whose cash flows are shown below:

Year	Project S	Project L
0	($2,000)	($2,000)
1	1,800	0
2	500	500
3	20	800
4	20	1,600

   The company's required rate of return is 9 percent, and it can obtain an unlimited amount of capital at that rate. What is the IRR of the better project? (Hint: Note that the better project may or may not be the one with the higher IRR.)

   a. 11.45%   b. 11.74%   c. 13.02%   d. 13.49%   e. 12.67%

10. The capital budgeting director of National Products Inc. is evaluating a new project that would decrease operating costs by $30,000 per year without affecting revenues. The project's cost is $50,000. The project will be depreciated using the MACRS method over its 3-year class life. It will have a *zero salvage value* after three years. The marginal tax rate of National Products is 34 percent, and the project's required rate of return is 12 percent. What is the project's NPV?

   a. $7,068   **b.** $8,324   **c.** $10,214   **d.** $11,326   **e.** $12,387

11. Your firm has a marginal tax rate of 40 percent and a required rate of return of 14 percent. You are performing a capital budgeting analysis on a new project that will cost $500,000. The project is expected to have a useful life of 10 years, although its MACRS class life is only 5 years. The project is expected to increase the firm's *net income* by $61,257 per year and to have a salvage value of $35,000 at the end of 10 years. What is the project's NPV?

   a. $95,356   **b.** $108,359   **c.** $135,256   **d.** $162,185   **e.** $177,902

12. The Board of Directors of National Brewing Inc. is considering the acquisition of a new still. The still is priced at $600,000 but would require $60,000 in transportation costs and $40,000 for installation. The still has a useful life of 10 years but will be depreciated over its 5-year MACRS life. It is expected to have a salvage value of $10,000 at the end of 10 years. The still would increase revenues by $120,000 per year and increase yearly operating costs by $20,000 per year. Additionally, the still would require a $30,000 increase in net working capital. The firm's marginal tax rate is 40 percent, and the project's required rate of return is 10 percent. What is the NPV of the still?

   a. $18,430   **b.** -$12,352   **c.** -$65,204   **d.** -$130,961   **e.** -$203,450

(The following information applies to the next three Self-Test Problems.)

As the capital budgeting director of Union Mills Inc. you are analyzing the replacement of an automated loom system. The old system was purchased 5 years ago for $200,000; it falls into the MACRS 5-year class; and it has 5 years of remaining life and a $50,000 salvage value five years from now. The current market value of the old system is $100,000. The new system has a price of $300,000, plus an additional $50,000 in installation costs. The new system falls into the MACRS 5-year class, has a 5-year economic life, and a $100,000 salvage value. The new system will require a $40,000 increase in the spare parts inventory. The primary advantage of the new system is that it will decrease operating costs by $40,000 per year. Union Mills has a 12 percent required rate of return and a marginal tax rate of 34 percent.

13. What is the initial investment outlay at Year 0?

   a. $350,000   **b.** $319,920   **c.** $295,000   **d.** $40,000   **e.** $23,200

14. What is the incremental operating cash flow in Year 1?

    a. $46,120   **b.** $43,950   **c.** $39,825   **d.** $33,350   **e.** $50,200

15. What is the net cash flow in the final year (Year 5)?

    a. $31,360   **b.** $43,060   **c.** $119,630   **d.** $121,930   **e.** $117,200

16. Initially, United Products has a beta of 1.30. The risk-free rate is 12 percent, and the required rate of return on the market is 18 percent. The firm now sells 10 percent of its assets, having a beta of 1.30, and uses the proceeds to purchase a new product line with a beta of 1.00. What is the new overall required rate of return for United Products?

    a. 15.11%   **b.** 16.24%   **c.** 17.48%   **d.** 18.00%   **e.** 19.62%

17. Consolidated Inc. uses a required rate of return of 12 percent to evaluate average-risk projects and adds/subtracts two percentage points to evaluate projects of greater/lesser risk. Currently, two mutually exclusive projects are under consideration. Both have a net cost of $200,000 and last 4 years. Project A, which is riskier than average, will produce annual after-tax net cash flows of $71,000. Project B, which has less-than-average risk, will produce after-tax net cash flows of $146,000 in Years 3 and 4 only. What should Consolidated do?

    a. Accept Project B with an NPV of $9,412.
    b. Accept both projects since both NPVs are greater than zero.
    c. Accept Project A with an NPV of $6,874.
    d. Accept neither project since both NPVs are less than zero.
    e. Accept Project A with an NPV of $15,652.

18. Union Industries, an all equity-financed firm, is considering the purchase of a plant that produces plastic products. The plant is expected to generate a rate of return of 17 percent, and the plant's estimated beta is 2.00. The risk-free rate is 12 percent, and the market risk premium is 6 percent. Union should make the investment.

    a. True   **b.** False

19. Diversified Products (DP) is considering the formation of a new division that will double the assets of the firm. DP is an all-equity firm that has a current required rate of return of 20 percent. The risk-free rate is 10 percent, and the market risk premium is 5 percent. If DP wants to reduce its required rate of return to 18 percent, what is the maximum beta the new division could have?

    a. 1.00   **b.** 1.10   **c.** 1.20   **d.** 1.25   **e.** 1.30

ANSWERS TO SELF-TEST QUESTIONS

1.	capital budget	27.	sunk cost
2.	Replacement decisions	28.	opportunity cost
3.	Expansion decisions	29.	Externalities
4.	Independent	30.	terminal
5.	Mutually exclusive	31.	old; tax
6.	payback period	32.	difference
7.	less	33.	incremental
8.	cash flows; ignored	34.	stand-alone; corporate (within-firm)
9.	discounted	35.	Stand-alone
10.	positive	36.	Corporate
11.	discounted payback	37.	Beta
12.	mutually exclusive; higher	38.	scenario analysis
13.	zero	39.	pure play
14.	hurdle	40.	risk-adjusted
15.	NPV; discount rates	41.	Capital rationing
16.	crossover	42.	Capital budgeting
17.	NPV	43.	firm
18.	required rate of return (cost of capital); internal rate of return	44.	asset valuation
		45.	less
19.	discount; cash flows; cost (or initial cost)	46.	zero
		47.	project size; scale; timing
20.	Multiple IRRs	48.	after-tax cash flows
21.	risk; liquidity	49.	Shipping; installation
22.	NPV	50.	inflation
23.	IRR	51.	repatriation of earnings
24.	cash flow estimation	52.	Exchange rate risk
25.	relevant	53.	Political risk
26.	outflow; inflow; end		

54.   a.   The more the cash flows are spread over time, the greater is the effect of a change in discount rate. This is because the compounding process has a greater effect as the number of years increases.

55.   a.   Project cash flows are substitutes for outside capital. Thus, the opportunity cost of these cash flows is the firm's required rate of return. The NPV method uses this cost as the reinvestment rate, while the IRR method assumes reinvestment at the IRR.

56.   b.   The computation of IRR is independent of the firm's required rate of return.

57.   a.   Both the NPV and IRR methods lead to the same accept/reject decisions for independent projects. Thus, the IRR method can be used as a proxy for the NPV method when choosing independent projects.

58.   b.   The net market value of land currently owned is an opportunity cost of the project. If

the project is not undertaken, the land could be sold to realize its current market value less any taxes and expenses. Thus, project acceptance means forgoing this cash inflow.

59. a. Incremental revenues, which are relevant in a capital budgeting decision, must consider the effects on cash flows in other parts of the firm (externalities).

60. b. In an incremental analysis, the cash flows assuming replacement are compared with the cash flows assuming the old asset is retained. If the old asset is retained, it will produce a salvage value cash flow that must be included, with tax effects, in the replacement analysis.

61. a. The addition of an asset with a beta of zero would normally lower the beta of the firm, thus lowering the firm's beta risk. (The starting beta of most firms is greater than zero.)

62. b. The only time this statement holds is when all independent projects being evaluated have the same risk as the firm's current average project. Otherwise, the required rate of return must be adjusted for project risk.

63. a. If we were to begin graphing the NPV profiles for each of these projects, we would know 2 of the points for each project. The Y-intercepts for Projects A and B would be $7,000 and $5,000, respectively, and the crossover rate would be 10 percent. Thus, from this information we can conclude that Project A's NPV profile would have the steeper slope and would be more sensitive to changes in the discount rate.

64. b. Statement a is false because the IRR is independent of the discount rate. Statement b is true; the situation identified is that of a project with unconventional cash flows, which has multiple IRRs. Statement c is false; multiple IRRs occur with projects that have unconventional cash flows not with mutually exclusive projects with different lives.

65. b. Statement b is true, the other statements are false. Note that IRR must be greater than the cost of capital; conflicts arise if the required rate of return is to the left of the crossover rate; and for some projects with unconventional cash flows there are two IRRs, so NPV and IRR could lead to conflicting accept/reject decisions, depending on which IRR we examine.

66. e. Statement e is correct, because both statements a and c are true. The IRR assumes reinvestment at the IRR, and since the discounted payback ignores cash flows beyond the payback period, it could lead to ranking differences.

67. b. Statement a is true; MACRS is an accelerated depreciation method, so Firm A will have a higher depreciation expense than Firm B. We are also given that both firms are identical, except for depreciation methods used. Net cash flow is equal to net income plus depreciation. In Year 1, Firm A's depreciation expense is twice as great as Firm B's; however, Firm A's lower net income is more than compensated for by the addition of depreciation (which is twice as high as Firm B's). Thus, in Year 1, Firm A's net cash flow is greater than Firm B's. Statement b is false; because Firm A's depreciation expense is larger, its earnings before taxes will be lower, and thus it will pay less

income taxes than Firm B. Finally, statements c, d, and e are all true.

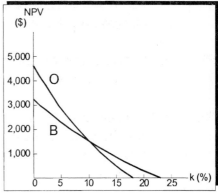

68.   c.   Institutional investors are well diversified and, therefore, more concerned with beta risk.

69.   c.   Statement c is correct. The opportunity cost of the building should be assessed against the new project, and that cost is what the company could currently get for the building, $50,000. All of the other statements are incorrect.

70.   e.   Statement e is the correct statement. Statement a is incorrect; stand-alone risk is a good proxy for market risk if the asset's returns are positively correlated with returns on other assets. Statement b is incorrect. After-tax cash flows are used in a capital budgeting analysis—it is cash that pays the bills and can be invested in capital projects. Statement c is incorrect; the pure play method can only be used for investments where the investment itself has characteristics similar to publicly traded firms.

SOLUTIONS TO SELF-TEST PROBLEMS

1.   c.   Unless you have a calculator that performs IRR calculations, the IRR must be obtained by trial and error or graphically. (Calculator solution: Input $CF_0 = -800000$, $CF_{1-2} = 700000$, $CF_3 = -400000$. Output: IRR = 25.48%.) Note that this project actually has multiple IRRs, with a second IRR at about -53 percent.

2.   c.   After Year 1, there is $5,000 – $2,085 = $2,915 remaining to pay back. After Year 2, only $2,915 – $2,085 = $830 is remaining. In Year 3, another $2,085 is collected. Assuming that the Year 3 cash flow occurs evenly over time, then payback occurs $830/$2,085 = 0.4 of the way through Year 3. Thus, the payback period is 2.4 years.

3.   b.   To solve graphically, construct the NPV profiles:

The Y-intercept is the NPV when k = 0%. For B, 4($2,085) – $5,000 = $3,340. For O, $9,677 – $5,000 = $4,677. The X-intercept is the discount rate when NPV = $0, or the IRR. For B, $5,000 = $2,085 × PVIFA$_{IRR,4}$; IRR ≈ 24%. For O, $5,000 = $9,677 × PVIF$_{IRR,4}$; IRR ≈ 18%. The graph is an approximation since we are only using two points to plot lines that are curvilinear. However, it shows that there is a crossover point and that it occurs somewhere in the vicinity of k = 10%. (Note that other data points for the NPV profiles could be obtained by calculating the NPVs for the two projects at different discount rates.)

4.   a.   Refer to the NPV profiles. When k = 14%, we are to the right of the crossover point and Project B has the higher NPV. You can verify this fact by calculating the NPVs. When k = 14%, NPV$_B$ = $1,075 and NPV$_O$ = $730. Note that Project B also has the higher IRR. However, the NPV method should be used when evaluating mutually

exclusive projects. Note that had the project cost of capital been 8 percent, then Project O would be chosen on the basis of the higher NPV.

5. a. After the first year, there is only $30 remaining to be repaid, and $50 is received in Year 2. Assuming an even cash flow throughout the year, the payback period is $1 + \$30/\$50 = 1.6$ years.

6. d. $NPV_L = -\$100 + \$10/1.10 + \$60/(1.10)^2 + \$80/(1.10)^3 = -\$100 + \$9.09 + \$49.59 + \$60.11 = \$18.79$. Financial calculator solution: Input the cash flows into the cash flow register, $I = k = 10$, and solve for $NPV = \$18.78$.

7. a. Input the cash flows into the cash flow register and solve for $IRR = 18.1\%$.

8. c. The NPV profiles plot as follows:

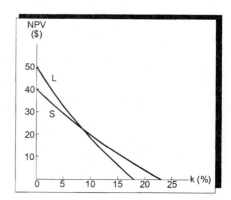

k	NPV_L	NPV_S
0%	$50	$40
5	33	29
10	19	20
15	7	12
20	(4)	5
25	(13)	(2)

By looking at the graph, the approximate crossover rate is between 8 and 9 percent.

9. b. Put the cash flows into the cash flow register, and then calculate NPV at 9% and IRR:

Project S: $NPV_S = \$101.83$; $IRR_S = 13.49\%$.
Project L: $NPV_L = \$172.07$; $IRR_L = 11.74\%$.
Because $NPV_L > NPV_S$, it is the better project. $IRR_L = 11.74\%$.

Alternatively, the PVIF table could be used to calculate the NPVs of both projects; however, calculating the IRR by trial and error would be tedious.

10. d. The only cash outflow is the $50,000 cost of the project. Cash inflows consist of the reduction in operating costs, equal to $30,000 per year. The depreciation allowances in each year are 0.33, 0.45, and 0.15 percent, respectively. After net income is calculated, depreciation is added back to arrive at the operating net cash flow.

$Dep_1 = \$50,000(0.33) = \$16,500$.
$Dep_2 = \$50,000(0.45) = \$22,500$.
$Dep_3 = \$50,000(0.15) = \$7,500$.

The project's cash flows are placed on a time line as follows:

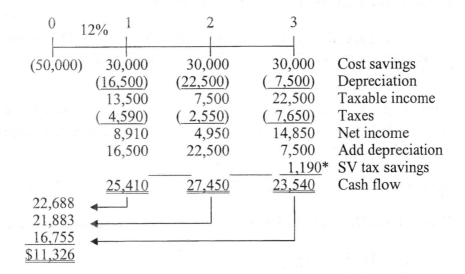

	0	1	2	3	
	(50,000)	30,000	30,000	30,000	Cost savings
		(16,500)	(22,500)	(7,500)	Depreciation
		13,500	7,500	22,500	Taxable income
		(4,590)	(2,550)	(7,650)	Taxes
		8,910	4,950	14,850	Net income
		16,500	22,500	7,500	Add depreciation
				1,190*	SV tax savings
		25,410	27,450	23,540	Cash flow

22,688
21,883
16,755
$11,326

*Salvage value tax savings. National has taken $16,500 + $22,500 + $7,500 = $46,500 in total depreciation, hence the book value at the end of the Year 3 is $50,000 – $46,500 = $3,500. Since the salvage value is $0, National can reduce its taxable income by $3,500, producing a 0.34($3,500) = $1,190 tax savings. Discount the cash flows individually at $k = 12\%$ to find the NPV.

Alternatively, input the cash flows into the cash flow register, input $I = 12$, and then solve for NPV = $11,326.

11. **e.** In this case, the *net income* of the project is $61,257. Net cash flow = Net income + Depreciation = $61,257 + Depreciation. The depreciation allowed in each year is calculated as follows:

$Dep_1 = \$500,000(0.20) = \$100,000.$
$Dep_2 = \$500,000(0.32) = \$160,000.$
$Dep_3 = \$500,000(0.19) = \$95,000.$
$Dep_4 = \$500,000(0.12) = \$60,000.$
$Dep_5 = \$500,000(0.11) = \$55,000.$
$Dep_6 = \$500,000(0.06) = \$30,000.$
$Dep_{7-10} = \$0.$

In the final year (Year 10), the firm receives $35,000 from the sale of the machine. However, the book value of the machine is $0. Thus, the firm would have to pay 0.4($35,000) = $14,000 in taxes; and the net salvage value is $35,000 – $14,000 = $21,000. The time line is as follows:

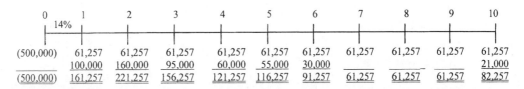

	0	1	2	3	4	5	6	7	8	9	10
14%											
	(500,000)	61,257	61,257	61,257	61,257	61,257	61,257	61,257	61,257	61,257	61,257
		100,000	160,000	95,000	60,000	55,000	30,000				21,000
	(500,000)	161,257	221,257	156,257	121,257	116,257	91,257	61,257	61,257	61,257	82,257

The project's NPV can be found by discounting each of the cash flows at the firm's 14 percent required rate of return. The project's NPV, found by using a financial calculator, is $177,902.

12. **d.** The initial net investment is $730,000:

Price	($600,000)
Transportation	(60,000)
Installation	(40,000)
Change in net working capital	(30,000)
Initial net investment	($730,000)

The annual operating cash flows are equal to net income plus depreciation. In Year 10, the firm will recover its investment in net working capital and gain the net salvage value. The depreciable basis is $700,000; thus, the annual depreciation is calculated as follows:

$Dep_1 = \$700,000(0.20) = \$140,000.$
$Dep_2 = \$700,000(0.32) = \$224,000.$
$Dep_3 = \$700,000(0.19) = \$133,000.$
$Dep_4 = \$700,000(0.12) = \$84,000.$
$Dep_5 = \$700,000(0.11) = \$77,000.$
$Dep_6 = \$700,000(0.06) = \$42,000.$
$Dep_{7-10} = \$0.$

The net salvage value is $10,000(0.6) = $6,000. Therefore, the time line is as follows:

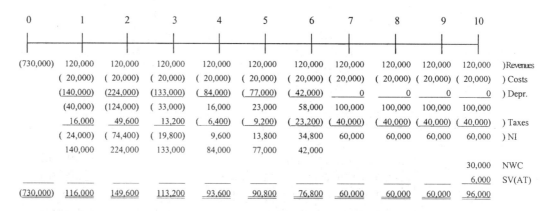

The project's NPV using a 10 percent required rate of return is -$130,961.

13. **b.**

Price of new machine	($300,000)
Installation	(50,000)
Sale of old machine	100,000
Tax on sale*	(29,920)
Increase in net working capital	(40,000)
	($319,920)

*The old machine has been depreciated down to $12,000 since it falls into the MACRS 5-year class and it has been in operation for 5 years. Now, the old machine has a market value of $100,000. The $88,000 (purchase price minus book value) is treated as ordinary income and is taxed at 34 percent. Thus, Union Mills must pay a tax of 0.34($88,000) = $29,920 on the sale of the old asset.

14.   a.   Costs decrease by $40,000. Net cash flow equals net income plus depreciation. The depreciable basis for the new machine is $350,000. Further, the MACRS depreciation allowance for Year 1 of a 5-year class asset is 20 percent. Thus, the depreciation expense on the new machine is 0.20($350,000) = $70,000. The old machine has not been fully depreciated, so its depreciation expense in Year 1 is $12,000, and the change in depreciation due to the replacement decision is an increase in depreciation of $58,000 ($70,000 − $12,000).

)Revenues	$40,000
)Depr.	(58,000)
	($18,000)
)Taxes (34%)	6,120
)NI	($11,880)
)Depr.	58,000
)NCF	$46,120

15.   c.   In the final year, Year 5, the net cash flow is composed of $40,000 in cost decreases and 0.11($350,000) = $38,500 in depreciation. Net income is calculated, depreciation is added back, and then the terminal cash flows must be determined.

)Revenues	$40,000
)Depr.	(38,500)
	$ 1,500
)Taxes (34%)	(510)
)NI	$ 990
)Depr.	38,500
)NCF	$39,490

Thus, we have the following:

NCF from operations	$ 39,490
Salvage value of new machine	100,000
Tax on new machine salvage value	(26,860)
Salvage value of old machine	(50,000)
Tax on old machine salvage value	17,000
Change in working capital	40,000
Net cash flow	$119,630

Note that the salvage value of the old machine is a cash outflow. This is an opportunity cost, since buying the new machine deprives Union Mills of the salvage value of the old machine. Additionally, salvage tax effects must be considered. Also note that the change in working capital considered at t = 0, an outflow, is exactly offset by an inflow at the end of the project. This is because it is assumed that the project will terminate and the increase in working capital is no longer required.

16. e. New $b = 0.9(1.30) + 0.1(1.00) = 1.27$.
New $k_s = 12\% + (18\% - 12\%)1.27 = 19.62\%$.

17. a. Look at the time lines:

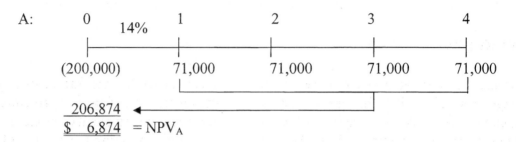

Alternatively, input the cash flows in the cash flow register, enter I = 14, and then solve for $NPV_A = \$6,873.57$.

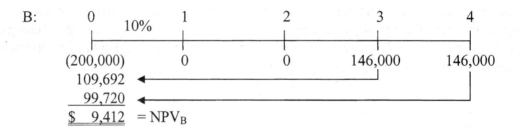

Alternatively, input the cash flows in the cash flow register, enter I = 10, and then solve for $NPV_B = \$9,411.93$.

Note that both discount rates are adjusted for risk. Since the projects are mutually exclusive, the project with the higher NPV is chosen.

18. b. The project's required rate of return on equity is 24 percent: $k_{proj} = 12\% + (6\%)2 = 24\%$. Since the expected return is only 17 percent, the plant should not be purchased.

19. c. First, find the current beta of the firm: $k_s = 10\% + (5\%)b = 20\%$, so $b = 2.00$.

Now find the beta required to lower the required rate of return to 18 percent:

$$k_s = 10\% + (5\%)b = 18\%, \text{ so } b = 1.60.$$

Finally, if the firm doubles its size with the formation of the new division, 50 percent of the expanded firm's assets will be old assets, while 50 percent will be assets from the new division. Thus, $0.5(2.00) + 0.5(b_{Div.}) = 1.60$; $b_{Div.} = 1.20$.

CHAPTER 14
CAPITAL STRUCTURE AND DIVIDEND POLICY
DECISIONS

OVERVIEW

In Chapter 12, when we calculated the weighted average cost of capital for use in capital budgeting, we took the capital structure weights, or the mix of securities the firm uses to finance its assets, as given. However, if the weights are changed, the calculated cost of capital, and thus the set of acceptable investments, will also change. Further, changing the capital structure will affect the riskiness inherent in the firm's common stock, and this will affect the return demanded by stockholders, k_s, and the stock's price, P_0. Therefore, choosing a particular capital structure is an important decision. In addition, decisions concerning the amount of earnings that are paid to stockholders as dividends affect the amount of internal equity financing a firm has available to support investments, and thus affect capital structure decisions. In this chapter, we discuss concepts relating to capital structure and dividend policy decisions.

OUTLINE

Capital structure policy involves a tradeoff between risk and return. Using more debt raises the riskiness of the firm's earnings stream, but a higher proportion of debt generally leads to a higher expected rate of return.

■ The *target capital structure* is the mix of debt, preferred stock, and common equity with which the firm plans to finance its investments.
~ This target may change over time as conditions vary.

■ The *optimal capital structure* is the one that strikes a balance between risk and return so as to maximize the stock price.

■ Four primary factors influence capital structure decisions:
~ *Business risk* is the amount of risk in a firm's operations if no debt is used.
• The greater the firm's business risk, the lower the amount of debt that is optimal.
~ A firm's tax position is important. A major reason for using debt is the fact that interest is *tax deductible*, which lowers the effective cost of debt.
• If much of a firm's income is already sheltered from taxes by accelerated depreciation or tax loss carryforwards, its tax rate will be low, and debt will not be as advantageous as it would be to a firm with a higher effective tax rate.

269

       ~ *Financial flexibility*, which is the ability to raise capital on reasonable terms under adverse conditions, is another consideration.

             • The potential future availability of funds, and the consequences of a funds shortage, have a major influence on the target capital structure.

             • When money is tight in the economy, or when a firm is experiencing operating difficulties, a strong balance sheet is needed to obtain funds from suppliers of capital.

       ~ *Managerial attitude (conservatism or aggressiveness)* with regard to borrowing influences the target capital structure a firm actually establishes.

             • This factor doesn't affect the optimal, or value-maximizing, capital structure.

■ Operating conditions can cause the actual capital structure to vary from the target at any given time.

Business risk is the uncertainty inherent in projections of future returns, either on assets or on equity, if the firm uses no debt or debt-like financing, including preferred stock. It is the risk associated with the firm's operations. Business risk is the single most important determinant of capital structure.

■ *Business risk* varies from one industry to another and also among firms in a given industry. It can also change over time. Smaller companies, especially single-product firms, also have relatively high degrees of business risk.

■ Business risk depends on a number of factors, the more important include: (1) *sales variability (volume and price)*, (2) *input price variability*, (3) *ability to adjust output prices for changes in input prices*, and (4) *operating leverage* (the extent to which costs are fixed).

       ~ A firm with greater operating leverage has greater business risk than a firm with lower operating leverage because its earnings will exhibit greater variability when sales vary.

       ~ Each of these factors is determined partly by the firm's industry characteristics, but each is also controllable to some extent by management.

Financial leverage refers to the firm's use of fixed-income securities, such as debt and preferred stock. Financial risk is defined as the additional risk, over and above basic business risk, placed on the common stockholders that results from using financial alternatives with fixed periodic payments.

■ The use of debt intensifies the firm's business risk borne by the common stockholders.

■ The degree to which a firm employs *financial leverage* will affect its expected earnings per share (EPS) and the riskiness of these earnings. Financial leverage will cause EPS to rise if the return on assets is greater than the cost of debt. However, the degree of risk associated with the firm will also increase as leverage increases.

■ At first, EPS will rise as the use of debt increases. Interest charges rise, but the number of outstanding shares will decrease as equity is replaced by debt. At some point EPS will peak.

Beyond this point interest rates will rise so fast that EPS is depressed in spite of the fact that the number of shares outstanding is decreasing.

■ Risk, as measured by the coefficient of variation of EPS, rises continuously, and at an increasing rate, as debt is substituted for equity.

■ The *EPS indifference point* is the level of sales at which EPS will be the same regardless of whether the firm uses debt or common stock.

■ The *optimal capital structure* is the one that maximizes the price of the firm's stock, and this always calls for a debt/assets ratio that is lower than the one that maximizes expected EPS.
  ~ The primary reason this relationship exists is because P_0 reflects changes in risk that accompany changes in capital structures and affect cash flows long into the future, while EPS generally measures only the expectations for the near term.

■ The expected stock price will at first increase with financial leverage, will then reach a peak, and finally will decline as financial leverage becomes excessive due to the importance of potential bankruptcy costs.
  ~ The optimal capital structure is found when the expected stock price is maximized.
  ~ Management should set its target capital structure at this ratio of debt/assets, and if the existing ratios are off target, it should move toward the target when new security offerings are made.

■ Managers are concerned about the effects of financial leverage on the risk of bankruptcy, and an analysis of this factor is therefore an important input in all capital structure decisions.
  ~ Accordingly, managements give considerable weight to financial strength indicators such as the *times-interest-earned ratio*, which is computed by dividing earnings before interest and taxes by interest expense.
    • The TIE ratio provides an indication of how well the firm can cover its interest payments with operating income (EBIT)—the lower this ratio, the higher the probability that a firm will default on its debt and be forced into bankruptcy.
    • In general, we know that with less debt, there is a much lower probability of a TIE of less than 1.0, the level at which the firm is not earning enough to meet its required interest payment and thus is seriously exposed to the threat of bankruptcy.
    •

The general theories of capital structure have been developed along two main lines: (1) tax benefit/bankruptcy cost tradeoff theory and (2) signaling theory.

■ *Tradeoff theory* as set forth by Modigliani and Miller states that, due to the tax deductibility of interest on debt, a firm's value rises continuously as it uses more debt, and hence its value will be maximized by financing almost entirely with debt.
  ~ This theory holds only under a very restrictive set of assumptions.
  ~ These assumptions, however, do not hold true in the real world.

- Debt costs rise as the debt ratio rises, EBIT declines at extreme leverage, expected tax rates fall and reduce the value of the tax shelter, and the probability of bankruptcy increases as the debt level rises.
- At some point, bankruptcy-related costs exceed the benefit of additional debt. This point denotes the target capital structure. However, researchers have not been able to identify these points precisely.

~ Many large, successful firms use far less debt than the theory suggests.

- This point led to the development of signaling theory.

■ *Signaling theory* recognizes the fact that investors and managers do *not* have the same information regarding a firm's prospects, as was assumed by tradeoff theory. This is called *asymmetric information*, and it has an important effect on decisions to use either debt or equity to finance capital projects.

~ One would expect a firm with very favorable prospects to try to avoid selling stock and, rather, to raise any required new capital by other means, including using debt beyond the normal target capital structure.

~ A firm with unfavorable prospects would want to sell stock, which would mean bringing in new investors to share the losses.

~ The announcement of a stock offering by a mature firm that seems to have multiple financing alternatives is taken as a *signal* that the firm's prospects as seen by its management are not bright. This, in turn, suggests that when a mature firm announces a new stock offering, the price of its stock should decline.

~ Firms, in normal times, maintain a *reserve borrowing capacity* that can be used in the event that some especially good investment opportunities come along. This means that firms should generally use less debt than would be suggested by the tax benefit/bankruptcy cost tradeoff theory.

■ In real life, capital structure decisions must be made more on the basis of judgment than numerical analysis.

There are wide variations in the use of financial leverage both across industries and among individual firms in each industry.

■ The times-interest-earned ratio is a good tool to gauge the degree of financial leverage used by a particular firm.

~ It gives a measure of how safe the debt is and how vulnerable the company is to financial distress.

~ The TIE ratio depends on three factors: (1) the percentage of debt, (2) the interest rate on debt, and (3) the company's profitability.

~ Generally, the least leveraged industries have the highest coverage ratios.

Dividend policy involves the decision to pay out earnings or to retain them for reinvestment in the firm. Dividend policy decisions directly affect (1) capital structure—all else equal, retaining earnings rather than paying out dividends increases common equity relative to

debt; and (2) cost of capital—financing with retained earnings is cheaper than issuing new common equity.

■   The *dividend irrelevance theory* is the theory that a firm's dividend policy has no effect on either its value or its cost of capital.
  ~   Proponents of this would contend that investors care only about the total returns they receive, not whether they receive those returns in the form of dividends or capital gains.
  ~   If dividend irrelevance theory is correct, there exists no optimal dividend policy, because dividend policy does not affect the value of the firm.

■   On the other hand, it is quite possible that, investors prefer one dividend policy over another. It has been argued that investors prefer to receive dividends today because current dividend payments are more certain than the future capital gains that might result from investing retained earnings in growth opportunities, so k_s should decrease as the dividend payout is increased.

■   Another factor that might cause investors to prefer a particular dividend policy is the tax effect of dividend receipts.
  ~   Depending on his or her tax situation, an investor might prefer either a payout of current earnings as dividends, which would be taxed in the current period, or capital gains associated with growth in stock value, which would be taxed when the stock is sold.
  ~   Investors who prefer to delay the impact of taxes would be willing to pay more for low payout companies than for otherwise similar high payout companies.
  ~   Those who believe the firm's dividend policy is relevant are proponents of the *dividend relevance theory*, which asserts that dividend policy can affect the value of a firm through investors' preferences.

Although researchers cannot tell corporate decision makers precisely how dividend policy affects stock prices and capital costs, the research has generated some thoughts concerning investors' reactions to dividend policy changes and why firms have particular dividend policies. Three of these views are: (1) the information content, or signaling, hypothesis, (2) the clientele effect, and (3) the free cash flow hypothesis.

■   It has been observed that a greater-than-expected dividend increase announcement is often accompanied by an increase in the price of the stock.
  ~   Managers do not raise dividends unless they anticipate higher, or at least stable, earnings in the future to sustain the higher dividends.
  ~   This means that a larger-than-expected dividend increase is taken by investors as a "signal" that the firm's management forecasts improved future earnings, whereas a dividend reduction signals a forecast of poor earnings.
  ~   In effect, dividend announcements provide investors with information previously known only to management. This theory is referred to as the *information content, or signaling, hypothesis.*

■ It has also been shown that it is very possible that a firm sets a particular dividend payout policy, which then attracts a *clientele* consisting of those investors who like the firm's dividend policy.

~ Some stockholders (for example, retirees) prefer current income to future capital gains; therefore, they would want the firm to pay out a high percentage of its earnings as dividends.

~ Other stockholders have no need for current income (for example, doctors in their peak earnings years) and they would simply reinvest any dividends received, after first paying income taxes on the dividend income. Therefore, they would favor a low payout ratio.

~ In essence, then, a *clientele effect* might exist if a firm's stockholders are attracted to companies because they have particular dividend policies.

~ We would expect the stock price of a firm to change if it changes its dividend policy, because investors will adjust their portfolios to include firms with the desired dividend policy.

■ According to the *free cash flow hypothesis*, all else equal, firms that pay dividends from cash flows that cannot be reinvested in positive net present value projects, which are termed free cash flows, have higher values than firms that retain such free cash flows.

~ According to the free cash flow hypothesis, the firm should distribute any earnings that cannot be reinvested at a rate at least as great as the investors' required rate of return, k_s.

~ The free cash flow hypothesis suggests the dividend policy can provide information about the firm's behavior with respect to wealth maximization.

The theories offer conflicting advice, yet managers must establish a dividend policy. The dollar amounts of dividends paid by firms follow a variety of patterns. Here are alternative dividend policies that are used in practice:

■ *Residual dividend policy* is based on the premise that investors prefer to have a firm retain and reinvest earnings rather than pay them out in dividends if the rate of return the firm can earn on reinvested earnings exceeds the rate of return investors can obtain for themselves on other investments of comparable risk. Further, it is less expensive for the firm to use retained earnings than it is to issue new common stock.

~ According to the residual dividend policy, a firm that has to issue new common stock to finance capital budgeting needs does not have residual earnings, and dividends will be zero.

~ Because both the earnings level and the capital budgeting needs of a firm vary from year to year, strict adherence to the residual dividend policy would result in dividend variability.

~ Following the residual dividend policy would be optimal only if investors were not bothered by fluctuating dividends.

■ A company's policy of *stable, predictable dividends* implies to shareholders that the regular dividend will at least be maintained and, accordingly, that earnings will be sufficient to cover it. A corollary of this policy is never reduce the annual dividend. There are two good reasons for following this type of dividend policy:

- ~ Given the existence of the information content, or signaling, idea, a fluctuating payment policy would lead to greater uncertainty, hence to a higher k_s and a lower stock price, than would exist under a stable policy.
- ~ Many stockholders use dividends for current consumption, and they would be put to trouble and expense if they had to sell part of their shares to obtain cash if the company cut the dividend.
    - As a rule, stable, predictable dividends imply more certainty than variable dividends, thus a lower k_s and a higher firm value.

- It would be possible for a firm to pay out a constant percentage of earnings, that is, a *constant payout ratio*.
    - ~ Because earnings surely will fluctuate, this policy would mean that the dollar amount of dividends would vary. This would normally result in an unpredictable dividend stream and would not please most investors.

- The policy of paying a *low regular dividend plus extras* is a compromise between a stable dividend (or stable growth rate) and a constant payout rate.
    - ~ This policy gives the firm flexibility, yet investors can count on receiving at least a minimum dividend.
    - ~ It is often followed by firms with relatively volatile earnings from year to year.
    - ~ The low regular dividend can usually be maintained even when earnings decline, and "extra" dividends can be paid when excess funds are available.

Firms usually pay dividends on a quarterly basis in accordance with the following payment procedures:

- *Declaration date.* This is the day on which the board of directors declares the dividend. At this time they set the amount of the dividend to be paid, the holder-of-record date, and the payment date.

- *Holder-of-record date.* This is the date the company opens the ownership books to determine who will receive the dividend; the stockholders of record on this date receive the dividend.

- *Ex-dividend date.* This is the date on which the right to the next dividend no longer accompanies a stock. It is usually two business days prior to the holder-of-record date. Shares purchased after the ex-dividend date are not entitled to the dividend. This practice is a convention of the brokerage business that allows sufficient time for stock transfers to be made on the books of the corporation.

- *Payment date.* This is the day when dividend checks are actually mailed to the holders of record. Recently, many firms have started paying dividends electronically.

Many firms have instituted dividend reinvestment plans (DRIPs) whereby stockholders can automatically reinvest dividends received to purchase more stock of the paying corporation.

Income taxes on the amount of the dividends must be paid even though stock rather than cash is received.

■   There are two types of DRIPs: (1) plans that involve only "old" stock that already is outstanding and (2) plans that involve newly issued stock.

Regardless of the debate on the relevancy of dividend policy, it is possible to identify several factors that influence dividend policy. These factors are grouped into four broad categories.

■   *Constraints on dividend payments*: (1) debt contract restrictions, (2) impairment of capital rule, and (3) cash availability.

■   *Investment opportunities*: (1) capital budgeting opportunities and (2) ability to accelerate or delay projects (flexibility).

■   *Availability and costs of alternative sources of capital*: (1) cost of selling new stock, (2) ability to substitute debt for equity, and (3) management's concern about maintaining control.

■   *Effects of dividend policy on k_s*: (1) stockholders' desire for current versus future income, (2) perceived riskiness of dividends versus capital gains, (3) the tax advantage of capital gains over dividends, and (4) the information content of dividends (signaling).

Although there is little empirical evidence to support the contention, there is nevertheless a widespread belief in financial circles that an optimal, or psychological, price range exists for stocks. "Optimal" means that if the price is within this range, the price/earnings ratio, hence the value of the firm, will be maximized. Stock dividends and stock splits are often used to lower a firm's stock price and, at the same time, to conserve its cash resources.

■   The effect of a *stock split* is an increase in the number of shares outstanding and a reduction in the par, or stated, value of the shares.
    ~   For example, if a firm had 1,000 shares of stock outstanding with a par value of $100 per share, a 2-for-1 split would reduce the par value to $50 and increase the number of shares to 2,000.
    ~   The total net worth of the firm remains unchanged.
    ~   The stock split does not involve any cash payment, only additional certificates representing new shares.

■   A *stock dividend* is similar to a stock split in that it "divides the pie into smaller slices" without affecting the fundamental position of the current stockholders.
    ~   It requires an accounting entry transfer from retained earnings to the common stock and paid-in capital accounts and an accompanying pro-rata distribution of new shares to the existing stockholders.
        •   Dollars transferred from retained earnings = Number of shares outstanding × Percentage of the stock dividend × Market price of the stock.

~ No cash is involved with this "dividend." Net worth remains unchanged, and the number of shares is increased.

■ If stock dividends and splits are accompanied by higher earnings and cash dividends, then investors will bid up the price of the stock.

   ~ If stock dividends are not accompanied by increases in earnings and cash dividends, the dilution of EPS and DPS causes the price of the stock to drop by the same percentage as the stock dividend.

   ~ The fundamental determinants of price are the underlying earnings and cash dividends per share, and stock splits and stock dividends merely cut the pie into thinner slices.

When capital structures of companies around the world are examined wide variations are found.

■ Different countries use somewhat different accounting conventions, which make comparisons difficult.

   ~ Still, even after adjusting for accounting differences, researchers find that Italian and Japanese firms use considerably more financial leverage than U.S. and Canadian companies.

   ~ The gap among the countries has narrowed somewhat during the past couple of decades.

■ The dividend policies of companies around the world also vary considerably.

■ Differential tax laws cannot explain the observed capital structure differences. Also, it has been found that differences in taxes do not explain the differences in dividend payout ratios among the countries.

■ An analysis of both bankruptcy costs and equity monitoring costs leads to the conclusion that U.S. firms should have more equity and less debt than firms in countries such as Japan and Germany, which is what we typically observe.

■ A recent study of dividend policy differences that exist around the world offers some insight.

   ~ All else equal, companies pay out greater amounts of earnings as dividends in countries with measures that help protect the rights of minority stockholders.

      • In such countries, though, firms with many growth opportunities tend to pay lower dividends, which is to be expected, because the funds are needed to finance the growth and shareholders are willing to forgo current income in hopes of greater future benefits.

   ~ In countries where shareholders' rights are not well protected, investors prefer dividends because there is great uncertainty about whether management will use earnings for self-gratification rather than for the benefit of the firm. Investors in these countries accept any dividends they can get.

SELF-TEST QUESTIONS

Definitional

1. Capital structure policy involves a tradeoff between _____ and _____.

2. The _____ _____ _____ is the one that strikes a balance between risk and return so as to maximize the price of a firm's stock.

3. Four primary factors influence capital structure decisions: _____ risk, a firm's tax position, _____ _____, and managerial _____ (conservatism or aggressiveness) with regard to borrowing.

4. A firm's _____ _____ _____ is the mix of debt, preferred stock, and common equity with which the firm plans to finance its investments, and it is generally set equal to the estimated optimal capital structure.

5. Business risk is the uncertainty inherent in projections of future _____ ____ _____, or of returns on equity, if the firm uses no debt or debt-like financing, and is the single most important determinant of a firm's capital structure.

6. Some of the factors that influence a firm's business risk include: (1) _____ variability, (2)
    input price variability, and (3) _____ leverage.

7. Business risk represents the riskiness of the firm's operations if it uses no _____; _____ risk represents the additional risk borne by common stockholders as a result of using debt.

8. _____ _____ refers to the firm's use of fixed-income securities, such as debt and preferred stock.

9. Expected EPS generally _____ as the debt/assets ratio increases.

10. The _____ _____ _____ is the level of sales at which EPS will be the same whether the firm uses debt or common stock financing.

11. As financial leverage increases, the stock price will first begin to rise, but it will then decline as financial leverage becomes excessive because potential _____ _____ become increasingly important.

12. The financial structure that maximizes EPS usually has _____ debt than the one that results in the highest stock price.

13. TIE ratios depend on three factors: (1) the _____ of debt, (2) the _____ _____ on debt, and (3) the company's _____.

14.   The general theories of capital structure have been developed among two main lines: _____ theory and _____ theory.

15.   _____ _____ occurs when managers have different (better) information about their firm's prospects than do outside investors.

16.   Firms, in normal times, maintain a(n) _____ _____ _____, that can be used in the event that some especially good investment opportunities come along.

17.   _____ _____ involves the decision to pay out earnings as dividends or to retain them for reinvestment in the firm.

18.   According to the _____ _____ theory, dividend policy can affect the value of a firm through investors' preferences.

19.   The _____ _____ theory states that a firm's dividend policy has no effect on either its value or its cost of capital.

20.   If the price of a firm's stock increases with a greater-than-expected dividend increase announcement, it may be due to the _____ content in the dividend announcement rather than to a preference for dividends over capital gains.

21.   The _____ _____ suggests that a firm establishes a dividend policy and then attracts specific individuals that are drawn to this dividend policy.

22.   According to the _____ _____ _____ _____, all else equal, firms that pay dividends from cash flows that cannot be reinvested in positive net present value projects have higher values than firms that retain these cash flows.

23.   _____ _____ _____ is based on the premise that investors prefer to have a firm retain and reinvest earnings rather than pay them out in dividends if the rate of return the firm can earn on reinvested earnings exceeds the rate of return investors can obtain for themselves on other investments of comparable risk.

24.   A company's policy of _____, _____ dividends implies to shareholders that the regular dividend will at least be maintained and, accordingly, that earnings will be sufficient to cover it.

25.   The policy of paying a(n) _____ _____ _____ _____ _____ is a compromise between a stable dividend and a constant payout rate.

26.   On the _____ _____ the board of directors set the amount of the dividend to be paid, the holder-of-record date, and the payment date.

27.   A firm with _____ earnings is most appropriate for using the policy of "extra" dividends.

28.   The ____-_____ date occurs two business days prior to the _____-____-_____ date and provides time for stock transfers to be recorded on the books of the firm.

29.   Actual payment of a dividend is made on the _____ date as announced by the _____ ____ _____.

30.   Many firms have instituted _____ _____ plans whereby stockholders can use their dividends to purchase additional shares of the company's stock.

31.   It is possible to identify several factors that influence dividend policy. These factors can be grouped into four broad categories: _____ on dividend payments, _____ opportunities, availability and cost of alternative sources of capital, and effects of dividend policy on k_s.

32.   _____ _____ refers to the ability to raise capital on reasonable terms under adverse conditions.

33.   _____, as measured by the coefficient of variation of EPS, rises continuously, and at an increasing rate, as debt is substituted for equity.

34.   The _____ _____ provides an indication of how well the firm can cover its interest payments with operating income.

35.   _____ _____ as set forth by Modigliani and Miller states that, due to the tax deductibility of interest on debt, a firm's value rises continuously as it uses more debt, and hence its value will be maximized by financing almost entirely with debt.

36.   _____ theory recognizes the fact that investors and managers do not have the same information regarding a firm's prospects.

37.   Dividend policy decisions directly affect _____ _____ and the _____ ____ _____.

38.   A(n) _____ are those investors who like the firm's dividend policy.

39.   A(n) _____ _____ increases the number of shares outstanding and reduces the par, or stated, value of the shares.

40.   A(n) _____ _____ is similar to a stock split in that it "divides the pie into smaller slices" without affecting the fundamental position of the current stockholders.

41. A dividend policy that calls for a firm to pay out a constant percentage of its earnings is called a(n) _____ _____ _____ policy.

Conceptual

42. As a general rule, the capital structure that maximizes stock price also

    a. Maximizes the weighted average cost of capital.
    b. Maximizes EPS.
    c. Maximizes bankruptcy costs.
    d. Minimizes the weighted average cost of capital.
    e. Minimizes the required rate of return on equity.

43. If investors prefer dividends to capital gains, then

    a. The required rate of return on equity, k_s, will not be affected by a change in dividend policy.
    b. The cost of capital will not be affected by a change in dividend policy.
    c. k_s will increase as the payout ratio is reduced.
    d. k_s will decrease as the retention rate increases.
    e. A policy conforming to the residual theory of dividends will maximize stock price.

44. Which of the following statements is correct?

    a. According to the asymmetric information, or signaling, theory of capital structure, the announcement of a new stock issue by a mature firm would generally lead to an *increase* in the price of the firm's stock.
    b. According to the asymmetric information, or signaling, theory of capital structure, the announcement of a new stock issue by a mature firm would generally lead to a *decrease* in the price of the firm's stock.
    c. If Firm A's managers believe in the asymmetric information theory, but Firm B's managers do not, then, other things held constant, Firm A would probably have the *higher* normal target debt ratio.
    d. There is no such thing as the asymmetric information theory of capital structure, at least according to the text.
    e. Both statements b and c are correct.

45. Which of the following statements is correct?

    a. The residual dividend policy calls for the establishment of a fixed, stable dividend (or dividend growth rate) and then for the level of investment each year to be determined as a residual equal to net income minus the established dividends.

    b. The basis of the residual policy is the fact that investors prefer to have the firm retain and reinvest earnings rather than pay them out in dividends if the rate of return the firm can earn on reinvested earnings exceeds the rate investors, on average, can themselves obtain on other investments of comparable risk.

    c. According to the text, a firm would probably maximize its stock price if it established a specific dividend payout ratio, say 40 percent, and then paid that percentage of earnings out each year because stockholders would then know exactly how much dividend income to count on when they planned their spending for the coming year.

    d. If you buy a stock after the ex-dividend date but before the dividend has been paid, then you, and not the seller, will receive the next dividend check the company sends out.

    e. Each of the above statements is false.

SELF-TEST PROBLEMS

1. Brown Products is a new firm just starting operations. The firm will produce backpacks that will sell for $22.00 each. Fixed costs are $500,000 per year, and variable costs are $2.00 per unit of production. The company expects to sell 50,000 backpacks per year, and its marginal tax rate is 40 percent. Brown needs $2 million to build facilities, obtain working capital, and start operations. If Brown borrows part of the money, the interest charges will depend on the amount borrowed as follows:

Amount Borrowed	Percentage of Debt in Capital Structure	Interest Rate on Total Amount Borrowed
$ 200,000	10%	9.00%
400,000	20	9.50
600,000	30	10.00
800,000	40	15.00
1,000,000	50	19.00
1,200,000	60	26.00

Assume that stock can be sold at a price of $20 per share on the initial offering, regardless of how much debt the company uses. Then after the company begins operating, its price will be determined as a multiple of its earnings per share. The multiple (or the P/E ratio) will depend upon the capital structure as follows:

Debt/Assets	P/E	Debt/Assets	P/E
0.0	12.5	40.0	8.0
10.0	12.0	50.0	6.0
20.0	11.5	60.0	5.0
30.0	10.0		

What is Brown's optimal capital structure, which maximizes stock price, as measured by the debt/assets ratio?

a. 10%   **b.** 20%   **c.** 30%   **d.** 40%   **e.** 50%

2. Tapley Dental Supplies Inc. is in a stable, no-growth situation. Its $1,000,000 of debt consists of perpetuities that have a 10 percent coupon and sell at par. Tapley's EBIT is $500,000, its cost of equity is 15 percent, it has 100,000 shares outstanding, all earnings are paid out as dividends, and its marginal tax rate is 40 percent. Tapley could borrow an additional $500,000 at an interest rate of 13 percent without having to retire the original debt, and it would use the proceeds to repurchase stock *at the current price*, not at the new equilibrium price. The increased risk from the additional leverage will raise the cost of equity to 17 percent. If Tapley does recapitalize, what will the new stock price be?

a. $17.20   **b.** $16.00   **c.** $16.50   **d.** $17.00   **e.** $16.75

3. Express Industries' expected net income for next year is $1 million. The company's target and current capital structure is 40 percent debt and 60 percent common equity. The optimal capital budget for next year is $1.2 million. If Express uses the residual theory of dividends to determine next year's dividend payout, what is the expected payout ratio?

a. 0%   **b.** 10%   **c.** 28%   **d.** 42%   **e.** 56%

4. Amalgamated Shippers has a current and target capital structure of 30 percent debt and 70 percent equity. This past year Amalgamated, which uses a residual dividend policy, had a dividend payout ratio of 47.5 percent and net income of $800,000. What was Amalgamated's capital budget?

a. $400,000   **b.** $500,000   **c.** $600,000   **d.** $700,000   **e.** $800,000

5. The Aikman Company's optimal capital structure calls for 40 percent debt and 60 percent common equity. The interest rate on its debt is a constant 12 percent; its cost of common equity from retained earnings is 16 percent; the cost of equity from new stock is 18 percent; and its marginal tax rate is 40 percent. Aikman has the following investment opportunities:

> Project A: Cost = $5 million; IRR = 22%.
> Project B: Cost = $5 million; IRR = 14%.
> Project C: Cost = $5 million; IRR = 11%.

Aikman expects to have net income of $7 million. If Aikman bases its dividends on the residual policy, what will its payout ratio be?

a. 22.62%   **b.** 14.29%   **c.** 31.29%   **d.** 25.62%   **e.** 18.75%

6. Ace Automotive Services Inc.'s stock trades at $120 a share. The company is contemplating a 5-for-3 stock split. Assuming that the stock split will have no effect on the market value of its equity, what will be the company's stock price following the stock split?

    a. $45.00   **b.** $58.00   **c.** $60.00   **d.** $72.00   **e.** $80.00

ANSWERS TO SELF-TEST QUESTIONS

1.	risk; return		**22.**	free cash flow hypothesis
2.	optimal capital structure		**23.**	Residual dividend policy
3.	business; financial flexibility; attitude		**24.**	stable, predictable
			25.	low regular dividend plus extras
4.	target capital structure		**26.**	declaration date
5.	returns on assets		**27.**	volatile (fluctuating)
6.	sales; operating		**28.**	ex-dividend; holder-of-record
7.	debt; financial		**29.**	payment; board of directors
8.	Financial leverage		**30.**	dividend reinvestment
9.	increases		**31.**	constraints; investment
10.	EPS indifference point		**32.**	Financial flexibility
11.	bankruptcy costs		**33.**	Risk
12.	more		**34.**	TIE ratio
13.	percentage; interest rate; profitability		**35.**	Tradeoff theory
14.	tradeoff; signaling		**36.**	Signaling
15.	Asymmetric information		**37.**	capital structure; cost of capital
16.	reserve borrowing capacity		**38.**	clientele
17.	Dividend policy		**39.**	stock split
18.	dividend relevance		**40.**	stock dividend
19.	dividend irrelevance		**41.**	constant payout ratio
20.	information			
21.	clientele effect			

42. d. The optimal capital structure balances risk and return to maximize the stock price. The structure that maximizes stock price also minimizes the firm's cost of capital.

43. c. If investors view dividends as being less risky than potential capital gains, then the cost of equity is inversely related to the payout ratio.

44. b. The asymmetric information theory suggests that investors regard the announcement of a stock sale as bad news: If the firm had really good investment opportunities, it would use debt financing so that existing stockholders would get all the benefits from the good projects. Therefore, the announcement of a stock sale leads to a decline in the price of the firm's stock. In order to reduce the chances of having to issue stock, firms therefore set low target debt ratios, which give them "reserve borrowing capacity."

45. b. Statement a is false; the residual dividend policy calls for the determination of the optimal capital budget and then the dividend is established as a residual of net income minus the amount of retained earnings necessary for the capital budget. Statement b is correct. Statement c is false; a constant payout policy would lead to uncertainty of dividends due to fluctuating earnings. Statement d is false; if a stock is bought after the ex-dividend date the dividend remains with the seller of the stock.

SOLUTIONS TO SELF-TEST PROBLEMS

1. b. The first step is to calculate EBIT:

Sales in dollars [50,000($22)]	$1,100,000
Less: Fixed costs	(500,000)
Variable costs [50,000($2)]	(100,000)
EBIT	$ 500,000

The second step is to calculate the EPS at each debt/assets ratio using the formula:

$$EPS = \frac{(EBIT - I)(1 - T)}{Shares\ outstanding}.$$

Recognize (1) that I = Interest charges = (Dollars of debt)(Interest rate at each D/A ratio), and (2) that Shares outstanding = (Assets – Debt)/Initial price per share = ($2,000,000 – Debt)/$20.00.

D/A	EPS	D/A	EPS
0%	$3.00	40%	$3.80
10	3.21	50	3.72
20	3.47	60	2.82
30	3.77		

Finally, the third step is to calculate the stock price at each debt/assets ratio using the following formula: Price = (P/E)(EPS).

D/A	Price	D/A	Price
0%	$37.50	40%	$30.40
10	38.52	50	22.32
20	39.91	60	14.10
30	37.70		

Thus, a debt/assets ratio of 20 percent maximizes stock price. This is the optimal capital structure.

2. a. Value of stock = [$500,000 – 0.1($1,000,000)](0.6)/0.15 = $1,600,000.

$P_0 = \$1,600,000/100,000 = \$16.$

After the recapitalization, value of stock is equal to [$500,000 – 0.1($1,000,000) – 0.13($500,000)](0.6)/0.17 = $1,182,353.

$P_0 = \$1,182,353/[100,000 - (\$500,000/\$16)] = \$17.20$.

3.　c.　The $1,200,000 capital budget will be financed using 40 percent debt and 60 percent equity. Therefore, the equity requirement will be $0.6(\$1,200,000) = \$720,000$. Since the expected net income is $1,000,000, $280,000 will be available to pay as dividends. Thus, the payout ratio is expected to be $\$280,000/\$1,000,000 = 0.28 = 28\%$.

4.　c.　Of the $800,000 in net income, $0.475(\$800,000) = \$380,000$ was paid out as dividends. Thus, $420,000 was retained in the firm for investment. This is the equity portion of the capital budget, or 70 percent of the capital budget. Therefore, the total capital budget was $\$420,000/0.7 = \$600,000$.

5.　b.　Maximum BP_{RE} = NI/Equity ratio = $\$7,000,000/0.6 = \$11,666,667$.

$WACC_1 = 0.4(12\%)(0.6) + 0.6(16\%) = 12.48\%$.

$WACC_2 = 0.4(12\%)(0.6) + 0.6(18\%) = 13.68\%$.

We see that the capital budget should be $10 million. We know that 60 percent of the $10 million should be equity. Therefore, the company should pay dividends of:

Dividends = NI – Needed equity = $\$7,000,000 - \$6,000,000 = \$1,000,000$.
Payout ratio = $\$1,000,000/\$7,000,000 = 0.1429 = 14.29\%$.

6.　d.　$P_0 = \$120$; Split = 5 for 3; New P_0 = ?

$$P_{0\ New} = \frac{\$120}{5/3} = \$72.00.$$

CHAPTER 15
WORKING CAPITAL MANAGEMENT

OVERVIEW

In this chapter, we discuss short-term financial management, also termed working capital management, which involves decisions about the current (short-term) assets and current (short-term) liabilities of a firm. A firm's value cannot be maximized in the long run unless it survives the short run. The principal reason firms fail is because they are unable to meet their working capital needs; consequently, sound working capital management is a requisite for firm survival.

OUTLINE

It is useful to begin a discussion of working capital policy by reviewing some basic definitions and concepts.

☐ *Working capital*, sometimes called *gross working capital,* generally refers to current assets, while *net working capital* is defined as current assets minus current liabilities.
   ~ Net working capital is a measure of a firm's liquidity.

☐ The *current ratio*, calculated as current assets divided by current liabilities, is also intended to measure a firm's liquidity.

☐ The best and most comprehensive picture of a firm's liquidity is obtained by examining its *cash budget*, which forecasts a firm's cash inflows and outflows.
   ~ The cash budget focuses on the firm's ability to generate sufficient cash inflows to meet its required cash outflows.

☐ *Working capital policy* refers to the firm's basic policies regarding target levels for each category of current assets and how current assets will be financed.

☐ Only those current liabilities that are specifically used to finance current assets are included in working capital decisions. Current liabilities that resulted from past long-term debt financing decisions are not working capital decision variables in the current period.
   ~ However, these current liabilities resulting from past long-term debt financing cannot be ignored, and they must be considered when managers assess the firm's ability to meet its current obligations using expected cash inflows.

Fluctuations in working capital requirements, and hence in financing needs, result from seasonal variations and business cycles. Working capital needs typically decline during recessions but increase during booms.

☐   For some companies, such as those involved in agricultural products, seasonal fluctuations are much greater than business cycle fluctuations, but for other companies, such as appliance or automobile manufacturers, cyclical fluctuations are larger.

The cash conversion cycle focuses on the length of time between when the company makes payments, or invests in the manufacture of inventory, and when it receives cash inflows, or realizes a cash return from its investment in production.

☐   The following terms and definitions are used:

~   The *inventory conversion period* is the average length of time required to convert materials into finished goods and then to sell those goods. It is the amount of time the product remains in inventory in various stages of completion.

$$\frac{\text{Inventory}}{\text{conversion period}} = \frac{\text{Inventory}}{\text{Annual cost of goods sold}/360}.$$

~   The *receivables collection period* is the average length of time required to convert the firm's receivables into cash, that is, to collect cash following a sale. It is also called the days sales outstanding (DSO).

$$\frac{\text{Receivables}}{\text{collection period}} = \text{DSO} = \frac{\text{Receivables}}{\text{Annual credit sales}/360}.$$

~   The *payables deferral period* is the average length of time between the purchase of raw materials and labor and the payment of cash for them.

$$\frac{\text{Payables}}{\text{deferral period}} = \frac{\text{Accounts payable}}{\text{Cost of goods sold}/360}.$$

~   The *cash conversion cycle,* which nets out the three periods just defined, equals the length of time between when the firm pays for (invests in) productive resources (materials and labor) and when it receives a return from the sale of products.

•   The cash conversion cycle equals the average length of time a dollar is tied up in current assets.

☐   Using these definitions, the cash conversion cycle is defined as follows:

$$\frac{\text{Inventory}}{\text{conversion period}} + \frac{\text{Receivables}}{\text{collection period}} - \frac{\text{Payables}}{\text{deferral period}} = \frac{\text{Cash}}{\text{conversion cycle}}.$$

~   To illustrate, suppose it takes a firm an average of 72 days to convert raw materials and labor to widgets and to sell them, and it takes another 24 days to collect on receivables, while 30 days normally lapse between receipt of materials (and work done) and payments for materials and labor. In this case, the cash conversion cycle is 72 days + 24 days – 30 days = 66 days.

☐   A firm should shorten its cash conversion cycle as much as possible without hurting operations. This would improve profits because the longer the cash conversion cycle, the greater the need for external financing and this financing has a cost.

    ~   The cash conversion cycle can be shortened by (1) reducing the inventory conversion period by processing and selling goods more quickly, (2) reducing the receivables collection period by speeding up collections, or (3) lengthening the payables deferral period by slowing down its own payments.

        •   To the extent that these actions can be taken without harming the return associated with the management of these accounts, they should be carried out.

Working capital policy involves two basic decisions: (1) What is the appropriate level for current assets, both in total and by specific accounts, and (2) how should current assets be financed?

☐   There are three alternative policies regarding the total amount of current assets carried. Each policy differs in that different amounts of current assets are carried to support a given level of sales.

    ~   A *relaxed current asset investment policy* is one where relatively large amounts of cash, marketable securities, and inventories are carried and where sales are stimulated by the use of a credit policy that provides liberal financing to customers and a corresponding high level of receivables.

    ~   A *restricted current asset investment policy* is one in which the holdings of cash, marketable securities, inventories, and receivables are minimized.

    ~   A *moderate current asset investment policy* lies between the two extremes.

    ~   The more certain a firm is about its sales, costs, order lead times, payment periods, and so forth, the lower the level of current assets it requires to support operations.

    ~   Generally, the decision on current assets levels involves a risk/return tradeoff.

        •   The relaxed policy minimizes risk, but it also has the lowest expected return.

        •   The restricted policy offers the highest expected return coupled with the highest risk.

        •   The moderate policy falls in between the two extremes in terms of both expected risk and return.

    ~   In terms of the cash conversion cycle, a restricted investment policy would tend to reduce the inventory conversion and receivables collection periods, resulting in a relatively short cash conversion cycle.

        •   Conversely, a relaxed policy would create higher levels of inventories and receivables, longer inventory conversion and receivables collection periods, and a relatively long cash conversion cycle.

        •   A moderate policy would produce a cash conversion cycle somewhere between the two extremes.

☐   Current assets can either be considered permanent or temporary.

    ~   *Permanent current assets* are current asset balances that do not change due to seasonal or economic conditions. These balances exist even at the trough of a firm's business cycle.

~ *Temporary current assets* are current assets that fluctuate with seasonal or economic variations in a firm's business.

☐ The second short-term financial decision is how to finance current assets. The manner in which the permanent and temporary current assets are financed is called the firm's *current asset financing policy*.
  ~ The *maturity matching, or "self-liquidating," approach* matches asset and liability maturities. This approach is considered a moderate current asset financing policy.
    • This strategy minimizes the risk that the firm will be unable to pay off its maturing obligations if the liquidation of the assets can be controlled to occur on or before the maturities of the obligations.
    • Two factors prevent exact maturity matching: (1) There is uncertainty about the lives of assets, thus when cash inflows will be received, and (2) some common equity must be used, and common equity has no maturity.
  ~ The *aggressive approach* is used by a firm that finances all of its fixed assets and some of its permanent current assets with long-term capital; the remainder of its permanent current assets and all of the temporary current assets are financed with short-term financing.
    • The aggressive approach is riskier than either of the other two approaches because the short-term credit used to finance the permanent current assets must be renewed each time it comes due. Thus, the firm is subject to dangers from rising interest rates as well as to loan renewal problems.
    • However, short-term debt often is cheaper than long-term debt, and some firms are willing to sacrifice safety for the chance of higher profits.
  ~ A *conservative approach* is a policy in which all of the fixed assets, all of the permanent current assets, and some of the temporary current assets of a firm are financed with long-term capital.
    • Most firms that follow this approach use some amounts of short-term credit to meet financing needs during peak-season periods. Even so, firms that use this strategy will have "extra" permanent funds during off-peak periods, which allows them to "store liquidity" in the form of short-term investments, called marketable securities, during the off-season.
    • This is a very safe, conservative current asset financing policy and generally is not as profitable as the other two approaches.

There are advantages and disadvantages to the use of short-term financing.

☐ A short-term loan can be obtained much faster than long-term credit.
  ~ Lenders insist on a more thorough financial examination before extending long-term credit.

☐ Short-term debt is more flexible than long-term debt.
  ~ Costs associated with issuing long-term debt are significantly greater than the costs of obtaining short-term credit.
  ~ Long-term debt can carry expensive penalties for prepayments.

~ Long-term loan agreements generally contain provisions, or covenants, that restrict the firm's future actions, whereas short-term credit agreements usually are much less onerous in this regard.

☐ Short-term interest rates are normally lower than long-term rates. Therefore, financing with short-term credit usually results in lower interest costs.

☐ Short-term debt is generally riskier than long-term debt for two reasons.
~ Short-term interest rates fluctuate widely, while long-term rates tend to be more stable and predictable, and hence the interest rate on short-term debt could increase dramatically in a short period.
~ Short-term debt comes due every few months. If a firm does not have the cash to repay debt when it comes due, and if it cannot refinance the loan, it may be forced into bankruptcy.

Short-term credit is defined as any liability originally scheduled for payment within one year. There are five major types of short-term debt: accruals, accounts payable (trade credit), bank loans, commercial paper, and secured short-term loans.

☐ One source of short-term funds is accrued wages and taxes, which increase and decrease spontaneously as a firm's operations expand and contract.
~ This type of debt is "free" in the sense that no explicit interest is paid on funds raised through *accruals*.
~ A firm ordinarily cannot control its accruals. Firms use all the accruals they can, but they have little control over the levels of these accounts.
• The timing of wage payments is set by economic forces and industry custom, while tax payment dates are established by law.

☐ *Accounts payable*, or *trade credit*, is the largest single category of short-term debt, representing about 40 percent of the current liabilities for the average nonfinancial corporation.
~ Trade credit is a *spontaneous* source of financing in the sense that it arises from ordinary business transactions.
~ The amount of trade credit used by a firm depends on the terms of the credit purchase and the size of the firm's operations.
• Lengthening the credit period, as well as expanding sales and purchases, generates additional trade credit.

☐ *Bank loans* appear on a firm's balance sheet as *notes payable,* and they are second in importance to trade credit as a source of short-term financing.
~ The banks' influence actually is greater than it appears from the dollar amounts they lend because banks provide *nonspontaneous* funds.
~ The bulk of banks' commercial lending is on a short-term basis.
~ When a firm obtains a bank loan, a *promissory note* specifying the following items is signed: the amount borrowed, the interest rate, the repayment schedule, any collateral

offered as security, and other terms and conditions to which the bank and the borrower have agreed.

~ Banks sometimes require borrowers to maintain *compensating balances* equal to 10 to 20 percent of the loan amount.

• In effect, the compensating balance is a charge by the bank for servicing the loan.

~ A *line of credit* is an arrangement in which a bank agrees to lend up to a specified maximum amount of funds during a designated period.

• When a line of credit arrangement is guaranteed, it is called a *revolving credit arrangement*.

• A revolving credit agreement is similar to a regular line of credit, except the bank has a legal obligation to provide funds requested by the borrower.

• The bank generally charges a *commitment fee*, a fee charged on the unused balance of a revolving credit agreement to compensate the bank for guaranteeing that the funds will be available when needed by the borrower.

☐ *Commercial paper,* another source of short-term credit, is an unsecured promissory note issued by large, financially strong firms. It is sold primarily to other firms, to insurance companies, to pension funds, to banks, and to money market mutual funds.

~ Using commercial paper permits a corporation to tap a wider range of credit sources, and this can reduce interest costs.

~ Maturities of commercial paper range from a few days to nine months, with an average of about five months.

~ A disadvantage of the commercial paper market vis-a-vis bank loans is that the impersonal nature of the market makes it difficult for firms to use commercial paper at times when they are in temporary financial distress.

☐ For a strong firm, borrowing on an *unsecured basis* is generally cheaper and simpler than on a secured loan basis because of the administrative costs associated with the use of security. However, lenders will refuse credit without some form of collateral if a borrower's credit standing is questionable.

~ Most secured short-term business borrowing involves the use of short-term assets, such as accounts receivable and inventories, as collateral.

~ When receivables are used as collateral for a short-term loan, the firm is said to be *pledging* its receivables. When receivables are sold to a financial institution, the firm is said to be *factoring* its receivables, and the buyer is called a *factor*.

• A principal difference between the two arrangements is that when receivables are pledged, the lender has both a claim against the receivables and *recourse* to the borrower.

• With recourse, the lender can seek payment from the borrowing firm when receivables' accounts used to secure a loan are uncollectible.

• With most factoring arrangements, if the receivable becomes uncollectible the factor that buys the receivable must take the loss.

~ A substantial amount of credit is secured by business inventories. If the firm is a relatively poor risk, the lending institution might insist upon security in the form of a *lien* against the inventory. There are three major types of inventory liens:

• A *blanket lien* gives the lending institution a lien against all of the borrower's inventories without limiting the ability of the borrower to sell the inventories.

- A *trust receipt* is an arrangement in which the goods are held in trust for the lender, perhaps stored in a public warehouse or held on the premises of the borrower.
- *Warehouse receipt financing* refers to arrangements in which inventory used as collateral is physically separated from the borrower's other inventory and then stored in a secured site located either on the premises of the borrower *(field warehousing)* or in a public warehouse *(terminal warehousing)*.

For any type of short-term credit, we can compute the interest rate, or cost, for the period that funds are used with the following equation:

$$\frac{\textbf{Interest rate}}{\textbf{per period (cost)}} = k_{PER} = \frac{\textbf{Dollar cost of borrowing}}{\textbf{Amount of usable funds}}.$$

☐ The numerator in the equation above includes interest paid, application fees, charges for commitment fees, and so forth.

☐ The denominator represents the amount of the loan that actually can be used (spent) by the borrower, which is not necessarily the same as the amount borrowed because discounts or other costs might be deducted from the loan proceeds.

~ When loan restrictions prevent the borrower from using the entire amount of the loan, the effective annual rate paid for the loan increases.

☐ The *effective annual rate* is calculated as

$$\text{Effective annual rate} = (1 + k_{PER})^m - 1.0.$$

☐ The *annual percentage rate* is calculated as:

$$\text{Annual percentage rate} = APR = k_{PER} \times m = k_{SIMPLE}.$$

☐ EAR incorporates interest compounding in the computation while the APR does not. Both computations adjust the percentage cost per period so that it is stated on an annual basis.

☐ A *discount interest loan* is one in which the interest, which is calculated on the amount borrowed (principal), is paid at the beginning of the loan period; interest is paid in advance.

☐ You should recognize that the cost of short-term financing is higher when the dollar expenses are higher or when the amount of the original loan that can actually be used by the borrower is lower.

~ In most cases, the effective interest rate of short-term financing is greater than its stated interest rate.

~ The effective interest rate of a loan is equal to the quoted rate only if the entire principal amount borrowed can be used by the borrower and the only dollar cost is interest charged on the outstanding balance of the loan.

Value, which we want to maximize, is based on cash flows. Thus, managing cash flows is an extremely important task for a financial manager. Cash is a "nonearning," or idle, asset that is required to pay bills. When possible, cash should be "put to work" by investing in assets that have positive expected returns. Thus, the goal of cash management is to minimize the amount of cash the firm must hold for use in conducting its normal business activities, yet, at the same time, to have sufficient cash to (1) pay suppliers, (2) maintain its credit rating, and (3) meet unexpected cash needs.

☐   *Cash* refers to the funds a firm holds that can be used for immediate disbursement—this includes the amount a firm holds in its checking account as well as the amount of actual currency it holds.

☐   Firms hold cash for the following reasons:
    ~ *Transactions balances* are held to provide the cash needed for day-to-day operations; the balances associated with routine payments and collections.
    ~ *Compensating balances* are often required by banks for providing loans and services.
    ~ *Precautionary balances* are held in reserve for unforeseen fluctuations in cash flows. The less predictable the firm's cash flows, the larger such balances should be. However, if it can borrow on short notice its need for precautionary balances is reduced.
    ~ *Speculative balances* are held to enable the firm to take advantage of any bargain purchase that might arise. Firms that have easy access to borrowed funds are likely to rely on their ability to borrow quickly rather than on cash balances for speculative purposes.

☐   Most firms do not segregate funds for each of these factors, but they do consider all four factors when establishing their target cash positions.

☐   In addition to these four motives, a firm maintains cash balances to preserve its credit rating by keeping its liquidity position in line with those of other firms in the industry.
    ~ A strong credit rating enables the firm to both purchase goods from suppliers on favorable terms and maintain an ample line of credit with its bank.

Most cash management activities are performed jointly by the firm and its primary bank, but the financial manager is ultimately responsible for the effectiveness of the cash management program. Effective cash management encompasses proper management of both the cash inflows and the cash outflows of a firm, which entails consideration of the following factors: Cash forecasts, cash flow synchronization, float, acceleration of receipts, and disbursement control.

☐   The most critical ingredient to proper cash management is the *cash forecast*, often referred to as the cash budget.
    ~ A firm needs to predict the timing of the cash inflows and the cash outflows to plan for investment and borrowing activities.

☐   *Synchronized cash flows* is a situation in which cash inflows coincide with cash outflows, thereby permitting a firm to hold low transactions balances.

~ Synchronizing cash inflows and outflows permits a reduction in the firm's cash balances, decreases its bank loans, lowers its interest expense, and increases profits.
  • The more predictable the timing of the cash flows, the greater the synchronization that can be obtained.

☐ *Float* is defined as the difference between the balance shown in a firm's (or individual's) checkbook and the balance on the bank's records. A firm's *net float* is a function of its ability to speed up collections on checks received (collections float) and to slow down collections on checks written (disbursement float). Net float = Disbursement float – Collections float.

~ *Disbursement float* is defined as the value of checks that have been written and disbursed but that have not yet fully cleared through the banking system and thus have not been deducted from the account on which they were written.

~ *Collections float* is the amount of checks that have been received and deposited but that have not yet been credited to the account in which they were deposited.

~ Delays that cause float arise because it takes time for checks (1) to travel through the mail (mail delay), (2) to be processed by the receiving firm (processing delay), and (3) to clear through the banking system (clearing, or availability, delay).

☐ A firm cannot use customers' payments until they are received and converted into a spendable form. The following techniques are used to manage collections:

~ A *lockbox arrangement* is a technique used to reduce float by having payments sent to post office boxes located near customers.
  • By having lockboxes close to the customers, a firm can reduce float because, at the very least, (a) the mail delay is less than if the payment had to travel farther and (b) checks are cleared faster because the banks the checks are written on are in the same Federal Reserve district.

~ A *pre-authorized debit system* allows a customer's bank to periodically transfer funds from that customer's account to a selling firm's bank account for the payment of bills.

~ *Concentration banking* is a technique used to move funds from many bank accounts to a more central cash pool in order to more effectively manage cash.

☐ Controlling funds outflows, or disbursements, represents the other side of cash management. Three methods commonly used to control disbursements include the following:

~ No single action controls cash outflows more effectively than *centralization of payables*, which permits the financial manager to evaluate the payments coming due for the entire firm and to schedule the availability of funds to meet these needs on a company-wide basis. It also permits more efficient monitoring of payables and the effects of float.

~ *Zero-balance accounts (ZBAs)* are special checking accounts used for disbursements that have balances equal to zero when there is no disbursement activity.
  • Typically, a firm establishes several zero-balance accounts in its concentration bank and funds them from a master account. As checks are presented to a ZBA for payment, funds are automatically transferred from the master account.

~ *Controlled disbursement accounts* are similar to ZBAs, except that controlled disbursement accounts can be set up at any bank. Controlled disbursement accounts are checking accounts in which funds are not deposited until checks are presented for payment, usually on a daily basis.

Marketable securities, or near-cash assets, are extremely liquid, short-term investments that permit the firm to earn positive returns on cash that is not needed to pay bills immediately but will be needed sometime in the near term. Although these securities typically provide much lower yields than operating assets, nearly every large firm has them. Two basic reasons for owning marketable securities are:

☐ *Marketable securities* serve as a substitute for cash balances. The securities are sold when cash is needed for transactions. Marketable securities offer a place to temporarily put cash balances to work earning a positive return.

☐ A second use of marketable securities is as a temporary investment.
  ~ Seasonal or cyclical operations may generate surplus cash at some times and deficits at other times. Marketable securities may be built up during one phase of the cycle and then liquidated to cover forecasted deficits.
  ~ Marketable securities may be used to accumulate funds for a known financial requirement, such as a bond redemption or a major tax payment.

☐ Depending on how long they will be held, the financial manager decides on a suitable set of securities, and a suitable maturity pattern, to hold as near-cash reserves in the form of marketable securities.
  ~ Long-term securities are not appropriate investments for marketable securities—safety, especially maintenance of principal, should be paramount when putting together a marketable securities portfolio.

The primary reason most firms offer credit sales is because their competitors offer credit. Effective credit management is extremely important because too much credit is very costly in terms of the investment in, and maintenance of, accounts receivable, while too little credit could result in the loss of profitable sales. Thus, to maximize shareholders' wealth, a financial manager needs to understand how to effectively manage the firm's credit activities. The major controllable variables that affect demand are sales prices, product quality, advertising, and the firm's credit policy.

☐ The *credit policy* consists of (1) the *credit standards*, (2) the *credit terms*, and (3) the *collection policy*.
  ~ *Credit standards* refer to the strength and creditworthiness a customer must exhibit in order to qualify for credit.
    • The major factors considered when setting credit standards relate to the likelihood that a given customer will pay slowly or perhaps even end up as a bad debt loss.
  ~ The *terms of credit* are the conditions of the credit sale, especially with regard to the payment arrangements.
    • Firms need to determine when the credit period begins, how long the customer has

to pay for credit purchases before the account is considered delinquent, and whether a cash discount will be offered.

- The *credit period* is the length of time for which credit is granted; after that time, the credit account is considered delinquent.
- *Cash discount* is a reduction in the invoice price of goods offered by the seller to encourage early payment.
- Because of the competitive nature of trade credit, most financial managers follow the norm of the industry in which they operate when setting credit terms.

~ *Collection policy* refers to the procedures the firm follows to collect its credit accounts.

It is important that firms examine their receivables periodically to determine whether customers' payment patterns have changed to the extent that credit operations are outside the credit policy limits.

☐ *Receivables monitoring* refers to the process of evaluating the credit policy to determine if a shift in the customers' payment patterns occurs. Traditionally, firms have monitored accounts receivable by using methods that measure the amount of time credit remains outstanding. Two such methods are the days sales outstanding (DSO) and the aging schedule.

~ The *days sales outstanding (DSO)*, sometimes called the average collection period (ACP), measures the average length of time required to collect accounts receivable.
- The DSO is calculated by dividing the receivables balance by average daily credit sales: DSO = Receivables/(Annual credit sales/360).
- The DSO can be compared with the industry average and the firm's own credit terms to get an indication of how well customers are adhering to the terms prescribed and how customers' payments, on average, compare with the industry average.

~ An *aging schedule* is a report showing how long accounts receivable have been outstanding. The report divides receivables into specified periods, which provides information about the proportion of receivables that are current and the proportion that are past due for given lengths of time.

☐ Management should constantly monitor the days sales outstanding and the aging schedule to detect trends to see how the firm's collection experience compares with its credit terms and to see how effectively the credit department is operating in comparison with other firms in the industry.

☐ Both the DSO and aging schedule can be distorted if sales are seasonal or if a firm is growing rapidly.

~ A deterioration in either the DSO or the aging schedule should be taken as a signal to investigate further, but not necessarily as a sign that the firm's credit policy has weakened.

~ If a firm generally experiences widely fluctuating sales patterns, some type of modified aging schedule should be used to correctly account for these fluctuations.

Changes in credit policy must be analyzed. For example, easing the credit policy normally

stimulates sales. As sales rise, costs also rise (1) to produce the extra required goods, (2) to carry the additional receivables outstanding, and (3) because bad debt expenses may rise.

☐ The question to answer when considering a credit policy change, therefore, is whether sales revenues will rise more than costs.

~ If the added benefits expected from a credit policy change do not exceed the added costs, then the policy change should not be made.

☐ You need to evaluate the effect the proposed changes will have on the firm's value.

~ To do this, you must compare the net present values (NPV) of the two credit policies.

☐ A great deal of judgment must be applied to the decision because both customers' and competitors' responses to credit policy changes are very difficult to estimate.

Inventories, which may be classified as raw materials, work-in-process, and finished goods, are an essential part of virtually all business operations. Most firms find it necessary to maintain inventory in some form because (1) demand cannot be predicted with certainty and (2) it takes time to produce a product that is ready for sale.

☐ *Raw materials* are the inventories purchased from suppliers that ultimately will be transformed into finished goods.

☐ *Work-in-process* refers to inventory in various stages of completion; some work-in-process is at the very beginning of the production process while some is at the end of the process.

☐ *Finished goods* are inventories that have completed the production process and are ready for sale.

☐ A *stockout* is a situation that occurs when a firm runs out of inventory and customers arrive to purchase the product.

The goal of inventory management is to provide the inventories required to sustain operations at the lowest possible cost. The first step in determining the optimal level of inventory is to identify the costs involved in purchasing and maintaining inventory, and then to determine at what point those costs are minimized. Inventory costs are generally classified into three categories: those associated with carrying inventory, those associated with ordering and receiving inventory, and those associated with running short of inventory (stockouts).

☐ *Carrying costs* are the costs associated with having inventory, and they generally increase in proportion to the average amount of inventory held.

~ Carrying costs associated with inventory include the cost of the funds tied up, storage costs, insurance, and depreciation.

~ The annual total carrying costs (TCC) are equal to the product of C = annual percentage carrying cost, PP = purchase price, or cost, per unit, and Q/2 = average number of units in inventory. Thus, TCC = (C)(PP)(Q/2).

☐   *Ordering costs* are the costs of placing and receiving an order. The cost of each order generally is fixed regardless of the order size.

~   Total ordering costs (TOC) are the product of O = fixed cost associated with ordering inventories and T/Q = number of orders, where T = total demand and Q = number of units purchased with each order. Thus, TOC = (O)(T/Q).

☐   Total inventory costs (TIC) equal the sum of total carrying costs and total ordering costs: TIC = TCC + TOC = (C)(PP)(Q/2) + (O)(T/Q).

☐   The average investment in inventory depends on how frequently orders are placed and the size of each order.

~   We can reduce ordering costs by ordering greater amounts less often, but then average inventory, thus the total carrying cost, will be high.

☐   There is a point where the total inventory cost, TIC, is minimized; this is called the *economic (optimum) ordering quantity (EOQ)*.

Inventories are obviously necessary, but it is equally obvious that inventory levels that are too high or too low are costly to the firm. The economic ordering quantity (EOQ) model can determine the optimal inventory level.

☐   The model, which is derived by minimizing total inventory costs, is

$$EOQ = \sqrt{\frac{2 \times O \times T}{C \times PP}}$$

where EOQ is the optimal quantity to be ordered each time an order is placed, O = fixed cost of placing and receiving an order, T = annual sales in units, C = annual carrying cost expressed as a percentage of average inventory value, and PP = purchase price the firm must pay per unit of inventory (raw materials).

☐   The primary assumptions of the EOQ model are as follows: (1) Sales are evenly distributed throughout the period examined and can be forecasted perfectly, (2) orders are received when expected, and (3) the purchase price of each item in inventory is the same regardless of the quantity ordered.

☐   At the EOQ, total carrying costs (TCC) equal total ordering costs (TOC). This always holds.

☐   Note that (1) as the amount ordered increases, the total carrying costs increase but the total ordering costs decrease, and vice versa; (2) if less than the EOQ amount is ordered, then the higher ordering costs more than offset the lower carrying costs; and (3) if greater than the EOQ amount is ordered, the higher carrying costs more than offset the lower ordering costs.

☐   Some of the assumptions necessary for the basic EOQ to hold are unrealistic. To make the model more useful, some simple extensions can be applied: safety stocks and quantity discounts.

~ A *reorder point* is the level of inventory at which an order should be placed.

~ *Safety stocks* are additional inventories carried to guard against changes in sales rates or production/shipping delays.

- The amount of safety stock a firm holds generally increases with (1) the uncertainty of demand forecasts, (2) the costs (in terms of lost sales and lost goodwill) that result from stockouts, and (3) the chances that delays will occur in receiving shipments.

- The amount of safety stock decreases as the cost of carrying this additional inventory increases.

~ A *quantity discount* is a discount from the purchase price offered for inventory ordered in large quantities.

~ In cases in which it is unrealistic to assume that the demand for the inventory is uniform throughout the year, the EOQ should not be applied on an annual basis. Rather, it would be more appropriate to divide the year into the seasons within which sales are relatively constant. Then, the EOQ model can be applied separately to each period.

The EOQ model can be used to establish the proper inventory levels, but inventory management also involves the establishment of an inventory control system. These systems vary from the extremely simple to the very complex, depending on the size of the firm and the nature of its inventories.

☐ One simple control procedure is the *redline method*. A red line is drawn inside the bin where the inventory is stocked. When the red line shows, an order is placed.

☐ Large companies employ much more sophisticated *computerized inventory control systems*. The computer starts with an inventory count in memory. As withdrawals are made, they are recorded by the computer, and the inventory balance is revised. Orders are automatically placed once the reorder point is reached and receipt of an order is also recorded.

☐ The *just-in-time system* coordinates a manufacturer's production with suppliers so that raw materials arrive from suppliers just as they are needed in the production process. Increased use of electronics has allowed firms to better coordinate orders with suppliers.

☐ Another important development related to inventories is *out-sourcing*, which is the practice of purchasing components rather than making them in-house. Out-sourcing is often combined with just-in-time systems to reduce inventory levels.

☐ Inventory control systems require coordination of inventory policy with manufacturing/ procurement policies.

The objectives of working capital management in the multinational corporation are similar to those in the domestic firm but the task is more complex.

☐ The objectives of cash management in the multinational corporation are to speed up collections and to slow disbursements—hence to maximize net float, to shift cash rapidly from those parts of the business that do not need it to those parts that do, and to obtain the highest possible risk-adjusted rate of return on temporary cash balances.

~ The same general procedures are used by multinational firms as those used by domestic firms, but because of longer distances and more serious mail delays, lockbox systems and electronic funds transfers are especially important.

- One potential problem a multinational company faces that a purely domestic company does not is the chance that a foreign government will restrict transfers of funds out of the country.
- Deteriorating exchange rates might make it unattractive for a multinational to move funds to its operations in other countries.

☐ Granting credit is riskier in an international context because, in addition to the normal risks of default, (1) political and legal environments often make it more difficult to collect defaulted accounts, and (2) the multinational corporations must worry about exchange rate changes between the time a sale is made and the time a receivable is collected. Hedging can reduce this type of risk, but at a cost.

~ Credit policy is generally more important for a multinational firm than for a domestic firm.

- Much of the United States' trade is with poorer, less-developed countries; thus, granting credit is generally a necessary condition for doing business.
- Developed nations whose economic health depends on exports often help their manufacturing firms compete internationally by granting credit to foreign countries.

☐ The physical location of inventories is a complex consideration for the multinational firm. The multinational firm must weigh a strategy of keeping inventory concentrated in a few areas from which they can be shipped, and thus minimize the total amount of inventory needed to operate the global business, with the possibility of delays in getting goods from central locations to user locations around the world.

~ Exchange rates, import/export quotas, the threat of expropriation, and taxes all influence inventory policy.

- Quotas restrict the quantities of products firms can bring into a country, whereas tariffs, like taxes, increase the prices of products that are allowed to be imported.

☐ In general, then, multinational firms use techniques similar to those described in this chapter to manage working capital, but their job is more complex because business, legal, and economic environments can differ significantly from one country to another.

SELF-TEST QUESTIONS

Definitional

1. Current assets are also referred to as _____ _____.

2. _____ working capital is defined as _____ assets minus current _____.

3. The _____ ratio, calculated as current assets divided by current liabilities, is intended to measure a firm's _____.

4. The most comprehensive picture of a firm's liquidity is obtained by examining its _____ _____, which forecasts a firm's cash inflows and outflows.

5. _____ _____ _____ refers to the firm's basic policies regarding target levels for each category of current assets and how current assets will be financed.

6. The _____ _____ _____ focuses on the length of time between when the company makes payments, or invests in the manufacture of inventory, and when it receives cash inflows, or realizes a cash return from its investment in production.

7. The _____ _____ _____ is the average length of time required to convert materials into finished goods and then to sell those goods.

8. The _____ _____ _____ is the average length of time required to convert the firm's receivables into cash.

9. The _____ _____ _____ is the average length of time between the purchase of raw materials and labor and the payment of cash for them.

10. A(n) _____ current asset investment policy is one where relatively large amounts of cash, marketable securities, and inventories are carried and where sales are stimulated by the use of a credit policy that provides liberal financing to customers and a corresponding high level of receivables.

11. _____ current assets are current asset balances that do not change due to seasonal or economic conditions.

12. _____ current assets are those that fluctuate with seasonal or economic variations in a firm's business.

13. The _____ _____ approach minimizes the risk that the firm will be unable to pay off its maturing obligations if the liquidation of the assets can be controlled to occur on or before the maturities of the obligations.

14. A(n) _____ approach to financing current assets is a policy in which all of the fixed assets, all of the permanent current assets, and some of the temporary current assets of a firm are financed with long-term capital.

15. Short-term borrowing will be less expensive than long-term borrowing if the yield curve is _____ sloping.

16. Short-term interest rates fluctuate _____ than long-term rates.

17. Long-term loan agreements generally contain provisions, or _____, that restrict the firm's future actions, whereas short-term credit agreements usually are much less onerous in this regard.

18. _____-_____ _____ is defined as any liability originally scheduled for payment within one year.

19. There are five major types of short-term debt: _____, _____ _____, _____ _____, _____ _____, and _____ short-term loans.

20. _____ wages and taxes are a common source of short-term credit. However, most firms have little control over the _____ of these accounts.

21. Accounts payable, or _____ _____, is the largest single category of short-term debt for most businesses.

22. Trade credit is a(n) _____ source of financing in the sense that it arises from ordinary business transactions.

23. Bank loans appear on a firm's balance sheet as _____ _____, and they are second in importance to trade credit as a source of short-term financing.

24. The instrument signed when bank credit is obtained is called a(n) _____ _____.

25. A(n) _____ _____ loan is one in which the interest, which is calculated on the amount borrowed (principal), is paid at the beginning of the loan period; interest is paid in advance.

26. Many banks require borrowers to keep _____ _____ on deposit with the bank equal to 10 or 20 percent of the loan amount.

27. _____ _____ is an unsecured promissory note issued by large, financially strong firms.

28. A(n) _____ loan is one where collateral such as _____ or _____ have been pledged in support of the loan.

29. A(n) _____ ____ _____ is an arrangement between a bank and a borrower as to the maximum loan that will be permitted during a specified period.

30. The fee paid to a bank to secure a revolving credit agreement is known as a(n) _____ fee.

31. _____ occurs when accounts receivable are sold, and the buyer generally has no recourse against the firm selling the receivables.

32. A(n) _____ _____ gives the lender a lien against all of the borrower's inventories without limiting the ability of the borrower to sell the inventories.

33. The goal of cash management is to _____ the amount of _____ the firm must hold for use in conducting its normal business activities.

34. _____ refers to the funds a firm holds that can be used for immediate disbursement—this includes the amount a firm holds in its checking account as well as the amount of actual currency it holds.

35. _____ _____ are held in reserve for unforeseen fluctuations in cash flows.

36. _____ _____ are held to provide the cash needed for day-to-day operations; the balances associated with routine payments and collections.

37. _____ _____ are held to enable the firm to take advantage of bargain purchases.

38. _____ cash flows is a situation in which cash inflows coincide with cash outflows, thereby permitting a firm to hold low transactions balances.

39. One method for speeding the collection process through the use of post office boxes is a(n) _____ arrangement.

40. The most effective method of controlling cash outflows is _____ ____ _____, which permits the financial manager to evaluate the payments coming due for the entire firm and to schedule the availability of funds to meet these needs.

41. The difference between a firm's balance on its own books and its balance as carried on the bank's books is known as _____.

42. A(n) _____-_____ _____ allows a customer's bank to periodically transfer funds from that customer's account to a selling firm's bank account for the payment of bills.

43. _____ _____, or near-cash assets, are extremely liquid, short-term investments that permit the firm to earn positive returns on cash that is not needed to pay bills immediately but will be needed sometime in the near term.

44. _____ _____ refer to the strength and creditworthiness a customer must exhibit in order to qualify for credit.

45. The _____ ____ _____ are the conditions of the credit sale, especially with regard to the payment arrangements.

46. The _____ is the length of time for which credit is granted; after that time, the credit account is considered delinquent.

47. A(n) _____ is a reduction in the invoice price of goods offered by the seller to encourage early payment.

48. _____ policy refers to the procedures a firm follows to collect its credit accounts.

49. Two commonly used methods for monitoring receivables are _____ and the _____.

50. _____ the credit policy normally stimulates sales.

51. _____ _____ refers to the process of evaluating the credit policy to determine if a shift in the customers' payment patterns occurs.

52. Inventories are usually classified as _____ _____, _____-____-_____, and _____ _____.

53. _____ are the inventories purchased from suppliers that ultimately will be transformed into finished goods.

54. _____-____-_____ refers to inventory in various stages of completion.

55. _____ _____ are inventories that have completed the production process and are ready for sale.

56. The goal of inventory management is to provide the inventories needed for operations at the _____ _____.

57. Storage costs, insurance, and other costs that _____ with larger inventories are known as _____ costs.

58. _____ _____ are generally fixed regardless of the order size.

59. The _____ _____ quantity minimizes the total costs of ordering and holding inventories.

60. When the level of inventories reaches the _____ _____, the EOQ amount should be ordered.

61. _____ _____ are additional inventory that must be maintained to guard against shipping delays and uncertainty in the rate of usage.

62. Inventory control systems that require suppliers to deliver items as they are needed are called _____-____-_____ systems.

63. _____-_____ is the practice of purchasing components rather than making them in-house.

64. A(n) _____ _____ is a reduction in the purchase price offered for inventory ordered in large quantities.

65. When a line of credit arrangement is guaranteed, it is called a(n) _____ _____ _____.

Conceptual

66. The matching of asset and liability maturities is considered desirable because this strategy minimizes interest rate risk.

    a. True   **b.** False

67. Other things held constant, an increase in the payables deferral period will lead to a reduction in the need for nonspontaneous funding.

    a. True   **b.** False

68. Generally, a firm should use short-term debt, rather than long-term financing, to minimize its interest expense.

    a. True   **b.** False

69. Accruals are "free" in the sense that no interest must be paid on these funds.

    a. True   **b.** False

70. A firm changes its credit policy from 2/10, net 30, to 3/10, net 30. The change is to meet competition, so no increase in sales is expected. The firm's average investment in accounts receivable will probably increase as a result of the change.

    a. True   **b.** False

71. An aging schedule is constructed by a firm to keep track of when its accounts payable are due.

    a. True   **b.** False

72. If a credit policy change increases the firm's accounts receivable, the entire increase must be financed by some source of funds.

    a. True   **b.** False

73. The economic ordering quantity is the order quantity that provides the minimum total cost; that is, both the ordering and carrying cost components are minimized.

a. True   **b.** False

74. Which of the following statements concerning commercial paper is correct?

a. Commercial paper is secured debt of large, financially strong firms.
b. Commercial paper is sold primarily to individual investors.
c. Maturities of commercial paper generally exceed nine months.
d. Statements a and b are correct.
e. None of the above statements is correct.

75. Which of the following actions would not be consistent with good cash management?

a. Increasing the synchronization of cash flows.
b. Using ZBA accounts in disbursing funds.
c. Using lockboxes in funds collection.
d. Maintaining an average cash balance equal to that required as a compensating balance or that which minimizes total cost.
e. Minimizing the use of net float.

76. Which of the following investments is not likely to be a proper investment for temporarily idle cash?

a. Commercial paper.
b. Treasury bills.
c. Recently issued long-term AAA corporate bonds.
d. Treasury bonds due within one year.
e. AAA corporate bonds due within one year.

77. Which of the following statements is most correct?

a. Other things held constant, the higher a firm's days sales outstanding (DSO), the better its credit department.
b. If a firm that sells on terms of "net 30" changes its policy and begins offering all customers terms of "2/10, net 30," and if no change in sales volume occurs, then the firm's DSO will probably increase.
c. If a firm sells on terms of 2/10, net 30, and its DSO is 30 days, then its aging schedule would probably show some past due accounts.
d. Both statements b and c are correct.
e. All of the above statements are false.

78. The costs of a stock-out do *not* include

    a. Disruption of production schedules.
    b. Loss of customer goodwill.
    c. Depreciation and obsolescence.
    d. Loss of sales.
    e. Statements c and d above.

79. The addition of a safety stock to the EOQ model

    a. Increases the EOQ proportionately.
    b. Raises the reorder point.
    c. Lowers the reorder point.
    d. Does not change the total inventory costs.
    e. Results in greater variability in the time required to receive deliveries.

80. Which of the following statements are primary assumptions of the EOQ model?

    a. Sales can be forecasted perfectly.
    b. Sales are evenly distributed throughout the period examined.
    c. Orders are received when expected.
    d. Statements a, b, and c are correct.
    e. All of the above statements are false.

SELF-TEST PROBLEMS

1. Price Industries Inc. has an inventory conversion period of 60 days, a receivables collection period of 35 days, and a payment deferral period of 28 days. What is the length of the firm's cash conversion cycle?

    a. 67 days   **b.** 82 days   **c.** 95 days   **d.** 104 days   **e.** 117 days

2. Refer to Self-Test Problem 1. If Price's sales are $972,000 annually, what is the firm's investment in accounts receivable?

    a. $72,450   **b.** $79,600   **c.** $85,300   **d.** $94,500   **e.** $100,000

3. On average, a firm sells 1.25 million in merchandise a month, and its cost of goods sold (CGS) is approximately 80 percent of sales. It keeps inventory equal to its monthly CGS on hand at all times. If the firm analyzes its accounts using a 360-day year, what is the firm's inventory conversion period?

    a. 360 days   **b.** 180 days   **c.** 60 days   **d.** 30 days   **e.** 15 days

4. A firm purchases raw materials on June 1st. It converts the raw materials into inventory by the last day of the month, June 30th. However, it pays for the materials on June 20th. On July 10th, it sells the finished goods for inventory. Then the firm collects cash from the sale one month later on August 10th. If this sequence accurately represents the firm's average working capital cycle, what is the firm's cash conversion cycle?

a. 45 days   **b.** 51 days   **c.** 61 days   **d.** 107 days   **e.** 30 days

(The following information applies to the next three Self-Test Problems.)

The Cairn Corporation is trying to determine the effect of its inventory turnover ratio and days sales outstanding (DSO) on its cash flow cycle. Cairn's sales (which were all on credit) were $750,000, and it earned a net profit margin of 12 percent, or $90,000. It turned over its inventory 9 times during the year, its DSO (receivables collection period) was 45 days, and the firm's cost of goods sold (CGS) was two-thirds of sales. The firm had fixed assets totaling $60,000. Cairn's payables deferral period is 30 days.

5. What is Cairn's cash conversion cycle?

     a. 25 days   **b.** 38 days   **c.** 55 days   **d.** 35 days   **e.** 65 days

6. Assume that Cairn holds negligible amounts of cash and marketable securities. What are its total assets turnover and ROA?

     a. 3.58; 37.45%   **d.** 3.58; 35.00%
     b. 4.03; 43.00%   **e.** 3.58; 43.00%
     c. 4.03; 48.83%

7. Suppose Cairn's managers believe that the inventory turnover can be raised to 12 times. Assuming that all other facts remain the same, what would Cairn's cash conversion cycle, total assets turnover, and ROA have been if the inventory turnover had been 12?

     a. 45; 3.00; 50.00%   **d.** 30; 3.00; 50.00%
     b. 30; 3.84; 46.06%   **e.** 45; 3.84; 50.00%
     c. 45; 3.84; 46.06%

(The following information applies to the next two Self-Test Problems.)

A firm buys on terms of 2/10, net 30, but generally does not pay until 40 days after the invoice date. Its purchases total $1,080,000 per year.

8. What is the *approximate* cost of the trade credit?

     a. 16.2%   **b.** 19.4%   **c.** 21.9%   **d.** 24.5%   **e.** 27.4%

9. What is the *effective* rate of the trade credit?

a. 16.2%   **b.** 19.4%   **c.** 21.9%   **d.** 24.5%   **e.** 27.4%

10. Lawton Pipelines Inc. has developed plans for a new pump that will allow more economical operation of the company's oil pipelines. Management estimates that $2,400,000 will be required to put this new pump into operation. Funds can be obtained from a bank at 10 percent discount interest, or the company can finance the expansion by delaying payment to its suppliers. Presently, Lawton purchases under terms of 2/10, net 40, but management believes payment could be delayed 30 additional days without penalty; that is, payment could be made in 70 days. Which means of financing should Lawton use? (Use the APR of trade credit.)

    a. Trade credit, since the cost is about 12.24 percent.
    b. Trade credit, since the cost is about 3.13 percentage points less than the bank loan.
    c. Bank loan, since the cost is about 1.13 percentage points less than trade credit.
    d. Bank loan, since the cost is about 3.13 percentage points less than trade credit.
    e. The firm could use either since the costs are the same.

(The following information applies to the next three Self-Test Problems.)

You plan to borrow $10,000 from your bank, which offers to lend you the money at a 10 percent quoted rate on a 1-year loan.

11. What is the *effective* interest rate if the loan is a discount loan?

    a. 11.1%   **b.** 13.3%   **c.** 15.0%   **d.** 17.5%   **e.** 20.0%

12. Assume the loan is a discount loan with a 15 percent compensating balance, and the firm has no checking account balances at that bank. How much would you have to borrow to have the use of $10,000?

    a. $10,000   **b.** $11,111   **c.** $12,000   **d.** $13,333   **e.** $15,000

13. What is the *effective* interest rate if the loan is a discount loan with a 15 percent compensating balance, and the firm has no checking account balances at that bank?

    a. 11.1%   **b.** 13.3%   **c.** 15.0%   **d.** 17.5%   **e.** 20.0%

14. Gibbs Corporation needs to raise $1,000,000 for one year to supply working capital to a new store. Gibbs buys from its suppliers on terms of 4/10, net 90, and it currently pays on the 10th day and takes discounts, but it could forgo discounts, pay on the 90th day, and get the needed $1,000,000 in the form of costly trade credit. Alternatively, Gibbs could borrow from its bank on a 15 percent discount interest rate basis. What is the *effective* annual rate of the *lower* cost source?

    a. 20.17%   **b.** 18.75%   **c.** 17.65%   **d.** 18.25%   **e.** 19.50%

15. The Brooks Company must arrange financing for its working capital requirements that total $100,000 for the coming year. Brooks can (a) borrow from its bank on a simple interest basis (interest payable at the end of the loan) for one year at a 10 percent rate; (b) borrow on a 3-month, but renewable, loan at a 9.5 percent rate; or (c) obtain the needed funds by no longer taking discounts and thus increasing its accounts payable. Brooks buys on terms of 1/20, net 60. What is the *effective* annual cost (*not* the approximate cost) of the *least expensive* type of credit, assuming 360 days per year?

    a. 9.84%   **b.** 10.17%   **c.** 9.47%   **d.** 7.64%   **e.** 8.91%

16. Your company buys on terms of 1/20, net 50, but it has not been taking discounts, so it has more accounts payable than if it did take discounts. It can borrow from the bank, begin taking discounts, and replace the "non-free" trade credit with bank debt. The firm will need to borrow $250,000. The bank will lend on two different bases: (a) 11 percent simple interest, where you repay the amount borrowed plus 11 percent interest at the end of one year; or (b) 10.5 percent simple, but with interest coming due each 6 months. What is your company's *lowest* cost source of credit *on an EAR basis*, considering the two types of bank loans and non-free trade credit? Assume 360 days per year.

    a. 11.00%   **b.** 10.78%   **c.** 8.28%   **d.** 9.24%   **e.** 9.83%

17. The Mill Company has a daily average collection of checks of $250,000. It takes the company 4 days to convert the checks to cash. Assume a lockbox system could be employed that would reduce the cash conversion period to 3 days. The lockbox system would have a net cost of $25,000 per year, but any additional funds made available could be invested to net 8 percent per year. Should Mill adopt the lockbox system?

    a. Yes; the system would free $250,000 in funds.
    b. Yes; the benefits of the lockbox system exceed the costs.
    c. No; the benefit is only $10,000.
    d. No; the firm would lose $5,000 per year if the system were used.
    e. The benefits and costs are equal; hence the firm is indifferent toward the system.

(The following information applies to the next two Self-Test Problems.)

Simmons Brick Company sells on terms of 3/10, net 30. Gross sales for the year are $1,200,000, and the collections department has calculated the firm's DSO as 27 days. Assume 360 days per year.

18. What is the current receivables balance?

    a. $60,000   **b.** $70,000   **c.** $75,000   **d.** $80,000   **e.** $90,000

19. What would be the new receivables balance if Simmons toughened up on its collection policy, with the result that the firm's DSO decreases to 24 days?

    a. $60,000   **b.** $70,000   **c.** $75,000   **d.** $80,000   **e.** $90,000

20. Furston Inc., a retail firm, currently has annual credit sales of $1 million. Current expenses for the collection department are $15,000, bad debt losses are 1 percent, and the days sales outstanding is 30 days. Furston is considering easing its collection efforts so that collection expenses will be reduced to $11,000 per year. The change is expected to increase bad debt losses to 2 percent and to increase the days sales outstanding to 45 days. In addition, sales are expected to increase to $1.3 million per year.

Should Furston relax collection efforts if the opportunity cost of funds is 13 percent, the variable cost ratio is 60 percent, and its marginal tax rate is 40 percent? Assume that any costs associated with the manufacture and sale of the product are made on the day of the sale.

    a. No, Furston should not relax collection efforts as it will lose $272.6 per day into perpetuity.
    b. Yes, Furston should relax collection efforts as it will gain $130.3 per day into perpetuity.
    c. No, Furston should not relax collection efforts as it will lose $95.0 per day into perpetuity.
    d. Yes, Furston should relax collection efforts as it will gain $272.6 per day into perpetuity.
    e. It doesn't matter what Furston does; both policies yield the same NPV.

21. Alan Linton, the new credit manager of Hodes Furniture, was alarmed to find out that the company sells on credit terms of net 60 days while industrywide credit terms have recently been lowered to net 35 days. Annual credit sales are $2.5 million. Linton estimates that tightening the credit terms to 35 days would reduce annual sales to $2 million, but days sales outstanding would fall from 72 days to 45 days.

Hodes' variable cost ratio is 75 percent, its marginal tax rate is 40 percent, and all costs associated with the production and sale of the product are paid on the day of the sale. If the interest rate on funds invested in receivables is 10 percent, should the change in credit terms be made?

    a. No, Hodes should not tighten its credit policy as the total value of the firm will decrease by $1,003,320 on a before-tax basis or by $601,992 on an after-tax basis.
    b. Yes, Hodes should tighten its credit policy as the total value of the firm will increase by $1,003,320 on a before-tax basis or by $601,992 on an after-tax basis.
    c. It doesn't matter which policy Hodes adopts; both policies will yield the same NPV. The value of the firm doesn't change.
    d. Yes, Hodes should tighten its credit policy as the total value of the firm will increase by $775,882 on a before-tax basis or by $465,529 on an after-tax basis.
    e. No, Hodes should not tighten its credit policy as the total value of the firm will decrease by $350,000 on a before-tax basis or by $210,000 on an after-tax basis.

(The following information applies to the next four Self-Test Problems.)

The South Florida Lawn Supply Company is reviewing its inventory policy regarding lawn seed. The following relationships and conditions exist:

- Orders must be placed in multiples of 100 bags.
- Requirements for the year are 16,200 bags.
- The purchase price per bag is $5.00.
- The carrying cost is 20 percent of inventory value.
- The fixed costs per order are $25.
- The desired safety stock is 300 bags; this amount is on hand initially.
- Five days are required for delivery.
- Assume 360 days per year.

22. What is the economic ordering quantity?

    a. 600 bags   **b.** 700 bags   **c.** 800 bags   **d.** 900 bags   **e.** 1,000 bags

23. How many orders should South Florida Lawn Supply place each year?

    a. 22   **b.** 20   **c.** 18   **d.** 16   **e.** 14

24. What is the reorder point?

    a. 750 bags   **b.** 525 bags   **c.** 345 bags   **d.** 300 bags   **e.** 225 bags

25. What is the average inventory level?

    a. 750 bags   **b.** 525 bags   **c.** 345 bags   **d.** 300 bags   **e.** 225 bags

(The following information applies to the next six Self-Test Problems.)

The Magnuson Company is trying to determine its optimal inventory policy. The following relationships and conditions exist for the firm:

- Annual sales are 120,000 units.
- The purchase price per unit is $500.
- The carrying cost is 20 percent of inventory value.
- The fixed costs per order are $600.
- The optimal safety stock is 500 units, this amount is already on hand.
- Assume 360 days per year.

26. What is the economic ordering quantity?

    a. 600 units   **b.** 800 units   **c.** 1,000 units   **d.** 1,200 units   **e.** 1,400 units

27. What is the maximum inventory the company will hold?

    a. 1,300 units   **b.** 1,400 units   **c.** 1,500 units   **d.** 1,600 units   **e.** 1,700 units

28. What is the average inventory the company will hold?

    a. 600 units   **b.** 850 units   **c.** 1,100 units   **d.** 1,200 units   **e.** 1,700 units

29. How often will the company order?

    a. Every 2.0 days   **d.** Every 2 weeks
    b. Every 3.60 days   **e.** Continually
    c. Every 5.25 days

30. What are the firm's annual total inventory costs disregarding the safety stock?

    a. $50,000   **b.** $120,000   **c.** $150,000   **d.** $170,000   **e.** $200,000

31. What are the annual total inventory costs including the safety stock?

    a. $50,000   **b.** $120,000   **c.** $150,000   **d.** $170,000   **e.** $200,000

ANSWERS TO SELF-TEST QUESTIONS

1.	working capital	24.	promissory note
2.	Net; current; liabilities	25.	discount interest
3.	current; liquidity	26.	compensating balances
4.	cash budget	27.	Commercial paper
5.	Working capital policy	28.	secured; receivables; inventories
6.	cash conversion cycle	29.	line of credit
7.	inventory conversion period	30.	commitment
8.	receivables collection period	31.	Factoring
9.	payables deferral period	32.	blanket lien
10.	relaxed	33.	minimize; cash
11.	Permanent	34.	Cash
12.	Temporary	35.	Precautionary balances
13.	maturity matching	36.	Transactions balances
14.	conservative	37.	Speculative balances
15.	upward	38.	Synchronized
16.	more	39.	lockbox
17.	covenants	40.	centralization of payables
18.	Short-term credit	41.	float
19.	accruals; accounts payable (trade credit); bank loans; commercial paper; secured	42.	pre-authorized debit
		43.	Marketable securities
		44.	Credit standards
20.	Accrued; size (amount)	45.	terms of credit
21.	trade credit	46.	credit period
22.	spontaneous	47.	cash discount
23.	notes payable	48.	Collection

49.	aging schedules; days sales outstanding (DSO)
50.	Easing
51.	Receivables monitoring
52.	raw materials; work-in-process; finished goods
53.	Raw materials
54.	Work-in-process
55.	Finished goods
56.	lowest cost
57.	increase; carrying
58.	Ordering costs
59.	economic ordering
60.	reorder point
61.	Safety stocks
62.	just-in-time
63.	Out-sourcing
64.	quantity discount
65.	revolving credit arrangement

66. b. The matching of maturities minimizes default risk, or the risk that the firm will be unable to pay off its maturing obligations, and interest rate reinvestment rate risk, or the risk that the firm will have to roll over the debt at a higher rate.

67. a. An increase in the payables deferral period shortens the cash conversion cycle, reducing the need for nonspontaneous funding.

68. a. Generally, the yield curve slopes upward, making the statement true. Even when the curve slopes downward, this suggests that rates are likely to fall, in which case interest expenses will fall if the firm uses short-term debt, but rates will be locked in (at a high level) if it uses long-term debt. Of course, if interest rates rise, the firm that financed with short-term debt may end up paying far more interest than a firm that obtained long-term funds when rates were lower.

69. a. Neither workers nor the IRS require interest payments on wages and taxes that are not paid as soon as they are earned.

70. b. No new customers are being generated. The current customers pay either on Day 10 or Day 30. The increase in trade discount will induce some customers who are now paying on Day 30 to pay on Day 10. Thus, the days sales outstanding is shortened which, in turn, will cause a decline in accounts receivable.

71. b. The aging schedule breaks down accounts receivable according to how long they have been outstanding.

72. b. Receivables are based on sales price, which presumably includes some profit. Only the actual cash outlays associated with receivables must be financed. The remainder, or profit, appears on the balance sheet as an increase in retained earnings.

73. b. The total cost, or the sum of ordering and carrying costs, is minimized, but neither of the component costs is minimized. For example, to minimize carrying costs, no inventory would be kept on hand at all.

74. e. Commercial paper is the unsecured debt of strong firms. It generally has a maturity from one to nine months and is sold primarily to other corporations and financial institutions. Rates on commercial paper are typically below the prime rate.

75. e. Management should try to maximize net float.

76. c. Long-term bonds have too much interest rate price risk for the firm's liquid asset portfolio.

77. c. If the firm sells on terms of 2/10, net 30, then its customers incur a cost of about 36 percent if they do not take discounts. Therefore, many customers will pay within 10 days and take discounts. So, if the DSO is exactly 30 days, then many customers must be paying well after 30 days because the DSO will be an average of 10 or less days plus the average payment time of the nondiscount customers.

Statement a is false because the better the credit department, the lower the DSO will be, other things held constant. Statement b is false because when the firm changes its terms to 2/10, net 30, some customers will start taking discounts, and that will lower its DSO.

78. c. Depreciation and obsolescence are inventory carrying costs.

79. b. The addition of a safety stock increases the reorder point by the amount of the safety stock.

80. d. Statements a, b, and c are all primary assumptions of the EOQ model.

SOLUTIONS TO SELF-TEST PROBLEMS

1. a. $$\text{Cash conversion cycle} = \frac{\text{Inventory}}{\text{conversion period}} + \frac{\text{Receivables}}{\text{collection period}} - \frac{\text{Payables}}{\text{deferral period}}$$

$$= 60 \text{ days} + 35 \text{ days} - 28 \text{ days} = 67 \text{ days}.$$

2. d. $$\text{DSO} = \frac{\text{Receivables}}{\text{Sales}/360}$$

$$35 = \frac{\text{Receivables}}{\$972,000/360}$$

Receivables = $94,500.

3. d. Inventory conversion period = Inventory/(CGS/360).

Annual sales = $1.25 million × 12 = $15 million.

CGS = 0.80 × $15 million = $12 million.

Inventory = $12 million/12 = $1 million.

Inventory conversion period = $1,000,000/($12,000,000/360) = 30 days.

4. b. Payables deferral period = 20 days (June 1 to June 20).

Inventory conversion period = 40 days (June 1 to July 10).

Receivables collection period = 31 days (July 10 to August 10).

Cash conversion cycle = 40 + 31 – 20 = 51 days.

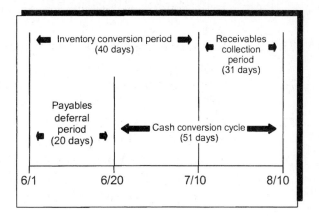

5. c. DSO = 45 days; Payables deferral period = 30 days.

Because inventory is turned over 9 times during the year, the inventory conversion period must be 40 days = (360 days)/9.

Alternatively, compute the average inventory balance:

Cost of goods sold (CGS) = $750,000(2/3) = $500,000.
Inventory = ($500,000)/9 = $55,556.

So, the inventory conversion period is:

$$\text{Inventory conversion period} = \frac{\text{Inventory}}{\text{CGS}/360} = \frac{\$55,556}{\$500,000/360} = 40 \text{ days.}$$

$$\begin{array}{c}\text{Cash conversion} \\ \text{cycle}\end{array} = \begin{array}{c}\text{Inventory} \\ \text{conversion period}\end{array} + \begin{array}{c}\text{Receivables} \\ \text{collection period}\end{array} - \begin{array}{c}\text{Payables} \\ \text{deferral period}\end{array}$$

= 40 days + 45 days – 30 days = 55 days.

6. e. We need to calculate receivables and inventory to determine total assets.

$$\text{DSO} = \frac{\text{Receivables}}{\text{Sales}/360}$$

$$45 = \frac{\text{Receivables}}{\$750,000/360}$$

Receivables = $93,750.

From Self-Test Problem 5, we know that Inventory = $55,556.

Total assets = Cash + Marketable securities + Receivables + Inventories + Fixed assets
= $0 + $0 + $93,750 + $55,556 + $60,000
= $209,306.

Now calculate Total assets turnover = Sales/Total assets and ROA = Net income/Total assets:

Sales/Total assets = $750,000/$209,306 = 3.58.

ROA = Net income/Total assets = $90,000/$209,306 = 43.0%.

7.   c.   DSO = 45 days; Payables deferral period = 30 days.

Inventory conversion period = (360 days)/12 = 30 days.

Cash conversion cycle = 30 days + 45 days – 30 days = 45 days.

Inventory = CGS/12 = ($500,000)/12 = $41,667.

Total assets = Cash + Marketable securities + Receivables + Inventories + Fixed assets
           = $0 + $0 + $93,750 + $41,667 + $60,000
           = $195,417.

Total assets turnover = Sales/Total assets = $750,000/$195,417 = 3.84.

ROA = Net income/Total assets = $90,000/$195,417 = 46.06%.

8.   d.   Periodic rate $= \dfrac{\$0.02}{\$0.98} = 0.020408.$

$$APR = 0.020408 \times \frac{360}{30} = 0.020408 \times 12 = 0.244898 = 24.49\% \approx 24.5\%.$$

9.   e.   The periodic rate is 2/98 = 2.04%, and there are 360/30 = 12 periods per year. Thus, the effective annual rate is 27.4 percent:

$$(1 + r_{PER})^{12} - 1.0 = (1.0204)^{12} - 1.0$$
$$= 1.2743 - 1.0 = 0.2743 = 27.4\%.$$

10.   c. $\dfrac{\text{Effective rate on}}{\text{the discount loan}} = \dfrac{(\$2,400,000)(0.10)}{\$2,400,000 - (\$2,400,000)(0.10)}$

$\dfrac{\$240,000}{\$2,160,000} = 0.1111 = 11.11\%.$

Credit terms are 2/10, net 40, but delaying payments 30 additional days is the equivalent of 2/10, net 70. Assuming no penalty, the approximate cost is as follows:

Periodic rate $= \dfrac{\$0.02}{\$0.98} = 0.020408.$

$$\text{APR} = 0.020408 \times \frac{360}{60}$$
$$= 0.020408 \times 6 = 12.24\%.$$

Therefore, the loan cost is 1.13 percentage points less than trade credit.

11.   a.   Effective rate $= \dfrac{\$10,000(0.10)}{\$10,000 - \$10,000(0.10)} = \dfrac{\$1,000}{\$9,000} = 11.1\%.$

12.   d.   Required loan $= \dfrac{\$10,000}{1 - 0.15 - 0.10} = \$13,333.33.$

$0.15(\$13,333) = \$2,000$ is required for the compensating balance, and $0.10(\$13,333) = \$1,333$ is required for the immediate interest payment.

13.   b.   Effective rate $= \dfrac{0.10(\$13,333.33)}{\$13,333.33 - [\$13,333.33(0.15 + 0.10)]} = \dfrac{\$1,333.33}{\$10,000} = 13.3\%.$

14.   c.   Accounts payable:

Periodic rate $= \$0.04/\$0.96 = 0.04167.$

APR $= (0.04167)(360/80) = 0.04167(4.5) = 18.75\%.$

EAR cost $= (1.04167)^{4.5} - 1.0 = 20.17\%.$

Notes payable: $\dfrac{(0.15)(\$1,000,000)}{\$1,000,000 - 0.15(\$1,000,000)} = \dfrac{\$150,000}{\$850,000} = 17.65\%.$

Thus, Gibbs should borrow from the bank as this is the lower cost source.

15.   c.   (a) *Simple interest loan:* $\left(1 + \dfrac{\$10,000}{\$100,000}\right)^{1} - 1 = 10\%.$

(b) *3-month loan:* Periodic rate $= 0.095/4 = 0.02375.$

$$\left(1 + \frac{0.02375(\$100,000)}{\$100,000}\right)^{4} - 1 =$$
$$\left(1 + \frac{\$2,375}{\$100,000}\right)^{4} - 1 =$$
$$(1.02375)^{4} - 1 = 9.84\%.$$

(c) *Trade credit:*

1/99 = 1.01% on discount if the firm pays in 20 days, otherwise the firm must pay at the end of Day 60. So, the firm gets 60 – 20 = 40 days of credit at a cost of 1/99 = 1.01%. There are 360/40 = 9 periods, so the effective cost rate is:

$(1 + 1/99)^9 - 1 = (1.01)^9 - 1 = 0.09467 \approx 9.47\%.$

16. b. (a) The 11 percent simple interest loan has an effective rate of 11 percent.

$$\left(1 + \frac{0.11(\$250,000)}{\$250,000}\right)^1 - 1 = 11\%.$$

(b) The 10.5 percent semiannual loan has an effective rate of 10.78 percent, found with this equation:

Periodic rate = 0.105/2 = 0.0525.

$$\left(1 + \frac{0.0525(\$250,000)}{\$250,000}\right)^2 - 1 = 10.78\%.$$

(c) The cost of non-free trade credit is found as follows:

$$\text{Periodic rate} = \frac{\$0.01}{\$0.99} = 0.0101.$$

$$\text{APR} = 0.0101 \times \frac{360}{30} = 0.0101 \times 12 = 0.1212 = 12.12\%.$$

This is the *approximate* cost of trade credit. To get the effective annual cost rate, proceed as follows:

$$\text{EAR} = (1 + \text{Cost per period})^{\text{No. of periods}} - 1.0 = (1.0101)^{12} - 1 = 12.82\%.$$

17. d. Currently, Mill has 4($250,000) = $1,000,000 in unavailable collections. If lockboxes were used, this could be reduced to $750,000. Thus, $250,000 would be available to invest at 8 percent, resulting in an annual return of 0.08($250,000) = $20,000. If the system costs $25,000, Mill would lose $5,000 per year by adopting the system.

18. e. Receivables = (DSO)(Sales/360) = 27($1,200,000/360) = $90,000.

19. d. Sales per day = $1,200,000/360 = $3,333.33.

Receivables = $3,333.33(24 days) = $80,000.00.

Thus, the average receivables would drop from $90,000 to $80,000. Furthermore, sales may decline as a result of the tighter credit and reduce receivables even more.

20.   d.   Analysis of change:

	Existing Policy	Proposed Policy
Annual amounts		
Sales	$1.00 million	$1.30 million
Bad debts—percent	1%	2%
Bad debts—dollars	$10,000	$26,000
Amount of sales collected	$990,000	$1,274,000
Variable costs (0.60 × Sales)	$600,000	$780,000
Collection expenses	$15,000	$11,000

	Existing Policy	Proposed Policy
Daily amounts = (Annual amounts)/360		
Sales	$2,777.8	$3,611.1
Bad debts	$27.8	$72.2
Amount collected	$2,750.0	$3,538.9
Variable costs	$1,666.7	$2,166.7
Collection expenses	$41.7	$30.6
DSO	30 days	45 days
Opportunity cost	13%	13%

Cash flow time line: Existing policy (daily sales)

```
 0                          30
 |____13%_____|
($1,666.7)              $2,750.00
   (41.7)
($1,708.4)
```

$$\text{NPV}_\text{Existing} = (\$1,708.4) + \frac{\$2,750.0}{\left(1 + \dfrac{0.13}{360}\right)^{30}} = (\$1,708.4) + \$2,720.4 = \$1,012.0.$$

Cash flow time line: Proposed policy (daily sales)

```
 0                                    45
 |____13%_____|
($2,166.7)                       $3,538.9
   (30.6)
($2,197.3)
```

$$\text{NPV}_\text{Proposed} = (\$2,197.3) + \frac{\$3,538.9}{\left(1 + \dfrac{0.13}{360}\right)^{45}} = (\$2,197.3) + \$3,481.9 = \$1,284.6.$$

If Furston adopts the new credit policy, its value will increase by $272.6 per day into perpetuity. As a result, the total value of the firm will increase by $272.6/(0.13/360) = $754,892 on a before-tax basis ($452,935 after taxes). The proposed credit policy should be adopted.

21. a. Analysis of change:

	Existing Policy	Proposed Policy
Annual amounts		
Sales	$2,500,000	$2,000,000
Variable costs (0.75 × Sales)	$1,875,000	$1,500,000
Daily amounts = (Annual amounts)/360		
Sales	$6,944.4	$5,555.6
Variable costs	$5,208.3	$4,166.7
DSO	72 days	45 days
Opportunity cost	10%	10%

Cash flow time line: Existing policy (daily sales)

```
0                                            72
 |————10%————————————————————————————————————|
($5,208.3)                              $6,944.4
```

$$\text{NPV}_{\text{Existing}} = (\$5,208.3) + \frac{\$6,944.4}{\left(1 + \dfrac{0.10}{360}\right)^{72}} = (\$5,208.3) + \$6,806.9 = \$1,598.6.$$

Cash flow time line: Proposed policy (daily sales)

```
0                          45
 |————10%———————————————————|
($4,166.7)            $5,555.6
```

$$\text{NPV}_{\text{Proposed}} = (\$4,166.7) + \frac{\$5,555.6}{\left(1 + \dfrac{0.10}{360}\right)^{45}} = (\$4,166.7) + \$5,486.6 = \$1,319.9.$$

If Hodes adopts the new credit policy, its value will decrease by $278.7 = $1,319.9 − $1,598.6 per day into perpetuity. As a result, the total value of the firm will decrease by $278.7/(0.10/360) = $1,003,320 on a before-tax basis ($601,992 after taxes). The proposed credit policy should not be adopted, because to do so would decrease the value of the firm.

22. d. $\text{EOQ} = \sqrt{\dfrac{2(\text{O})(\text{T})}{(\text{C})(\text{PP})}} = \sqrt{\dfrac{2(\$25)(16,200)}{0.20(\$5)}} = \sqrt{\dfrac{\$810,000}{\$1.00}} = 900$ bags.

23. c. $\dfrac{16,200 \text{ bags per year}}{900 \text{ bags per order}} = 18$ orders per year.

24. b. Daily rate of usage $= 16,200/360 = 45$ bags.

Reorder point $= 300 + 5(45) = 525$ bags.

Thus, South Florida Lawn Supply Company will have 1,200 bags on hand immediately after a shipment is received, will use 45 bags per day, will reorder when the stock is down to 525 bags (which is 5 days' requirement, plus the safety stock), and will be down to 300 bags just before a shipment arrives.

25. a. Average inventory level $=$ EOQ/2 + Safety stock $= 900/2 + 300 = 750$ bags.

Note that the inventory fluctuates between 1,200 and 300 bags.

26. d. $\text{EOQ} = \sqrt{\dfrac{2(O)(T)}{(C)(PP)}} = \sqrt{\dfrac{2(\$600)(120,000)}{0.20(\$500)}} = \sqrt{\dfrac{\$144,000,000}{\$100}} = 1,200$ units.

27. e. Maximum inventory $=$ EOQ + Safety stock $= 1,200 + 500 = 1,700$ units.

28. c. Average inventory $=$ EOQ/2 + Safety stock $= 1,200/2 + 500 = 1,100$ units.

29. b. $\dfrac{120,000 \text{ units per year}}{1,200 \text{ units per order}} = 100$ orders per year.

$\dfrac{360 \text{ days per year}}{100 \text{ orders per year}} = 3.60$ days.

The firm must place one order every 3.60 days.

30. b. $\text{TIC} = (C)(PP)(Q/2) + (O)\left(\dfrac{T}{Q}\right)$

$= 0.2(\$500)(1,200/2) + \$600\left(\dfrac{120,000}{1,200}\right)$

$= \$60,000 + \$60,000 = \$120,000.$

Note that total carrying costs equal total ordering costs at the EOQ.

31. d. Now, the average inventory is EOQ/2 + Safety stock $= 1,100$ units rather than EOQ/2 $= 600$ units.

$\text{TIC} = 0.2(\$500)(1,100) + \$600\left(\dfrac{120,000}{1,200}\right) = \$110,000 + \$60,000 = \$170,000.$

Another way of looking at this is TIC= Cost of working inventory + Cost of safety stock

$$= \$120,000 + 0.2(\$500)(500)$$
$$= \$120,000 + \$50,000 = \$170,000.$$

CHAPTER 16
INVESTMENT CONCEPTS

OVERVIEW

This chapter discusses the various approaches investors must choose from implementing their investment objectives to achieving their investment goals. Our discussions focus on investing, not speculating, and on individuals rather than institutions. The investment process is described, examining investment objectives and investors' attitudes toward risk. Investment alternatives are considered, and the role of the brokerage firm relative to financial intermediaries in securities trading is discussed. Sources of investment information are discussed, and an explanation on how to read an investment's price quotation is given. We discuss measuring returns on individual assets, such as stocks and bonds, as well as market indexes, which are used to measure the returns for combinations of securities such as stock and bond markets. Finally, we outline alternative investment strategies such as buy-and-hold, margin trading, and short selling.

OUTLINE

From an economic standpoint, investors are defined as individuals who forgo current consumption to increase future wealth and consumption.

☐   There are two general types of investors:
  ~   Those who purchase investments with current savings in anticipation of relatively stable growth on average, or in the long-term, are usually referred to as *investors*.
  ~   Those who try to make a quick profit based on short-term market adjustments are called *speculators* because they gamble, or speculate, on whether financial assets are actually mispriced and market prices will adjust accordingly.
    •   Speculating is riskier than investing.

Investing should be viewed as a continuous process. There are many different financial instruments, each of which serves a somewhat different purpose, available to investors. Before an investor can determine what investment to purchase, he or she must identify the reason(s) for investing.

☐   The major reason people invest is *retirement planning*.
  ~   Depending on what point in an individual's career he or she starts planning for retirement determines the strategy the investor will follow.
    •   Beginning early in one's career enables a person to invest in instruments that

promise long-term growth; starting later might dictate investing in instruments that offer greater short-term stability.

~ People also use investments to *supplement current income.*

- Appropriate investments include those that offer steady dividend or interest payments called *income securities.*
- Preferred stock and interest-bearing bonds generally are considered good income-producing investments.

~ Another reason people invest is to *shelter current income from taxes* using tax write-offs or other provisions of the Tax Code.

- Investors attempt to legally defer or avoid paying taxes on income that is not needed in the current period.

~ People often save current income to *achieve future goals* such as a home purchase, attending college, or travel.

☐ For the most part, investors are risk averse; thus, they demand greater returns for taking on greater levels of risk.

~ The degree of risk aversity exhibited by investors varies among individuals at any point in time and changes across time.

~ In order to determine what instruments are appropriate to achieving investment objectives, it is important to examine one's ability and willingness to take on risk when investing.

~ Maximizing returns associated with investments is a universal goal, but remember that higher returns are accompanied by higher risks.

~ The ability and willingness to tolerate risk, called your *risk tolerance level*, depends on existing economic conditions, current socioeconomic position, and expectations about your socioeconomic position in the future.

- When the economy is performing well and funds are not needed for current expenses or existing investment goals, investors will probably be willing to invest in riskier securities than if the economy is performing poorly and the funds are needed for specific reasons.

☐ Once realistic goals have been formulated based on investment objectives and risk attitudes, it is necessary to implement the decisions that have been made.

~ Implementation involves the selection and purchase of specific investment instruments to achieve the desired goals.

~ This is a costly process because *transaction costs*, or commissions, must be paid to acquire investments.

- Transaction costs are the costs associated with trading securities, which include the costs of time, effort, and phone calls, as well as broker commissions that are incurred.

~ Depending on an investor's risk tolerance level and propensity to control investment decisions, an investor might prefer to either actively select investments or rely on the advice of an investment professional (passive management).

~ An investor should always be aware of the composition of his or her *investment portfolio*, the combination of investment assets held, because the allocation of investment funds to various types of assets in the portfolio is an important decision.

~ When determining the appropriate *asset allocation*, the proportion of funds invested in various types of assets, the investment goal should always be held in the forefront.

~ In most cases, investors allocate funds according to three basic categories of financial assets:

- Short-term debt instruments, or money market securities (cash and near-cash items);
- Long-term debt, or bonds; and
- Stocks.

~ Asset allocation is important because it affects the return earned on the investment portfolio, and it is a dynamic process. As conditions in the financial markets change, so do the asset allocations in investment portfolios.

- When markets become more unstable and unpredictable than normal, many professional investment managers shift their allocations into the asset categories that are considered safer, such as money market instruments and debt.
- Similarly, as individuals move through life, there is a tendency to become more conservative, and thus, there is a shift into less risky asset categories.

☐ After the investment strategy has been implemented, the investment position must be monitored to ensure the goals are being met. It is vitally important that investor regularly reexamine their goals and strategies and their investment positions to determine whether modifications are needed.

~ Changing economic and legal conditions warrant the periodic evaluation of investment positions.

~ Changing attitudes toward risk or socioeconomic positions change investment strategies.

There are many different instruments available to help individuals meet their investment goals, whether low or high risk, for short or long-term periods. Additionally, new investments continue to evolve as investors' needs (demands) change and as investors' demographics change.

Most of the investment transactions entered into and not related to savings instruments from financial institutions require the assistance of a middleman, or agent, called a broker.

☐ The role of a *broker* is to help his or her clients trade financial instruments, especially stocks, bonds, and derivatives.

~ A broker must be licensed by the exchanges on which the traded securities are listed, and must abide by any licensing or registration requirements of the state in which he or she trades and by ethical standards established by the SEC.

☐ In the strictest sense, a brokerage firm is not considered a financial intermediary.

~ Financial intermediaries literally manufacture a variety of financial products, such as mortgages, automobile loans, and so forth, to allow savers to indirectly provide funds to borrowers.

~ Brokerage firms do not create savings instruments, or financial securities; rather, they help investors trade such securities, which are created by corporations and governments.

- Brokers allow savers to directly provide their funds to users. This is not part of the intermediation process.

~ Some brokerage firms have ventured into areas customarily associated with financial intermediaries, such as offering their own money market funds with checking privileges, credit cards, and other services.

- This trend will probably continue in the future enabling brokerage firms to better compete in the financial marketplace.

☐ In general, brokerage firms are classified into one of two categories:

~ *Full-service brokerage firms* offer a variety of services to their clients, including results from research projects, monthly publications containing investment recommendations, and advisory services.

~ *Discount brokerage firms* offer their clients only basic services associated with trading securities, such as trade executions and related reporting requirements.

- Because discount brokerage firms offer fewer amenities, they are able to charge substantially lower commissions to execute trades.

☐ Although most security trades are completed either by telephone or in person, many large brokerage firms now offer electronic trading. Advantages to electronic trading include:

~ An order can be placed any time, even when the markets are closed.

~ Commissions are generally lower than dealing with a traditional or discount stockbroker, because, in effect, electronic orders can be placed directly with the representative of the brokerage firm that completes the trade.

- Although most commissions are still derived from traditional trading mechanisms, it is evident that a virtual Wall Street is evolving.

☐ Regardless of the means, executing a trade involves the same general process— instructions are given concerning the security to be traded, which include an indication of the number of units, or shares, to be traded, when the trade should take place, and any limitations associated with the trade.

~ When securities are traded on exchanges, they are traded in multiples of 100 shares called *round lots*.

- Investors can also trade in *odd lots*, multiples of less than 100 shares, handled by special *odd-lot dealers,* who "bundle together" odd lots to create round lots that can be traded on the exchanges.

- The additional processing of odd lot trading increases the relative cost compared with round-lot trades.

~ Transactions to buy and sell stocks are executed according to orders submitted by investors.

- The most common type is a *market order* to execute a transaction at the best price available when it reaches the market.

~ Conditions and limitations concerning how and when a buy or sell transaction can be executed can also be included in an order.

- A *stop order* specifies the price at which an order to buy or sell at the market price (a market order) is initiated. A stop order instructs the broker when to begin executing a transaction; it doesn't guarantee, or limit the price of the transaction.
- To restrict the price of a transaction, an investor can use a *limit order* to buy or sell at no worse than a specified price.
- Orders that have price restrictions can also have time limitations. A stop order can be placed so that it is canceled if the price conditions are not met by the end of the trading day—a *day order (DO)*.
- The order can remain *good 'til canceled (GTC)*, which means the order is active until the price limitations are met or until the investor cancels it (reconfirmed by the broker every six months).
- An investor can place a *fill or kill order*, which instructs the broker to cancel the order if it cannot be executed immediately, sometimes with a time limit attached.
- ~ Evidence of stock ownership can be accomplished by possession of a stock certificate or by allowing the brokerage firm to hold the stock for the investor.
  - Stock that is registered to the brokerage firm in the investor's name is referred to as *street name stock*, with the firm's records indicating the investor is the "real" owner of the stock.
  - Allowing the brokerage firm to hold the stock in street name provides for easier transfer of shares when sold and also provides safekeeping of the investment.
- ~ Nearly every brokerage firm purchases insurance through the Securities Investor Protection Corporation (SIPC), which insures the cash and securities of investors held by the brokerage company from theft or loss of the security to a maximum of $500,000.

Ignorance can be very costly when making investment decisions—both advantages and disadvantages should be investigated beforehand.

- There are many sources and forms of investment information. Newspapers, magazines, company reports, investment research organizations, and the Internet are all sources of information.
  - ~ Publicly traded companies are required to prepare and publish annual reports that contain financial statements and other information.
  - ~ *Value Line Investment Survey, Moody's Investment Services,* and *Standard and Poor's,* among others, provide financial data as well as some of the results from analyses conducted by their research staffs.
  - ~ Newspapers of larger cities such as the *New York Times,* as well as other papers such as *The Wall Street Journal, Barron's,* and *Investor's Business Daily* report financial news and related business information.
  - ~ Various magazines include *Business Week, Forbes, Fortune,* and *Money.*
  - ~ The Internet provides a mechanism for investors to find and contact numerous additional sources, such as the web sites of individual companies and brokerage firms, the SEC, and the Federal Reserve.
  - ~ Numerous databases and programs to analyze investments are available on the Internet, as well as software packages available to investors for their own PCs.

- The PC has revolutionized the ability of individual investors to evaluate investment strategies and alternatives available to meet investment goals.
- As a result, individual investors are able to perform much more sophisticated investment analyses today than 20 or 30 years ago, and make more informed investment decisions.

☐ To compute the return associated with an investment, the price of the investment must be determined from reading its price quotation.
~ *The Wall Street Journal* is considered by many investors to be the premier source of daily quotations for stocks and bonds.
~ Quotes represent trading activity from the previous trading day.
~ Stock prices are denominated in decimal form such that they are reported in dollars and cents.
- The *stock symbol* is the designation that represents the trading initials of the company.
~ The interpretation of bond quotations is somewhat different than stock quotations. The closing "price" of a bond does not represent a dollar amount because *bond values are stated as a percentage of the face value.*
~ The prices of bonds issued by the Treasury and government agencies are quoted differently than corporate bonds.
- Like a corporate bond, the price of a Treasury bond (or note) is stated as a percentage of the face value; unlike corporate bonds, price fractions are always stated as 32nds.
- Two prices are given in the quote—the "Bid" and the "Asked," called dealer bid/asked prices because they represent the amount government bond dealers bid (what they are willing to pay) to purchase the bonds from investors and the amount they ask (what they are willing to take) for selling their bonds to investors.
- The only difference between Treasury notes and bonds is their maturities when they are originally issued—notes have original maturities from greater than one year to ten years, and bonds have original maturities greater than ten years.

An important part of monitoring investments includes determining the return that has been earned.

☐ The return on an investment is generated by (1) any income produced by the investment and (2) any change in the value, or price, of the investment. Thus, the *dollar return* earned from an investment is simply the income received plus any change in value, which can be stated as follows:

$$\text{Dollar return} = \frac{\text{Income}}{\text{received}} + \frac{\text{Ending value}}{\text{of investment}} - \frac{\text{Beginning value}}{\text{of investment}}$$
$$= \text{INC} + P_1 - P_0.$$

~ Here INC represents the income received from the investment, whether it is interest from a bond or dividends from a stock, P_1 is the investment's value at the end of the period for which the return is computed, and P_0 is the value of the investment at the beginning for the period for which the return is computed.

☐ The *rate of return* on an investment for a particular period can then be computed as follows:

$$\text{Rate of return} = k = \frac{\text{Income received} + \left(\text{Ending value of investment} - \text{Beginning value of investment}\right)}{\text{Beginning value of investment}}$$

$$= \frac{\text{INC} + (P_1 - P_0)}{P_0} = \text{Holding period return (HPY)}$$

~ This computation is often referred to as the *holding period return (HPR)* because it is used to calculate the return earned over the period of time the investment was held.
- The holding period return is the actual, or realized, rate of return, k.
~ The numerator includes the income received from the investment and the change in value, or the *capital gain (loss)*, associated with the investment.
~ In most cases returns are stated on an annual basis so that alternative investments are more easily compared. To adjust the holding period on an annual basis, the formula is rewritten as:

$$\text{Annualized rate of return} = k = \frac{\text{INC} + (P_1 - P_0)}{P_0} \times \left(\frac{360}{T}\right).$$

- Here T represents the number of days the investment is held.
- 360 days is used for simplicity.

☐ Generally when examining the returns associated with an investment that has been held for many years, the *average annual return* is desired.
~ To calculate the average annual return (return per period), first compute the annual HPR for each year the investment was held, then find the average.
~ Two techniques for computing the average return for an investment held for more than one year (period) are: the simple arithmetic average and the geometric average.
~ The *simple arithmetic average return* is computed by summing each return and then dividing by the number of returns:

$$\text{Simple arithmetic average return} = \bar{k}_A = \frac{k_1 + k_2 + \Lambda + k_n}{n}$$

$$= \frac{\sum_{t=1}^{n} k_t}{n}.$$

- Here $\bar{k}_A$ is the simple arithmetic average return, k_t is the holding period return for Year t, and n is the number of years the investment has been held.
~ The *geometric average return* considers compounded rates.
~ The geometric average return is found as follows:

$$\text{Geometric average return} = \bar{k}_G = [(1 + k_1) \times (1 + k_2) \times \ldots \times (1 + k_n)]^{1/n} - 1.0$$

$$= \left[\prod_{t=1}^{n} (1 + k_t) \right]^{1/n} - 1.0.$$

- Here $\bar{k}_G$ is the geometric average return. The Greek symbol, $\prod$, which is pronounced "pie," means to multiply, or take the product of, a series of numbers. And, when an equation is raised to the 1/n power, it means take the nth root of the result, which can be accomplished by using the y^x key on your calculator.

~ Because the simple arithmetic average return does not consider compounding, its value will always be equal to or greater than the geometric average return.
  - This relationship exists because, all else equal, it takes a greater rate of return to reach a particular future value if funds are not compounded.
  - The simple arithmetic average return and the geometric average return will be equal only if the annual returns are constant.

~ Although the simple arithmetic average return should not be used to compute the average annual return for an investment over a multiple-year period, it can be used to compute the average return for a group of investments at one point in time.

☐ The *expected return* on a portfolio is the weighted average of the expected returns on the individual stocks included in the portfolio.
  ~ The same principle applies when computing the historical return of a portfolio—determine the weighted average of the actual returns on each individual stock, with the weights being the fraction of the total portfolio invested in each stock at the beginning of the investment (holding) period. The formula to compute the historical return of a portfolio is:

$$\bar{k}_p = \left(\frac{\text{Value of Security 1}}{\text{Portfolio value}} \right) \cdot k_1 + \left(\frac{\text{Value of Security 2}}{\text{Portfolio value}} \right) \cdot k_2 + \Lambda + \left(\frac{\text{Value of Security n}}{\text{Portfolio value}} \right) \cdot k_n$$

$$= w_1 \cdot k_1 + w_2 \cdot k_2 + \Lambda + w_n \cdot k_n$$

$$= \sum_{j=1}^{n} w_j \cdot k_j .$$

  - Here the wj's are the weights based on market values at the beginning of the investment period, and there are n stocks in the portfolio.
  ~ Annual returns for the portfolio can be calculated by determining the change in the total value of the portfolio each year.

Market indexes are used to measure the returns for combinations of securities, or "baskets" of investments, such as stock markets and bond markets.

☐ Market indexes measure performance in the financial markets much like economic indexes measure performance in the economy.

☐ One of the most often quoted market indexes is the Dow Jones Industrial Average, or DJIA, which measures the aggregate return, or performance, for the 30 largest industrial firms in the United States.

~ Although the Dow includes only 30 stocks, less than one percent of the total number of stocks listed on the NYSE, many believe it provides a very good picture of the stock market's performance because the companies in the Dow are extremely large industrial firms that account for nearly one-fifth of the total market value of NYSE firms.

~ The Dow is considered the stock market's bellwether barometer.

☐ Another very well-known family of indexes includes those published by Standard & Poor's—the S&P 500, S&P 400, S&P Industrials, and so forth.

~ The S&P indexes are more general, with broader coverage, than the Dow because they include more companies.

☐ The NYSE, AMEX, and NASDAQ indexes contain even broader coverage as they include all the stocks listed on the exchanges.

☐ The Russell 3000 and the Wilshire 5000 are indexes that were created in an attempt to measure the performance of more general groups of stocks, not just those listed on particular exchanges.

☐ Returns differ fairly significantly among the indexes due to two major reasons:

~ Not every index measures the same group of stocks. Thus, it makes sense there would be some variation among the different index results.

~ Indexes are not constructed the same.

• A *price-weighted index* is constructed by adding the price of one share of stock and then dividing by the number of stocks in the index.

• A major criticism of this type of index is that a change in price of a very high-priced stock will influence the index more than the other stocks that have much smaller prices.

• One way to mitigate the influence high-priced securities have on the value of a price-weighted index is to compute a *value-weighted index,* which is based on the total value of the stock of each firm rather than the price of a single share.

• *Market capitalization* is the total market value of a firm's stock, which can be computed by multiplying the number of shares outstanding by the market price per share.

☐ The method used to construct an index can make a considerable difference in the results that are indicated for market performance.

~ The indexes reported in the media do not always measure the same event.

• In reality, however, market indexes are very highly correlated, regardless of how they are constructed or the specific group of securities used.

☐ Indexes have several important uses.

- ~ They provide investors with an indication of how well the general economy is doing.
  - When the market is rising it is referred to as a *bull market*, which suggests the economy is performing well.
  - When the market is falling it is called a *bear market*, which suggests the economy is performing poorly.
- ~ Market indexes are used as benchmarks by individual investors and mutual fund managers when determining how well their portfolios have performed.
- ~ Indexes are also used to estimate the betas for securities.
  - Beta represents the relationship between a stock's returns and the market's returns; thus, it is a measure of the systematic risk associated with the stock.
- ~ Indexes are used as investment instruments and as the basis for other investments, such as options.

Investors construct investment portfolios by holding different positions in different financial assets.

☐ Most individual investors follow a *buy-and-hold strategy*, which means they purchase securities with the intent to hold them until either their goals are met or modifications are needed in their portfolios to ensure future goals are met.
  - ~ This strategy is usually considered a long-term rather than a short-term investment position.
    - When investors buy securities, regardless of the intended holding period, they are said to be *going long* and, clearly, they hope that prices increase.
    - When investors sell securities they own, they are said to be *going short*, which generally occurs when they believe prices will drop in the future.

☐ *Margin trading* permits an investor to borrow from his or her broker some portion of the funds needed to purchase securities.
  - ~ The amount that can be borrowed is based on the *margin requirement*, which represents the minimum amount of personal funds (initial equity) an investor must have to purchase securities.
  - ~ The margin requirement, which is set by the Federal Reserve, is currently 50 percent.
  - ~ When an investor borrows funds from a brokerage firm to purchase securities, he or she signs a *hypothecation agreement*, which assigns the securities as collateral for the margin loan. The hypothecation agreement allows the broker to liquidate the stocks to repay the loan if the investor defaults.
    - Investors who borrow funds to purchase securities are charged interest on their margin loans. The interest rate, called the *broker loan rate*, is based on the rate a brokerage firm is charged by its lenders.
    - Margin trading magnifies the gains when the value of the investment increases at a rate greater than the broker loan rate; but, margin trading also magnifies losses associated with a decline in value.
    - To determine the amount of stock an investor can purchase on margin, first consider how the actual margin, or percentage of investor's equity, is computed:

CHAPTER 16—INVESTMENT CONCEPTS

$$\frac{\text{Actual}}{\text{margin}} = \frac{\text{Percentage of}}{\text{investor's equity}} = \frac{\text{Investor's equity}}{\text{Market value of investment}}.$$

- The *actual margin* must equal the margin requirement when the stock is purchased.
- The amount the investor owes the broker does not change when the market value of the stock changes.
- At any point, an investor's equity position is represented by the actual margin associated with the existing market price of the stock. An investor's equity position is calculated:

$$\text{Actual margin} = \frac{\text{Investor's equity}}{\text{Market value of investment}}$$

$$= \frac{\left[(\#\text{ of shares}) \times (\text{Price per share})\right] - \text{Amount borrowed}}{(\#\text{ of shares}) \times (\text{Price per share})}.$$

- The broker will require the investor to provide additional funds when the actual margin decreases to a certain percentage or lower, issuing a *margin call*—the call for more funds.
- The price at which a margin call is issued depends on the *maintenance margin*, which represents the lowest actual margin, or percentage equity, the brokerage firm permits its margined investors to possess at any time.
- To determine the price at which a margin call will be issued, we can set the actual margin in the above equation equal to the *maintenance margin* and rearrange the equation as follows:

$$\frac{\text{Margin call price}}{(\text{per share})} = \frac{\text{Amount borrowed}}{(\#\text{ of shares})(1 - \text{Maintenance margin})}.$$

☐ If an investor believes the price of a stock (or other security) is going to decrease in the future, a profit could be made by *short selling* the stock—borrowing the stock of another investor, selling it, promising to replace, or repay, the borrowed stock at a later date.

~ If the price of the borrowed stock falls, the investor can buy it back and replace it at a lower price, hence make a profit.

~ The objective of short selling is to "sell high and buy low."

~ Restrictions to short selling make it unattractive to many investors. An investor cannot short sell a stock if its latest trade results in a price decrease, called a *downtick*.

- Short sales can be placed only after uptick or zero-plus tick trades. An *uptick* trade occurs when the price of the most recent trade is higher than the previous trade, and a *zero-plus tick* trade occurs when the price of the most recent trade equals the price of the previous trade but exceeds the price from one trade earlier.

~ A second restriction is that the initial proceeds generated from the short sale cannot be used freely by the investor; instead, the proceeds are kept by the broker as collateral for the stock that was borrowed.

- The investor must "deposit" funds with the brokerage firm to ensure the stock can be repurchased if its price increases.
- If the price of the stock increases by too much, the investor will receive a "margin call" from the brokerage firm that will require him or her to provide additional funds to cover possible future price increases.

~ At times, investors short sell stock they also own, said to be *shorting against the box*.

- The name originated in earlier times when an investor held securities in a safety deposit box.
- In the past, investors shorted against the box to delay tax payments associated with liquidating an investment until some future period.
- Revisions made to the Tax Code in 1997 have essentially eliminated the tax benefits associated with such an investment strategy.

~ The restrictions along with the unpredictability of stock price movements make short selling a very risky investment strategy used by sophisticated investors.

SELF-TEST QUESTIONS

Definitional

1. _____ are individuals who forgo current consumption to increase future wealth and consumption.

2. Those who try to make a quick profit based on short-term market adjustments are called _____ because they gamble on whether financial assets are actually mispriced and market prices will adjust accordingly.

3. The major reason people invest is _____ _____.

4. Investments that offer steady dividend or interest payments are called _____ _____.

5. Your _____ _____ level depends on existing economic conditions, current socioeconomic position, and expectations about your socioeconomic position in the future.

6. _____ costs are the costs associated with trading securities, which include the costs of time, effort, and phone calls, as well as broker commissions that are incurred.

7. _____ _____ is the proportion of funds invested in various types of assets.

8. Most of the investment transactions entered into and not related to savings instruments from financial institutions require the assistance of a middleman, or agent, called a(n) _____.

9.   _____ brokerage firms offer their clients only basic services associated with trading securities, such as trade executions and related reporting requirements.

10.   When securities are traded on exchanges, they are traded in multiples of 100 shares called _____ _____.

11.   A(n) _____ _____ is an order to execute a transaction at the best price available when the transaction reaches the market.

12.   A(n) _____ ____ _____ order instructs the broker to cancel the order if it cannot be executed immediately, sometimes with a time limit attached.

13.   Stock that is registered to the brokerage firm in the investor's name is referred to as _____ _____ stock.

14.   The _____ _____ is the designation that represents the trading initials of the company.

15.   The _____ _____ return is the return earned over the period of time an investment is held.

16.   Two techniques for computing the average return for an investment held for more than one year are: the _____ _____ average and the _____ average.

17.   _____ _____ are used to measure the returns for combinations of securities, or "baskets" of investments, such as stock markets and bond markets.

18.   A(n) _____-_____ index is constructed by adding the price of one share of stock and then dividing by the number of stocks in the index.

19.   One way to mitigate the influence high-priced securities have on the value of a price-weighted index is to compute a(n) _____-_____ index, which is based on the total value of the stock of each firm rather than the price of a single share.

20.   _____ _____ is the total market value of a firm's stock, which can be computed by multiplying the number of shares outstanding by the market price per share.

21.   When the market is rising it is referred to as a(n) _____ market, which suggests the economy is performing well.

22.   When the market is falling it is called a(n) _____ market, which suggests the economy is performing poorly.

23. Most individual investors follow a(n) _____-_____-_____ strategy, which means they purchase securities with the intent to hold them until either their goals are met or modifications are needed in their portfolios to ensure future goals are met.

24. _____ _____ permits an investor to borrow from his or her broker some portion of the funds needed to purchase securities.

25. _____ _____ is a type of trade that allows an investor to borrow the stock of another investor and then sell it, but with a promise to replace the stock at a later date.

26. Investors can trade in _____ _____, multiples of less than 100 shares of stock.

27. A(n) _____ _____ instructs the broker when to begin executing a transaction; it doesn't guarantee, or limit the price of the transaction.

28. The _____ _____ return considers compounded rates.

29. When investors buy securities, regardless of the intended holding period, they are said to be _____ _____.

30. A(n) _____ _____ assigns the securities as collateral for the margin loan.

31. The _____ _____ represents the lowest actual margin, or percentage equity, the brokerage firm permits its margined investors to possess at any time.

Conceptual

32. When markets become more unstable and unpredictable than normal, many professional investment managers shift their allocations into the asset categories that are considered riskier, such as preferred and common stocks.

    a. True   **b.** False

33. The role of a broker is to help his or her clients trade financial instruments, especially stocks, bonds, and derivatives.

    a. True   **b.** False

34. The holding period return is an expected rate of return.

    a. True   **b.** False

35. The formula used to calculate holding period returns is not adjusted for holding periods not equal to a year.

    a. True   **b.** False

36. Which of the following statements is *false?*

    a. A stop order specifies the price at which an order to buy or sell at the market price is initiated.
    b. Electronic trading commissions are generally higher than dealing with a traditional or discount stockbroker, because electronic orders have to be placed directly with the representative of the broker firm that completes the trade.
    c. Financial intermediaries literally manufacture a variety of financial products to allow savers to indirectly provide funds to borrowers.
    d. Discount brokerage firms offer their clients only basic services associated with trading securities.
    e. Depending on an investor's risk tolerance level and propensity to control investment decisions, an investor might prefer to either actively select investments or to rely on the advice of an investment professional.

37. Which of the following statements is correct?

    a. The closing price of a bond in a bond quote is represented as a dollar amount.
    b. The dealer asked prices in government bond quotations represent the amount government bond dealers are willing to pay to purchase the bonds from investors.
    c. Brokerage firms do not create savings instruments, or financial securities; rather, they help investors trade such securities, which are created by corporations and governments.
    d. Investors can trade in round lots, which are multiples of less than 100 shares. These round lots are "bundled together" to create odd lots, which are more easily traded.
    e. Stock prices in quotations are denominated to the nearest 1/8 of a dollar but stated as a simplified fraction (i.e., 2/8 is simplified to 1/4).

38. Returns differ fairly significantly among the major indexes for which of the following reasons?

    a. Some market indexes are not good gauges for determining how well the stock market is performing. Thus, market indexes are not highly correlated with one another so their returns would be expected to differ significantly from one another.
    b. Not every index measures the same group of stocks. Because of this there would be some variation among the different index results.
    c. The indexes are not all constructed the same.
    d. Statements a, b, and c are all valid reasons for the differences in returns among the major indexes.
    e. Only statements b and c are valid reasons for the differences in returns among the major indexes.

39. Which of the following statements is *false?*

    a. A hypothecation agreement assigns the securities as collateral for a margin loan. It allows the broker to liquidate the stocks to repay the loan if the investor defaults.

    b. The interest rate on margin loans, called the broker loan rate, is based on the rate a brokerage firm is charged by its lenders.

    c. At times, investors short sell stock they also own, said to be shorting against the box. The name originated in earlier times when an investor held securities in a safety deposit box.

    d. The objective of short selling is to "sell low and buy high."

    e. The margin requirement represents the minimum amount of personal funds an investor must have to purchase securities.

40. Which of the following statements represents an important use of market indexes?

    a. They provide investors with an indication of how well the general economy is doing.

    b. Market indexes are used as benchmarks by individual investors and mutual fund managers when determining how well their portfolios have performed.

    c. Indexes are used to estimate the betas for securities.

    d. Indexes are used as investment instruments and as the basis for other investments, such as options.

    e. Statements a, b, c, and d all represent important uses of market indexes.

SELF-TEST PROBLEMS

The problems in this section do not take into consideration the impact of taxes or commissions on investment returns. For simplicity, we assume there are no taxes and no commissions.

(The following information applies to the next three Self-Test Problems.)

Adrian Smith bought 300 shares of HBH Enterprises for $20 per share. One year later, Adrian sold the stock for $25, just after she received a $1.00 cash dividend from the company.

1. What is the total *dollar* return earned by Adrian for the year?

    a. $6   **b.** $300   **c.** $1,000   **d.** $1,500   **e.** $1,800

2. What is the *rate* of return Adrian earned?

    a. 5%   **b.** 15%   **c.** 25%   **d.** 30%   **e.** 50%

3. What is the dividend yield and the capital gain that Adrian earned by holding HBH for one year?

   a. 5%; 0%   **b.** 5%; 10%   **c.** 5%; 25%   **d.** 0%; 30%   **e.** 10%; 20%

   (The following information applies to the next three Self-Test Problems.)

   According to the XYZ Composite Index, the stock market returns from 2003 through 2007 were as follows:

Year	XYZ Return
2003	28.5%
2004	15.3
2005	45.7
2006	-7.9
2007	4.4

4. What is the simple arithmetic average return for the XYZ Composite Index for the 5-year period?

   a. 15.6%   **b.** 17.2%   **c.** 18.9%   **d.** 20.4%   **e.** 22.7%

5. What is the geometric average return for the XYZ Composite Index for the 5-year period?

   a. 12.92%   **b.** 13.85%   **c.** 14.72%   **d.** 15.24%   **e.** 15.73%

6. What is the dollar value an investor would have at the end of 2007 if he or she invested $1,000 in the XYZ Composite Index at the beginning of 2003?

   a. $1,598   **b.** $1,874   **c.** $2,076   **d.** $2,412   **e.** $2,689

   (The following information applies to the next three Self-Test Problems.)

   Three years ago James Vaughn purchased 250 shares of Tidy Kleen Inc. for $75 per share. The company does not pay dividends. Now the market value of the stock is $120.

7. What is the total dollar return James has earned since he bought Tidy Kleen?

   a. $3,500   **b.** $7,500   **c.** $9,000   **d.** $12,500   **e.** $15,000

8. What is James' 3-year holding period return?

   a. 25.25%   **b.** 66.67%   **c.** 33.33%   **d.** 50.00%   **e.** 75.00%

9. What is the average annual return James earned? (Hint: You know the beginning value and ending value of the stock, so you can use the time value of money concepts we discussed in Chapter 9 to solve this problem.)

    a. 18.56%   **b.** 5.00%   **c.** 7.55%   **d.** 12.50%   **e.** 15.72%

(The following information applies to the next two Self-Test Problems.)

The following table gives information about the five stocks that have traded on the Small Investors Stock Exchange (SISE) since it started 2 years ago:

| | | Price per share | | |
Stock	Number of Shares	Beginning of Year 1	End of Year 1	End of Year 2
Hanratty	250	$ 30.00	$ 33.00	$ 40.00
Smythe	50	225.00	227.25	230.00
XLV	500	10.00	13.33	12.85
Twain	2,500	1.50	1.35	2.70
MMT	150	50.00	55.00	49.50

None of the stocks pays a dividend.

10. Using all the stocks, construct a simple price-weighted market index. What is the price-weighted index at the end of Year 2?

    a. 51.720   **b.** 65.986   **c.** 67.010   **d.** 70.950   **e.** 26.880

11. Using all the stocks, construct a value-weighted market index. What is the value-weighted index at the end of Year 2?

    a. 5,000   **b.** 6,194.48   **c.** 6,984.00   **d.** 7,625.25   **e.** 8,420.00

(The following information applies to the next two Self-Test Problems.)

Assume that Coca Cola is selling for $150 per share and that you short sell 300 shares of the stock.

12. What would be your dollar return if the price of Coca Cola drops to $135 per share?

    a. -$1,000   **b.** -$3,000   **c.** $1,500   **d.** $4,500   **e.** $6,000

13. What would be your dollar return if the price of Coca Cola increases to $160 per share?

    a. -$1,000   **b.** -$3,000   **c.** $1,500   **d.** $4,500   **e.** $6,000

(The following information applies to the next four Self-Test Problems.)

Sharon wants to purchase 2,000 shares of SST Inc. that is selling at $2.50 per share. SST does not pay dividends because all earnings are reinvested in the firm to maintain its successful R&D department. The brokerage firm will allow Sharon to borrow funds with an initial margin requirement equal to 60 percent and a maintenance margin of 30 percent. The broker loan rate is 12 percent. Assume that Sharon borrows the maximum allowed by the brokerage firm to purchase the SST stock.

14. How much of her own money must Sharon provide to purchase 2,000 shares of SST?

   a. $3,000   b. $2,000   c. $4,000   d. $0   e. $5,000

15. To what price can SST drop before Sharon receives a margin call from her broker?

   a. $0.25   b. $0.77   c. $1.43   d. $0.55   e. $1.25

16. If the price of SST's stock is $3.75 in 1 year, what rate of return would Sharon earn from her investment position?

   a. +10.55%   b. +25.35%   c. +56.75%   d. +75.33%   e. +81.22%

17. If the price of SST's stock is $2.00 in 1 year, what rate of return would Sharon earn from her investment position?

   a. -15.00%   b. -25.25%   c. -41.33%   d. -50.00%   e. -56.87%

ANSWERS TO SELF-TEST QUESTIONS

1.	Investors	17.	Market indexes
2.	speculators	18.	price-weighted
3.	retirement planning	19.	value-weighted
4.	income securities	20.	Market capitalization
5.	risk tolerance	21.	bull
6.	Transaction	22.	bear
7.	Asset allocation	23.	buy-and-hold
8.	broker	24.	Margin trading
9.	Discount	25.	Short selling
10.	round lots	26.	odd lots
11.	market order	27.	stop order
12.	fill or kill	28.	geometric average
13.	street name	29.	going long
14.	stock symbol	30.	hypothecation agreement
15.	holding period	31.	maintenance margin
16.	simple arithmetic; geometric		

32. b. Investment managers will shift their asset allocations into the asset categories that are considered safer, such as money market instruments and debt.

33. a. This statement is correct.

34. b. The holding period return is the actual, or realized, rate of return, k.

35. b. The holding period return formula is adjusted when the holding period does not equal a year. The adjusted formula is:

$$\text{Rate of return} = \frac{INC + (P_1 - P_0)}{P_0} \times \left(\frac{360}{T}\right).$$

36. b. Electronic trading commissions are generally lower than those of either the traditional or discount stockbrokers. The remaining statements are true.

37. c. Statement a is false; the closing price of a bond is stated as a percentage of face value. Statement b is false; the dealer asked price is the amount he or she is willing to take for selling their bonds to investors. Statement d is false; odd lots are multiples of less than 100 shares that are bundled together to create round lots. Statement e is false; stock prices in quotations are denominated in decimal form.

38. e. Statement a is false; the market indexes are used as gauges for determining how well the stock market is performing and there is a high correlation among the indexes, regardless of how they are constructed or the specific group of securities used to create them. Statements b and c are valid reasons for the differences in returns among the major indexes, so statement e is correct.

39. d. Statement d is false; the objective of short selling is to "sell high and buy low." The other statements are true.

40. e. All of the statements represent important uses of market indexes.

SOLUTIONS TO SELF-TEST PROBLEMS

1. e. Dollar return $= INC + P_1 - P_0$
$= 300(\$1.00) + 300(\$25.00 - \$20.00)$
$= \$300.00 + \$1,500.00$
$= \$1,800.00.$

2. d. Rate of return $= \dfrac{INC + P_1 - P_0}{P_0}$

$= \dfrac{300(\$1.00) + 300(\$25.00 - \$20.00)}{300(\$20.00)}$

$$= \frac{\$1,800}{\$6,000} = 30\%.$$

3. c. Dividend yield $= \dfrac{\$1.00}{\$20.00} = 0.05 = 5\%.$

Capital gains yield $= \dfrac{\$25.00 - \$20.00}{\$20.00} = \dfrac{\$5.00}{\$20.00} = 0.25 = 25\%.$

4. b. Simple arithmetic average return $= \dfrac{28.5\% + 15.3\% + 45.7\% + \text{-}7.9\% + 4.4\%}{5}$
$$= 17.2\%.$$

5. e. Geometric average return $= [(1.285) \times (1.153) \times (1.457) \times (0.921) \times (1.044)]^{1/5} - 1.0$
$$= 1.1573 - 1.0 = 0.1573 = 15.73\%.$$

6. c. 2003: $\$1,000 \times 1.285 = \$1,285.00.$
2004: $\$1,285 \times 1.153 = \$1,481.605.$
2005: $\$1,481.605 \times 1.457 = \$2,158.6985.$
2006: $\$2,158.6985 \times 0.921 = \$1,988.1613.$
2007: $\$1,988.1613 \times 1.044 = \$2,075.6404 \approx \$2,076.$

Alternative solution:

$\$1,000(1.1573)^5 = \$1,000(2.07601) = \$2,076.01 \approx \$2,076.$

7. d. Dollar return $= INC + P_1 - P_0$
$$= 250(\$0) + 250(\$125.00 - \$75.00)$$
$$= 250(\$50.00) = \$12,500.$$

8. b. Rate of return $= \dfrac{INC + P_1 - P_0}{P_0}$
$$= \dfrac{\$0 + 250(\$125 - \$75)}{250(\$75)}$$
$$= \dfrac{\$12,500}{\$18,750} = 0.6667 = 66.67\%.$$

9. a. $FV_n = PV(1 + k)^n$
$250(\$125.00) = \$250(\$75.00)(1 + \text{Annual return})^3$
Annual return $= \left(\dfrac{\$125}{\$75}\right)^{1/3} - 1.0 = 1.18563 - 1.0 = 18.56\%.$

10. c.

			Year 1		Year 2	
			Mkt.		Mkt.	
Stock	Shares	Price	Capital	Price	Capital	
Hanratty	250	$ 33.00	$ 8,250.00	$ 40.00	$10,000.00	
Smythe	50	227.25	11,362.50	230.00	11,500.00	
XLV	500	13.33	6,665.00	12.85	6,425.00	
Twain	2,500	1.35	3,375.00	2.70	6,750.00	
MMT	150	55.00	8,250.00	49.50	7,425.00	
		$329.93	$37,902.50	$335.05	$42,100.00	

$$\text{Price-weighted index, Year 1} = \frac{329.93}{5} = 65.986.$$

$$\text{Price-weighted index, Year 2} = \frac{335.05}{5} = 67.010.$$

11. e. From the table calculated in Self-Test Problem 10, we can calculate a value-weighted index:

$$\text{Value-weighted index, Year 1} = \frac{37,902.50}{5} = 7,580.50.$$

$$\text{Value-weighted index, Year 2} = \frac{42,100.00}{5} = 8,420.00.$$

12. d.
Sell 300 shares @ $150/share =	$45,000
Buy 300 shares @ $135/share =	40,500
Gain	$ 4,500

13. b.
Sell 300 shares @ $150/share =	$45,000
Buy 300 shares @ $160/share =	48,000
	($ 3,000)

14. a. 2,000 shares × $2.50 = $5,000.

Sharon must put up $60\% = 0.60 \times \$5,000$
$$= \$3,000.$$

Amount borrowed = $5,000 − $3,000 = $2,000.

15. c. $$\text{Margin call price} = \frac{\text{Amount borrowed}}{(\# \text{ of shares})(1 - \text{Maintenance margin})}$$

$$\text{Margin call price} = \frac{\$2,000}{(2,000)(1 - 0.3)} = \$1.4286 \approx \$1.43.$$

16.   d.   Purchased 2,000 shares @ \$2.50 = \$5,000.
           Sold 2,000 shares @ \$3.75 = \$7,500.
           Borrowed \$2,000 @ 12%; Interest = \$240.

           Total dollar return = 2,000(\$3.75 − \$2.50) − \$240
                           = \$2,260.

$$\text{HPR} = \frac{\$2,260}{\$3,000} = 75.33\%.$$

17.   c.   Purchased 2,000 shares @ \$2.50 = \$5,000.
           Sold 2,000 shares @ \$2.00 = \$4,000.
           Borrowed \$2,000 @ 12%; Interest = \$240.

           Total dollar return = \$2,000(\$2.00 − \$2.50) − \$240
                           = -\$1,240.

$$\text{HPR} = \frac{-\$1,240}{\$3,000} = -41.33\%.$$

CHAPTER 17
SECURITY VALUATION AND SELECTION

OVERVIEW

Common stock does not legally obligate the firm to make any future cash distributions; rather, investors view common stock as an implied contract with the firm that value will be maximized and cash distributions will be made when the firm exhausts its positive growth opportunities. Thus, even though the concept of valuation is fairly intuitive, in reality, trying to determine the value of investments such as common stock is not so straightforward; in fact, it can be a formidable task.

In this chapter, we describe some of the approaches that are used to value and select securities such as common stock. This chapter presents an overview of available valuation and selection methods. Traditionally, the techniques used to value common stock have been divided into one of two categories—fundamental analysis or technical analysis. The chapter begins with a description of both these approaches, and then it provides an overview of some of the popular valuation techniques used by both types of analysts.

OUTLINE

Traditionally, the techniques used to value common stock have been divided into one of two categories—fundamental analysis or technical analysis.

☐ *Fundamental analysis* is the practice of evaluating the information contained in financial statements, industry reports, and economic factors to determine the intrinsic (economic) value of a firm. The analysis integrates evaluations of the company, its industry, and the economy.

~ *Fundamentalists,* analysts who utilize fundamental analysis, attempt to forecast future stock price movements by examining factors that are believed related to the market values of stocks.

~ Factors that are examined can be grouped into one of three categories:

● *Company conditions,* such as earnings, financial strength, products, management, and labor relations.

● *Industry conditions,* such as maturity, stability, and competitive conditions.

● *Economic and market conditions.*

☐ *Technical analysis* is based on analyses of supply/demand relationships for securities to determine trends in price movements of stocks or financial markets.

- ~ *Technicians* search for trends by examining charts or by using computer programs that evaluate information about historical movements in trading volume and prices for stocks and for financial markets as a whole.
- ~ In the past, technicians have been referred to as *chartists* because they have been known to pore over charts.
- ~ The approach technicians take is based on their belief that movements in the financial markets are caused by investors' attitudes toward various economic and financial factors and other psychological circumstances, which, in many instances, result in actions that are fairly predictable.

The condition of the economy affects the performances of businesses and thus their securities in the financial markets. When forecasting movements of the financial markets and firms' performances, it is important to analyze economic conditions and determine when to expect changes in the business cycle.

- ☐ The *business cycle* is defined as the direction in which aggregate economic activity is moving.
  - ~ Increasing economic activity is called an *expansion,* while decreasing economic activity is called a *contraction*.
  - ~ We generally gauge economic activity using the *gross domestic product (GDP)*, which is a measure of all the goods and services produced in the economy during a specific time period.
  - ~ The GDP is stated both in nominal terms, meaning the value is not adjusted for inflation, and in real terms, which means the value is inflation-adjusted.
  - ~ The real GDP allows economists to determine the actual growth in the economy.

- ☐ Movements in the financial markets are closely related to business cycles.
  - ~ Good estimates of changes in the business cycle should enable one to forecast movements in financial markets such as stocks and bonds.
  - ~ Using historical economic information to predict future cycles is difficult because past business cycles have been irregular, and financial markets are not perfectly related to business cycles.

- ☐ Economists define a *recession* as two consecutive quarters of economic contraction, or decline, in the GDP.
  - ~ According to the National Bureau of Economic Research, there have been five recessions since 1970.
  - ~ The stock market decreased during each of these recessions; however, the two most notable declines within the last 20 years occurred during economic expansions.
  - ~ There is no pattern associated with these recessions—their lengths and effects as well as the expansionary periods between them vary considerably.

- ☐ Examining economic indicators published by the government and determining the general tenor of professional analysts are keys to predicting future recession or expansion periods.
  - ~ *Composite indexes* are aggregate measures that include various economic variables

grouped into one of three categories:

- *Leading economic indicators* are economic measures that tend to move prior to, or precede, movements in the business cycle.
- *Lagging economic indicators* are economic measures that tend to move after, or follow, movements in the general economy.
- *Coincident indicators* are economic measures that tend to mirror, or move at the same time as, business cycles.

~ The most familiar leading indicator included in the composite index is stock prices. They are considered a leading economic indicator because the prices of stocks are based on *forecasted* future cash flows.

~ For the most part, the indexes have performed as expected:

- The index of leading indicators declines prior to the start of recessionary periods;
- The index of coincident indicators declines when the recessions begin; and
- The index of lagging indicators declines after recessionary periods begin and sometimes not until after the recessions end.

~ For the most part, the composite indexes seem to provide indications of general business cycles, but the timings and magnitudes of the cycles are very difficult to forecast—the lead and lag times vary from one recession to another.

☐ Most large brokerage firms and financial service organizations have divisions that analyze economic data to provide their clients with estimates of future business activity.

☐ The monetary policy carried out by the Federal Reserve and the fiscal policy of the government can significantly affect business cycles.

☐ *Monetary policy* refers to the means by which the Federal Reserve influences economic conditions by managing the nation's money supply.

~ The Fed changes the money supply through reserves at financial institutions in its effort to promote stable economic conditions with moderate growth.

☐ *Fiscal policy* refers to government spending, which is primarily supported by the government's ability to tax individuals and businesses.

~ Conceptually, government fiscal policy should have the same goal as monetary policy—promote economic stability with moderate growth.

~ Since the 1960s, the fiscal policy in the United States has been dominated by *deficit spending*, which occurs when the government spends more than it collects in taxes (i.e., expenses exceed revenues).

~ Evaluating the government's spending behavior is important when determining economic expectations.

☐ Economic conditions affect financial markets; thus, it is important to perform an economic analysis when making investment decisions.

The stock market consists of many different segments called industries, which include companies with like characteristics. Although industries are usually defined by product classifications, firms are also differentiated according to their general sectors—industrial, service, technology, financial, and so forth. All industries do not perform the same in different business cycles.

☐ It is necessary to examine industry conditions to determine the attractiveness of the firms classified in the industry relative to firms in other industries.

☐ A basic industry analysis should include evaluations to determine (1) the relationship between the general performance of the industry and economic conditions and (2) the potential for future growth with respect to where the industry is in its life cycle.

☐ Every firm is affected by economic, or market, conditions, and changes in business cycles do not affect every firm the same.

~ Some industries are referred to as *cyclical industries* because they tend to be directly related to business cycles such that they perform best during expansions and worst during contractions.

~ In contrast, some industries are *defensive*, or *countercyclical, industries* because they tend to be the best-performing industries when the economy is in a contraction or recession, but they are generally the poorest-performing industries in expanding economies.

~ To determine the sensitivity of an industry to the economy, one can use computer models that are based on sophisticated statistical methods, or observe the direction an industry's stock prices move when major economic factors, such as interest rates and consumer prices, change.

☐ An *industry life cycle* is defined as the various phases of an industry with respect to its growth in sales and its competitive conditions. Generally, three distinct stages of industry life cycles can be described:

~ The *introductory stage* begins with the birth of the industry.

• Growth is very rapid, with few barriers to keep new competition from entering the industry, and survivorship is relatively low.

• Most firms have "bare bones" operations as they are trying to carve out a competitive niche, and generally all earnings are reinvested in the firm to support growth.

~ The *expansion stage* includes firms that survived the introductory stage.

• Operations become more sophisticated as firms move into larger facilities to meet their expanded needs.

• Growth begins to slow because the product is no longer a novelty.

• Sales are still increasing, but at a decreasing rate.

• Competitive barriers increase because firms have begun to carve their competitive niches and customers become more brand loyal.

• Because of fewer investment growth opportunities, at the end of this stage firms generally begin to pay dividends.

~ The *mature stage* is characterized by firms that are well entrenched.

- It is difficult for newcomers to enter the industry because competitive niches that are hard to break through have been established—competitive barriers are high.
- Growth in the industry begins to flatten, thus much of the earnings is paid out as dividends.

☐ Industries do not progress through the life cycle stages at the same pace.

~ Some industries, such as biotechnology, move through the stages relatively quickly, or an industry may never reach the mature stage of the industry life cycle, such as one that continuously produces large amounts of innovative technology.

☐ It is important for an investor to understand where in the life cycle an industry is currently operating and evaluate the characteristics of the investment opportunities in each of the three stages.

~ Investing in industries in the expansion and mature stages is less risky than investing in the introductory stage.
~ Industries in the mature stage are often characterized by large, stable firms with income-producing stocks (i.e., stable dividends).

The ultimate goal of investment analysis is to value the firm's security. Valuation requires an estimation of the future cash flows expected to be generated by the investment. The current financial condition of the firm issuing the security must be examined to forecast its future prospects.

☐ Financial statement analysis is used to evaluate the financial condition of a firm.

~ The purpose of financial statement analysis is to determine the attractiveness of an investment by identifying the strengths and weakness of the firm and projecting how its operations will change in the future.
~ Financial statement analysis involves a comparison of a firm's operating performance and financial position with that of other firms in the same line of business.

☐ The primary use of financial statement analysis as an analytical tool is to help investors form expectations about the future cash flows and the risks associated with an investment.

☐ The most important and most difficult input to successful ratio analysis is the judgment used when interpreting the results to reach an overall conclusion about the firm's financial position.

☐ Qualitative factors, such as labor conditions, management tenure, brand loyalty, and so forth, are examined in addition to financial statements when forming opinions about a firm's financial position and in predicting the future strength of its financial position.

Three basic stock valuation techniques are used by investors to find mispriced and fast-growing stocks as well as to make strategic decisions about the general compositions of their portfolios. These three techniques are: (1) Dividend discount model (DDM), (2) P/E ratio, and (3) Economic value added (EVA) approach.

▢   The most appropriate approach to stock valuation is finding the present value of, or discounting, future cash flows.

~   Most existing stock valuation models were derived from the *dividend discount model (DDM)*, which applies the discounted cash flow principle to the dividends expected to be received from investing in a stock.

$$\text{Value of stock} = V_s = \hat{P}_0 = \text{PV of expected future dividends}$$

$$= \frac{\hat{D}_1}{(1 + k_s)^1} + \frac{\hat{D}_2}{(1 + k_s)^2} + \cdots + \frac{\hat{D}_\infty}{(1 + k_s)^\infty}$$

$$= \sum_{t=1}^{\infty} \frac{\hat{D}_t}{(1 + k_s)^t}.$$

~   In this equation, $\hat{D}_t$ represents the dividend payment expected in period t, and k_s is the rate of return investors require for similar risk investments.

~   If the firm grows at a constant rate, the DDM is rewritten in the following simplified form:

$$\hat{P}_0 = \frac{\hat{D}_1}{k_s - g}.$$

●   Here g represents the constant growth rate in dividends.

●   The application of the equation requires that the firm's growth is constant today and forever into the future.

●   Additionally, three variables must be estimated: (1) the next period's dividend payment, (2) the constant growth rate, and (3) the appropriate required rate of return.

~   The DDM model can be used to get a ballpark value for common stock.

~   The nonconstant growth DDM is written as:

$$\hat{P}_0 = \sum_{t=1}^{N} \frac{\hat{D}_t}{(1 + k_s)^t} + \frac{\hat{P}_N}{(1 + k_s)^N}.$$

●   Here $\hat{P}_N$ is the future stock price at the point where constant growth begins, which is computed as:

$$\hat{P}_N = \frac{\hat{D}_{N+1}}{k_s - g_{norm}}$$

where g_{norm} is the growth rate when normal, or constant, growth begins.

~   Valuation methods like the DDM are most effective when forecasts of future dividends are accurate and when the assumptions associated with the CAPM and the DDM are not violated.

▢   Many analysts consider the P/E ratio, also referred to as the earnings multiplier, to be a good indicator of the value of a stock in relative terms.

~   The *P/E ratio* is computed by dividing the current market price per share, P_0, by the earnings per share, EPS_0.

~ The higher (lower) the P/E ratio, the more (less) investors are willing to pay for each dollar the firm earns.

~ The P/E ratio is similar to the payback method used in capital budgeting. If P/E ratios are viewed as measures of payback, then, all else equal, lower earnings multipliers are better.

~ It has been suggested that firms with low P/E ratios relative to other firms in their industries can earn above average risk-adjusted returns, and vice versa.

- The rationale is that if the P/E ratio is too low relative to similar firms, earnings have not been fully captured in the existing stock value; thus, the price will be bid up.

- Similarly, if the P/E ratio is too high relative to similar firms, the market has overvalued current earnings; thus, the price must decrease.

☐ P/E ratios can be used to value common stocks when a value determined appropriate for the P/E is multiplied by the firm's EPS to estimate the stock price.

~ Depending on the company analysis, such as evaluation of financial statements, the P/E ratio might need to be adjusted to reflect expectations about the firm's performance in the future.

~ Although the adjustment process is somewhat arbitrary, P/E ratios are higher (lower) for firms with higher (lower) expected earnings growth and lower (higher) expected required rates of return.

☐ The *economic value added (EVA) approach* is one of the newest approaches used to measure financial performance and evaluate the attractiveness of a firm's stock. This method is used to evaluate if the earnings generated by a firm are sufficient to compensate the suppliers of funds—both the bondholders and the stockholders.

~ The basic approach, developed by Stern Stewart Management Services, is to utilize basic financial principles to analyze a company's performance to value the firm.

~ The general concept behind EVA is to determine how much a firm's economic value is increased by the decisions it makes. Thus, the basic EVA equation is as follows:

$$EVA = (IRR - WACC) \times (\text{Invested capital})$$
$$= EBIT(1 - T) - (WACC \times \text{Invested capital}).$$

- In this equation, IRR represents the firm's internal rate of return, WACC is the firm's weighted average cost of capital, T is the marginal tax rate, and invested capital refers to the amount of funds provided by investors.

~ The equation can be used to evaluate the value of the firm as a whole or in terms of individual projects. If the EVA is positive, the actions of the firm increase its value, but if the EVA is negative, the actions of the firm decrease its value.

~ The EVA concept can be used to determine the maximum dividend that can be paid to stockholders before the firm's value would be threatened, by dividing the computed EVA by the number of outstanding shares.

☐ The EVA approach has gained attention as a valuation technique because it is based on the fundamental principle of wealth maximization, the goal of every firm.

~ EVA is also attractive because it outlines the value creation process in simple terms:

- Changing the capital structure can change value because the WACC is affected.
- Increasing the efficiency of the firm through reductions in operating expenses or increases in revenues will increase operating income and thus increase value.

The valuation techniques used in fundamental analysis focus on what factors determine values and why values change. Technical analysis, on the other hand, focuses on predicting when values will change. Technical analysts believe it is possible to identify shifts in the supply/demand relationships associated with investments that result in persistent trends for either individual stocks or the market as a whole. More importantly, however, technical analysts believe that investors behave in a predictable manner when faced with current situations similar to ones that occurred in the past.

☐ Technical analysis is based primarily on the belief that trends exist in the stock market. One of the ways technical analysts attempt to identify trends in the stock market is by examining charts and graphs of historical prices, trading volume, and so on.

☐ One example of a chart that technical analysts might use is a *bar chart,* a graph that indicates the high, low, and closing price movements for a stock during a specified period.
  ~ A *trend line* indicates the direction of the stock price movement. It is drawn so that it touches either high or low prices for some of the trading days.
  ~ The point at which the trading line crosses the trend line is called the *trend line penetration.* If the penetration is either significant or persistent, the suggestion is that there is pressure for the previous trend to reverse.
  ~ The most critical, as well as the most difficult, part of charting is interpreting the graphs in an attempt to find trading patterns and to determine the timing reversals in any patterns that are found.

☐ Technical analysts also use measures and indicators that they believe gauge both the trading activity and the tenor of the market.

☐ Structured technical analysis was introduced in the late 1890s by Charles Dow, who developed the *Dow theory.*
  ~ According to this theory, there are three types of market movements:
    - Primary, or broad, trends that last from several months to many years;
    - Secondary, or intermediate, trends that last from a few weeks to three or four months; and
    - Short-term movements represented by daily price movements.
  ~ The primary objective of the Dow theory is to identify the reversal of primary trends by examining the movements of the Dow Jones Industrial Average, which includes stocks of the largest 30 industrial firms, and the Dow Jones Transportation Average, which includes stocks of 20 transportation firms.
    - It is believed that these two indexes reflect the most important factors that drive market movements, including market psychology, or the general attitude of investors.

~ The theory states that as long as the industrial index and the transportation index move in the same direction, indications are that the market will continue its current trend.

☐ Technical analysts often examine the patterns of average stock prices for a fixed time frame, or window, over a particular period of time—measures called *moving averages*.
~ The windows generally range from 30 days to one year. The results of the moving averages for a particular time period are graphed and then interpreted much like bar charts—when the moving average crosses over, or penetrates, a previously established series, a reversal in the trend might be expected.

☐ *Technical indicators* are measures used by technical analysts to help forecast future movements in stock prices. Technicians believe these indicators behave much like leading economic indicators.
~ There are two basic types of indicators: those that measure the *breadth* of the market and those that measure the *sentiment* of the market.

☐ *Market breadth indicators* are used to measure the trading volume and the range of trading that takes place in the market.
~ One of the most often quoted measures is the *advance/decline line*, constructed by graphing the result of computing the difference between the number of advancing and declining stocks over a given time period.
  ● The advance/decline line is used to track whether there is upward or downward pressure in the market.
  ● If the line moves in the same direction as the market, the belief is that the market will continue in the same direction.
  ● If the line moves opposite the market trend, the indication is that the market is weakening and a reversal might soon occur.
~ Other breadth indicators, such as the overbought/oversold index, the traders index, and various other volume indexes, are also used to provide indications of future price changes in the market.

☐ *Sentiment indicators* are used to monitor the "mood," or psychology, of the market.
~ One group is based on observations of the recommendations made to, and the behavior of, the average individual investor.
  ● Many technical analysts believe the average investor makes decisions to buy or sell in the stock market at the wrong time. Therefore, when odd-lot buying increases or recommendations made by investment newsletters subscribed to by investors are bullish, analysts suggest that the market is expected to decline in the near term.
~ Another group is based on observations of the trading behavior of investment experts and sophisticated investors.
  ● Technical analysts believe that the amount of short selling done by professional investors is a good indicator of which direction they expect the market to move—when professionals increase their short positions, it is a sign that the market might decline in the future, and vice versa.

☐ Fundamental analysts argue that technical analysis can only reveal what is already known (movement of historical prices), not what we want to know (movement of future prices).

Many different criteria, or screening techniques, for selecting stocks have been developed by numerous investment professionals. Some approaches emphasize growth potential, while others focus on value and stability. Most factors evaluated are considered part of fundamental analyses, while some are classified as technical indicators; yet they share commonalities.

☐ To date, no single "perfect" stock selection technique has been discovered. Many investors use screening, or selection, techniques in hopes of finding stocks that will "beat the market" on a risk-adjusted basis. Stocks are classified in two categories—growth stocks and value stocks.
   ~ *Growth stocks* are defined as stocks of firms that have many positive net present value opportunities; that is, the firms' values should increase as these projects are undertaken. They are the stocks of firms that exhibit sales and earnings growths that significantly exceed the industry averages.
   ~ *Value stocks* are defined as stocks of firms that are mispriced, especially those that are undervalued.

☐ Similarities are found among the different quantitative and qualitative stock selection criteria.
   ~ Each of the criteria requires some type of an evaluation of the firm's earnings; the P/E ratio appears to be the most commonly used valuation measure.
   ~ Professional investors prefer firms that exhibit stable growth in earnings.
   ~ Firms with financial strength are favored—those that have low amounts of debt relative to the industry norm and the ability to meet current obligations.
   ~ Investors who favor institutional ownership—ownership by pension funds, insurance companies, and so forth—believe it adds liquidity to a firm's stock, while those who prefer a lower institutional presence believe that contributes to stocks selling at bargain prices.
   ~ A general consensus is that an investor should have some knowledge of a company's product line and its general operations before investing in it, in order to understand the reasons for its stock price movements.
   ~ Professional investors favor firms that have carved competitive niches resulting from patents, brand loyalty, or other competitive barriers.
   ~ Professional investors clearly do not recommend that investors speculate or try to time market movements; instead, the common theme is to hold an investment until it no longer satisfies the investor's goals.
      • The consensus of the professionals is to "buy and hold" until either personal goals or market conditions change.

If the markets are efficient with respect to information, then investors cannot use investment selection criteria to consistently earn abnormal returns.

☐   *Abnormal returns* are returns that exceed returns earned by similar-risk investments.

☐   Three general forms of market efficiency include weak-form efficiency, semistrong-form efficiency, and strong-form efficiency.
  ~   If *weak-form efficiency* exists, then existing market prices reflect all historical information, including past price movements and trading volume data.
     • Most of the results of various empirical tests indicate the markets are weak-form efficient.
  ~   *Semistrong-form efficiency* asserts that existing market prices reflect all publicly available information, including information contained in historical data and in current financial statements. Using fundamental analysis techniques to earn abnormal returns would prove futile.
     • Test results have been inconclusive—some seem to prove semistrong-form efficiency exists, while some indicate it does not.
  ~   *Strong-form efficiency* asserts that existing market prices reflect all information, whether public or private. Thus, if the markets achieve this form of efficiency, then even corporate insiders would be unable to earn abnormal returns on a consistent basis.
     • Empirical tests of this form of market efficiency have produced results suggesting insiders can consistently earn abnormal returns; thus, the evidence fails to prove strong-form efficiency exists.

☐   The investment selection approaches included in this chapter are useful for reasons beyond earning abnormal returns.
  ~   Evidence suggests it is difficult, if not impossible, to accomplish the objective of earning abnormal returns on a consistent basis.
  ~   Generally, investors should conduct appropriate investment analysis—rather than randomly selecting stocks—utilizing valuation and selection approaches to evaluate particular investments to determine their risk level and whether their investment goals are being met.

SELF-TEST QUESTIONS

Definitional

1.   Traditionally, the techniques used to value common stock have been divided into one of two categories--_____ analysis or _____ analysis.

2.   _____ analysis is based on analyses of supply/demand relationships for securities to determine trends in price movements of stocks or financial markets.

3.   _____ attempt to forecast future stock price movements by examining factors that are believed related to the market values of stocks.

4. The _____ _____ is defined as the direction in which aggregate economic activity is moving.

5. Increasing economic activity is called a(n) _____, while decreasing economic activity is called a(n) _____.

6. We generally gauge economic activity using the _____ _____ _____, which is a measure of all the goods and services produced in the economy during a specific time period.

7. Economists define a(n) _____ as two consecutive quarters of economic contraction, or decline, in the GDP.

8. _____ _____ _____ are economic measures that tend to move prior to, or precede, movements in the business cycle.

9. _____ _____ are economic measures that tend to mirror, or move at the same time as, business cycles.

10. _____ _____ refers to the means by which the Federal Reserve influences economic conditions by managing the nation's money supply.

11. _____ _____ refers to government spending, which is primarily supported by the government's ability to tax individuals and businesses.

12. The stock market consists of many different segments called _____, which include companies with like characteristics.

13. Some industries are referred to as _____ industries because they tend to be directly related to business cycles such that they perform best during expansions and worst during contractions.

14. Some industries are _____, or _____, industries because they tend to be the best-performing industries when the economy is in a contraction or recession, but they are generally the poorest-performing industries in expanding economies.

15. There are three distinct stages of industry life cycles: the _____ stage, the _____ stage, and the _____ stage.

16. The _____ _____ _____ applies the discounted cash flow principle to the dividends expected to be received from investing in a stock.

17. Many analysts consider the _____ _____, also referred to as the earnings multiplier, to be a good indicator of the value of a stock in relative terms.

18.   The _____ _____ _____ _____ is used to evaluate if the earnings generated by a firm are sufficient to compensate the suppliers of funds—both the bondholders and the stockholders.

19.   _____ _____ _____ are used to measure the trading volume and the range of trading that takes place in the market.

20.   _____ _____ are used to monitor the mood, or psychology, of the market.

21.   _____ stocks are defined as stocks of firms that have many positive net present value opportunities.

22.   _____ stocks are defined as stocks of firms that are mispriced, especially those that are undervalued.

23.   _____ returns are returns that exceed the returns earned by investments with similar risks.

24.   _____-_____ _____ asserts that existing market prices reflect all information, whether public or private.

25.   _____ _____ occurs when the government spends more than it collects in taxes.

26.   _____ analysis is the practice of evaluating the information contained in financial statements, industry reports, and economic factors to determine the intrinsic (economic) value of a firm.

27.   _____ search for trends by examining charts or by using computer programs that evaluate information about historical movements in trading volume and prices for stocks and for financial markets as a whole.

28.   _____ _____ are aggregate measures that include various economic variables grouped into one of three categories.

29.   _____ _____ _____ are economic measures that tend to move after, or follow, movements in the general economy.

30.   A(n) _____ _____ _____ is defined as the various phases of an industry with respect to its growth in sales and its competitive conditions.

31.   The point at which the trading line crosses the trend line is called the _____ _____ _____.

32. According to the _____ _____ there are three types of market movements: primary trends, secondary trends, and short-term movements.

33. _____ _____ are measures used by technical analysts to help forecast future movements in stock prices. Technicians believe they behave much like leading economic indicators.

34. If _____-_____ _____ exists, then existing market prices reflect all historical information, including past price movements and trading volume data.

35. _____-_____ _____ asserts that existing market prices reflect all publicly available information, including information contained in historical data and in current financial statements.

36. The gross domestic product is stated both in _____ terms, meaning the value is not adjusted for inflation, and in _____ terms, which means the value is inflation-adjusted.

Conceptual

37. Fundamental analysis is the practice of evaluating the information contained in financial statements, industry reports, and economic factors to determine the intrinsic value of a firm.

    a. True   b. False

38. Composite indexes are aggregate measures that include various economic variables grouped into one of three categories: technical indicators, primary trends, and sentiment indicators.

    a. True   b. False

39. Technicians search for trends by examining charts or by using computer programs that evaluate information about historical movements in trading volume and prices for stocks and for financial markets as a whole.

    a. True   b. False

40. The expansion stage of an industry life cycle is characterized by firms that are well entrenched.

    a. True   b. False

41. If the weak-form efficiency exists, existing market prices reflect all publicly available information, including that contained in historical data and in current financial statements.

a. True   **b.** False

42. Which of the following is *not* one of the distinct stages in an industry life cycle?

    a. Contraction stage.
    b. Mature stage.
    c. Introductory stage.
    d. Expansion stage.
    e. All of the above represent distinct stages in an industry life cycle.

43. Which of the following statements is *false?*

    a. Lagging economic indicators are economic measures that tend to move after, or follow, movements in the general economy.
    b. In the expansion stage of industry life cycles competitive barriers increase because firms have begun to carve their competitive niches and customers become more brand loyal.
    c. Economists define a business cycle as two consecutive quarters of economic contraction, or decline, in the GDP.
    d. The gross domestic product (GDP) is a measure of all the goods and services produced in the economy during a specific time period.
    e. The most familiar leading indicator included in the composite index is stock prices. Stock prices are considered a leading economic indicator because the prices of stocks are based on forecasted future cash flows.

44. Which of the following statements is most correct?

    a. The monetary policy carried out by the Federal Reserve and the fiscal policy of the government have little or no effect on business cycles.
    b. Although industries are usually defined by product classifications, firms are also differentiated according to their general sectors—industrial, service, technology, financial, etc.
    c. In the introductory stage of industry life cycles it is difficult for newcomers to enter the industry because competitive niches that are hard to break through have been established—competitive barriers are high.
    d. The higher the P/E ratio, the less investors are willing to pay for each dollar the firm earns.
    e. Technical analysis focuses on what factors determine values and why values change, while fundamental analysis focuses on predicting when values will change.

45. Which of the following statements is most correct?

    a. According to the Dow theory, there are three types of market movements: primary, or broad, trends that last from several months to many years; secondary, or intermediate, trends that last from a few weeks to three or four months; and short-term movements represented by daily price movements.

    b. Market breadth indicators are used to monitor the mood, or psychology, of the market.

    c. Many investors use screening, or selection, techniques in hopes of finding stocks that will beat the market on a risk-adjusted basis.

    d. Statements a and c are correct.

    e. Statements a, b, and c are correct.

SELF-TEST PROBLEMS

(The following information applies to the next two Self-Test Problems.)

Starr Enterprises has paid a dividend for more than 50 years, and this practice is expected to continue for a long time to come. Analysts have evaluated the financial position of Starr and discovered that past dividends have grown by a constant rate of 5 percent each year. The most recent dividend payment, which was made yesterday, was $2.00 per share. The company has not been able to calculate the rate of return required by its shareholders. But, the following information about market conditions has been gathered:

Risk-free rate	6.00%
Market return	14.00%
β for Starr Enterprises	1.1

1. According to the Capital Asset Pricing Model (CAPM), what is the rate of return required by Starr's stockholders?

    a. 6.0%   **b.** 9.2%   **c.** 13.8%   **d.** 14.8%   **e.** 15.6%

2. Using the constant growth version of the dividend discount model (DDM), what should be the current value of Starr's common stock?

    a. $15.75   **b.** $21.43   **c.** $18.95   **d.** $22.50   **e.** $24.66

(The following information applies to the next four Self-Test Problems.)

Auto Hut Inc.'s common stock currently is selling for $55.00, which is 14 times its earnings per share, EPS. The most recent dividend paid by Auto Hut was $1.75 per share.

3.   What is Auto Hut's current EPS?

   a. $1.25   **b.** $1.88   **c.** $2.22   **d.** $3.15   **e.** $3.93

4.   What is Auto Hut's current dividend payout ratio? (Hint: Remember that the payout ratio refers to the percent of earnings that are paid as dividends.)

   a. 24.25%   **b.** 37.50%   **c.** 44.53%   **d.** 50.00%   **e.** 55.44%

5.   Assume that Auto Hut has achieved constant growth and investors require a 12 percent return to invest in Auto Hut's stock. What are the dividend yield and the growth provided by Auto Hut's stock? (Hint: The dividend yield is the dividend divided by the current market price of the stock.)

   a. 2%; 10%   **b.** 2.5%; 9.5% **c.** 3.2%; 8.8% **d.** 3%; 9%   **e.** 4.5%; 7.5%

6.   The industry P/E ratio is 12.5×. Using this industry average, what is the price at which Auto Hut should sell?

   a. $47.500   **b.** $49.125   **c.** $50.950   **d.** $53.750   **e.** $55.000

7.   The current price of ABC's stock, P_0, is $16.00, and the company is expected to pay $1.76 next year. If the appropriate required rate of return for ABC's stock is 16 percent, what should be the price of the stock in one year, P_1? Assume the company has achieved constant growth.

   a. $15.50   **b.** $16.00   **c.** $16.45   **d.** $16.80   **e.** $17.25

8.   BDT Corporation has $650,000 invested capital, 55 percent of which is in the form of debt. With this capital structure, the company has a weighted average cost of capital equal to 11 percent. According to BDT's latest income statement, operating income is about $125,000, and its marginal tax rate is 40 percent. What is the firm's EVA?

   a. $3,500   **b.** $2,250   **c.** $0   **d.** $4,125   **e.** $5,000

(The following information applies to the next three Self-Test Problems.)

The stock of SSR Inc. is currently selling for $135.00, which equates to a P/E ratio of 25×.

9.   Using the P/E ratio, what is the current EPS of SSR?

    a. $2.25   **b.** $3.75   **c.** $4.50   **d.** $5.00   **e.** $5.40

10.   Assume earnings next year increase by 15 percent, but the P/E ratio drops to 20×, which is more in line with the industry average. What will be the price of SSR stock next year?

    a. $124.20   **b.** $128.00   **c.** $130.00   **d.** $132.75   **e.** $135.50

11.   If an investor purchases the stock today for $135.00 and sells it in one year at the price computed in Self-Test Problem 10, what rate of return would be earned? Assume no dividend is paid.

    a. 0%   **b.** +5%   **c.** -8%   **d.** -2%   **e.** +8%

(The following information applies to the next two Self-Test Problems.)

Taylor Industries reported that its net income was $130,000 last year. Interest expense was reported to be $80,000, and its marginal tax rate was 35 percent. According to the company's balance sheet, invested capital equals $1,600,000. Taylor's WACC is 10 percent.

12.   What is the operating income (EBIT) Taylor Industries generated last year?

    a. $250,000   **b.** $280,000   **c.** $300,000   **d.** $325,000   **e.** $350,000

13.   What is the EVA generated by Taylor Industries last year?

    a. $12,500   **b.** $15,250   **c.** $18,500   **d.** $22,000   **e.** $25,000

ANSWERS TO SELF-TEST QUESTIONS

1.	fundamental; technical	10.	Monetary policy
2.	Technical	11.	Fiscal policy
3.	Fundamentalists	12.	industries
4.	business cycle	13.	cyclical
5.	expansion; contraction	14.	defensive; countercyclical
6.	gross domestic product	15.	introductory; expansion; mature
7.	recession	16.	dividend discount model
8.	Leading economic indicators	17.	P/E ratio
9.	Coincident indicators	18.	economic value added approach

19.	Market breadth indicators		28.	Composite indexes
20.	Sentiment indicators		29.	Lagging economic indicators
21.	Growth		30.	industry life cycle
22.	Value		31.	trend line penetration
23.	Abnormal		32.	Dow theory
24.	Strong-form efficiency		33.	Technical indicators
25.	Deficit spending		34.	weak-form efficiency
26.	Fundamental		35.	Semistrong-form efficiency
27.	Technicians		36.	nominal; real

37.   a.   This statement is correct.

38.   b.   Composite indexes are grouped into one of the three following categories: leading economic indicators, lagging economic indicators, and coincident indicators.

39.   a.   This statement is correct.

40.   b.   The expansion stage includes firms that survived the introductory stage, while the mature stage is characterized by firms that are well entrenched.

41.   b.   Semistrong-form efficiency asserts that existing market prices reflect all publicly available information, while weak-form efficiency asserts that existing market prices reflect all historical information.

42.   a.   Statements b, c, and d are the three distinct stages in an industry life cycle.

43.   c.   Statements a, b, d, and e are correct. Statement c is the definition of a recession and not a business cycle.

44.   b.   Statement a is false because both monetary policy and fiscal policy can have a significant effect on business cycles. Statement c is false; this statement applies to the mature stage of an industry life cycle. Statement d is false; the higher the P/E ratio, the more investors are willing to pay for each dollar the firm earns. Statement e is false; the statement has been reversed.

45.   d.   Statement b is false; this is the definition for sentiment indicators. Statements a and c are true; therefore, statement d is correct.

SOLUTIONS TO SELF-TEST PROBLEMS

1.   d.   CAPM $k = 6\% + (14\% - 6\%)1.1$
$\qquad\qquad = 14.8\%.$

2.   b. $\hat{P}_0 = \dfrac{\hat{D}_1}{k_s - g}$

$$= \frac{\$2.00(1.05)}{0.148 - 0.05}$$

$$= \frac{\$2.10}{0.098} = \$21.43.$$

3.   e. $P_0 = 14(EPS)$

        $\$55.00 = 14(EPS)$

        $\$3.93 = EPS.$

4.   c.   Payout ratio $= \dfrac{DPS}{EPS}$

$$= \frac{\$1.75}{\$3.93}$$

$$= 0.4453 = 44.53\%.$$

5.   c.   Dividend yield $= \dfrac{\$1.75}{\$55.00} = 3.18\% \approx 3.2\%.$

        Total return $=$ Dividend yield $+$ Growth rate

            $12\% = 3.18\% + g$

               $g = 8.82\% \approx 8.8\%.$

6.   b. $P_0 = EPS \times P/E$

          $= \$3.93 \times 12.5$

          $= \$49.125.$

7.   d. $k =$ Dividend yield $+ g$

        $16\% = \dfrac{\$1.76}{\$16.00} + g$

        $16\% = 11\% + g$

           $g = 5\%.$

        $\hat{P}_1 = P_0(1 + g)$

        $\hat{P}_1 = \$16(1.05)$

        $\hat{P}_1 = \$16.80.$

8.   a. $EVA = EBIT(1 - T) - (WACC \times$ Invested capital$)$

          $= \$125,000(1 - 0.40) - (0.11 \times \$650,000)$

          $= \$75,000 - \$71,500$

          $= \$3,500.$

9.   e. $EPS = \dfrac{\$135.00}{25}$

EPS = $5.40.

10.   a. $EPS_1 = \$5.40(1.15) = \$6.21.$

$\hat{P}_1 = EPS_1(P/E)$

$\hat{P}_1 = \$6.21(20)$

$\hat{P}_1 = \$124.20.$

11.   c. $\hat{P}_1 = \$124.20;\ P_0 = \$135.$

$$Return = \frac{\$124.20 - \$135}{\$135}$$

$$= \frac{-\$10.80}{\$135}$$

$$= -0.08 = -8\%.$$

12.   b.

EBIT	$280,000	
INT	80,000	
EBT	$200,000	$130,000/0.65
Taxes	70,000	$200,000 × 0.35
Net income	$130,000	

13.   d. EVA = EBIT(1 − T) − (WACC × Invested capital)

             = $280,000(1 − 0.35) − (0.10 × $1,600,000)

             = $182,000 − $160,000

             = $22,000.